W9-CMT-872

Into the Carpathians:
A Journey Through the Heart and
History of Central and Eastern Europe
Part 1: The Eastern Mountains

by Alan E. Sparks

© Copyright 2015 Alan E. Sparks

ISBN 978-1-63393-153-4

All rights reserved. No part of this publication may be reproduced, stored in a retrieval system, or transmitted in any form or by any means—electronic, mechanical, photocopy, recording, or any other—except for brief quotations in printed reviews, without the prior written permission of the author.

Map on pages 3-4 © Laura Sparks

Published by

◣ köehlerbooks™

with

Rainy Day Publishing

Boulder, Colorado

Into the Carpathians

A Journey Through the Heart and
History of Central and Eastern Europe

Part 1: The Eastern Mountains

Alan E. Sparks

VIRGINIA BEACH
CAPE CHARLES

TABLE OF CONTENTS

PREFACE:
A Journey Inspired by Wolves

The wolf began its odyssey by exploring the territory of its pack in Romania, deep in the enchanted mountain forests of Transylvania. Now it wanders further, loping along the misty valleys, tumbling rivers, and ragged ridges of the Carpathian Mountain chain — the spine of Central and Eastern Europe. I invite you to follow this wolf: to see what it saw, hear what it heard, feel what it felt, and learn what it learned. . . and maybe, just maybe, to love what it loves.

On a late winter day in 2003, wolf tracker Peter Sürth negotiated his Isuzu Trooper up a steep, icy forest road into the Bucegi Mountain Range of Transylvania. Peter and I were following the steady beep from a radio collar that indicated a female wolf and its mate were resting somewhere up on the rocky ridge above, perhaps after making a kill the night before.

We were in the midst of a thirty-day predation study being conducted by a team of scientists, students, and volunteers called the Carpathian Large Carnivore Project (CLCP)—an experience I describe in my previous book, *Dreaming of Wolves*. I had been in Romania for three weeks: a volunteer, brought by the loss of my job, a search for meaning, and a deep interest in wolves. Peter had been with the project for seven years: a professional, brought by a degree in wildlife management, the project's need for a jack of all trades, and a passion for adventure. Peter was now the CLCP's chief wolf tracker and technician, but the project was coming to an end. In another month he would be out of a job. As the car lurched and spun up the slippery slope, I asked Peter what he would to do next. I suspected that opportunities for wolf trackers weren't crawling out of the woodwork.

"I'm thinking about hiking the Carpathians."

I paused for a moment, wondering what was new about that.

"The whole way," Peter continued. "From Romania to Germany. Next year if I can get sponsors."

I had no map in front of me, but I knew enough geography to know this would be no trivial undertaking. Was he serious or just dreaming? After having chased wolves with Peter for several days in this rugged Transylvania terrain, I figured if anyone could do it, it would be him. I had met the durable German only two weeks earlier—after receiving due warning of both his pace and intensity—and he is an incredibly serious man not given to chitchat. Nevertheless, Peter and I had developed a bond while trudging for hours through snow up to our waists, up and down precipitous slopes and across deep ravines and through dense thickets on the trail of wolves. Peter covered rough terrain faster than anyone with whom I had ever hiked; he seemed to almost fly above earthly resistance. *Maybe he is serious.*

"That's a long way," I replied.

"*Ya*, more than two thousand kilometers. I'll get eco-volunteers to join me. We'll collect scat. Maybe build a genetic inventory of wolves, bears, and lynx. We'll see where they live and learn how they move. Identify corridors. Maybe we can also raise public awareness about the mountains and the wildlife. Promote eco-tourism in the Carpathians."

"Wow! What an idea! Maybe you could even establish a route that could be built into a trail, like the Appalachian Trail in America."

"*Ya*, I was thinking of that."

"It's crazy!"

Peter smiled, and after a pause in which it became clear he would offer no dispute, I added, "Do you think I could come? For a while anyway?"

"*Ya*, I think so."

It took a year longer than he had hoped, but by 2005 Peter had found sponsors to provide camping and backpacking gear. Then he assembled a support team to handle the day-to-day logistics: Jürgen Sauer, a forty-nine year old ex-high-tech worker from Germany, and me, a forty-eight year old ex-high-tech worker from America. Eco-volunteers would fund the expedition by paying a weekly fee to join us.

We would start from a gorge deep in the Southern Carpathians near Zarneşti, Romania (where wolves have lived for millennia) on April 1 and were expected to arrive sixteen weeks later as special guests for the festivities of "Wolf Day" in Rietschen, Germany, deep in the pine flats just across the border with Poland (where wolves have recently returned). Peter called the expedition "The Way of the Wolf." This is one of its stories.[1]

To fully experience a landscape, one must travel through time as well as space, and through the imaginations as well as the realities of its inhabitants. Thus, along with descriptions of spectacular terrain, colorful people, stunning wildlife, and extraordinary experiences while on the *Way of the Wolf*, herein I offer vignettes of the ever-fascinating history and folklore of the mountain people of the Carpathians.

In selecting from a dazzlingly rich past, I admit a bias towards the foundations of the nations along our route (or the *nationalities*—for not all the nations have had states), both because they are fascinating, and because they may not be well known by many readers in the West. History classes when I was in school did not cover the geneses of these nations, even though several developed into the largest states in Europe in their times, and even though at least sixteen million people of Romanian, Polish, Ukrainian, Slovakian, and Czech descent now live in North America. As well, given the way things have gone during much of the modern era, these early days are often viewed as golden ages, in whose glow national psyches along the Carpathians still bask.

The amount I write about each country is also strongly influenced by its linear hold on our path—the time we spent traveling through it: four weeks in Romania and three weeks in Ukraine (for this volume, Part 1), and three weeks in Slovakia, one week in the Czech Republic, and five weeks in Poland (for the next volume, Part 2); the depth of my coverage is in no way indicative of the relative fascination that each nation holds. In the case of Romania, I have chosen not to repeat treatments in *Dreaming of Wolves* that are valuable for understanding the cultural landscape of the country; in particular: brief histories of the ancient Dacians, the Roma (also known as Gypsies), and Vlad the

Impaler (also known as Dracula), and a synopsis of Transylvanian vampire folklore.

INTRODUCTION

Rising at the heart of Europe like a giant serrated shield above the grassy plains—magnificent ridges and snow-capped peaks tossing up clouds and catching moisture to quench the thirst of shadowy forests and luxuriant meadows where wild flowers and wild beasts and the animals of man flourish—the Carpathian Mountains have deeply shaped the natural and cultural history of Europe, as well as the history of the collective human imagination. Their intimidating slopes and impervious woods have splintered waves of Proto-Indo-Europeans, guided the expansion of the earliest Slavs, and harbored the aspirations of peoples called Dacians, Celts, Romans, Huns, Goths, Gepids, Vandals, Moravians, Poles, Hungarians, Slovaks, Rusyns, Gorals, and many more. Carpathian ridges have defended mighty kingdoms, Carpathian passes have channeled stalwart armies, and Carpathian peaks have separated diverging societies—a sundering legacy seen today in the numerous national and provincial boundaries that Carpathian crests still form.

Yet the Carpathian Mountains are not well known in the West. If they conjure up images at all, we likely picture them in caricature, as an exclusively vertical landscape, bristling with precarious castles perched atop improbable crags, where swirling mists shroud the depredations of vampires and werewolves, and where blinding flashes of lightning animate bodies assembled by deranged professors with strong accents and hunchbacked assistants. Even in nearby Western Europe, the term "Carpathians" is still sometimes used as North Americans might use the term "sticks" or "boondocks" to refer to remote and inaccessible places.

If we examine a geophysical map of Europe, however, the Carpathian Mountains look like a natural extension of the familiar peaks to their west, the Alps. There is only a small break between the two, at a narrowing of the Danube basin, in the area where Hungary, Slovakia, the Czech Republic, and Austria meet (known as the Little Hungarian Plain). From here—almost literally from the cobblestone courtyard of the imposing Bratislava Castle in the capital city of Slovakia—oak and beech-covered hills roll up from the banks of the Danube, continuing in the same direction the Alps left off, towards the northeast. They rise hill upon hill and steepen to ridge after ridge and fracture into range after range, their crests rising and falling in great undulations on a long and majestic sweep back to the Danube, far downstream where in a last grasp for dominance they choke the waters with cliffs called the Iron Gates. Heaving splendid heights into the skies of eight countries— Romania, Slovakia, Ukraine, Poland, Hungary, Czech Republic, Serbia, and Austria—the Carpathians wrap the Transylvanian Plateau, cradle the Pannonian Basin, and part the waters of central Europe, dividing those destined for the Baltic from those flowing south and east to the Black Sea. The mountains precipitate twice as much moisture as the surrounding lowlands, discharging innumerable torrents that collude into such great and venerable courses as the Vistula, the Dniester, the Tisza, the Prut, the Siret, the Mureș, and the Olt.

Today, throughout much of their 930-mile (1,500 km) length and 77,220-square mile (200,000 km²) area (both ranking second in Europe), and among their 16 to 18 million human inhabitants, the Carpathian Mountains preserve final vestiges of the "old life" of Europe. Springtime still brings the sounds of bells, yells, whistles, and barks to the mountain slopes as shepherds and dogs guide cows, sheep, and goats to the lower pastures. Summer finds the flocks grazing higher, on flowery alpine meadows where their tenders camp in drafty huts and make cheese, fend off wolves, and tell tales of vampires around their fires. In the fall, enormous red-tasseled horses pull wobbly wooden carts along dusty roads, stacked high with ricks of hay or bundles of sticks, or filled with scythe-grasping harvesters bound for the fields; in winter, the same horses pull the trunk of trees down the icy slopes. Near villages the scent of things burning almost always fills the air; as well the sounds of clucking hens, crowing roosters, and, during the holidays, screaming pigs.

As the Carpathian Mountains shape the lives of their human inhabitants, so they shape the lives of the wild. Home to the largest populations of large predators in Europe west of Russia, the forested highlands are a carnivore's delight. Some four thousand Eurasian gray wolves (*Canis lupus lupus*), eight thousand Eurasian brown bears (*Ursus arctos arctos*), and three thousand Eurasian lynx (*Lynx lynx*) hunt the hills, where a feast of spritely roe deer (*Capreolus capreolus*), stately red deer (*Cervus elaphus*), earthy wild boar (*Sus scrofa*), or dashing hare (*Lepus europaeus*) is seldom far off; a scramble up a steep rocky slope might even yield a rare and agile chamois (*Rupicapra rupicapra*).

From high airy circles the rare Eastern imperial eagle (*Aquila heliaca*) scouts for hares, hamsters, and pheasants; and here is one of the few remaining refuges where the European wildcat (*Felis silvestris silvestris*) can avoid the genes of its domestic cousin. The European bison (*Bison bonasus*; also known as *wisent*)—the largest surviving wild land animal in Europe and once extinct in the wild—has recently been reintroduced, as has the Eurasian beaver (*Castor fiber*), which thrives along upland streams and rivers.

With some 1158 square miles (3000 km²) of forest still virgin, and the southern Carpathians of Romania guarding the largest contiguous forest remaining in Europe west of Russia, the Carpathian Mountains harbor the last significant relic of the great primeval woodlands that once spanned the continent. For now, their dark sylvan halls, unruly fields, and lofty alpine meadows provide a vital corridor between the wild remnants of northern and southern Europe. But for how long? Logging—legal and otherwise—is shrinking the old-growth forests. Roads, vacation homes, ATVs, and ski resorts are invading the highlands. Tractors, pesticides, and factory farms are replacing horses, hoes, and farmsteads. Only about sixteen percent of the wild Carpathian landscape is formally protected, enforcement is spotty, and poaching of wildlife is common. . .

> *Wolves are quintessential emblems of wildness, symbolic of an*
> *absence of human domination, a reminder that we do not control the*
> *cosmos. Wolves are part of the landscape, as surely as the trees, the cliffs,*
> *and the rivers. And wolves must perceive a landscape as it* **is** *in order*

to survive. But wolves must also be able to learn from the past. They must be able to temper unpredictability with experience. To perceive a landscape as a wolf, then, is to perceive it as it is: shaped by the past, but ever changing. To perceive a landscape as a wolf is to perceive it as it is—and will never be again.

A Note about Nomenclatures

The nomenclature of the ranges, ridges, and peaks of the Carpathian Mountains is as puzzlingly convoluted as the landscape. Appendix A provides a summary of several systems of names along with the major geological divisions of the chain. Although I will sometimes use one or another local name of a mountain or range to refer to where we are on the expedition, one can enjoy this narrative without getting caught up in the multifarious and sometimes contradictory Carpathian labels. I will usually also provide the names of the nearest human constructs—counties, towns, and villages—when I know them, and often the more universal names of rivers.

ROMANIA

March 25. Denver International Airport.

Here I am again, on a plane, heading to London. . . and then what?

Why such dread, when the unknown is precisely what adventure requires? It has been there, churning in my stomach for the last two weeks, ever since I made my final commitment: "Yes, I will work on the 'backup team' (as Peter called it) for *The Way of the Wolf* expedition." "Yes," I could have added, "I will sleep in a tent for the next four months, at who knows what uncomfortable and awkward spots along the length of the Carpathian Mountains, amongst who knows what kind of bandits and bears, finding food and water who knows where, cleaning myself and my clothes who knows how, negotiating roads dominated by who knows what kind of crazy drivers" (see *Dreaming of Wolves*).

How will I shower? I really must shower once a week at least, especially when it's warm. In fact, my main concern is not how cold and frozen it might be in the beginning, but how hot and muggy it will be at the end.

My nights have crawled with fears, some reasonable, most not, but my mind blowing them all out of proportion into anxious nocturnal shrapnel. Or so it seemed when I arose and came to my senses. Riding along to the airport, I had a faint hope the bus would spring a flat. I'd miss the plane and that would be that. A face-saving excuse, surely.

I'm even more apprehensive than two years ago. Is it because I know more now? Or do I just have the attitude of a hobbit: Why put myself through hardship and uncertainty when I can stay safe and comfortable at home?

The answer is obvious. After my last experience in Romania, it's safe to say I'll never again feel satisfied staying safe and comfortable at home. *Is a need for adventure coded in our genes? I suppose risk takers, over time, may have the better chance to propagate. . . if they survive.*

Full moon over the wing,
the dark expanse of Nebraska below.

I was under no obligation. Peter had found someone else for the backup team after I declined back in January. His original plan of doing the expedition a year ago had fallen through when he failed to get enough sponsors. I had moved on, even contemplating a return to a software job, when he contacted me last fall. I was tempted—my old reliable backpack fighting the computer screen for my loyalty—but after several exchanges with Peter, wherein I asked lots of reasonable questions about how we would pull it off, I balked: "Well, I'd like to, but I don't think it will work out. . . " I mitigated my disappointment in myself, and my guilt, by writing and editing publicity pieces for the expedition.

Then the software prospect fell through: All my conscience needed to start asking, "Why not?" Of course I could find lots of reasons why not. But they were not enough. Not enough to stop me from dreaming of wolves again. How many evenings had I lain awake nostalgic for Transylvania? For the moon riding the clouds above the silvery ramparts of Piatra Craiului; for the plaintive howls of Poiana and Crai asking to join Curly and me as we strolled along the pot-holed road; for the cow bells, sheep bleats, and yells and whistles of the shepherds. . . I even missed the constant scent of things burning. I was nostalgic for spontaneity and a close connection with the earth. Had I forgotten the difficulties? Yes, of course. We always forget the difficulties.

As the bus rolled along to its inevitable destination at Denver International Airport and I accepted the fact that its tires would remain inflated, my nerves finally quieted. The decision had been made, I was on my way, there was no backing out. . . I was at peace. Then, another wave of anxiety. *Are the Buddhists right? Is there no real "self"?*

My self was being swept back and forth by violent tides—inconsistent thoughts, feelings, desires, and fears, from one moment to the next. Part of me wanted to go, part of me didn't. *So who am I? Am I a single being? Or is inconsistency a proof of free will?*

"I can still back out," I thought. "Just don't get on the plane. Do what you want and only what you want. What does it matter what others think?

"But what do **I** think?

"I'm going, that's what I think. Stop imagining the negative, start imagining the positive. This adventure is beginning now. I'm taking the long way home. . . "

But why this feeling I won't come back?

Monday, March 28, Aarad, Romania

Jürgen, Thilo, and I are at a "two-star" hotel (according to the sign outside) in Aarad, Romania, just over the border from Hungary. The room is austere, with stark blue walls, somber brown carpet, small rickety beds, and a bathroom whose cracked and missing tiles, moldy grout, wall-less shower, and rusty running sink make you wonder whether you'd be any cleaner for cleaning there. But we had little choice, arriving late last night after an all-day drive from Munich.

Crossing the border yesterday was abrupt, like walking through the wardrobe of Narnia, except into a land of wondrous squalor rather than wondrous enchantment. I remember Thilo uttering a subdued moan as he scanned the roadside, where mud, rust, and poverty ruled the landscape. Dilapidated shacks and the shells of houses and lots of smoke—I don't remember Romania being this bleak. Maybe part of it is the season, with no snow and no greenery to hide the mud and marrings of humans. Or maybe border towns are particularly decrepit. Or maybe it was just something I had previously become used to.

After our passport check at the crossing lots of unsavory looking characters were hanging about, grouped under glaring neon lights and looking ready to pounce, so we drove on through fatigue and the blackness of night. We took the first hotel a few kilometers beyond the border, feeling lucky to have found one.

I'm in a jetlag-induced fog as I try to remember the events following my arrival two days earlier. Jürgen was waiting in the terminal of the Frankfort airport, holding a white poster with "The Way of the Wolf" neatly inscribed in big black letters. Presaging a fountain of practicality, Jürgen noted in very hesitant and broken English that we'll be needing the sign for four months. "For eco-volunteers."

Yes, of course. Good idea.

With thick whitening hair, a pleasant though tentative smile, and a glint in his eyes, Jürgen seemed nice enough. But he was older than I expected (my age), and seemed a tad too rotund for months in the outdoors.

"Sorry. Thirty-five years before I learn English. Not much since. Some in Asia," he said in his apologetic tone.

"Your English is better than my German. I'm happy to meet you, and thanks for picking me up." I tried to speak slowly and enunciate clearly.

A little more small talk was followed by an uncomfortable silence as we navigated though the terminal. *Well, I'm in it now*, I thought, as we grabbed my suitcase and backpack. The airport was my last link to my comfortable, *known* life. The only honorable way home now will be through four long months, thousands of kilometers, and surely many difficulties. As we walked along to his car hauling my luggage, I stole furtive measuring glances at my new companion.

That first night we stayed at Jürgen's parents' neat townhouse in the small neat town of Babenhausen. Jürgen's parents were at least as pleasant as Jürgen, if a bit more rotund. His father spoke only a few words of English, his mother a few more, but their hospitality was wonderful. His mother had made a memorable road tour through the Western US—the Zion, Bryce, and Grand Canyon route. As jovial and maternal as a mother could be, she immediately adopted me, quickly and efficiently serving up a much appreciated and ample German meal for this travel-starved guest, with lots of potatoes, eggs, and sausages. Although at home I try to eat only meat that has been "humanely raised" (which hopefully also means humanely killed)—whenever I'm a guest I generally take an attitude attributed to Gautama Buddha: I eat what I'm offered.

In the evening, we viewed slides of Jürgen's motorcycle trip last summer through the Czech Republic, Slovakia, and northern Romania to visit a friend. Apparently we'd be passing near the friend's cabin during the expedition, where maybe we could even cop a shower and sleep on a bed. The knot of fear I had been carrying in my stomach started to ease. Maybe this whole thing is doable after all. Maybe it'll just be a long road trip.

Next day, it was on to Munich in the project's Passat station wagon to pick up Thilo, a photojournalist who will be joining us for the first two months. Thirty years old, with straight and fine dark blond hair, Thilo is very slender and very intense. His English is pretty good, polished by a recent photography jaunt in the States, although his words occasionally come with a piercing stare.

Jürgen and I dropped our bags onto Thilo's floor, and then we all went out for food and drink. Munich beer *is* indeed good.

That night Jürgen and I slept on Thilo's sofas, where I got my first introduction to Jürgen's thunderous snore. In the morning we loaded Thilo's rather prodigious photography gear and off we went, already feeling the camaraderie of heading into the unknown together.

Tuesday, March 29, Zarneşti, Romania

Peter's house in Zarneşti. The place is still Spartan. A bed in the bedroom and a table in the main room and not much else. Zarneşti (pronounced "Zarneshte") is a red-tile-roofed town of about 25,000[2] souls residing in rows of old stucco houses and a few decaying Communist-era apartment blocks. The town lies below the soaring snow-dusted coniferous slopes of Piatra Craiului and is the former home of the CLCP.

Yesterday as we drove down the hill into town I was pelted by familiar scenes: the same muddy, potholed streets; the same bundles of sticks on red roofs (storks' nests); the same swarms of chickens strutting about; the same scraggly dogs lounging around; the same grey skies of March. I felt I was returning home. But I did spot a new restaurant on the road near the Prombergers' former residence. Development is invading even this remote Carpathian outpost.

Today I play tour guide, happy to revisit old haunts with Jürgen and Thilo and revive my Romanian language skills. Visiting Cabanna Lupului (the solid and cozy log "Wolf Cabin") and Poiana and Crai (the two captive wolves I had cared for two years earlier) is nostalgically sad. The wolves don't disappear up the bushy slope as they would with strangers, but neither do I get a warm and enthusiastic reception. They are aloof, tentative, and shy. I guess two years is a long time for a wolf.

The cabin has been sold to a local entrepreneur—the bike renter who once loaned me a bike—and although people occasionally stay here (so I'm told), the place is empty now. Formerly a home of activity, life, and warmth, the cabin is now deserted and neglected, with its large ceramic stove cold and dead, and trash scattered about the forlorn yard. The new owner is caring for the wolves until the Prombergers can relocate them to new facilities in nearby Sinca Noua, where they are establishing an equestrian-based ecotourism business.

I notice with some satisfaction that the log rail fence I resurrected around the cabin yard has held up, and the new house being built just upstream is yet only a few concrete blocks that look hurriedly slapped together.

We leave the cabin and hike across the valley and up the slopes to the cave monastery, Coltii Chiliei, in the same fog and drizzle of two years ago. Two dark, twisted strands of scat bristling with wild boar hair lay in the middle of the icy road leading up to the cave, almost surely left by a wolf. A monk, who looks not particularly monkish in his trim jacket and dark wool beanie, comes out to greet us and lead us to the sacred cave. I don't know what sins of my companions were forgiven, but since I had already been through the natural stone arch, mine were immutable (see *Dreaming of Wolves*).

Later we pay the obligatory visit to "Dracula's Castle" in Bran, where Thilo and Jürgen become sincerely interested tourists, climbing the narrow stairs, ducking through low passageways, and photographing the imposing gothic hilltop fortress and the less imposing but quaint and rustic peasant cottages of the open air museum. We then finish the day with a celebratory and delicious dinner at Moserel's guesthouse. There we meet Markus, our eco-volunteer from Switzerland who will join us for the month-long Romanian leg of the expedition, our only paying member for the first two weeks. Fiftyish, with short thinning-graying hair and glasses that magnify and a moustache that punctuates a sense of humor in his face, he appears fit and shakes our hands quite vigorously. I'm told he stays in shape via prodigious hiking in the mountains of his homeland. Markus can't tell me this himself because he speaks no English.

Poiana and Crai. © Jürgen Sauer.

Bran Castle, also known as Dracula's Castle. © Oana Vinatoru / istockphoto.com.

Wednesday, March 30, Zarneşti, Romania

At a planning meeting in a forestry administration building in Braşov[3], we go over maps and discuss plans with some important looking officials, and meet Ana and Cata, the two Romanian members of our team for the first month. Peter lays down a few rules:

1. We are to <u>always</u> store our most vital piece of equipment,

Peter's laptop, in the Land Rover, which we are <u>never</u> to leave unattended. If the laptop is stolen, the expedition will be over. It is our only means of communication with eco-volunteers—both those who have already signed on and those (hopefully) yet to come—who are funding our expedition. The eco-volunteers will come and go usually on Fridays, and tentative agreements have been, or will be, made as to what airports, train stations, or bus depots we will pick them up and drop them off. With so much uncertainty we must stay flexible and responsive, so our ability to communicate with both committed and prospective eco-volunteers is critical.

2. Those of us who drive the vehicles are not to exceed speed limits, where there are speed limits, and in any case we are to drive conservatively, "not Romanian style" (see *Dreaming of Wolves*).

3. This is an international expedition and therefore we are all to speak English as much as is practical, at least in group conversation.

Thursday, March 31, Zarneşti

Tomorrow, April Fool's Day, is the Big Day. We'll start from Zarneşti Gorge, where some kind of media event is planned. As the expedition's immensity in time and place looms, I know the milestones with which I will measure my life will now be short, modest and simple: keep myself fed, hydrated, and reasonably clean, dry, and warm. If I can manage these on a daily basis (at least), I'll be fine. I hope.

Last night Peter funded our second delicious dinner, this time at the other CLCP-affiliated guesthouse, *Pensiunea Elena*, run by Gigi Popa, his wife Elena, and their daughter Beatrice. Gigi, a tall man with dark, receding hair and a long, sharp nose popping out from a thick, active moustache, took the head of the table. He kept our glasses filled with schnapps, and between frequent tilts of his own, accompanied by insistent gestures, smiles, and pleading looks to tilt ours, directed particularly towards me (I was sitting next to him), entertained us with guitar playing and singing. His rendering of American classics such as John Denver's "Country Road" was awkward and uninspiring, but when he covered Romanian folk songs his crooning became beautiful and evocative, and I couldn't help adding my tears to his. As he encouraged us to drink, so I encouraged him to perform.

It was a fun and convivial evening, yet accompanied by a strange loneliness. The six of us were the only diners in the large, echoing room, which was dark and cold excepting the area of our table. Since Markus spoke no English and is our single paying client, and since everyone besides me spoke German, the team quickly broke rule number three. I felt a little left out, but since our opportunities for meals have been sporadic, I was content to concentrate on eating. I also resisted as much as possible Gigi's wordless but persistent pleas to imbibe.

I only partially succeeded.

This morning I feel the effects, not only of last night's revelry and lack of sleep but also lingering jet lag. Jürgen, Thilo, and I are camping out on Peter's floor. For us the expedition has already begun. But of all the dangers I had imagined, I hadn't considered a snorer to be one of them. Earplugs help, but not enough. The floor literally vibrates in resonance with Jürgen's breathing. I'm exhausted and have a headache and a sense of dread about the prospect of ongoing sleep deprivation.

The weather has been grey since we arrived, but a couple of inches of fresh snow this morning have brightened things up. In the afternoon, Thilo, Jürgen, and I take a break from the growing stress and revisit the wolf cabin. Our photographer wants some shots of the wolves. This time I get the reception I had been expecting: Poiana and Crai are affectionate, even demanding pats through the fence. They give Thilo ample opportunities, looking well fed and healthy in their thick winter coats, but Peter says they don't receive much social interaction with humans these days. I feel guilty when we leave: Will I ever see them again after we depart tomorrow?

Daylight ends with a wash of the Land Rover. A spiffy start won't hurt. Then I organize, loading my backpack with what I think I'll need during spring conditions in the mountains and putting the rest in my suitcase for later life on the road. We haven't enough boxes and bags and backpacks, so still many odds and ends to squeeze into the vehicles, and still many questions about how things will work. I guess we'll figure it out as we go.

Jürgen, Thilo, and I are on our own for dinner tonight, so I buy onions, tomatoes, potatoes, and beans fresh off the vine at an open market to make a soup. This will be a big role for me, dreaded in my normal life: shopping.

Since Ana and Cata will be with us in Romania, I won't have to always drive, so I'll start off tomorrow with the hiking team. This pleases me. My body has dutifully obeyed my mind's directive to exercise almost every day for the past twenty-five years, and is now craving activity.

Saturday, April 2. Near Sinca Noua, Romania.

Driving up the gorge to our start early yesterday morning was like driving backwards in time into an earlier and darker hour and an earlier and colder season, as the browns and greens of a promising spring morning froze into the blues and whites of a pre-dawn winter. We stopped where several vans and SUVs were parked at a widening of the snowy track, dwarfed and shadowed by soaring, frosted cliffs.

Hopping from our warm seats we zipped up our coats, donned our hats and gloves, and enthusiastically hoisted our carefully prepared packs onto our backs for the start of our epic journey. Then we stood waiting in the cold. We watched our frozen breaths hang in the air while Romanian and German TV and radio technicians adjusted their cameras and microphones, and the reporters interviewed Peter and the mayor and other dignitaries. A few cliques of excited and shy children—middle-school-aged students, I guessed—hung about on the periphery, hands in their pockets and puffs of fog punctuating their words.

Finally, just as my toes were starting to freeze, Peter finished talking, waved for us to start, and set off down the road with a grin as big as day. The vehicles started up with belches of blue exhaust above the white snow and passed us by, leaving a sudden hush that let the sounds of crunching snow and giggling children echo off the canyon walls. We followed with all the pent up energy of weeks of planning and anticipation, practically bounding down the gorge.

Several of the braver children hustled closer for a chat. They spoke English surprisingly well, and the bravest and most curious, a girl named Christina, tentatively asked between hurried breaths, "Where are you from?"

"America."

Almost leaping with joy, "Please, tell me about America!"

"Well, it's not all like you see in the movies..."

The rest of the children ventured nearer to hear our talk, which continued all the way to back down to the warm and sunny spring morning waiting on the outskirts of Zarneşti.

We're off! Peter, the author, and the Romanian children. © Jürgen Sauer.

Skirting the town, we took a path that cut across open terraces to join the road to the wolf cabin. On our left the beige valley floor curved into an ever steepening and whitening evergreen forest that lifted the frosty gray cliffs of Piatra Craiului vertically into the clouds. Hurrying to meet our final appointment with the media at the cabin, Peter strode along far ahead. "He *is* a fast walker," Ana observed. Peter's reputation had apparently reached the Romanian members of our team.

Reporters stood ready at the cabin with cameras and microphones, and at our sight they rushed to interview the students, who in turn interviewed Peter, all under Poiana's and Crai's cautious gaze. We hobnobbed with the paparazzi and celebrities (so I imagined) for what seemed too long, those of us who could grabbing a bite to eat, until the crowd finally began to disperse. Then Peter, Ana, Markus, Thilo, and I hoisted our packs, while Jürgen and Cata climbed into the vehicles and drove off to set up a camp, somewhere on the far side of a mountain ridge, somewhere near the village of Sinca Noua. It was about 2:00 p.m. We were an hour behind schedule.

Jürgen under the northern edge of
Piatra Craiului. © Jürgen Sauer.

Shepherd watches The Way of the Wolf go by. © Jürgen Sauer.

With the hubbub behind us, we walked in the sound of our
own thoughts, and in the glow from our well-wishers and the warm
afternoon sun, suddenly this whole thing no longer seemed so
intimidating. We walked briskly for about eight kilometers along the
flat, easy road of the valley, the forbidden one that led to the *Cold
Mountain* artificial village film site. I finally got to walk it—and so had
a bear, who had flaunted the privilege by impressing its large paws in

the mud alongside the road. Somewhere before the alleged village, we turned aside to the right (east), cut up a sloping meadow, and stopped to rest briefly in the sunshine. Taking seats on relatively dry patches of straw, we soothed our bare feet in the snow.

Then we began to climb. Our route took us up a slope that steepened sharply into a thickly wooded wall, until the only possible path was an ice-choked creek bed: one long semi-frozen waterfall trickling down through the brush. The time for Thilo to easily roll his wagon full of photography equipment was over—surely a dubious strategy from the get-go.

So Thilo hoisted the front of the wagon while Peter took one rear corner and Markus the other. I wanted to help, but it was obvious my leather hiking boots weren't appropriate for the watery conditions of the streambed, and both Peter and I knew that if I soaked them through, it would be days before I could hike again. With no hindrance from the wagon, I at least had some hope of picking a route through the snow on the sides of the waterfall that might spare my boots.

Wrestling the wagon up what had become essentially a cliff slowed our pace. The porters tired, and we all knew our rendezvous with the backup team before dark was in jeopardy. At a break in the action I suggested we leave the tangled ice flow and try what might be a more reasonable slope to the left of the ravine. It was still steep, but mature trees had begun replacing impenetrable brush and it was covered with mere snow rather than water and ice. Its contour also hinted of rounding to a knoll, and anyway in the snow I could also help with the wagon. I seized a corner and we scrambled quickly up the bank.

Our new route paid off, and we even stumbled upon an old forest road near the top of the ridge. Then, as we were stomping through the deep snow, we hit our Holy Grail (!): a set of fresh wolf tracks slashing through the deep powder, punctuated by a pile of scat resting against a tree. Our anxiety at the fading day was swept aside by this "... record of wild intelligence, efficiency, and mystery so recently cast in the sparkling snow of [the] still forest."[4] Peter dumped his pack, retrieved a glass tube, and carefully scraped a sample of the fecal matter using his sterilized popsicle-sticks.

Weak golden-red sunrays slanting horizontally across boles and branches put us soon on our way. We continued plowing through the snow, traveling single file like wolves—though much less efficiently—until the road and the daylight faded. So did any hope I had for dry feet—the wet snow had finally produced its inevitable effect—and after we topped the ridge and started down, the wagon with its attached people tugged and twisted me this way and that until my knees began to kill.

We kept coming upon extreme slopes thick with underbrush and fallen trees, completely impassable with the wagon. I scouted ahead, but nothing was working. Darkness and cold were falling fast, and we were exhausted and soaked from snow and sweat. Peter scanned the terrain, looking for some lighter channel through the wood that might reveal a path, or some recognizable undulation of the landscape. He had expected a trail down from the ridge, but only a dense and chaotic cavalcade of trunks surrounded us. We had no phone connection, so no way to know the support team's location. In our optimistic preparations, to condition ourselves for the rigors ahead we had packed our sleeping bags and pads, but not our tents or tarps, and now there was not a flat or dry spot in sight. I discreetly searched Peter's face for some hint of confidence. It was obvious that four months of this would be impossible.

Meanwhile, the here and now demanded a change in strategy. We wouldn't make it out before dark to the relative comfort of a camp—to something resembling the images of dry tents and warm food that were beginning to pervade my imagination—if we kept descending blindly into dead ends.

The wagon. If it wasn't for the wagon, we could slip and slide down about anything.

"Should we ditch it?"

My companions looked at me with puzzled expressions.

"What?"

Sorry. I'm trying to avoid idioms, but this one slipped out.

"The wagon...should we leave it here? We could climb back up and get it tomorrow."

I avoided Thilo's gaze, already figuring he wouldn't be pleased with the idea of leaving his entire net worth at some uncharted spot in this wilderness, even if just for a night. And a sour glance from Peter, who is never loquacious, acknowledged the response I already expected: Losing a day to retrieve the wagon would seriously hamper his ambitious schedule of trekking twenty-five kilometers a day, six days a week, over the difficult mountainous terrain of the Carpathians, some of it trackless wilderness. We desperately needed a good start in order to believe in our entire plan for the next four months. To lose the first day wouldn't be it.

My suggestion fell into the darkening silence. Not a dead dry leaf nor living green needle stirred.

Suddenly Peter broke the spell.

"Ana and I will go down. Others stay here. If we find the road, Ana will go get the backup team. They will bring the Land Rover while I find a good path back up from below."

Peter didn't say what would happen if they couldn't find the road before they couldn't see, or how he could find a path clear enough for the wagon. But if there was any light at all, even only starlight, it should be easier to find a path from below than from above. I could think of no better plan, and nods and "okays" confirmed that neither could anyone else.

As Peter and Ana disappeared into the gloom, Markus, Thilo, and I took a few longing steps in their direction, towards a slightly less intimidating grade, perhaps a better spot to spend the night in case the plan didn't quite work. If it didn't, I knew I was in for trouble. My feet were soaked, and not only did we not have shelter, but my sleeping bag was of the light summertime variety. I had only room for one, and when I packed back in my comfortable home in the States, I was more worried about summer heat than winter cold. I thought I could simply don lots of warm clothes during the few nights in April when it might be cold.

We stood and waited, for complete darkness or Peter's voice, whichever would come first. I guessed we had about thirty minutes until the former. There was no moon, and we didn't really think Peter would be able to find us after that, although I supposed hollering might help.

It won't take much to set up a camp. We have little to set up. Take off my waterlogged boots, put on the few dry winter clothes I have in my pack, crawl into my bag and try to avoid sliding down the slope. I just hope the dampness will take its time soaking me. At least the cold has stopped the snow from melting. . .

We spoke in low voices, not only to listen, but because disturbing the terrible frozen twilight seemed a weighty and needless task. I wiggled my toes to fight off the numbness that I knew would be the end of them. As the minutes passed, we became ever more still, until merely shifting our weight on our feet in the crunching snow seemed to produce an uproarious din. The light was all but gone, and I was thinking about my sleeping bag when I thought I heard a sound.

"Did you hear that?" Thilo whispered.

"I'm not sure. . . maybe," I whispered back.

We held our breaths. Again, a faint sound. Suddenly a tremendous whistle rent the stillness. It was Thilo. Then again, a little more certain now, definitely a faint yell. We waited until we could locate the sound, then we leaped down through the snow, Thilo's wagon alternately pushing and dragging him. Finally, through the darkness I detected motion. It was Peter.

Raising our arms against invisible branches, we all crashed through the wood, Peter leading the way down to the bottom of the slope and then along a creek bed. When we finally got to the forest road, we thought the worst was over.

Although the afternoon had been sunny, now there was no hint of a star or light of any kind. The total blackness was disorienting. I suppose the road might have been some small iota less black than the stygian woods on our sides, but we had to feel our way. The track was rough and rutted, far too rough for Thilo to pull his wagon, so he lifted the front while Markus and I took the rear.

We groped along for what seemed like hours, each step searing pain into my knees, my soaked feet, and my shoulders, which now burned from the weight of my pack. A wolf, observing from the black void of the forest, might reasonably observe, "That is not my way," as we stumbled past with an occasional groan. We halted at intervals so Markus and I could switch sides to relieve the asymmetry of our torment. Yearning for the lights of the Land Rover, as something like time passed, my expectation just settled into a vague will to complete the next step.

Waves of fatigue and pain suddenly rolled into a light. Then two lights. Two bright lights bouncing in the darkness. *A vehicle is approaching! Yes! Yes! Yes!*

But, what is this? Not a Land Rover? What the hell is a strange vehicle doing out here in the middle of this wild blackness of Transylvania!?

We couldn't know or care. We just trudged on—until, after some new black eternity, more lights. *Another mirage?* No, this time it was a Land Rover. It was real, and dear Jürgen was in it!

We had not the energy to celebrate. We peeled our packs from our backs and threw them and the wagon into the vehicle while Jürgen frantically explained that he had been searching for us for hours, driving up many a rough forest road. "It's ok, man!"

The Land Rover filled so I still had to walk to our camp, but without the weight of my backpack and Thilo's wagon, and with the knowledge I only had about a kilometer to go before a campfire, warm food (hopefully), and dry tents, my final slog felt like a joyful skip.

Our much appreciated backup team did indeed have a camp set up, much as I had envisioned, with a fire going, soup boiling, and tents pitched. We had survived the first day. But how much more of this could we take? Glancing up from my cup and watching my exhausted companions standing around the fire shoveling steaming spoonfuls into their months with gloved hands (there was only one place to sit), I began to wonder: *Has anyone else done this? Has anyone else traversed on foot the entire length of the Carpathian Mountains?*

I suppose we can never know whether some unknown nomad unwittingly accomplished the feat sometime in the distant past while on an extended hunt, or forced migration, or merely a protracted aimless wander, but given the physical hurdles, the paucity of motivating factors, and the fact that the mountains have been perpetually cut by numerous and usually conflicting tribal, cultural, and political divisions, it is safe to doubt it. During their reign of terror in the Middle Ages, marauding bands of Tartars on raids from their Crimean base into Central Europe for slaves and booty would have covered a portion of the general route, but to ensure the swift passage of their small horses, they would likely have kept to the mountains' feet. And during most of the last century, when the idea of hiking for the sake of hiking—hiking for recreation—first arose in the human psyche, brutal invasions, insurgencies, counter-insurgencies, and intimidating national borders would have made it highly improbable. Even today there is no single trail, no chain of campgrounds, no established potable water sources, no accommodations or conveniences of the kind that have come to be expected by most modern trekkers. I suppose it could be compared to hiking the Appalachian Trail before there was an Appalachian trail, with the added complication that one must pass through a multiplicity of cultures, languages, and nations.

Yes, staring into the flames and shuffling aching knees and sore feet, I couldn't help but wonder. *Will we, or at least I, really make it?*

Our four tents, all donated by Marmot, are two-person jobs, and Peter will share his with the canine member of our team, Shira. Terrified of Jürgen's snore, and realizing that precedent may endure, I claimed a tent with Thilo. Then I shivered mightily through the entire night. A woolen base layer, a woolen shirt, a woolen sweater, a winter coat (fleece liner and double nylon shell), fleece pants, a self-inflating open-cell pad, my 45° sleeping bag, and the tent were no match for the bitter, damp cold which rose like a reanimated corpse from the hard, frozen ground.

We awaken to a thick layer of frost covering everything that is anywhere near the river, which is steaming. It is minus 13° C (about 9° F). The hiking team—Peter, Thilo, and Markus today—gets underway by about 10 a.m. We are proceeding northward along a range of relatively low, rounded mountains known as the Munţii Perşani (Persian Mountains, part of the Căliman-Harghita Mountains of the Inner Eastern Carpathians), which is about sixty kilometers long, the highest peaks reaching near a thousand meters above sea level.

In the afternoon Ana and I scout for a campsite along a highway (E68) west of Braşov. The land is mostly open, and dry and straw-colored, and after we've run the course of a quiet gravel side road without any prospects (no water and no cover), Ana asks if she can drive the Passat. Around thirty and petite with very short, blond hair, Ana grew up in the mountains of western Romania. She now lives in Braşov, and speaks English very well, and has travelled throughout Europe to participate in rock climbing competitions. Wiry and waiflike, I'm not surprised to hear she won a few, but is now retired. She's experienced at living and working in the outdoors as a rock climbing and hiking guide, but is coming along primarily to help us navigate Romania's human landscape.

Ana allows that she hasn't had much experience driving a standard, and since neither of our vehicles are automatics, I guess it's time to see if she can manage. After she starts the engine and tries to tease our car along the track, I can see she indeed doesn't have much experience. She evidently doesn't have any at all, and while the car lurches forward and starts negotiating a six or seven point turn I offer a variety of suggestions. We eventually jolt back to the highway, but just as Ana's about to gun us on, I notice another side road branching off that I'd like to check out. "Turn!" I shout.

My urgency was a mistake. We pitch into the angle between the road and the highway and halfway into a ditch. By now Ana has had enough of my driving lessons and is nearly in tears. I take the wheel. And the blame: There's no question I've been too impatient. I apologize and silently assuage my guilt by concluding that the start of an expedition is not the best time for driving lessons.

We finally find a place to camp in a sheep pasture—with no water and no cover.

Sunday, April 3. Bogata pass on E60, Romania.

Except for a shepherd and a flock of sheep last night, we've been left alone at our campsites, but this afternoon we set up on a small sheltered depression just off a busy mountain highway. It is next to a small stream, and a group of frolicking picnickers have dropped in to enjoy an hour or two of warm afternoon sunshine.

The others are all off, and I'm watching over our campsite. Peter and Markus have started trekking, while Jürgen, Cata, and Ana have joined Thilo on a photographic tour back at Piatra Craiului. I want to hike, but my knees won't allow it. I'll try tomorrow. With no springs or clear running water for two days now, I'm putting my Katadyn filter to work on the tiny muddy brook.

I'm still wearing the same clothes I started with, even though I sweated heavily the first day. With limited luggage space and more concern about sweating in summer than spring, I didn't bring many changes of winter clothing.

Living out of two packs (a daypack and a backpack) in a two-person tent with two people makes for a cramped lifestyle. The going would be easier if I could remember in the morning where I had put things in the darkness of night, and if I could remember in the darkness of night where I put things in the morning. Then I'd only have to pull everything out of one of my packs half the time instead of pulling everything out of both of my packs all the time. I expect that soon I'll have a system down.

After everyone's in camp and the campfire is lit and darkness has fallen and cars and trucks buzz by on the road above, we enjoy a meal of polenta with tomatoes, onions, garlic, and Thilo's lousy cheese. He had bought a large wad at an open market in Braşov, but it is barely edible. We figure it will go down easier if it is melted in with the tastier ingredients.

This is fortunate for more than culinary reasons, as it turns out.

Camp 2: Shepherd's Camp. © Jürgen Sauer.

Monday, April 4. Bogata Pass.

Last night was very cold once again, but I added another layer and either didn't shiver all night or wasn't conscious of it if I did. I was wrapped so tightly in clothes not designed to go over other clothes and stuffed into a sleeping bag not designed for a person with so many layers that maybe I didn't have room to vibrate. In any case, I finally slept fairly well. Except I was interrupted when Thilo kicked me so I would stop snoring. Only I wasn't snoring. It was Jürgen, whose vibrations had no chance of staying confined to the Land Rover, where he has taken to sleeping. I tried squirming my lower half over to kick Thilo back, but I was too mummified.

In the morning our tents and cars and anything left outside are covered with a thick layer of frost. And stamped in the icy mud about a hundred meters from our tents is a set of very fresh bear tracks. European brown bear tracks. The same species as the American grizzly. Thus our good fortune at ridding ourselves of the pungent cheese, tasty or not.

After the sun climbs high enough into this ravine to warm us up, Peter, Thilo, Markus, and I hit the trail, continuing northwards along the Perşani. We jaunt up a gentle slope leading into a park-like beech forest.

Tuesday, April 5. Near Vârghiş, Romania.

Back in Colorado, the feasibility of Peter's plan to hike eighteen to twenty-four straight-line kilometers a day, six days a week for four months across the convoluted terrain of the Carpathians, up and down steep slopes, along treacherous ridges, through snow and mud and dense forest—some of it trackless—was a subject of doubt amongst my friends and me, experienced hikers and backpackers all. I can't say there was much debate; our skepticism was universal. Yesterday I learned how, just maybe, it can be done. I'll call it Extreme Power Hiking (EPH). Ten straight hours of marching fast, with one maybe thirty-minute break for a bite to eat and a couple of brief pauses if we're lucky enough to spot wildlife or the sign of wildlife (we spied foxes, roe deer, red deer, an owl, and lynx tracks). No other stops. Not even for a moment. If you stop to take off a layer, or tie your laces, or relieve your bladder, you'll have to utilize your momentary deliverance as a source of inspiration to quicken your step, or you'll be left behind.

At first the trails were marked and mannerly and the grade gentle. The naked canopy, each leafless tree its own fractal wonder, let in a fair amount of sun, so there wasn't much snow. The ground was covered instead by an amiable blanket of yellow, orange, and brown leaves: condensed glories of summers past, which, rustled by our steps, released a scent of fertile decay.

Then things began to change. The trails began to get unruly, contradicting our map or simply fading into unmarked, wandering aisles that forced us to bushwhack until we stumbled upon another line of blazes. The ground steepened, and regardless of angle the trail rarely bothered to switchback. We trudged straight up and down steep slopes so many times I lost count. After four or five hours—just about when we learned that our next campsite was still at least nine straight and level kilometers away—my knees began to ache. My strength was up to the pace, which now quickened even more so we might be out before dark, but the pain in my knees on declines seared through me like fire. I began sidestepping the descents to reduce the pain, which slowed me a bit, so I yelled to the others, who were not waiting, to not wait, I would catch up on the climbs.

Extreme Power Hiking. © Thilo Brunner

We had no energy for chatting, but once when I caught up with Thilo, he turned and managed a rare admission. "I'm running out of power." Not surprising, since his huge green pack stuffed with photography equipment looked like a small refrigerator. I offered him the Red Bull he had given me to carry, but he declined. "You can have it."

We slogged on, experiencing that perpetual fantasy on hikes in the mountains when you're hurting and tired: the next ridge must surely be the last. Wrong at least a half-dozen times during the last three kilometers or so, I hobbled along on wounded knees. These were now allied with sore feet, and I tried other strategies to descend the slopes—such as kicking out my unbent legs like a soldier on parade—and by the time darkness had completely wrapped me, I had fallen permanently behind. Alone and now with no need to keep up, I slowed until I finally stumbled onto a wider forest road with a gentler slope that I figured must be right. The dark wood began to lift, I spotted a flickering orange glimmer in the distance, and I dragged my feet a little quicker.

Limping into the camp I recognized most of our team from the shadowy faces wavering in the weak glow of the Primus stoves, which reflected faintly off the orange tents. Jürgen had obviously been at work, but where were Cata and Ana?

Turns out they took an alternate route, which was lengthened several hours by road washouts or some such thing. We had no campfire, nor cut vegetables, so we just tossed in some noodles and instant soup for a few quick swallows before hitting our bags. We had covered over twenty-five kilometers as the (very lucky) crow flies: At least thirty as the Carpathian wolf lopes, ever up and down. Extreme Power Hiking.

The night turned cold and left its frozen white coat to dress this morning, which the sun is now removing. Shira is curled up and conked out in the warm sunshine. Maybe she's dreaming of staying put long enough to pounce on field mice, as she likes to do when given the chance. Does the oblivious dog know what she has signed on for?

We have extra time to break camp this morning, and whenever we have it, we seem to need it. We have it because today we are *all* riding to a small village called Vârghiş. Even Peter, who is thus abandoning his plan of hiking every meter to Germany, although it is a matter of only a few kilometers. We are crossing a break in the woods, and I guess Peter sees no point in trudging along a flat dusty road where wolves wouldn't likely tread, at least in daytime.

We find a place to camp on a grassy slope, the side of a ravine above the village. This is our first time setting up in the light of day, and we have a broad vista of the valley, which stretches between deciduous orange-gray hills on one side and evergreen hills on the other to a hazy plain glittering with the silver steeples of distant villages. We'll stay here tonight and all of tomorrow. The hiking team needs rest, especially their feet, and anyway we are about a half-day ahead of schedule. We'll pick up the trail again in nearby Vârghiş Gorges National Reserve the morning after tomorrow.

Further up the road, two loggers are working with chain saws and a horse team. Soon after spotting us, they desert the large brown horses, which show their concern by contentedly munching the still dormant grass, and come down to chat, their arms loaded with fresh cut firewood. The wood is green, but trim and neat and stacks wonderfully. We compensate each with a cigarette, extras brought along for such purposes at the advice of Cata and Ana. As the loggers shield the little white sticks in large calloused hands and light up and let go a few puffs from out of their whiskered cheeks, their content seems to imply they got the better deal. They offer us as much wood as we want, and one of them tells us of his dream to build a guesthouse for the many tourists and climbers whom he hopes will someday be drawn to the nearby caves and cliffs.

Some seven and a half kilometers of limestone has been leached out of the ground underneath the two-hundred-meter cliffs of Vârghiş Gorge. The largest cave, a 1.4-kilometer long gash known as the Almas Cave (or alternatively, the Mereşti Cave), is the stuff of legend. According to the local version of the story, this is the hole from which the Pied Piper and his young charges emerged at the end of their long subterranean parade all the way from Hamelin, Germany, in 1284. The story probably has its roots in the march of real "Saxons,"[5] who were invited to Transylvania by Hungarian kings seeking to bolster their southeastern defenses, beginning in the twelfth century and picking up after the land was depopulated by the Mongols in 1241.

The Saxons would go on to build the "seven fortified cities of Transylvania"[6]—hence the region's German name, *Siebenbürgen* ("Seven Cities")—as well as stout churches in many a country village. The Germanic immigrants not only helped defend Transylvania[7], but their energy and craftsmanship brought prosperity, and they were able to maintain their culture—their neat, solid, and defendable houses; austere but pragmatic habits; modest dress; and language—reportedly less changed than that of the kinsfolk they left behind—until well into the twentieth century. Most returned to Germany in a migration that started with the upheavals of World War II, continued after the downfall of Hitler in 1945 (when they became welcomed as German citizens), and gained steam after the downfall of Ceauşescu in 1989 (when they became freer to leave[8]). Their influence remains, however, in the architecture of the many Saxon villages and towns that dot the Transylvanian Plateau (including Zarneşti), and in the tongues of a few.

The logger-entrepreneur wants to know our opinion of his guesthouse concept. *Sounds good to us.*

"Ah, maybe. But do you know that 150 bears from Braşov were recently brought into the area? This might complicate my plans," he says. "And yours, too," he adds, nodding towards our flimsy tents. We shrug and exchange furtive glances. *Bears will be bears; what can we do?* Surely an incredulous story, which later both Peter and Cata, whom would know, confirm is not true.

In the afternoon, my first clothes-washing the very old-fashioned way: Not even a washboard to scrub a couple of cotton t-shirts and a pair of wool socks; just some swishes and squeezes in Jürgen's portable "bucket" (a nylon sack), then wrung and hung to dry in the sun and breeze on a pole wedged in the forks of two sticks planted in the ground.

Usually when I hurt my knees, they are fine the next day. Not this time. It was that first day. The wagon tug-of-war definitely inflicted some damage. I think I'll be on the backup team for a while.

Wednesday, April 6. Near Vârghiş.

Jürgen made The Way of the Wolf sign. Jürgen brought the camp shower. Jürgen brought the portable water bucket and the nylon cord we use to hang things on or lash things together. Jürgen brought the indispensable straps we use to secure our storage boxes, poles, and other miscellaneous items to the top of the Land Rover. Jürgen brought the only camp chair we have, so at least one person can sit when we eat and no dry horizontal spot can be found. Jürgen brought the fire-starter we use when no dry kindling can be found. Jürgen brought fire gloves and the metal grate we use to grill over the fire.

In these early days of the expedition I often feel lost as we set up camp, not knowing what should be done next. Jürgen always knows. Or if not, he soon finds something. As the days pass, it becomes more and more clear that this whole operation would be impossible without not only Jürgen's equipment but also his ample foresight and practical knowledge. Of similar ages, Jürgen and I seem to have been thrown into this experience by similar circumstances. Like me, he was employed by a large high-tech corporation for many years until he was laid off when the tech-bubble burst, although unlike me, he was not an engineer. But Jürgen has an additional excuse: He was recently divorced from his wife of more than twenty years. They have two sons in their early twenties, and I have gathered from various comments that the divorce was not his idea. We have other differences already alluded to: Jürgen is a fountain of practicality, I am not; and Jürgen masks his doubts, if he has any, with at a veneer of confidence (at least), while mine are exposed for all to see.

Another relaxed morning. The hiking team, today reduced to Peter and Markus by Thilo's injured toe, sets off late, Jürgen dropping them off about halfway (5 km) to the gorge. They'll be on their own tonight, camping somewhere up on the bluffs, while we stragglers stay put, resting aching joints, waxing boots, and hanging clothes (washed or not) and sleeping bags. After a morning fog recedes, the sun dries us all.

Yesterday we thought our only source of water was a tiny, muddy runnel flowing down through the tussocks at the far side of our slope, so I spent a good deal of the afternoon filtering. But today when returning from the village, we notice a pipe sticking from a wall of the ravine, gushing crystal clear water. The first clean source we've found, Jürgen and I waste no time grabbing our five-liter plastic water bottles and trotting down the hill. The bottles are leftover from water we buy, which we reuse until they are beaten into misshapen blobs. In between fills I shuck my travel-literature-induced paranoia and drink the refreshing liquid straight from the pipe.

Thus far I have seen no evidence that we, or at least those of us who wish to, will have an opportunity for a shower once a week or so, as I had hoped and had been semi-assured. I mean a real shower, with hot water and walls and a floor cleaner than mud. But here we make do with the next best thing: a solar (i.e., black) shower bag. Brought by who else?

We construct a small enclosure from a tarp and several long, straight poles we cut from saplings (which we'll keep for the duration of our adventure). We hang the shower bag along the side of the Land Rover, which forms the fourth wall, and spread a few sticks to keep our feet off the mud. Only the first can expect a sprinkling anywhere near warm, since the water requires at least a couple of hours of full sun to warm up. I'm not first, so mine is just a brief, cold, wetting, followed by a brief, cold soaping, followed by a brief and even colder rinse. But a frigid shower is better than no shower at all, and after five days of living, working, and sweating in the dirt, dust, and mud, I almost feel I resemble my indoor self.

In the afternoon, Jürgen and I join Thilo on a photographic tour. Along the coarse road leading towards the gorge we pass a rustic farmstead, with a rickety pen full of prostrate sheep and a recently plowed field undergoing further leveling. A team of two large bony horses is dragging a wooden harrow under the guidance of a cone-capped man in knee-high rubber boots, all under the rambunctious direction and encouragement of a small tawny dog. In sharp contrast, a bit further on, a brand spanking new though apparently vacant log house, with a dormered balcony, an eave-covered porch, and a handsome peach-colored roof, sits in the middle of a solid, fenced-in yard. With no driveway and no neighbors, this is apparently one of the new vacation homes beginning to invade the Carpathian countryside.

We then visit the villages back down in the dusty plain, and become semi-lost amidst their similarity. Each hosts a gleaming, silver-tipped steeple rising above the plain, and rows of white stucco houses and hipped red-tile roofs either side of the streets, behind solid walls of tall wooden fences pierced by even taller, ornately carved, painted, and even roofed gates.

As the sun starts to sink towards the wood behind us, we don't have to figure out where the hiking team might finish for the day. We've received no text messages modifying a plan we made in the morning. We don't need to gather enough food for seven people, nor must we find a suitable campsite with enough flat, dry, relatively brush-free ground for four tents. Nor must we set up tents and hurriedly cook the food, which, although it is not supposed to be always and entirely our job, is the only polite thing to do when the hiking team comes stumbling in after dark—cold, weary, and hungry after ten hours of EPH. So we, the support team, have our first opportunity for a carefully prepared evening meal, and we make the most of it. Ana begins simmering beans in late afternoon, and by twilight we have turned them into a tasty and robust vegetarian chili meal. As innumerable stars begin to light the infinite black dome above us, our food, chatter, and fire keep the biting chill slightly at bay.

Thursday, April 7.
On the road from Vârghiş to Vlâhiţa.

We arise a little late on our familiar slope, play a game of horseshoes with a single rusty horseshoe found in the mud while our tents and sleeping bags dry, examine a set of fresh bear tracks nearby, and then set out for a town called Vlâhiţa (pronounced "Vlahitsa"), some forty kilometers on, where we expect to meet the hiking team tomorrow night. Along the way Ana will investigate any guesthouses we might encounter, interviewing the owners to build our database.

First we stop at a tiny *magazine* (shop) in Vârghiş to say a moist-eyed goodbye to a helpful and friendly clerk with whom we have bonded during our day-and-a-half dalliance above her village. Around thirty with dark hair—was that longing for a pre-Trianon past we saw in her proud blue eyes when she told us of her Hungarian heritage? (There are still claims of discrimination, though nothing as blatant as occurred during the 1980s, for example, when Ceaușescu's officials didn't allow Hungarian names for newborn babies.) Or does she simply want more than this remote outpost can offer? She speaks more than a few words of English, although she didn't let on until our struggles with Romanian had had the chance to brighten her face with smiles.

The gravel road to Vlâhiţa dictates caution, but we are in no danger. Cata, who leads in the Passat with Ana, takes his responsibility seriously. Thus we often tool along at about ten kilometers an hour.

It's another sunny day, and the earth is parched and the road dusty. Around midday we arrive in a village called Ocland, the seat of a "commune" 9 by the same name. We pull into a surprisingly trim establishment amidst the mud, a large yellow stucco house with a bright red tile roof and an elegant colonnaded porch capped by a white-balustered balcony; its sign in red, white, and blue proudly declares "*Siculus Pensiune.*"

The proprietors welcome us warmly, and while Ana interviews the wife, the husband, whose name is Csabo, a forty-something amiable and slightly round and balding well-dressed businessman, shows us around the dusty village. According to him Ocland is a "sister city" of its apparently famous namesake in America: Oakland, California. (This might surprise the residents of the latter, for I have found no evidence that Oakland has a sister city anywhere in Romania).

Ocland sits in the midst of Szekely Land (also called Széklerland)— an informal designation for this region of Transylvania where most of the Szekely people of the world reside, and where they form a majority of the population10. Széklers are a Hungarian ethnic group, who, according to legend, descend from Attila the Hun. In this they join a sizable club, but it could hold some truth. When Attila ruled the jumble of "barbarians" that formed the Hunnic Empire in the fifth century A.D., the Great Hungarian Plain, just down the rivers from Transylvania, was his preferred base. And in summer, if the Hun king wasn't out slaughtering, he probably fled the searing plain for these cool Carpathian hills. Refugees from his oppression, meanwhile, slunk to remoter alpine recesses. Until the tables abruptly turned.

From the time an explosion of war technology—the saddle, the composite recurve bow, and mass-produced bronze arrowheads—first enabled lots of riders to shoot lots of arrows from atop galloping horses with some accuracy (around 600 B.C.), farmers and pastoralists working the slanting pastures and rippled fields of eastern Carpathian slopes lived ever in fear of clouds of dust and thunder of hoofs rising above the eastern plains. Scythians[11], Sarmatians[12], Huns, Avars[13], Bulgars[14], Magyars[15], Pechenegs[16], Cumans[17], Mongols, and Tartars[18] all would come in their turn, but it was the Huns —towing cities of felt and hordes of livestock—who first made it substantially up and over the passes.

According to Maenchen-Heflen[19], a leading scholar of the Huns, the main army of nomads made it down onto the Great Hungarian Plain, sometime around 410 A.D., by descending the valley of the Tisza River, which cuts through the mountains along the northern border of Romania. This would put them crossing the Carpathian divide by way of the *Yablonitsky* Pass (also transliterated "*Jablonica*", and also called the Tartar Pass), at the headwaters of the Prut River in today's Ukraine.

As the pointy-capped warriors led their short, sturdy, thick-necked steeds (something like Przewalski's horses) up the stony path, the cold mountain winds ruffling the patchwork fur of their rodent-skin coats[20], they were likely anxious for the other side, for someplace flat and open where they could continue terrorizing from the backs of horses. Like other equestrian invaders to come, the Huns didn't much care for treed slopes, where they couldn't array themselves in large, mobile formations or engage in feigned retreats, and where their enemies could hide behind trees, rocks, and ridges and shoot back[21]. Enticed by rumors of wealth for the taking along the frontier of the now divided Roman Empire, however, the Huns must have sensed paradise when they finally broke onto the plains on the other side. It was a perfect place to graze their livestock, raise their families in their tents and wagons, and raid the wealthy imperialists the other side of the Danube. So that is where they set up shop.

The Huns had first reached the steppes of Ukraine a generation earlier, after, according to legend, they had been guided across the enigmatic "Maeotic Marshes"[22] by a doe they were meaning to eat. Once through, they left the deer and drove other bands of barbarians (so called by "civilized" folks who cheered from stadium seats while humans were torn apart by large carnivores imported from around the world) ahead of them like a bow wave in front of a rushing ship[23]. Swollen with recently conquered reinforcements such as Alans[24] and Goths, the tumultuous tide crashed against the foothills of the Carpathians, forcing less compliant barbarians through the valleys and over the passes until they (the other barbarians) washed up against the Roman limes[25]. Thus, when the Huns finally started up into the hills themselves, they encountered straggling Gothic and Sarmatian refugees, a related Germanic tribe already there known as the Gepids, and remnants of previous glories: "Free Dacians" such as the Carpi (see below) and the Germanic Vandals[26]—an assortment of survivors eking out a living on the rugged landscape, isolated from the intrigues and travails of the lowlands below. Though the Huns quickly set straight who was boss, they didn't much bother with the stubborn highlanders, except for collecting tribute and forcing conscripts to join their battles.

In those days (as always), martial advantage went to those with the best weapons, the most determination, ruthlessness, and discipline, and the best leaders—i.e., those with the best motivational, organizational, and tactical skills. The Hunnic warriors effectively thrust lances, tossed lassos, and fought in close with swords. In their later campaigns against the fortresses of the Romans, they launched boulders, battered gates, and scaled walls with engines and towers designed by engineers plucked from the ranks of their Roman prisoners. But it was shooting arrows from the backs of horses that was the forte of the Huns. They reportedly did it better than anyone else at the time. Their composite bows, strengthened with laminates of bone and sinew, were not new, but they were longer than anyone else's by a foot and a half, producing more power and better range. When you can hit without being hit, you win.

With enduring reputation, the Huns were ruthless (though this was before the era of chivalry in Europe: there were no gentlemen soldiers). Roman observers—not exactly unbiased—described the invaders as short and stocky (probably not a disadvantage on horseback) and added many an uncomplimentary attribute: "savage," "cruel," "ugly," "barely human," and comparable to those other savage beasts—evil incarnate throughout the ages—wolves. But the Huns were not likely concerned with their image. After all, they inflicted disfigurations upon their young: forcing their heads to grow into unnaturally oblong dimensions, and scarring their cheeks and chins with swords (of the males at least) to prevent the growth of beards[27].

For most of their century in Central Europe, the Huns were not particularly aligned in their goals. Roving bands operated independently, going around hitting those from whom they could take and helping those from whom they could take[28]. Attila, however, changed this MO. After killing his brother in 434 A.D., most Huns (though not all) and their many subject peoples fell into line behind their first singular leader as he led them on rampages all over Europe. From Constantinople to Paris, Attila's army helped one foe fight another, while seizing booty and slaves and extorting ransoms and bribes.

The fun was not to last. Some nineteen years after Attila had topped the Hunnic ladder—and some three years after his western ambitions had been halted by a Roman and Visigoth alliance at the Battle of the Catalaunian Plains—the "Scourge of God" suddenly died, reportedly from a nosebleed after an amply lubricated matrimonial celebration[29]. This was certainly not the first of Attila's nuptial engagements—the ruler of central Europe was used to getting what he wanted, which was always gold, but also numerous women, who gave him many children. In a story attributed to Priscus, a contemporary Eastern Roman historian, Attila's invasion first into Gaul and then into Italy was at least partially motivated by his desire to claim the hand of a Roman princess—Honoria, the daughter of the Emperor Valentinian I—who had offered herself to him, or so he assumed when she asked him for help, and who would presumably bring a handsome dowry. She wanted the Hun to somehow prevent her forced betrothal to a Roman senator, and perhaps spite her imperious brother who had made the arrangement[30].

Valentinian threw a fit and the wedding never happened, but plenty of others did, until the last, in 453 A.D., reportedly to a young Gothic beauty. An ironic end for the alpha-male warrior-king who set Europe astir for centuries. (Whether the bride spiced herself up with black lipstick, eye shadow, and nail polish was not recorded, although a report some years later identified her, rather than a nosebleed, as Attila's likely killer.)

To find the resting place of Attila, not to mention the site of his "palace"—which may have been nothing more substantial than a glorified tent—somewhere down below on the fertile plains of Hungary, perhaps somewhere along the Tisza River, has been the lifetime goal of many an archeologist, the transcendental quest of many a treasure seeker, and the dreamy fancy of many a rustic plower of soil. For, according to the poetic image painted originally by Priscus[31] and since embellished by legend, after Attila's entourage had duly cut their hair and slashed their faces and rode circles around the silken tent where his body lie in state, singing praises and lamentations, they interred the body in a coffin of gold within a coffin of sliver within a coffin of iron. Then, under darkness of night, they took the heavy burden to a river, temporarily diverted the waters, dug a hole, and lowered the shiny coffin along with reams of treasure into the ground. Those who did the dirty work were then put to death so no one living would know the location.

With Attila gone, discord among his sons spurred the subjected peoples who had stayed relatively hidden and independent in the mountains—especially the Goths and Gepids—to come down out of the Transylvanian hills. Led by a Gepid king named Ardaric, formerly a right-hand man of Attila[32], they routed the bewildered Huns. A few refugees probably managed to hide themselves in the wooded highlands, and it was these who, according to their ancient legends, eventually became the Széklers. Modern historians are fairly confident of different origins, either Finno-Ugric (an early branch of Magyars who settled the Carpathian foothills of eastern Transylvanian before their kinsmen reached the Great Hungarian plain further west at the turn of the ninth century) or Turkic (possibly a group of Avars who had sought refuge from Charlemagne a century earlier).

Whoever they were and however they ended up along the Carpathian borders, the Széklers were tasked by Hungarian kings to secure the frontier; their label may derive from the Hungarian word for "border" or "margin," as well as "ledge"—"szegély"—and came to mean "frontier keeper" or "watchman." In return for their services, Székler peasants avoided serfdom and Székler nobles got special privileges, the latter joining the Saxons and Magyars (and sometimes the Romanians—known as *Vlachs* at the time) as one of the three (sometimes four) "nations" of medieval Transylvania[33]. Over time, if they did not already, the Széklers came to have much in common with the Magyars—who outsiders called Hungarians—and they still speak a dialect of Hungarian today.

Descendants of Attila or not, the Széklers suffered their own devastations—particularly from the Mongols in the thirteenth century and the Ottoman Turks beginning in the sixteenth century—but they also successfully repelled many a Tartar raid, which occurred intermittently until the eighteenth century. (Attacks often came through the Buzău Pass, just east of Brașov, which came to be known as another "Tartar Pass.") They used their nomadic steppe heritage against nomadic steppe invaders, riding and fighting effectively as light, mobile cavalry along with their Saxon, Vlach, Slav, and more heavily armored Hungarian and (for a very brief time) Teutonic Knight[34] allies. They were key in repelling the second Mongol invasion of Hungary in 1285-86, when Carpathian snows also came to the rescue.

The Széklers were not always victorious, however, and whenever they were about to be overwhelmed, they sought sanctuary in their stone-walled churches, or the steep forested slopes, or in deep, dark caves. Emily Gerard, the writer whose book *Land Beyond the Forest* inspired Bram Stoker to place his vampire in Transylvania, relates a legend in which a resourceful Székler woman thwarts a Tartar siege by taunting the attackers with a large, apparently sumptuous-looking cake attached to the end of a long pole held above a defensive wall. The Széklers were holed up in the Almas cave, both sides were starving, and the "cake" was nothing more than water and ashes mixed with the last few spoonfuls of their flour. Seeing this burnt offering so demoralized the Tartars that they gave up and moved on.

While Széklerland is mostly a Roman Catholic island floating in a Romanian Orthodox sea, about 600 of the 1400 residents of Ocland are Unitarian—a statistic Csabo proudly shares as he guides us around a splendid, heavenly-blue church. The church was originally built in the twelfth century A.D., raised in the solid and defendable Romanesque style to save Catholics in both body and soul. Its lines and arches converted to the airier Gothic style about three hundred years later, and its congregation to Unitarian about a hundred years after that. The nascent denomination had been founded in 1568, in Transylvania, by the previously Calvinist bishop Ferenc Dávid, and Széklers in particular were flocking to the unitary, as opposed to triune, conception of the Christian God (a concept an Italian physician by the name of Biandrata had recently brought to the Transylvanian court, with slightly earlier shoots sprouting among the Polish Brethren in Poland).

The Unitarian church had been granted charter by the

Transylvanian Diet, under the Eastern Hungarian King John II (John Sigismund Zápolya), but the next Prince of Transylvania, Stephen Báthory, a Catholic and husband of the Queen of Poland, was not its friend; devotees were persecuted and Dávid died in prison. More indignities came four hundred years later, when the Communists seized the property of all minority religions in Transylvania, and exiled, executed, or sent recalcitrant clerics to labor camps.

When we finish the tour, Csabo conjures up a calendar, leafs through a dozen images of famous murals lining the church's walls, and hands it to me, with the pride of centuries of improbable survival seeming to reflect in his moist eyes.

On the way back to the *pensiune*, beaming behind the wheel of his sleek new Mercedes van, Csabo describes his plans to buy and refurbish a few traditional houses. He'll place them next to the two tiny new log cabins already on his one-hectare lot behind the main guesthouse, to enhance the cultural experience for his guests. Mindful of Transylvania's vile roads, he personally drives his customers to and from Bucharest, Braşov, and Budapest. Brimming with ambition and hospitality, Csabo's entrepreneurial spirit—and probably the industry of his wife—is clearly reflected in the condition of their guesthouse, whose shiny tile floors, freshly painted walls, and trim and modern furniture stand out in a village otherwise dominated by mud.

After Ocland the road degrades even more into a ruddy trail of ruts and mogul-like bumps, seemingly even rougher than the tussocky terrain off to the sides. If a thick yellow line on our map represents intermediate quality, I shudder to think what the thin gray squiggles imply. As we swerve between rocks and boulders up the side of an open valley, columns of smoke rise here and there from the plain. A haze in fact hangs over the rolling fields and scattered clumps of trees in the distance, but whether the obscurity is mostly smoke or humidity is unclear.

We roll into Vlâhiţa by mid-afternoon. The little town consists of a few rows of stucco houses strung along small streams—ditches really, diverted from the main stream, and, judging by the odor, important carriers of waste. Goats browse the weeds while chickens scamper about the streets and yards pecking the dust. The village is not drab, however, as the houses are colored with a cheery variety of blues, greens, and pinks—albeit with the stucco of many chipping away. As a town, Vlâhiţa has the highest proportion of people of Hungarian heritage in Romania—mostly Széklers—and is famous for its orchestra of 140 children.

In search of a campsite, we follow one of the wider of the narrow lanes up a gentle slope behind the main street, past more houses and finally along the main creek where women are washing their laundry with buckets and scrub-boards next to a melting snow bank. A few more kilometers of highland scrub bring us to a jewel of a place to camp. Just below tree and snow line, in a grassy alpine meadow surrounded by the Harghita Mountains, our new campsite lies along, or more precisely amidst, the many channels of the same creek that washes Vlâhița. These are the headwaters of the Vârghiș River, and they are swelled and churning with clear running snowmelt.

A gusty wind whips the grass and chills our bones, and to be heard above the howl of air and water requires force be given to both words and thoughts. But the mountain air cleansed by pristine peaks and primeval forests provides a refreshing reprieve from the hazy day behind us. This is more the experience I wanted.

Doing laundry in Vlâhița. © Jürgen Sauer.

After the hiking team has staggered into camp and we've gotten settled, Cata tries to dig an "eco-friendly" pit for our campfire. I am responsible for dinner this night and I semi-patiently wait, but the stony ground doesn't cooperate, and by now darkness is not far off, so after Cata storms off to smoke a cigarette, Jürgen and I rush to collect a few rocks and build a blaze.

Campfires are the core of our outdoor life. Preparing a spot to contain the flames, gathering deadwood, cutting it if necessary, with Jürgen's saw or Thilo's hatchet, arranging a small pyramid of kindling, lighting it, keeping it lit, feeding it until it grows into a flickering, self-sustaining, all-consuming, orange-red organism, cooking on it (although we more often cook with our gas stoves), drying our soaked boots and socks near it, warming our bodies around it, staring into it, contemplating through it, and conversing about it—the fire is the soul of our adventure. And tonight, with the hiking team in camp, we add something more. Along with dancing red tongues and flying yellow sparks we send song into the howling windblown night: mostly English-language songs from Peter's songbook, well-known numbers by John Denver, Bob Dylan, and the Beatles, as well as some old traditional American folk songs. We sing a few German favorites as well, but I am surprised by the strong influence of American music on European campfires.

Whatever our singing lacks in harmony of voice is more than compensated by its contribution to harmony of spirit, for tensions have been building. When the hiking team arrived this afternoon, I was sitting in the Passat, editing the English version of Peter's expedition diary on the laptop while the others performed various camp chores. I wrapped up what I was doing and walked over to greet Peter, who was sitting in his tent, looking rather haggard as he peeled off his boots. Just today, he had extreme-power-hiked around twenty-six kilometers.

"Hello. How did it go? Any sign of wolves?"

Peter looked up from examining his bare feet with an expression of annoyance. "Will you do something?"

"Sure. What do you want me to do?"

"Will you do... *something?*"

I gaped at him a moment, startled. It is true that sometimes during the rushes of our early morning tear downs or late evening set ups, especially during the first few days, I felt a bit like a fifth wheel, while most of the others operated, or at least appeared to operate, if not like a well-oiled machine, then at least like a machine, hustling about doing this and that while I stood a bit dumbfounded. Actually, in my opinion too many people were trying to do too few things, practically tripping over themselves to complete their favorite task, getting in each other's way and having too many conflicting ideas about how things should be done, as though it were a competition to prove who was the most camp-worthy. So I often just stepped back, figuring my best contribution was to get out of the way. I know how to camp, of course, and if I were on my own I surely would succeed in making and breaking camps as well as the next person, but here I was often a step behind. And how many times had I loaded all the tents and tarps and boots and hiking poles quite effectively into the large cargo box on top of the Passat, only to have Thilo or Peter gape at it with a frown, take it all out, and pack it in some other but no more efficient arrangement? Or how many times had Thilo sighed in frustration while I flipped my end of the collapsed tent from one side while he flipped it from the other? Even as I became more proficient, others would too often rush over to "help" me when I would have done better myself. I occasionally even found myself joining the fray, if only to complete my task before someone's help would cause it to take twice as long.

Recently, however, I've become more adept, fitting in smoothly and specializing in certain tasks, and as far as today is concerned, I had surely done my share to help set up camp. But Peter hadn't been here, and we found ourselves with spare time before the hiking team arrived, so as the others gathered firewood or hung their clothes to dry, I chose to work on the expedition diary, a task Peter had asked me to stay on top of.

Now, as our leader resumed inspecting his feet, I walked away, feeling about ready to do *something* like quit the expedition. But then I did my best to rationalize Peter's gruffness.

I'm sure he feels responsible for this whole show. From whether we avoid car crashes, broken ankles, and trespassing arrests to whether we get enough eco-volunteers to be able to eat. He's stressed and exhausted. Let it go.

I suppose I was also stung by my own disappointment that my knees aren't allowing me to do what I would enjoy more, and surely what Peter would respect more, than finding and setting up camps—trekking. But the support team's role is proving to be no piece of cake, and while it might seem less glorious, it is obviously just as important. Or it *should* be obvious.

Other signs of tension have been popping up. Two nights ago at the Vârghiş campsite, Ana chewed me out for offering a strategy for cooking the beans and then adding salt to her wound by suggesting that the chili could use a bit more, well, salt. And today, Cata went ballistic over his failed fire pit, kicking tussocks into the air as he stormed away.

Such frictions are to be expected amongst a team of people living and working together under intense conditions outdoors, but they can become heavy psychic burdens, and I've begun to wonder how we'll make it for three and a half more months. Jürgen, with the most amiable disposition of us all, seems to be the only one unaffected. So far.

There was no snow on their route, and the only large carnivore spoor the hiking team found over the last two days was the tracks of lynx frozen in the mud. *I want to see a Carpathian wolf in the wild. But they are elusive. Even here, on* The Way of the Wolf, *it's unlikely I'll see one. So why put up with this bleakness and bickering? Why should I stay?*

From here at the start of the Harghita Mountains, we expect snow ahead. Not only better for sign, but I love the sparkling silencing beauty of snow.

Friday, April 8. "Windy Camp,"
Near Vlâhiṭa, Romania.

We've made it one week! This pleasant and invigorating campsite has become a balm for our souls, just when we need it. We also need an effective balm for our lips. They are all seriously chapped and blistered. I've been applying a balm that I had thoughtfully packed, but it's not helping.

I slept well last night in spacious opulence, the first night in my own tent, enabled by Ana's and Cata's new habit of sleeping in the Passat. But tonight I must yield my new digs to Sandra. I'm not feeling particularly chivalrous about this, since I had diligently selected what I think is the best spot, a relatively rock-free patch of turf somewhat away from the others. I've enjoyed the peace, comfort, and solitude, but it turns out I do have a neighbor. Last night after I left the warm glow of the fire to make my way to my tent, a pair of eyes reflected my headlamp back from the wild blackness just beyond its beam. I froze and exchanged gazes with the greenish orbs, which existed only for an instant. I assume it was a fox, and am comforted by its living presence somewhere nearby in the windy, freezing, inhospitable void.

We are staying put another day while Peter goes to Braşov to pick up Sandra, a new eco-volunteer who will be with us for two weeks. So we're washing clothes and constructing another shower, this time adding the luxury of a soft floor from wide strips of bark that we find peeling from a stack of cut and weathered logs. After cleaning, we take advantage of the auditory seclusion offered by the constant wind and rush of water. The white noise also apparently comforts several roe deer that come strolling through our camp.

In the afternoon Jürgen and I walk down the road to the village to dine at the guesthouse restaurant. The village has a third-world feel with dogs chasing each other, horses pooping in the street, and chickens ruling the side lanes. Wood smoke, livestock, horseshit, cow manure, dust, and sewerage all add pungency to the atmosphere—a sharp contrast to the clean air we have just left. Yet the blue-jean-clad school children, book packs dangling from their shoulders and mobile phones plastered to their ears, look every bit like middle-class American kids; occasionally a sleek, polished Mercedes soars by, leaping potholes and outracing the dust; and the church is splendidly ornate.

Back at camp with the sun lowering, I'm happily cutting a log with a saw for the evening's firewood. I'm progressing well enough through the stubborn fiber, not really paying much attention to the details of my technique, when Cata, wearing his camouflaged forest service fatigues, looks at me from his rock seat at the smoldering fire, stamps out his cigarette and shakes his head. A tall, lanky, forestry student in his early twenties, Cata has strong opinions about how things should be done (no exception there), and he is not stingy with his advice (no exception there either), although he usually coats it with a veneer of almost too-formal politeness. Ever since I first let him have the wheel of the Passat a few days ago, he's insisted that he retain the role, which is fine with me. It gives me a chance to see the countryside. Interestingly, Cata is the antithesis of many drivers in Romania: he is cautious and, well, very slow. And that is also fine with me. It gives me a chance to see the countryside. Anyway, Cata is a very serious young man, and he's already employed part-time by the forestry administration, and so a forester he will be. And a good one, I have no doubt. He will do anything we ask of him, usually with enthusiasm (although he rarely does more). Whenever we thank him, he replies with a "For nothing" in an aw-shucks tone.

As I continue pushing and pulling the saw, Cata walks over and with a condescending smile explains that I should place the log so that the support, which is a large rock, will be behind where I'm cutting instead of in front, so the end will pull away from and take pressure off the blade. Having a background in physics and a fair amount of experience sawing campsite logs, I'm actually a little embarrassed that I was operating so thoughtlessly, and I express my appreciation for Cata's guidance. My advisor reclaims his rock seat, and as he lights another cigarette and takes a long triumphant draught, I suspect he is wondering how I have made do for so many years. Actually, I could start sawing on the sides once the blade begins to catch, but not wanting to insult my young mentor, who is sneaking glances to gauge my wisdom, I move the heavy pivot (the log is heavier still, part of a large trunk) and saw until the two foot section of wood finally drops. I wipe the sweat off my brow and appreciate a saying we have back in Maine: "Wood warms twice."

Saturday, April 9.

At last night's fire Markus related that he had pulled a tick off his arm. This has me concerned, as I couldn't get a vaccination for tick-borne encephalitis in the States and didn't have time here. After Markus's revelation, the conversation proceeded to some other European tick-inspired illness that sounds even worse than TBE, possibly not manifesting for years. (Upon further research I've concluded they were either pulling my leg or were indeed talking about TBE.) To the descriptions of convulsions and useless limbs, our new volunteer, Sandra, a woman of Asian heritage around thirty from Germany, just stared into the flames, her thoughts hidden by orange reflections off her frameless eyeglasses.

The night was warmer but windy—it is eternally windy here—and I didn't sleep well on the lumpy floor of my new tent; or I should say my old tent, back with Thilo. Exacerbating matters was the condition of my sleeping pad. Yesterday morning I decided to increase its inflation, and when I entered the tent in mid-afternoon, the almost brand-new normally inch-thick pad had morphed into a large blue balloon. I guess it caught whatever of the sun's infrared radiation passes uninhibited through tent fabric and heated until the expanding air separated the outer shell. I wrestled with the unruly bladder throughout the night, trying to keep some portion of the liberated air between myself and the ground, but it was worse than useless. Peter has a spare I can use until I can replace mine, but any ill-equipped eco-volunteers will have priority.

From here the hiking team (Peter, Thilo, Markus, and Sandra) will trek for two days through the snow. My knees still don't allow me to go.

Breaking camp this morning feels like routine drudgery, for the first time, really. At least by now we're learning to do things efficiently. *But where is the adventure in cleaning pots?* I soon find out. Always careful to use and rinse soap away from running waters (although I seem to be the only one who makes the effort), while scrambling away from the creek with dishes in one hand and J's bucket of rinse water in the other, I slip on the rocks and fall in to my knees. So much for the socks I have patiently dried by our campfire.

We depart our windy sanctuary with some regret, then make for Miercurea-Ciuc to buy supplies, find an internet café to catch up with email, and search for a new sleeping pad—profane goals compared to those of the hundreds of thousands pilgrims who make their way here at Pentecost each year: the Székler and Hungarian Roman Catholic faithful who come to a nearby monastery (Şumuleu Ciuc) and battlefield to commemorate the victory by their genetic and spiritual forebears over an army sent by King John II Sigismund of (Eastern) Hungary in 1567 to make them all Protestant. Within a year of his triumph, John II's Unitarian counselor Ferenc Dávid helped the monarch see the wisdom of at least some religious toleration, and he issued the Edit of Torda allowing preachers to "preach and explain the Gospel each according to his understanding of it"[35]. In addition to its famous paintings, organ, and huge bell, the monastery's baroque church houses a wooden Weeping Mary, representing she whom the monks and pilgrims believe had more than a little to do with the victory.

While in the city I experience a minor miracle of my own: a foam pad buried under blankets and burners high on a shelf in a tiny, cramped sporting goods shop near the city centre. My triumph at finding the thin, low-tech treasure is gradually deflated, however, by our next bone-jarring ride: a sixty-kilometer haul through the hills on another rough, winding, yellow road (Route 12), north to Gheorgheni.

Our route skirts an open valley with a bleak, reddish, Mars-scape sort of beauty: a landscape so desolate that it seems the thirteenth-century Mongols might have just finished their work. The sky is neither clear nor menacing, just hazy and insipid, which casts a grey dreariness over the land and our spirits. Although we have just had a two-day reprieve, we are all feeling tired, cranky, and downbeat.

While the Mongols, who bounced on horseback across four thousand miles before seizing the heart of Europe, were nomads to the core, we apparently are not. In spite of our own distant origins, we are growing weary of always moving on.

In the late afternoon, after Ana fails for some reason to interview the owner of the next *pensiune* on her list, in a city called Lazarea, just beyond Gheorgheni, we regroup in the parking lot of a *magazine*. We are far from woods and know it is time, but none of us feel inspired to set up camp and cook at some random place alongside the road, so we make a heretical decision: We'll look for a place with a roof.

At the guesthouse where Ana has just struck out, we have no better luck getting a room. It is full. Ana has another on her list located somewhere nearby, but no luck with that either. We can't find it. We don't feel like randomly wandering through the city or surrounding towns, so we head up another yellow road into the hills above town where Ana sort of remembers a place she once stayed.

After we have long passed Ana's memory and any light, something resembling a *pensiune* goes by. Then something resembling a motel. Some attraction must be hiding in the blackness beyond the swath of roadside lit by our headlights. We pull into the motel, but it is a sleek establishment lit with black lights and vibrated with disco music and managed by a slick young salesman, totally incompatible with our mood and budget. So back to the potential *pensiune*, where a cheery, robust woman of around forty-five, with round face under a thick crop of short wavy unnaturally red hair comes out of a two-story log A-frame and greets us warmly.

We get quickly to the point. A two-bedroom "suite" will cost 200,000 lei each. About six dollars. A short tour reveals a neat and clean establishment, with two log cabins for rent. Comforting knotty-pine walls, a kitchen, and two bedrooms, each with a couple of small but clean-looking cots; a stove to cook on, a table to eat on, chairs to sit on, and a bathroom with toilet and shower. The deal is sealed without debate. We'll have a comfortable end to this long, dreary, frustrating day.

The last warm shower I had was a dousing from a rubber hose in Peter's bathtub back in Zarneşti a week and a half ago. I turn on the electric water heater, reorganize my backpack, and separate out the things that are washable. Then I take a short tour of the backyard, to the riffs of *Take Me Home, Country Roads* booming from a neighboring house. John Denver's voice occasionally manages to transcend the multi-gendered, Romanian-accented shouts, hoots, hollers, and screams that accompany the familiar and comforting melody. Take me home indeed.

Impatience leads to a lukewarm but much appreciated shower, then I don some not-recently-worn clothes, wash what I can fit in the sink, and hurry over to help Ana with the onions and carrots. She already has a pot of rice boiling and soya diced and wants no help, not with the cooking nor the cleaning up afterwards. Jürgen and I later speculate that she wants to compensate our personal cover of the bill for her and Cata (there being no room in the project's budget for interior accommodations).

While we are enjoying our repast, feeling very comfortable and maybe even a bit smug sitting on chairs and eating at table, in rushes our hostess, whom we take to calling "Mama," carrying a bottle of homemade wine. We assuage our guilt with many a toast and lots of good cheer.

The Land Rover safely parked behind a gate, earplugs are my only defense from Jürgen's snore. They can't stop the low-frequency rumbles shaking the floor between our beds, but still I sleep like I haven't slept since leaving my home in the States some immeasurable time ago.

Sunday, April 10. Somewhere along Route 12,
South of Gheorgheni, Romania

In the morning Mama returns to fatten us up with pickled green tomatoes and sausages that resemble miniature hot dogs. They are "on the house." In fact, our hosts (Mama and her almost invisible husband) have been paragons of hospitality, even giving access to their ancient PC, which sits on a small desk in someone's private bedroom, which reeks of cigarette smoke. While I wait the five or six minutes for the PC to boot and the three or four minutes for my email page to load, I can't help doing what I always do when I see a bookcase lined with books: snoop the titles. Most are in Romanian, but a sociology textbook has an English title, and I surmise the name *Dracula* is universal.

Peter calls in late morning to ask us to pick up the hiking team, so Jürgen has left to comply. Meanwhile, Cata is off querying nearby Parcul National Cheile Bicazului - Hasmas (Bicaz Gorges—Hasmas

Mountain National Park) headquarters about a possible stay for the night. I take advantage of the rare moment of leisure and lounge around the backyard. Fronting a wood plank fence and a hedge of still leafless trees and bushes, a small stream slices along the back edge of the property, channeled by white birch logs lining the banks and spanned by two miniature wooden footbridges. The water is rushing, singing in its jubilance as it cascades over a small waterfall and into a pool in front of one of the bridges. Clothes are soaking in a couple of buckets near the pool's edge, waiting their turn to hang and freeze stiff on a line running from a tree to a corner of the main house. I sit on a small log and am enticed into entertaining a new friend with a wagging tail, who looks like a German Shepherd-Airdale mix. Dogs in Romania, it seems, are very quick to notice who will give them affection.

Although the earth still rests in the grey-brown dormancy of early spring, this is as idyllic a backyard as one can imagine, tucked away here in this rural corner of Romania, sheltered by wood and water. And as I hear the proprietors conversing, I am struck again by the Latin music of the Romanian language.

While Transylvania is called "The Land Beyond the Forest" (*trans*, Latin for "beyond"; *sylva*, Latin for "forest"), being fairly ringed by Carpathian woods, it might just as well be called the "The Land of Many Peoples." Arriving (or arising) successively through enormous spans of prehistory—Acheulean (maybe)[36], Mousterian, Aurignacian, Gravettian, Sauveterrian, Tardenoisian—we can only classify the earliest hominid presence by species and barely detectable cultures. With resolutions limited to large swaths of Europe and tens of millennia, we can identify them only by a few bones and the most durable art and artifacts. The first we can distinguish with any confidence we call Mousterian: Neanderthals who typically sheltered in mountain caves, hunted mammoths, deer, and maybe horses, and left a few chipped flint tools in a rocky corner or crevice now and then.

It wasn't until a mere 37,800 years ago that the first modern humans showed up in Transylvania, smaller-boned creatures who first left a few skulls in a cave at the far western end of the southern Carpathians, among the earliest remains of *Homo sapiens* found in Europe. These weaker but perhaps more nimble newcomers may have had to evict a few cave bears with their sticks and projectiles, but they seemed to have won over the resident Neanderthals by love[37].

As millennia passed, human beings invented, used, and then abandoned progressively better (and more) tools, and with less time for disintegration we are able to distinguish cultures with greater frequency and less expanse. In a cave near the town of Râşnov (which is near Zarneşti), for example, around 30,000 years ago someone chopped firewood with one of the earliest stone axe heads ever glued with tar to a handle in Europe[38].

By the late Stone Age, the first people to grow crops and herd livestock in Central Europe brought their agricultural ways northwards from out of the Balkans and across the Danube Basin and up the valleys of the Mureş and Körös Rivers onto the Transylvanian Plateau, arriving by around 6,000 B.C. The Starčevo–Criş (if I may imprecisely use the names we give to cultures for the people who possessed them) were early adopters if not innovators on many fronts, building sophisticated single room post and beam houses with plaster walls; growing peas, barley, millet, and wheat; harvesting crops with sickles made from red deer antlers embedded with flint blades; herding cattle; planting plum orchards; cooking hot wheat cakes; and weaving textiles with the new technology of warp-weighted looms. They were also the first to take advantage of the hard, shiny resources of the Carpathians, forging rudimentary copper ornaments and collecting gold from mountain streams.

(The Starčevo–Criş thus initiated Transylvania's role as one of the most productive sources of precious metals in the ancient world. Transylvanian metals fed mints and adorned necks in societies as scattered in space and time as the ancient Egyptians, classical Romans, and modern Indians: Transylvania still contains the largest gold and silver reserves in Europe[39].)

In one of the great ironies of history, Starčevo–Criş agriculture spread eastward over the Carpathian passes and down the lush slopes and river valleys (while a parallel transmission skirted the southern mountains). Picked up and run with by the peoples of the open steppes, the herding of livestock enabled the nomadic lifestyle, surplus, and land greed that was to power so many later invasions from the opposite direction[40].

As time went by, innovation continued flourishing in and about the Carpathians. The Vinča came next, the earliest users of copper for tools and inscribers of symbols for communication we know of, who founded the largest settlements in Europe throughout the Balkans, the

Danube Basin, and Transylvania by around 5,000 B.C. The Vinča were followed by a quickening succession of creativity, including cultures we call Linear Pottery, Petreşti, Cucuteni-Trypillian, Baden, and Coţofeni.

Inscription on a clay amulet from a site near the town of Sălіştea, near the Mureş River in Transylvania, dated to between 5,500 and 5,300 BC. These etchings, considered a form of "proto-writing", predate Summerian pictographic writing—usually considered the earliest true writing— by more than a thousand years. (Author: Nikola Smolenski, GNU Free Documentation License.)

With the beginning of true writing, we gain an even deeper sense of the attraction of Transylvania. The ancient Greeks inform us first of the Dacians (whom they called *Getae*[41]), who coalesced by at least the sixth century B.C. The Dacians founded a kingdom; revered a messianic, Pythagorean, vegetarian, and holistic-healing[43] man, king, high priest, or god named *Zalmoxis*[42], who reportedly promoted the immortality of the soul; and traded, mingled, and clashed with Celts and Romans.

After the Dacians succumbed to Trajan in 106 A.D., settlers rushed in from all corners of the Empire, enticed not only by the productive fields, quenching rivers, sheltering forests, and precious minerals of the cool Transylvania highlands, but also by the reassuring sight of the head and right hand of Decebalus on display in the Roman Forum. From his sacred mountaintop fortress *Sarmizegetusa Regia* in the Apuseni Mountains (the "thumb" of the Carpathians—see Appendix A), the "ten-man strong" Dacian king, with the aid of steep slopes, dense forests, and fierce warriors, had held off two emperors for decades. His was the most spirited and successful resistance to date, and when the end finally came, to avoid a humiliating capture he cut his own throat.

Funded by perhaps the richest haul of gold, silver, and slaves in the history of their empire[44], the Romans infused the new province with roads, cities[45], gods, and the Latin language. They exploited the mines of gold, silver, iron, copper, and salt; used the mountainous rim for a barbarian shield; soaked in the mineral and hot springs; and assimilated the locals. But the fun was not to last: Goths and other miscellaneous agitators (including the irrepressible "Free Dacians"[46]) forced the imperialists to abandon their investment after only 165 years.

Once the legions were gone, the parade speeds up: Goths, Sarmatians, Vandals, Gepids, Huns, Slavs[47], Avars, Bulgars, Magyars, Pechenegs, Cumans, Mongols, Tartars, Saxons, Vlachs (returning Daco-Romans, see below), Jews, Turks, Roma, Greeks, and Armenians[48] all scrambling over Carpathian passes or up Transylvanian valleys during the ensuing centuries, seeking shelter, peace, sustenance, plunder, power, the resources of nature, or to pass through to greater glories.

How many descendants of the Latin-speaking and by now Eastern Christian inhabitants of Dacia—the people who would eventually be called Romanians[49]—survived in the rugged sylvan sanctuaries of Transylvania before and after the Magyars came and made it part of Hungary has been a matter of dispute, with more than just historical curiosity at stake. During the last thousand years Magyars and Romanians alternated being the majority (albeit by village or micro-region), so who has the prior claim on Transylvania as a homeland? To which state does Transylvania most legitimately belong (if not its own)? (And the important corollary question: To which nation does Transylvanian's greatest hero, John Hunyadi—legendary nemesis of fifteenth century Turks, with Romanian blood and Hungarian allegiance—belong?) For most of the past millennium, Hungary staked the claim (with occasional interruptions from the Ottoman Empire and Austria). Transylvania didn't become part of Romania until the Austro-Hungarian Empire was shredded in 1918. (See endnote 50 for a brief political history of Transylvania since the foundation of the Kingdom of Hungary[50].)

By then, Romanians were in the majority (except in Széklerland). Many had started returning from their long exile beyond the eastern and southern rim of the Carpathians in the twelfth century, when they were known as *Vlachs* or *Wallachians*. For although Dacia had been centered in Transylvania, the realm often stretched from the northern

Carpathians to the Danube in the south, and from the Tisza in the west to the Dniester in the east (and maybe sometimes beyond—see Appendix B), and many Daco-Roman descendants had survived beyond the mountains. They were shepherds and peasants mostly, trickling in for the next few centuries, with occasional surges driven by Cumans and Ottoman Turks. They were also mostly Orthodox, and they came despite a certain inhospitality: A decree by the Hungarian King Louis I in 1366, for example, was designed to get rid of them, at least from the ranks of the nobles, to which some were arising, by requiring them to be Catholic[51]. Some Romanians therefore continued northward and westward, moving their flocks along the mountains into "Carpathian Ruthenia" (see next chapter) and Moravia, where the word "vlach" became synonymous with "shepherd"[52]. Nevertheless, by the eighteenth century, Romanians had become the majority in Transylvania.

What to do about Transylvania with its mingle of nationalities was a thorny problem for the negotiators struggling to redraw the map of Europe after two World Wars[53]. To Romanians, the acquisition of Transylvania in 1920 by the Treaty of Trianon was a "reunification." To Hungarians, it was an "amputation," quoting Fermor, still greatly resented when the young adventurer took his walk across Europe in 1934[54]. For those Hungarians who stayed "beyond the forests" (around one and a half million, while about 200,000 migrated to Hungary), cultural survival was at stake, as the varied Romanian governments of the twentieth century tried sometimes brutal methods of assimilation[55]. Nor does the matter rest today. On October 27, 2013, thousands of ethnic Hungarians demonstrated in Romania and Hungary, petitioning both the European Union and Romania for political autonomy for Széklerland[56], in hopes of preserving their culture and restoring what they see as lost opportunity resulting from continued discrimination.

Thus have many colored the landscape and language of Transylvania. The Romanian language contains Slavic, Turkish, Greek, and Hungarian words, as well as Slavicisms in its grammar, phonetics, and prefixes and suffixes; for a time, it was even written in Cyrillic. Yet, amazingly, surrounded as it is by non-Romance seas and encompassing the Land Beyond the Forest and the Land of Many Peoples, in Romania still resounds the music of an essentially Latin tongue.

The tensions we hoped we left back at Vlâhiţa resume when Jürgen arrives with the hiking team tightly packed in the Land Rover. Whether there is annoyance at our night under a roof, or budgetary concerns (unawareness that Jürgen and I used our personal funds), or the reigning minimalist philosophy, or just a natural consequence of (now) eight people living (mostly) outdoors for ten days, once the hikers unload, loaded questions fly through the air like arrows.

What have we been doing for a day and a half? We dried the tents at the last campsite, navigated extremely rough roads at about fifteen kph for seven or eight hours, and searched for *pensiune* owners to interview, as planned. *Why didn't we have a campground ready for tonight?* We didn't arrive here until well after dark last night, it is now only early afternoon, we didn't previously know where and when we would meet, Jürgen had to pick you guys up, and we're awaiting word from Cata about staying at the park headquarters.

Most of this transpires in German, but I catch the gist and hear the details later. I also hear about other attitudinal challenges. The hiking team has had a hard go of it, having to pick their way through windfalls, trek through deep snow on snowshoes, and camp without tent poles that were somehow lost.

After Cata returns and the air clears enough for everyone to squeeze into our two vehicles, we proceed to the National Park headquarters. There, to my chagrin, the plan becomes to pitch our tents on the parking lot. When I was exchanging emails with Peter while trying to decide about this crazy undertaking, he mentioned that we might camp at some "unusual" sites. We thought most of the trouble wouldn't come until relatively populated and developed stretches in Poland. Yet here we are only ten days in, still amidst the wilds of Romania, and already forced to sleep on concrete. I'd rather sleep in a tent in the snow without poles.

But then a break. Those who want can sleep in beds in the administration building. Jürgen must stay in the Land Rover, Cata has claimed the Passat, Peter chooses to keep with the spirit of "The Way of the Wolf," and most everyone else also seems content to lie for the night on the unforgiving surface. But I already know that my thin foam pad would provide little comfort on concrete, and for me sleep is more important than pride. I accept the offer. Ana is the only other person also willing to lose some status. When I ask Peter what time I should arise, his answer is curt. "Early."

Cooking and eating in the parking lot, we have nothing to sit on besides Jürgen's single camp chair, which no one lacks enough pride to use. So everyone alternately stands or sits on the pavement, shuffling and shifting to relieve bones and feeling exposed away from our usual wooded haunts.

Peter and Markus navigate windfalls. © Thilo Brunner

Monday, April 11. Mountain Pass near Toplița, Romania.

I don't feel much like writing but I have the time so here it is. I am sitting in the Passat with Cata waiting for the hiking team at a cold, windblown, fog-enshrouded mountain pass. This morning we drove the hiking team (Peter, Thilo, Markus, and Sandra) into the National Park at a place called Alba for their start under the guidance of a game warden and biologist. Once the slant and ice of the forest road became too much for the Passat, Cata and I turned and headed for Gheorgheni, where we bought supplies, then proceeded northward to a small mountain town called Toplița (pronounced "Toplitsa", meaning "hot springs"), and then northeastward up a winding mountain road to this pass to set up a camp. Cata continued distorting my diligently acquired image of drivers on twisting mountain roads in Romania, slowing to a crawl rather than passing wildly on blind curves. There being many blind curves on the road, it is already getting dark.

Water drips from everything: the branches, the needles, the grass. We'll have no campfire tonight. We've found a small but relatively well-drained and snow-free patch of earth resting under spruce trees and perched a few meters above the road, at the final switchback before the pass. Our tents will be exposed—to the wind as well as the eyes and noise from passing cars and trucks—but soon the gloom will hide us. Earlier I plowed through deep drifted snow, searching for a flow of water more substantial than a drip. The contours of the terrain guided me to a gurgle under a trough in the snow that took me down a steep ravine until I was halted by a tiny exposed spout between icefalls. I soaked myself to the waist hanging from a tree trunk in wet snow while my water bottle very slowly filled.

As Cata and I await further darkness, the recent negative attitude—the constant pressure to do everything perfectly and the complaining when things are not done to someone else's definition of what that is—hangs over me heavier than the mist. The eco-volunteers don't have this attitude, and it's not a strong tendency in Jürgen, and Peter usually expresses displeasure only with silent glares (or in German), but it is expressed copiously by everyone else (and in English, at least when I'm about). I'm trying to stay detached and let the criticisms bounce, but I'm suddenly feeling homesick. It doesn't help that I'm the only native English speaker here and the frequent breaking of rule number three makes me feel an outsider.

Then Suzanne Vega comes on the radio, and *Luka* from my homeland soothes me. (Suzanne Vega and Tinita Tikaram are quite popular on Romanian radio).

We finally set up the tents, and in near darkness I slide back down to get more water for cooking and cleaning. By the time I return, the entire team is shivering in the complete darkness around our vehicles. Turns out the maps misdirected the hiking team's stomp through snow, fog, and mist, and they had to quit.

It also turns out that Cata and I missed what could be one of the highlights of the expedition. Just after we had left in the morning, as the hikers were hoisting on their packs, Markus noticed a movement up the sparsely treed slope. Wolves! Apparently everyone caught a glimpse of the four sleek grey-brown blurs dashing up the slope and into the forest, leaving a shredded and gutted roe deer lying sprawled on the frozen ground.

Cold slopes near cold camp. © Thilo Brunner

The wolves of the Carpathians are a subspecies of gray wolf, *Canis lupus lupus*, also called "Eurasian wolves." Like all gray wolves, Eurasian wolves are believed to descend from canids that migrated from the North American continent across the Bering land bridge, possibly in multiple waves, beginning at least two million years ago. (After evolving "in the direction" of gray wolves, some migrated back to North America, possibly also in multiple waves.[57]) Eurasian wolves once inhabited most of the vast supercontinent (and its islands), from Ireland to the Pacific coast[58], until humans became especially adept at getting rid of them. They reached a low point by the mid twentieth century, after they had been eradicated from most of Central and Western Europe, and the Carpathian Mountains became their most significant refuge[59]. Today, with greater tolerance and legal protections, Eurasian wolves are making a comeback; they can now be found in almost every country on the continent, although the Carpathians still provide their most suitable habitat west of Russia.

Driven by thermodynamic reality (the smaller surface area to volume ratios of larger bodies produce slower heat loss), the average size of wolves in both Eurasia and North America generally increases towards the north, just like that of their prey. Thus Carpathian wolves are intermediate in size, most adults weighing between 75 and 130 lbs. The relatively ungulate-rich forests of the Carpathians result in relatively small packs (around five) and territories (between 80 and 300 km²)—smaller than those typical of gray wolves in North America (west of the eastern forests).

Wolves are opportunists and will eat whatever creatures are worth the effort to kill, which include in the Carpathians small mammals such as hares (*Lepus europaeus*), foxes (*Vulpes vulpes*), and rodents; wildcats (*Felis sylvestris*); chamois; and when the opportunity arises, livestock and dogs. They will also munch vegetation now and then, including fruit, berries, and grass, and they will scavenge inanimate remains—as demonstrated by the CLCP when it found a pack specializing in the offerings of a garbage dump in the city of Brasov. But the primary diet of most wolves most of the time in the Carpathians consists of the region's largest and most available wild protein, ungulates all: roe deer, red deer, and wild boar. A study in Slovakia, for example, found that red and roe deer comprised 68 percent of wolves' diet, and wild boar 26 percent[60].

Immediately after World War II around 5,000 wolves roamed the forests and fields of Romania, not only in the mountains but throughout most of the country. Some, at least, had probably even thrived on the corpses of fallen soldiers. Once guns ceased being fired at humans, however, they were aimed at wild game, wild ungulates became scarce, wolves turned to livestock, and Communists came to power. The new authorities had little toleration for four-legged partisans who took what they wanted regardless of central planning—the fittest getting the most, uncomfortably like capitalists—so wolves were hunted, trapped, and poisoned, and dens raided and bounties paid, until by 1967 there were only about 1,550 left, confined almost entirely to Carpathian slopes.

Then an unlikely savior came along. The new dictator, Nicolae Ceauşescu, was a small man who liked to puff himself up by hunting bears. He liked it so much, in fact, that he made Romania his personal hunting reserve. To enhance the quantity and quality of his bag, he ordered bears be fed, but he also banned firearms (except for him and his cronies) and poisons and seriously protected habitat. (For more about Ceauşescu's bear hunting and its effects on wildlife, see *Dreaming of Wolves*). Predator and prey of all kinds benefited, and by the time Ceauşescu was executed in 1989, wolves had rebounded significantly. So had bears—to around 8,000—far too many for the natural habitat to support.

The revolution left the large predators unprotected, however, exposing them to the same pressures that had decimated their numbers in the rest of Europe, until visions of the European Union brought Romania into conformance with European biodiversity and conservation goals. In 1993, Romania ratified the Bern Convention on the Conservation of European Wildlife and Natural Habitats and restored protection to wolves in 1996 (with quota-based hunting allowed and enforcement spotty).

Today, viable wolf range in Romania, entirely in the mountains, is essentially saturated, which means that around thirty percent of wolf mortality is caused by intra-specific strife. Around 300 wolves are legally shot each year, an unknown number poached (often by poison, targeted at wolves believed guilty of specializing in livestock), and there have been proposals to allow landowners to kill wolves regardless of whether they are actively depredating domestic animals (wolves and bears together take about 1.2% of percent of the five million sheep that graze within their Romanian territory each year[61]). Nevertheless, while there has been a modest decline recently, probably due to increased livestock operations and poaching of wild ungulates, the official population has been holding fairly steady over the past dozen years at about 2,500 wolves. Some conservationists argue that the wolf-counting system is flawed both technically and politically, and that the true number of wolves in Romania is significantly lower, but in any case most experts believe it is the destruction of suitable habitat that is the greatest threat now facing wolves in Romania.[62]

We prepare a minimal meal and silently stand around with our hoods up against the swirling mist and our gloved hands shoveling steaming noodles flavored with dehydrated soup into our shivering mouths.

Tuesday, April 12. Cold camp,
near Toplița, Romania.

I awake to the sound of rain on the tent, in no hurry to crawl from my cold sleeping bag into the colder tent. The drops are actually not rain but drips snared from the rushing fog by the twining branches above.

I have recently started a tradition of naming each campsite, picking my own or querying the team for ideas around our campfires. Not only is this a pleasant amusement at the end of long days, but it gives us a convenient way to refer to earlier experiences. The name of this camp is unanimous: "Cold Camp." As we stand eating our breakfast of muesli and bread and sipping warm tea, it may not be as cold as our first few nights to a thermometer, but the wind and mist cut through our clothes like we're naked. Actually I for one am not sipping my tea. I'm taking it directly into my muesli so my frozen hands will have only one steel cup and a spoon to clean.

After packing up, it's on to Toplița, where spilling from our crowded vehicles we're accosted by begging Roma children. We escape with strong talk from Cata and Ana and a brisk walk to shop for food. We have much to buy since our next campsite will be a four-day halt nowhere near a town. It has become obvious that our hikers will not be able to traverse the high ridges of the next range, the Caliman Mountains (Munți Câlimani)[63]. This winter and spring have been wetter and colder than normal and the snow lies too deep—well over a meter in places—and too wet. Not only is the snow obstinate, but there is danger of avalanche. So our next campsite will be a base camp: Those who want can hike by day, assuaging any disappointment they may have with a more thorough survey for spoor than usual.

Our hiking team must still go on from here, keeping to the lower slopes, so we drop them off just west of Toplița, at a forest road that wends up a narrow valley. My knees keep me car-bound and longing as I watch our shrinking team—today only Peter and Markus—disappear into the dripping woods, their raincoats shedding the persistent drizzle. I love to walk in the rain.

The rest of us drive another twenty kilometers westward until another rough track shoots northward into another dense evergreen forest that ascends the Caliman spine, somewhere near where Peter and Markus should arrive tomorrow. The road is gated and guarded, but Cata has arranged our permissions. Peter wants us to settle near the road's foot, to save time and gas, but an active bear hunt pushes us at least five kilometers beyond, and no clearing big enough for our tents pushes us several more through the deepening snowbound forest, until a small turnoff dips down to a level spit of snow and ice between the road and a wildly gushing river.

Jürgen sensibly hesitates about driving onto the ice, which seems likely to span something less solid, but Thilo is in a hurry. He urges Jürgen on with his usual vigorous manner. So onto the ice we go—and through the ice we fall. The Land Rover settles down in two or three more crunching drops until the undercarriage finally suspends, three out of four wheels having nothing but watery mud, or muddy water, in which to spin. What are we going to do? Has the expedition just ended here on this bland patch of ice? We have no winches, or capable ropes or chains, and we are likely far from any help.

Or so we thought. After hours of digging and chopping through snow and ice, and throwing scavenged rocks and logs into the mire, and pushing and prying and praying while we are spattered with a concoction of mud, water, and ice flying from the wheels, with little to show other than further sinking, an old Dacia pickup truck comes bouncing and belching along the snowy lane. There is no hesitation— this man is all business as he hops out, silently listens to Cata's details, grabs a chainsaw from the back, cuts down a medium-size spruce tree, and efficiently trims the branches. Once he's finished, we use the trunk and other large pieces of tree to create a huge lever and fulcrum. We pry up one wheel at a time, shove into the muck the long, sturdy planks the man conveniently has in the truck, and Jürgen guns our vehicle out of its hole.

After we've loaded the planks back into their place, our savior speeds off with barely a word. *Multsemesc* ("thank you") to another kind Romanian stranger—and a collective sigh of relief as we gather up our useless implements scattered on the snow.

A more solid place to camp reveals itself a bit further up the road: a flat pan of open ground between the woods and the river where most of the snow has melted. The newly liberated waters are rushing to join the Mureş, that great waterway of Transylvania that once drew the Starčevo–Criş up from the plains, floated copper to ancient foundries, and refreshed summering Huns. We're wet, muddy, and exhausted from our struggles with the Land Rover, which could be a problem when the cold night falls, so we waste no time gathering stones and deadwood and igniting a blaze.

After one does a camp chore often enough, one eventually owns it, and the responsibility of finding drinking water has now become unofficially mine. It is a role I cherish, especially since I've been unable to join the hiking team. It allows me to escape the bustle of the camp and explore our surroundings. Sometimes I have company, and this time it is Sandra. Several long days of Extreme Power Hiking have taken their toll, so she's taking a couple of days off. I remember her staggering into camp one evening, planting her hiking poles into the earth, plopping onto a log, looking at her watch through fogged-up glasses, letting go a sigh, and barely getting out over her breath, "Nine and a half hours..."

Sandra and I walk up the road looking for a spring, or a lay of the land that might imply a spring, but we come up empty. We are surrounded by water—unruly and cloudy in the river, frozen and silent on the ground—finding some good enough to drink should not be a problem. We'll try again tomorrow.

I've acquired another role by default. Living outdoors does not exempt us from that dilemma faced by mothers and housewives, fathers and househusbands, partners and the lonely, each day the world over: *What's for dinner?* Ana and I seem to be the ones whose bluff is always called, the ones too hungry to wait out the others in getting an evening meal underway. So, while most of the team usually helps once we begin—lighting the stoves, boiling the water, cutting the vegetables—the responsibility for design usually falls to us. We usually swap, and tonight is my turn. I've decided we'll dine on noodles seasoned with dehydrated cream of mushroom soup along with stir-fried carrots and onions. I hope my creativity, especially in avoiding rice, is appreciated.

Wednesday, April 13. Camp of the Frogs,
somewhere in the Caliman Mountains, Romania.

Last night cleared by the time of our evening meal, and I caught my first glimpse of the Transylvanian moon since I've been in Romania: a startling white crescent shedding silvery dust amidst the blue-black sea of stars. Thus my surprise when I awoke in the middle of the night to heavy rain rattling the tent. This morning is cloudy and damp, with intermittent light rain, but the skies clear again by midday. I guess we better appreciate these brief intervals of dry, for they are just that—brief.

We now feel settled in this pleasant though damp camp next to the hypnotizing river, so it is with some reluctance that we decide to move back to the foot of the forest road, where we couldn't camp yesterday because of the alleged twenty-four-hour bear hunt. Supposedly, Peter and Markus won't have to walk as far, but I argue against the move, as I like the river and our pristine surroundings, and I'm not all that confident that people will voluntarily give up shooting at what they think might be bears. I remember from my work on the Carpathian Large Carnivore Project that poaching of large carnivores in Romania is far from unheard of. I also point out that we're already here (i.e., the gasoline is already burnt), and anyway we don't know exactly where the hiking team will come out. But the weight of Peter's directive prevails.

Now I'm sitting on a rock next to the raging waters while the others drive down the road to scope out a site. The river dashes by, clinging madly to its trembling whitewater forms with a deafening, incessant din. Gray-brown with sediment and frothing, the water seems bent on washing away the banks while tree roots desperately hold on.

We've been at this for only two weeks. Seems like ages. I wonder: Do we measure time by the novel? Everything we encounter is new. When we awake in the morning, we seldom know where we'll lay our heads at night. Even the mundane tasks of living are uncertain and require unusual planning and effort. Ever on the move, our passage through space also seems magnified. Our focus is so immediate—worrying about the plan each morning, figuring out what spot on the map we need to get to by the end of the day and where we can get food and other supplies on the way, and then navigating over fickle roads—we often don't know exactly where we are. We unfold only that portion of our maps that concerns the day, tracing our route across the green and white blotches and squiggly brown contours by pencil. (Thankfully, our expedition occurred before affordability made adventure-reducing GPS navigation gadgets ubiquitous.)

Yet the trees yield their wet evergreen scents; the snow moistens and chills the air; the mud tugs at our feet; the river roars its freedom. . . Our path is real. But I'd like to know more. I'd like to know what has happened here. *What events of triumph or tragedy have transpired in these woods? What ghosts of soldiers who met their end in frozen grips of agony lurk on these slopes? What renowned castles or towns lie on the other side of these ridges? What hero may have been evolved there? Did John Hunyadi or Vlad III Dracula trod this path on prancing horse, armored and helmeted with feathery plumes on the way to battle Ottomans? (And to impale them, in the case of Vlad.)* When I'm traveling in the States, I usually have a pretty good idea, a context for where I am. But not here. Here in the misty Carpathian

Mountains, I am adrift.

Later, Peter and Markus intersect the road not far from our campsite. We're staying put after all.

We've designated this site the "Camp of the Frogs," in honor of the teeming throngs of amorous amphibians squeezed into the swamps just up the road, taking advantage of what must be the very first thaw. The females are larger and redder than the (mostly) green-tinged males they tolerate on their backs. Readers of *Dreaming of Wolves* may recall the newts that crowd the puddles and roadside runnels in the late Transylvanian spring. It's nice to see amphibians doing well in the Carpathians, at least[64]. And while I love the sound of the river, I regret it masks the peeping nighttime serenades.

Though green, the tree that was sacrificed to rescue our Land Rover is also rescuing us from the cold, the dark, and the wet. Much appreciated, although I suppose the tree's double merit is beyond reward in this world. But what draws us to fire like moths to light? Could we survive without campfires? We'd certainly have a lot less work to do, and our footprint would be smaller. Today, as we search for more firewood and break and cut it up, I find myself annoyed by our dependency, although maybe I am influenced by the gradually warming weather: this is the first night I've felt comfortable in just shirt, sweater, and green nylon anorak. Or maybe it's because when I hung my wet socks on sticks over the flames last night, my impatience burnt holes in a few of them.

In addition to yesterday's disaster, we seem to have lost our better camp shovel, which as creator and concealer of our temporary toilets is a critical device. We have another, but it's a tiny collapsible contraption that likes to fold just when we need it most.

Our food has been lacking in fresh fruits and vegetables, which I'm now craving. I ate next to nothing for lunch because I couldn't bear another meal of bread and cheese. Thus my energy is low. Now it is raining hard, and we cannot enjoy the fire, but most of us stay outside under the tarp with Ana and Cata, who must defer their repose until Peter finishes updating his field notes in the Passat.

Thursday, April 14. Camp of the Frogs, Romania

In the morning, Jürgen and I carry our seven empty water bottles

up the icy road looking for a spring as well as any less predictable
diversions. The road follows the river up the valley, but eventually
veers from the uproar, and after a couple of kilometers, a steep, mossy
slope veneered with an almost invisible sheet of falling water replaces
the river on the left. But no spout allows us to fill our bottles cleanly, so
we continue a little further on, until we arrive at the end of the track,
where are nestled, to our surprise, a few rustic buildings. An ornately
carved wooden cross sprouting from the snow signifies a monastery.
We walk onto the premises, where my "*Buna siua*" to a passing monk
doesn't elicit a glance. Is he a renunciate under a vow of silence, or
does he just want to avoid this profane foreigner?

We slither back to the road, wondering what such remote peace-
seekers do for water, and whether we should disturb them to find out.
It is tedious to filter all that we need from a small tributary close to
camp. Glancing back, we spy a monk exiting one of the buildings with
a bucket in hand. Is he going for water? We duck behind a leafless
bush and freeze while he comes out to the road, crosses to the dripping
slope, and fills the bucket.

Once the coast is clear we discover his secret: a runnel carved in a
small split log that barely peaks out from the undergrowth. While not
a spring bubbling from the sacred, sanitizing earth, it's close enough,
and if it's good enough for the monks, it's good enough for us. We
quench our thirst, fill our bottles, and offer silent thanks to the monks.

Later, Sandra and I hike for about three hours looking for sign
of large carnivores. Fresh bear tracks have turned up in the snow not
more than a hundred meters from our camp, and fresh wolf scat lay on
the road near our water source. We scramble up the same steep slope
that's giving us our drinking water, through wet snow and slippery
mud. With only a light backpack, my knees hold up fairly well, which
gives me encouragement, but my feet get totally soaked. I'll try not to
burn my socks tonight. (During our four days of exploring about this
remote hideaway, we will find lots of scat, tracks, and scratchings of
wolf, bear, roe deer, red deer, and wild boar.)

Come nighttime, it is raining steadily again. I get caught in the
downpour while walking after an early dinner without my raincoat
because it is in the Passat, which has left to pick up a new eco-volunteer.
My tent is the only option for drying off, so in I crawl, early by the clock.

Drip, drip, drip. Each raindrop dissolves forever in an instant, splattered by the tent. Sometimes I lament almost to the point of total despair that I cannot embrace each moment with complete awareness and retain it with perfect memory. I cannot rescue even a simple raindrop from the tyranny of time. But does time pass us, like this river rushing madly past our tents, or are we the *creators* of time, which, if our minds are open to the novelty of each moment—to the proud note in a bird's song as it announces its masterful new nest, or the sparkling gleam of a crystal on a frozen forest floor, or a warm breeze carrying the scent of spring—provides all the adventure, beauty, and wonder of existence?

Friday April 15, Camp of the Frogs, Romania

What a couple of days! Rain off and on. Last night, mostly on. We are existing in a matrix of mud, water, and melting snow. I now thank God for fire.

Last night Cata and Sandra drove 120 kilometers to Sighisoara to pick up our newest eco-volunteer, Klaus, who was supposed to arrive by bus at 9:00 p.m. They didn't return until seven this morning. The bus was an hour late, but the real trouble occurred on the return. On the rural roads of Romania at night, especially after heavy rain, holes pop up (or down) like obstacles in a video game. Not just rounded dips we might call potholes, but deep, steep-sided craters, which appear only when headlights happen upon them. Cata, who is no mercurial driver, hit at least three, since that is how many flat tires the poor Passat endured on its return. All in the middle of the night, with only one spare. I heard something about the waking of at least one set of presumably sleepy but very considerate Romanians to get the other tires repaired.

Meanwhile, Jürgen and Ana, while on some errand, got stranded at the foot of the forest road because the gate got closed for the night. Since their sleeping bags had been stored in the wayward Passat, they had to make do in the Land Rover with just their coats, and it was not a warm night.

Capping it all off, this morning Peter ups and leaves in the Land Rover without a word. This might not seem particularly onerous, and one can certainly sympathize with the project leader not wanting his every move approved, until one recalls that we are all living out of the two vehicles, so it's not unusual for something useful to go missing with an auto. Like raincoats and sleeping bags.

The expedition's minimalist attributes, or at least its minimalist budget, are adding to the strain. Complaints are coming even from the eco-volunteers, most of whom are presumably reluctant to register grievances about an endeavor that was never advertised as being cushy. But they are paying for their experience, and there's not enough of everything, especially food (especially since our fresh bread tends to get devoured before our older bread). I've always been amazed at how little Peter consumes for the amount of energy he expends. As someone with a physics background, I'm even tempted to formally study the phenomenon. But not everyone can emulate Peter's meager diet while living and extreme power hiking in the cold and wet outdoors. Although it's usually the backup team's responsibility to purchase food, Peter controls the purse strings, and we constantly feel pressure to stay within budget. Due to other pressing matters, we often miss what could be called lunch anyway, and there are never leftovers at our evening meals.

So spirits are down and team issues are coming to a head once again. Maybe the constant work and little sleep are also taking their toll. Even Jürgen is getting discouraged. He was brought down by his sleeping arrangements last night, and, like me, is tired of dealing with everyone wanting everything exactly their own way. This evening he confides to me that he is glad I am here, and would have left by now if I wasn't. "I might anyway," he adds.

There's no way this endeavor works without him. None of the others know the expedition hangs on this thread, and perhaps my most valuable contribution at this point is to keep Jürgen in it.

"Well, if you leave, then I leave. Then it will be over."

I let silence drive home the point. We've both put a lot into this.

Jürgen takes a deep breath and releases it with a sigh. "Well, maybe I just make a holiday at Mihai's. My friend in Maramureş. Maybe ten days."

I wouldn't much like his absence for one day, let alone ten. Not only does he make things work, but we've become close friends—although he was annoyed with me yesterday when I did not agree with moving the camp.

Whenever I can, I escape into the hypnosis of churning rapids; the river swells further every day, oblivious to our travails.

In the afternoon, Thilo attempts a photo expedition higher in the mountains with some of the others in the Land Rover; they don't get very far, hindered by snow and ice.

The forest is often shrouded in mist, and tonight the smoke from our campfire hangs almost motionless throughout the valley, like a spooky white veil drifting in the dark blue Transylvanian twilight. There is Something about The Night in these lonely mountains...

According to Emily Gerard, whose writings back in the nineteenth century ignited the worldwide reputation for strange goings-on in the thick forests and craggy landscape of the Transylvanian Carpathians (albeit indirectly, by way of Bram Stoker), the local people had a propensity for superstition. As reason number one, Gerard offers this:

> *"First, there is what may be called the indigenous [i.e., Dacian] superstition of the country, the scenery of which is particularly adapted to serve as background to all sorts of supernatural beings. There are innumerable caverns whose depths seem made to harbor whole legions of evil spirits; forest glades, fit only for fairy folk on moonlight nights; solitary lakes, which instinctively call up visions of water-sprites; golden treasures lying hidden in mountain chasms,— all of which things have gradually insinuated themselves into the minds of the oldest inhabitants, the Romanians, so that these people, by nature imaginative and poetically inclined, have built up for themselves, out of the surrounding materials, a whole code of fanciful superstition, to which they adhere as closely as to their religion itself."* (Gerard 1888, 366).

(Bram Stoker, using Gerard as a source, popularized it this way: *"I read that every known superstition in the world is gathered into the horseshoe of the Carpathians, as if it were the centre of some sort of imaginative whirlpool. . . "* (Stoker 1897, 3))

Ms. Gerard goes on to cite the imported folklore of Saxon and Gypsy immigrants as adding spicy potency to a folkloric mix that was already brewing in a cauldron of Dacian, Celtic, Roman, and Slavic pagan stock. Thus out of history and the Transylvanian night crawl demons (*samca*), witches (*strigoaică*), ghosts (*stafie*), goblins, and various shades of vampires (*strigoi, moroi, nosferatu*), as well as more benign entities such as wizards (*solomonars*), fairies (*zână, sânziană*), and sprites—all romping about the Transylvanian landscape and haunting its ancient hilltop castles—several of which, along with certain bridges, according to legends and ballads, had someone, usually female—like the wife of the master mason—interned alive as the stones went up, lured into their predicament through some kind of trickery and sacrificed to procure an auspicious future for the rising structure.

Other villains of Transylvanian folklore arise from barely natural roots. Especially wolves—ever portrayed as treacherous, malicious, and dangerous fiends (although also sometimes considered the enemies of vampires)—and those humans who choose, or are doomed, to emulate them: *pricolici* (or alternatively, *vârcolac*, from the Slavic for "wolf-skin"[65]). Werewolves. Still dreaded in the Carpathians today.

Imagine you're a peasant living in the mountains in late sixteenth century Europe. Your little daughter—the one you carried in your womb for nine long months while you and your husband struggled to feed your family, the one you nursed through disease and fever, the one who grew into a precocious, curious, and happy little girl, the light of your world who never complained of the cold or hunger, who would bravely march out into the dark of night to break the ice off your well while your little cabin shook and rattled in the howling wind—imagine she left one morning before the crack of dawn to exchange a few eggs with the miller for a sack of flour, your family's first in a month. And imagine she never came back. You, your family, and neighbors frantically search the open meadows and thick woods until finally your little child is found, half buried under leaves and dirt behind a hut that sits on a mountain slope high above the village. Her body lies twisted and eviscerated and missing a leg. A recluse is known to dwell in the hut, an evil-favored man with a stooped posture and thick protruding eyebrows that meet above the nose, a man who the children say leers at them from the primeval darkness of the forest as they tend their flocks in the pastures.

This horror of horrors, the brutal murder of a child, happens occasionally today, and has probably happened since humanity came down from the trees (at least). But if it happened in Europe during a three-hundred-year stretch, between the late fifteenth and the mid-eighteenth centuries—at the same time ecclesiastic and civil inquisitors were falling over themselves putting witches to the flame[66], and before detectives and forensic scientists were around to ferret out facts, and psychologists were employed to offer theories about the origins of such evil—and especially if it happened where wolves were common—there's a strong chance the killer was a werewolf.

Not just an outlaw, or a boorish man racked with evil cravings, who might derisively be labeled a werewolf by the local villagers, but a man whose skin suddenly sprouts a thick layer of fur (sometimes on the inside of the skin), whose nails change into claws as he goes down on all fours, whose jaws extend into a bone-crunchingly powerful snout, and whose belly is ravenously hungry for raw flesh. After all, such monsters have been revealed by many a famous prosecutor in many a famous trial.

Now imagine you're the hermit living in the hut. Maybe you're a shepherd whose sheep are fatter and woolier and milkier than those of the incompetent fool staked out on the next hill, who now declares he's seen you change into a wolf. Or maybe you're a peasant just barely scraping by, uneducated and illiterate and a little slow on the uptake. Maybe you're even starving, reduced to eating grass as famine ravages the countryside due to a long spell of wet, cold weather that has recently rotted the crops[67]. Yes, you sometimes watch the young shepherds. But not to commit the unspeakable act of devouring a child. You're just hoping for a scrap they leave behind, or maybe even to steal a sheep.

Heaven forbid you also be seized with epileptic fits. Or have a wound where an accuser says one of his dogs bit the fiend who was attacking his sheep just last week. Because if you're suspected of a heretical crime like transforming into a wolf, your fate is about to get horrid. Just as horrid as *your* lungs being ripped out by a supernatural beast. Because—not only to put a stop to the evil acts, but for the sake of your own soul—you must *confess*.

So you've been held in chains interminably in a dark, dank dungeon, and now you're shown the implements: the thumb screws, the Spanish boots, the rack, the pulleys to hang you by your arms until they separate from their sockets[68]. . . True, the penalty for being a werewolf is the flame, if not many tortures besides[69], so you might reasonably wonder what benefit a confession.

The rack or the fire. Not much of a choice. But the former will surely lead to the latter anyway, and you've been made to understand that if you confess, you'll be mercifully strangled before you're mutilated and burned. So you answer the inquisitor's leading questions.

"Yes, I made a deal with a dark man. He promised to help me."

"Yes, he gave me the skin of a wolf."

"Yes, I stripped naked and he rubbed on me a foul ointment and told me to put on the pelt."

"Yes, he also chanted strange words."

"Yes, I became a wolf. I had the paws of a wolf and the jaws of a wolf."

"Yes, I craved raw meat."

"Yes, I copulated with wolves. I enjoyed it as much as with my wife."

"Yes, I killed and ate the girl."

"Yes, yes, and many others besides. But little girls taste best. And if I couldn't get a live one, corpses from the cemetery would do."

"Yes, I could hardly move from fatigue after I was finished running and killing and had regained my human form."

Just like all the others. *Case closed.*

Stories and legends about werewolves have been common throughout history, just about everywhere in the world there are (or have been) wolves. Shape-shifting into animals, or simply being part animal, was a typical feature of many an early god of man, and many origin myths portray tribal descent from animals or animal-like beings. Carpathian highlanders tell stories in the other direction as well: bears, bees, and voles descending from people[70]. And common is the theme that animals and humans once spoke the same language. There seems to be an innate recognition that human and non-human animals are kin. Especially when it comes to mammals: we all have four limbs, and heads with a nose, two eyes, and two ears. And if you look inside, which meat eaters and warriors are wont to do, you find the same basic structure: the same organs and tissues, all bathed in red blood.

But why the emphasis on wolves? Well, over most of their territory, as far as early hunters and pastoralists were concerned, wolves were the most bad-ass predators out there[71]. They were fierce and efficient competitors for the same prey as humans; they hunted in groups like humans; they killed the animals of humans; and sometimes they killed humans. And as they tore into soft underbellies for the steaming, nutrient-rich organs, and ripped off chunks of raw muscle with shakes of their tremendous necks, and crunched bones and sinew with twice the force of any domestic dog[72]—all the while fending off pretenders with snarls, growls, and snaps—wolves were pure primal power incarnate.

So early hunter and warrior societies emulated wolves in hopes for some of their mojo. Prior to hunts (which may have often been timed with the lunar cycle, at least in part to avoid the cyclic bleeding of women), hopeful nimrods donned wolf skins and danced around fires, whipping themselves into frenzies as they imitated wolf postures, movements, and howls. Nervous warriors—especially initiates—did likewise, and kept the skins on for raids, both to terrify enemies and soften incoming blows[73]. Those who fought spiritual battles—the shamans—also invoked the power of the great predator, taking the form of wolves on their entranced journeys to the other world[74]. The dreaded and yet magnificent wolf even nurtured great founders and heroes, like Romulus and Remus and an ancestor of Genghis Khan.

Sure, witches could morph into cats and jump fences and slink about doing their dirty work; and more than one legendary fool was turned into an ass; and the *berserkers* of the Norse[75] could do damage in the guise of bears as well as wolves[76]. But no creature was as cunning and vicious as the wolf. Wolves were so terrible—in fact, they were the enemy of the Lamb, the Christ—that sometimes the devil himself took their shape.

The first written reference of shape-shifting into wolves occurs in one of the earliest surviving works of literature, the *Epic of Gilgamesh*, a poem written in eighteenth century B.C., in Mesopotamia. The epic has themes, details, and proverbs that seem to have infiltrated both the Old Testament and the works of Homer, and amidst its stories of flood and odyssey is a tale of a shepherd, who after sacrificing to Ishtar—goddess of love, war, fertility, and sex—is turned into a wolf. Apparently not a particularly big, bad, wolf, as he is subsequently devoured by his dogs.

Herodotus, writing in the fifth century B.C., tells of a tribe called the Neuri, living somewhere in what is now northern Ukraine (and who therefore may have been a proto-Slavic people—see the next chapter), who temporarily changed into wolves once a year. In one of the oldest werewolf myths, an ancient Arcadian king named Lycaon tries to feed Zeus a meal of his own baby son, supposedly to test the top god's power of discernment. Zeus is not fooled and punishes the skeptic and would-be cannibal-maker by turning him into that most feared, ferocious, and insatiable devourer of flesh, a wolf.

Not all werewolves of European folklore were unambiguously malicious. Rather than serving the devil, some eastern werewolves battled him and his witches over the produce or fertility of the fields[77]. These disputes usually occurred during the Christmas season or other religious feast days, such as those of St. Lucy, Epiphany, St. George, and St. John (which coincide with pagan days of the dead and also include the winter and summer solstices[78]). Other, eastern werewolves seemed at least as interested in partying as killing and cannibalizing[79], and even in the West, before cavorting with witches made them nothing but bad, certain literary werewolves were famously portrayed as semi-sympathetic figures: men shaped into wolves by life's tragedies, such as having unfaithful wives, who might take vengeance on their betrayers, but who were otherwise benevolent and loyal friends. And the trials do not inform us of the unwilling unfortunates transformed by spurned witches or hired sorcerers, or by indifferent heredity, who more often behaved as whimpering victims seeking pity than fierce marauders seeking blood[80].

In their efforts to stamp out pagan beliefs, the churches, especially the western churches, began forcing all but their own supernatural beings towards unambiguous evil. Early on, even to believe in werewolves was declared heretical, since it implied doubt that such acts of material creation as changing a man into a wolf were God's alone[81]. But werewolf folklore was widespread and stubborn, and theologians, especially under the influence of St. Thomas Aquinas, began to suspect that the devil could indeed work in mysterious ways.

Thus by the fifteenth century—around the same time Europe was racked by political, social, and religious violence and extreme poverty to the point of occasional famine and even cannibalism—certain dedicated inquisitors and jurists began enhancing their prestige by penning detailed demonologies outlining just how and why people became witches and werewolves, and what to do about it[82]. Werewolves became decidedly depraved, vicious, and real, and to become one, at least voluntarily[83], you now had to do more than the heretofore sufficient strategies of walking through water and donning wolf skins in the light of the full moon. You had to make a pact with the devil, and you had to do something to demonstrate your subservience, like apply a foul ointment or repeat unspeakable incantations.

Real wolves, meanwhile, were doing well. During the fourteenth century, the Black Death had put a 30–60% dent in the population of their two-legged nemesis, triggering a recovery from an earlier decline probably caused by vast agricultural clearings. As the forests returned, so did the wolves, coming down from the mountains and from the north and having plenty to eat in the form of poorly disposed human corpses. They defeated all attempts by kings and lords to get rid of them, including bounties and massive hunts, and they discovered another promising food source as sheep became important to the livelihood of Europe.

Wolves sometimes wreaked havoc on livestock and occasionally, especially during very cold winters, on people. A few bad actors became especially famous, such as the Wolf of Gubbio, which allegedly killed and ate people until St. Francis intervened. The Wolves of Paris reportedly penetrated gaps in the city walls during the winter of 1450 and killed forty people before the citizens of the city lured them to the front of Notre Dame Cathedral and stoned and speared them to death. (Occasional wolf attacks on humans in Europe and Asia are reported today—typically more in one year than in North America over a century—perhaps due to millennia of habituation to the greater proximity of humans, including corpses left during frequent wars and plagues. Most cases today, however, involve rabid or captive wolves, or wolves defending themselves.)

So we have the word "scapegoat;" maybe we should add "scapeperson" for projecting onto some unlucky, sullen, down-and-out man what real wolves may have done[84]. And it surely went the other way as well. There may have always been people who believe they become wolves, and there surely have always been serial killers amongst us.

Thus the trials during the sixteenth and early seventeenth centuries of people (usually but not always men) accused of, and often confessing to, such heinous and sensational crimes as raping and eating women and children in the form of wolves, including such famous werewolves as Pierre Burgout, Michael Verdun, Peter Stump (or Stubb), Giles Garnier, the Gandillon family, Jacques Roulet, and Jean Grenier.

The leading jurists of the day were conflicted regarding the nature of the crime for which they were condemning people to torture and death. For example, Henri Boguet (1550 - 1619), perhaps the most famous witch-hunter of all, who claimed to have successfully prosecuted 600 witches and werewolves and who wrote the standard text for witch-hunting prosecutors (*Discours des sorciers*), believed on the one hand that werewolves were real enough, and on the other that they were delusions caused by the devil. He and many others went to great lengths and twists of logic to explain the possibilities, drawing inspiration from a cauldron of real events, imaginations, folklore, religion, and perhaps a few lying (or hallucinating) witnesses: *The devil deludes people into believing they commit evil acts in the form of wolves, and deceives their victims and witnesses as well. The devil entrances people to sleep, fills their dreams with the acts of real wolves under devilish control, and inflicts fatigue and any necessary sympathetic wounds as well (echoes of shamanism). The devil commits the acts at the behest of a sleeping "witch." The devil creates "an aerial effigy of a beast"* (Summers 2003, 121) *around a person committing the crimes. The devil, although he cannot create perfectly, can create imperfectly, so the transformations are real but if one looks closely, the creatures lack tails.* All ultimately, of course, as just punishment from God[85].

The trials of werewolves began to wane during the seventeenth century as prosecutors started to believe that werewolves, even those who confessed, could not materially change into wolves, nor were they necessarily possessed by demons. Rather, they were simply people deranged, lying, or framed. After all, most confessions that were unforced (e.g., Roulet) or even boastful (e.g., Grenier) came from obviously unbalanced folks. And maybe the nascent rational and scientific approach would uncover other causes, such as rabies[86], the strange ointments[87], ergot poisoning[88], or mere physical deformities[89]— maybe even under the peculiar influence of the moon (lunacy).

Sentences thus began to favor imprisonment over death by torture and fire, and by the eighteenth century the reborn science of psychology started making one of its oldest diagnoses (going back to its roots in ancient Greece)—*clinical lycanthropy*, taken from the myth of Lycaon—a form of mental illness in which a person believes he or she is a wolf and acts accordingly: crawling about on all fours, barking and howling, or even having an urge to kill and consume people or animals or to hang out in graveyards; a form of madness which occurs even to this day[90].

Is Something out there? © Jürgen Sauer.

Sunday, April 17. Camp of the Flies,
Piatra Fântânele, Romania.

Yesterday morning we departed the amphibious world of the Camp of the Frogs. It was the first time the entire team of now nine of us squeezed into the two vehicles for the sixty- kilometer drive, and it was not pleasant. Fitting everyone in required careful packing, and many of us had to hold full backpacks on our laps, or boxes of food, or a trail-weathered dog. We were compensated with the sight of three or four free-ranging roe deer browsing on the slopes, who lifted their heads in unison and twitched their ears as our stuffed cars sped by.

The restocked and rejuvenated hiking team (Peter, Thilo, Markus, Sandra, and Klaus) finally spilled out onto a muddy track near a couple of log houses on the outskirts of a village called Vătava, shouldered their packs in a downpour, and strode into the forest of a small ravine— the dim, gray skylight glistening off their ponchos. As they disappeared into yet another dripping mystery, how I wanted to go with them!

The rest of us continued westward on the only motorized route around the Caliman range. This took us some distance from the mountains, and onto a stretch of rolling farmland, where the burgeoning earth, the season's first green leaves, and our relieved quarters lifted our spirits.

Arriving at Bistrița[91] in early evening, we resupplied our meager food stocks, using all of the money Peter had allocated for us plus some of our own. Bistrița, which name derives from a Slavic word meaning "fast moving water," referring to the river which tumbles through it, is another locale that should be familiar to readers of *Dracula*. This is where Count Dracula's dutiful if uneasy legal advisor from England, John Harker, spent his second night in Romania on the way to visit his mysterious client. Harker's hotel, the Golden Krone, was fictional at the time, but a real version has since sprung from the page to satisfy the expectations of vampire fans.

After shopping we headed northeast on Highway 17, back into the dull late-winter browns and grays and the brilliant whites of the mountains, to the vicinity of our next planned hookup with the hiking team, a village called Piatra Fântânele. Upon our arrival, we found a spattering of humble buildings strung along the highway on top of a mountain pass. The sun was sinking into a cloud-lined golden-violet blaze behind tiers of receding, hazy hills, and precedent having been set, we settled into a quaint, mountaintop *pensiune* for the night.

Daylight brings to the hamlet of Piatra Fântânele a grand prospect of rolling hills mottled by patches of evergreen and meadow with a backdrop of spectacular snow-capped peaks—the Calimans to the south and the Bargau Range (*Munţii Bârgăului*[92]) to the north. The view is breathtaking, and it's natural to conclude that this quiet village is destined to become a resort. In fact, the process has already begun. At the bottom of a high hill immediately adjacent the village, a chairlift begins its ascent straight up a steep white slope. A couple of trim *pensiunes* are popping up along the winding highway on the outskirts of the village proper, and just down the road looms a large complicated stoney structure at the end of a parking lot, an establishment designated "Hotel Castel Dracula."

Straddling the border between Transylvania and the historical region of Bukovina (the "land of beech trees"), this mountain pass is called the Tihuţa Pass in Romanian. In Hungarian it is called Borgo Pass, and this is where John Harker is picked up and whisked away to Dracula's castle in a carriage pulled swiftly by four black horses. The imaginary journey requires only four hours, so although the castle back in Bran can claim the historical Dracula—that is, Vlad III, also known as Vlad Ţepeş (Vlad the Impaler)—as its most famous if not most welcome guest, this "Dracula's Castle" can claim a closer proximity to, if not the actual location of (which it does), the fictional vampire's abode—an arrow in its quiver as the two establishments battle it out for tourists drawn by rumors of surreptitious bloodletting during the menacing blackness of Transylvanian nights.

Bukovina, which today is divided between Ukraine and Romania[93], can also claim another distinction: Just down the slopes to the east, between the Siret River flowing along the mountains' feet and the Prut River a few dozen kilometers beyond, once dwelt a people who left an enduring legacy unrelated to the undead.

By the middle of the second century A.D., when the forested foothills and rivers valleys of the eastern Carpathian piedmont lay just outside the border of the Roman Empire, a collection of Dacian tribes had organized themselves, and together with Sarmatian allies had expelled a Germanic-speaking people called the Bastarnae[94]. This new meta-tribe took, or was given by the Romans, the name "Carpi".

Unlike their Dacian kin on the western side of the mountains, the Carpi never succumbed to Trajan. Instead, they raised just enough ruckus to be treated as a "client state" of the empire[95], which meant they got special trading privileges and payoffs to abstain from raiding while supplying conscripts for the imperial army and maybe a few hostages to boot. There was little trouble for about a century—after all, the new Roman citizens in the salient province of Dacia, this side of the mountains, were their relatives—until the coming of the Goths.

This Germanic menace from the north, especially a branch known as the Tervingi, along with a few of their like-speaking allies such as Vandals, caused so much trouble for the Roman citizens of Dacia, raiding from their hideouts in the Carpathians, that the Empire was forced to pull its border all the way back to the Danube, abandoning Dacia to the barbarians in 271 A.D[96].

The Goths pressured the Carpi as well, and the Carpi, sometimes in alliance with the newcomers and sometimes seeking relief, began to also seriously harass the Empire. The Romans would bend no further, however, and decided to fight, and although it took about fifty years of intermittent, brutal warfare, they finally subdued the Carpi. Most of the survivors were herded onto the plains of Pannonia the other side of the Danube and made Roman citizens, some certainly welcoming the reprieve from the Goths, while a few escaped into the hills to harbor with the Dacians or flee even further into the misty mountains.

The refuge of the Carpi: The Carpathian Mountains.

(This is but one theory, and seems to be contradicted by the fact that Ptolemy first uses the label about a hundred years earlier. In his *Geographia*, Ptolemy labels what roughly seem to be the Western Carpathians, *Carpates Mons*. But Ptolemy deviates more from reality the further he gets from the Mediterranean, and physically separates the *Carpates Mons* from the Eastern Carpathians, which he calls *Sarmatici Mons*. Slightly earlier geographers had the mountains as one chain, but without a name. Perhaps it was this lexical similarity—*Carpates* and *Carpi*[97]—that helped unify the Carpathian Mountains and seal their name in classical minds. See Appendix A for more theories.)

Caliman Mountains from the Tihuţa Pass. © Jürgen Sauer.

A rare morning sun begins to warm the day, although high clouds move in by late morning. Jürgen and I are waiting at a potential campsite along a dusty side road about a kilometer from the village, while Cata and Ana go back to the *pensiune* to see if we can find the owners of this property. This small field of compressed dead grass seems to be the only flat, dry patch of land around, but it also seems to be someone's yard. A tottering split-rail fence corrals it next to a sprawling old barn just across the road from a large house. The buildings are silent, but those are lacey white curtains and not cobwebs in the windows of the old house, so maybe this is someone's seasonal country home, and for the first time we feel compelled to seek permission.

A weathered picnic table foreshadows dining without the need of standing or folding ourselves onto hard, cold rocks. Three or four crows watch us from the fence, occasionally pecking at each other as though anticipating the renewal of ancient disputes over crumbs. We sit at the table absorbing the first true sunny heat of the expedition, but so do hordes of nagging flies. Hence the name of this camp, which we begin setting up after we receive word that it "should" be okay: "The

Camp of the Flies." In the afternoon, a couple of horse-drawn carts carry two men and a boy along the road, and I'm glad we sort of got permission.

Monday, April 18, Piatra Fântânele, Romania

Cloudy with a soft fog this morning. Last night Cata, Ana, Jürgen, and I took the time to prepare a delicious meal of noodles and dehydrated cream of mushroom soup enhanced with fresh onions, carrots, rutabagas, chili peppers, and garlic (which Ana often eats raw). With this more riveting fare, and without the responsibilities and conflicts of the larger team, we enjoyed a more intimate bonding experience than usual. We enveloped the crackling fire with talk about our lives, dreams, and frustrations; the health and blood-preserving properties of raw garlic (from loss to both ticks and vampires); and a story we heard the previous evening from the *pensiune* owners. Seems a "new species" of wolf is invading from Ukraine: an especially malicious variety that eats only dogs and small children. Maybe the species is new, but the stories are not: this sounds a lot like the *pricolici. Are Romanians pushing their fearsome legends to a safe distance across the border?* Rain, thunder, and lightning sent us scurrying to our beds around ten, the question unresolved.

Have werewolves had a special affinity for the dark forests and precipitous slopes of Transylvania?

They seem to have prowled this terrain for a long time. Transylvanians as ancient as the Vinča (sixth millennium B.C.) left evidence of imitating wolves, and Dacian warriors—long-haired, thick-bearded men (according to the images on Trajan's column) who may have referred to themselves as wolves and who charged into battle under their infamous wolf-headed standard the *draco*—surely did so[98]. (Ironically, the Dacian warriors, at least the most devout of them, may have limited their carnivorous impulses to the battlefield, refraining from eating animals under the advice of their god Zalmoxis). And although the most famous werewolf trials of the early modern era took place in Western Europe, some two thousand witch and werewolf trials also occurred in Hungary—which at the time included Transylvania. Stories of werewolves are still told amongst Carpathian mountain folk today. But why is *Transylvania* so closely linked with werewolves in the modern *global* imagination?

Turns out there is a distinctly Eastern species of werewolf, and it is closely related to the undead. In the Carpathians, werewolves have long hobnobbed with vampires.

In fact, according to certain Eastern European folklore[99], werewolves and vampires are varied aspects of the same beast, the primary difference being that the one is alive and the other is undead; and with a corollary dietary difference: werewolves consume people living or dead, whereas the victims of vampires are exclusively alive— filled with living blood, that is—albeit briefly. Vampires indeed can take the form of wolves (as well as that of other nocturnal predators, such as cats, bats, and owls), and if one is a werewolf in life, one will necessarily become a vampire in death. Like vampires, most eastern werewolves do not volunteer, and in most Slavic countries werewolves and vampires are called by the same name, e.g., *vulkodlak, volkodlak, vlkodlak, vrkolak*.

Perhaps this bond between werewolves and vampires originally arose from real wolves being spotted in the act of digging up corpses: Easy to mistake for werewolves, rising vampires, or both. . . or even werewolves struggling with rising dead—which might explain the completely contradictory belief among some easterners that werewolves are the mortal enemies of vampires.[100]

In any case, once Bram Stoker set the vampires of Transylvania astir, werewolves went along for the ride. And once Hollywood got into the act, the Transylvania link became even stronger. Werewolf movies not only gave the monsters new characteristics—for example, most film versions don't bother to go down onto all fours, and a silver bullet is a common antidote—but they also emphasized a lycanthropic (and vampiric) base in the Carpathian Mountains: for example, such influential films as *Werewolf of London* (1935), wherein the bad guy is a botanist with a degree from the (mythical) University of Carpathia; and *I Was a Teenage Werewolf* (1957), wherein the person most capable of ID'ing a werewolf is a janitor from the Carpathians.

In the middle of the night I awoke to the sound of something rustling. Dragging myself from visions of werewolf invaders, I rose and quietly unzipped my wall and tentatively stepped out and vaguely spied in my headlamp what I hoped was a large fox running off. Whatever it was paused and peered back over it shoulders for an instant, revealing two flashy orbs, a lot like the creature near Vlâhiţa. *Too small for a werewolf. But is Gollum on our trail?*

The morning brings a clue: A bag of garbage torn open and strewn about. We really must remember to store our trash in a car.

This afternoon Jürgen and I walk to the village. A dog joins us, craving affection but terrified of any of our moves to give it. It finally seems content strutting along ahead of us, proudly guiding us through the muddy backstreets of its turf.

We pass the low buildings and tall crosses of a monastery and then stumble upon Hotel Castel Dracula. Did we have a choice? Like the magnetism of Dracula's eyes, would all the village roads pull us to it? It is a rambling edifice of wings and stone facades and nonsensical steep pitched roofs, whose dark windows glare from far above its large parking lot. But it is closed for renovation, which, judging by all the scaffolding, beams, and stones lying about, is structural as well as cosmetic. Yet a kitschy souvenir shop is open, its carved wooden motorcycle rockers and velvet portraits of Vlad the Impaler spilling from the large log cabin on the edge of the lot, and we buy a hand-carved wooden spoon that we think will be handy.

Author reassures Piatra Fântânele guide. © Jürgen Sauer.

On our return we stop for a beer at a dilapidated bar. There's not much inside except a counter and a couple of wobbly round tables to break the echoing monotony of a stark high-ceilinged chamber with pea-green cinderblock walls, so we opt for a weathered wooden bench outside. We watch the passing traffic and gathering clouds, gulp the last of our beer, and try to beat the storm. Failing, we catch shelter from the worst of it under the eaves of a forlorn, unfinished house. The water pours and the wind blows so hard that we are soaked by rain, mist, and splatter.

After the deluge is over and birds are chirping to celebrate, Jürgen and I go the other way from our camp on a search for potable water. About a mile up the road we happen upon a waterworks almost hidden in the woods: a cascading sequence of split-log runnels that brings crystal clear water down and out from a steep, brushy, moss-covered slope and channels it alongside a platform of small round logs that even has the luxury of hand rails. Another Carpathian sluice.

Just before we arrive at camp lugging our full bottles, a huge chestnut horse comes plodding along tugging a cart full of logs. Upon the big logs sits a big logger, whose graying hair is escaping his small camouflage hat and whose ample belly is escaping his large camouflage jacket. The recon-ready logger's plump face is all kindness as he stops the horse and shakes his head and conveys to us with words and gestures that there is a spring much nearer our camp. He will come by later to show us.

I'm sitting at the picnic table, gazing at the snow-capped Caliman Mountains and swatting at flies. *How did I get here?* An infinity of paths could have brought me from my birthplace in Portland, Maine some forty-nine years ago to this weathered table sitting astride the Borgo Pass of Transylvania. Does it matter which I have followed? I suppose the effects of my route—all the places I've been and things I have done, all the pleasures and pains, triumphs and tragedies—linger as patterns encoded in my brain cells and in the condition of my body. They make a difference, don't they? All my regrets, fears, and dreams dissolving into the warm sun on my face and the flies buzzing through the air and the breeze whispering through the evergreens carrying a cold, snowy scent from the peaks... in this moment it seems they do not.

Tuesday, April 19, 2005, Piatra Fântânele, Romania

Last night came another rainy reminder that our home is never far from the damp, the mud, and the cold. Today is overcast and windy, around 40°F. One begins to feel truly imbued with cold when one is *always* in it. My entire being has become torpid. While never easy for my hands to keep pace with my thoughts, writing in my journal with my cold fingers has been slow and awkward for so long now that I hardly notice, and I wonder whether my thoughts are slowing to match.

Our hikers came into camp late afternoon yesterday looking very beat, but their two-day trek went more smoothly than usual. The trail was "nice"—they even found fresh bear tracks less than a kilometer from camp—and other than some stretches that were strewn with fallen trees, not particularly demanding. Oddly, the trail maps were accurate and the route well marked. Their pleasant hike, along with the comfortable camp and warm food that were waiting, lifted their spirits to match ours, and the campfire mood last evening was of rare cheer (for the whole team).

We've acquired a camp dog that comes slinking around looking for scraps, which probably explains the large size of the "fox" I saw the other night. Not the same dog who guided us through town, we have tried to befriend it, but it is also very wary.

This morning Jürgen, Thilo, and I go off to observe and photograph the logging operation up the road. Two lumbermen, including our water consultant, are working the old-fashioned way, using chainsaws to cut, axes to limb, and the horse to haul. Once our photographer's preference for the real hero of the operation becomes obvious, the men seem bent on upstaging the horse, striking poses amidst the defeated timber whilst holding axes with vigor.

In the afternoon, while Peter is off meeting with Caliman National Park officials in Varta Dornei, Klaus, Sandra, and I chuck Extreme Power Hiking and take a leisurely hike on a gentle forest path. The spruce-wood is dark, cool, quiet, fragrant, and absent of flies, with the only sign of wild mammals being the tracks of red deer. Upon our return we learn that we will break camp and ride to a new site around midday tomorrow. The park officials and the local mountain rescue team warned Peter of deep snow and high avalanche danger in the Rodnei Mountains ahead. Once again, conditions have stymied Peter's plan. Once again, we must stuff all of ourselves into our vehicles: Another squished ride with eight or nine opinions about how to pack everything in. I wish I could fly.

In early evening our lumbermen friends pull up, toss an immense log from off their cart (which lifts the head of the doleful horse), and manufacture firewood for us with their chainsaw and axes.

Trees to be felled.
© Jürgen Sauer.

Proud loggers. © Jürgen Sauer.

Thursday, April 21. Vadu Izei, Romania.

More rain and mud. Two days more. We broke the Camp of the Flies yesterday morning in fog and light showers, drove back down to Bistriţa and then headed north into the Rodnei Mountains. This range is contained within the Rodna National Park and Biosphere Reserve and at about fifty kilometers in length comprises one of the longest continuous ridges in Romania. Its highest peak, Pietrosul Rodnei, soars into a 2303-meter (7556 feet) cone that is currently as white as a cloud. Apparently the current deep-snow conditions are not unusual for April, as this range is known to hold a skiable amount of snow well into June and sometimes July. In addition to its lofty backbone, the Rodnei Range also features a contrary geological attraction: one of the deepest caves in Romania, Izvorul Tăuşoarelor, which delves 1512 feet (461 meters) over its length of eleven miles.

We dropped off the hiking team (Peter, Klaus, and Sandra; Markus was sidelined by an ailing stomach) not far from the town of Năsăud for a two-day hike on the western flank of the mountains. Again they marched off into a misty wooded aisle, again in the rain, and again I was envious.

The rest of us motored northward, taking lunch in a dilapidated, smoke-filled hovel of a restaurant in a small village called Telciu. As we stepped into the dark wooden interior, music was blaring into the ears of the only occupants, a waitress and a bartender who, tapping their cigarettes, met our entrance with blank if not unfriendly stares. Many minutes after we took our rickety seats, the waitress sauntered over. With Ana's help we placed our orders and then wondered what we'd get. To my surprise, the food was truly excellent. The French fries, cut from real potatoes and smothered with cheese to boot, were the best I've ever had.

Thilo at work. © Jürgen Sauer.

We had a notion we'd stay at a "chalet" arranged through Mihai, Jürgen's friend in Maramureş (pronounced "Maramuresh"). Maramureş is now a county along Romania's northern edge, but the name used to refer to a larger county of the Kingdom of Hungary that began at the Setref Pass ahead and extended beyond the Tisza some fifty kilometers into Ukraine[101]. It was from Maramureş, legend has it, that Dragoş set out in pursuit of aurochs in the mid-fourteenth century. This viovode (governor) of Maramureş was led by these now extinct progenitors of cattle over Carpathian passes to an "uninhabited" land so filled with springs and streams and so beautiful and bountiful that he couldn't bear to leave, and so he invited his kinsmen to join him, and thereby founded the Principality of Moldavia. The story may have evolved both to establish greater Romanian unity (a quaint linkage between all sides of the Carpathians) and explain the auroch in the coat of arms of Moldavia; a less fabled version has King Louis I of Hungary sending Dragoş over the mountains to merely defend against the Mongol Golden Horde.

So up the Setref pass we went, to an open and alpine saddle that forms the junction between three mountain ranges: the Rodnei to the west, the Suhard to the east, and the Maramureş to the north. At 817 meters (2680 feet), the pass offers vistas of silver-ribboned valleys snaking between green-brown hills that roll up to white peaks, and on the very top sits a small A-frame braced against the wind. Inside, shelves jammed with beer and cigarettes as well as a few trinkets and packages of stale junk food and candy bars lined a corner behind a counter. The rest of the room was stuffed with a small dining table, a few smaller tables in other corners, and an ancient TV and VCR. Several small shelves dug into the walls, whose clutter tried to hide behind see-through curtains, and lots of pictures of traditionally attired mountain folk hung from the ceiling. The proprietor was a towering man who came to a point in a Tyrolian hat, and he was all smiles as he conversed with my friends in German and gathered up a few chocolate bars and bags of chips in what seemed to be a corner of his living room.

After collecting our goods, we waited outside for a man who was to guide us to the cabin. Upon arriving, he pointed to the only trail leading from the parking lot—a muddy, deeply rutted track that traversed a steep slope shooting up from the pass—and told us to follow it to the end.

We got underway in pouring rain. The road was soggy and soft, and the only ground that wouldn't inhale our boots was a six-inch wide bank from which the slope fell precipitously away. It soon became clear there was no way we could negotiate even our Land Rover over this spongy route, and chatter began about giving up our plan. Apparently the cabin was another mile or so in, we'd be staying for a two days, and we'd have to bring Sandra and Klaus out and new eco-volunteers in. We needed a place with easier access.

I for one wanted to continue. Enough level ground for four tents was nowhere in sight—never mind dry or well-drained turf—so this looked like the only reasonable alternative for the night. As hikers we had backpacked much further over more difficult terrain, and certainly we had camped in less pleasing environs. We could deal with any back-

and-forth to the road as needed. Someone suggested looking for a *pensiune* in the town at the foot of the pass, but we were already here, so with a few more complaints that we were wasting our time, on we trudged.

The "chalet" was a rough-hewn hut perched at the bottom of a steep grassy slope and near the foot of two declivitous, wooded ravines. It had an imposing corrugated metal roof, but the ground level seemed an afterthought compared to the overhanging loft. Indeed, the structure seemed more appropriate for its equestrian tenants whom we could hear snorting and neighing on one side than for any human kind who might be hiding in a small corner compartment—identifiable by bright blue trim surrounding three curtained windows and a door—on the other. A couple of knocks, however, dispelled any doubt. The door opened, along with a blast of unbelievably hot air.

A boy of around twelve stood in the entrance to the tiny room, which was dominated by an overqualified wood stove on one side and a man lying crumpled on an undersized cot on the other. The man was snoring away, unshaven and unkempt (his clothes were filthy, actually)—and way too tall for the cot. A small table with a couple of chairs completed the furnishings, and together with the cot and the piping hot stove left little space for us five newcomers. The cot was the only horizontal accommodation of any kind, and a quick glance at the dirty floor immediately convinced me that we wouldn't have a roof over our heads this night. Even if one or two of us could fit on the floor, they (it was not going to be me) would likely be roasted by morning. I thought we should escape before the man awoke.

The boy gave the man a gentle poke, which provoked a stir and an even louder snore, and then he gave him another. With a yawn and a robust stretch the man finally arose, his face gradually lighting with awareness and welcome. He urged us to sit, oblivious of the fact that there were three more of us than chairs, and introduced himself as Ion (pronounced roughly as "Yawn").

Ion spoke loudly and exuberantly as we exchanged introductions and pleasantries and proceeded to a discussion about how, when, where, and whether we would stay. He spoke without pausing for Ana's translation, but I grasped snatches on my own, and from both word and bearing one point became reinforced and another immediately clear: There was no way we could stay in the cabin, and this man was not going to easily take no for an answer.

Ion began to plead with an exaggerated demeanor, explaining

all the reasons his abode was better than our tents. He began with the obvious: *It is cold and wet outside, it is dry and warm inside (definitely true).* With a nod at Ana: *Surely we wouldn't force a woman to sleep on the ground under a cloth.* He pantomimed how we could sleep on the floor (*like sardines,* did he add?), and emphasized the natural beauty surrounding us, and how much he loved being here away from the onerous bustle and crowd of cities and towns. He spoke emphatically but not offensively, gestured comically and smiled continuously, and while we suspected he was inebriated, there was something very likeable about this unusual man. Whether he was desperate for more than our companionship I wasn't sure, but we had all agreed it wouldn't be appropriate to pay for his hospitality: he was a friend of a friend of one of us, he hadn't asked for anything when the offer was made, and it would be insulting in his culture.

I suddenly felt claustrophobic and overwhelmed by the infernal air, and sensing that the inevitable "*tsweeger*" (shot of homemade schnapps) was about to come, which I didn't feel up to at the moment, I excused myself and squirmed for the door. It was now late afternoon, I knew we had better get moving, and I hoped my exit would speed things along; I'd leave it to the others to maneuver a politer escape. As I stepped outside and filled my lungs with cool, fresh air, I did notice the flat, well-drained patch of grass adjacent to the cabin, just big enough for three or four tents. But no, the man inside was just too strange, too determined.

My reprieve was brief. Ion rushed out the door, all smiles, apparently having deduced that I was the one to convince. Changing expression as quick as a clown, he pointed to various features of his domain—the trees, the streams in the ravines, a small square wooden structure that apparently served as an alternative abode for the horses— and earnestly explained all he was going to do. The Communists had cut the trees (now he was crying), but he was going to let them grow (smiling). They had killed the animals (wailing), but he was going to let them live (laughing). He was going to create his own kingdom of beautiful nature (ecstatic). As his mimed soliloquy continued, Jürgen came out and confirmed with a tilt that they did indeed have a toast.

Suddenly Ion waxed jovial again and started across the open slope towards the closest ravine, explaining that there we could get water— clean and sparkling, as I'm sure he added. I was reluctant to follow, thinking that once we started there'd be no escape, but he was going whether we followed or not, and his friendly enthusiasm and sincerity were impossible to resist. I even felt that maybe we had better save him from himself.

Jürgen and I looked at each other, and with mutual shrugs that we're here for adventure, started after our eccentric guide. As we crossed the sharp incline and entered the woodsy ravine, where slippery wet leaves plastered the muddy ground and made footholds difficult, Ion started slipping and sliding. Dismayed not in the least, he scrambled eagerly on towards the stream, falling down and collecting mud on knees, hips, elbows, hands, and face as he continued raving about his beautiful trees; after he had literally come out of his shoes a couple of times, he simply ditched them.

Unsure whether we were trailing a fool, a drunk, or a prophet, we followed, until Jürgen suddenly pulled up short and asked with an uncertain grin, "Alan, what are we doing?" We watched the barefoot man scrambling and bumbling on ahead, and then let go three weeks of tension, nearly falling over with laughter. Ion came to a stop, caressed and kissed several small saplings like they were his babies, and then let loose a long, mournful wail lamenting the abuse of previous powers.

I couldn't help believing in the sincerity and innocence of this man's passion and started asking him questions with gestures and broken Romanian: How long had he had the property, where were the boundaries, etc. He was thrilled to explain, and his gestures and hand signals were easy to understand. When we finally made it to the stream, we discovered a swelled and muddy torrent. Ion assured us that we'd have clean running water "*dimineatsa*" (tomorrow morning).

We clambered back to the cabin, where Thilo, Ana, and Markus were waiting with skeptical expressions. Had we succumbed to the spell of a lunatic? We hadn't wavered in our decision, but as we, and especially Ana, tried to find a graceful way to finalize our decline of Ion's offer—which by now included his house in the village for two of us—we were somehow ushered into the horses' quarters and then up to the hay-filled loft. Apparently our wannabe host had another epiphany: We could sleep comfortably in the hay, even like babies, as he so aptly demonstrated by diving into the piles of straw and bouncing about like a child.

Once this last strategy failed, Ion's pleas ceased, although his demeanor barely changed. He made clear he wasn't angry and offered to give us a ride out by horse-cart. But the path snaking up the slope proved too slippery even for Ion's hooved friends, so this Tom Bombadil[102] of Maramureş walked along beside us while we trod the soggy path. The view of the white-streaked mountains and greening brown hills enshrouded in gray-white banks of cloud and fog was enchanting, but prospects for outdoor sleeping were bleak.

As we walked and discussed our options for the night, Ion, occasionally grabbing a stem to chew, was mostly quiet, and by the time we made it out to the road, his quiescence may have helped endow our only feasible decision: Thilo, Markus (who was still quite sick), Ana, and I would pack our camping gear back to Ion's cabin and pitch all the tents on the only patch of level turf we had seen. Jürgen would sleep, as usual, in the Land Rover and Cata in the Passat, both parked at the pass.

Ion, needless to say, was ecstatic. But as he strode along the path with us back to his cabin, he became pensive once more, and I concluded that he was neither drunk nor crazy, but just might be the world's most hospitable man. Thus the name for our new camp, "Camp of the World's Most Hospitable Man." "Ion's Camp" for short.

By the time we reached the cabin, night was setting in. We got the tents up—one for each of us (Thilo, Markus, Ana, and I)—just in time to escape a wind-driven downpour. While the rain battered and the wind rattled the fly of my tent, I removed my soaked, mud-encased hiking shoes, and then realized I was thirsty, and low on drinking water, and we had neglected to bring our tarps. We'd have no place to dry, cook, and eat. I guessed I'd call it a night: wet, thirsty, and hungry.

Then I heard the sound of singing and someone bustling about. Although the rain had let up, surely none of my companions had cause for such joy, so I stuck my head out of the tent to see what was up. There was Ion, happily tossing firewood into the small barn-like structure near our tents.

Spying my mug sticking out of the tent flaps, Ion waved for me to come further out, so I slipped my feet into my cold, wet shoes, tiptoed over, and entered the barn. In the dim light I could see the boy—whose name turns out to be George and who is not Ion's son as I had assumed—tossing stacked wood from the sides to the center of the open dirt floor, directly below a vent in the peaked roof.

So we'd have a dry place to cook and eat after all! And there were even several large logs to sit on! Rejuvenated, I roused Thilo and Ana (Markus was in agony and would not leave his tent), and then made the slippery journey to the ravine to get cooking water from the stream, now even more swelled and muddy than before.

Upon my return Ion and George had a fine blaze going, and they were hustling about, raking brush and wood chips out of the way, throwing more logs onto the fire, showing us nails on the walls where we could hang our wet clothes, and generally trying to be helpful. Ion beamed, and danced in his movements, taking a few extra spins to change directions and lifting his knees a few extra inches in his marches, with George cracking up all the while. Once Thilo, Ana, and I began to boil water and cut vegetables, however, Ion and George left us to cook and eat our meal in peace. The world's most hospitable man, indeed.

As we ate, the wind and rain returned, along with thunder and lightning, and we were feeling fortunate indeed at finding ourselves dry and eating around a warm fire. Soon Ion and George slyly poked their heads through the opening. They were shedding water, and we waved them in with our forks and gestures towards our pots, and in they came, dripping, steaming, and grinning in the warm glow of the fire.

Ion pulled a bottle of schnapps from under his coat and pushed it towards us, and then began to sing and dance. He seemed to swell in the flickering firelight as he kicked his legs side-to-side and held a hand over his head and spun like a top and opened his mouth and yodeled like a goat, all the while George clapping and rolling over laughing. Some songs were happy and others sad, but Ion's singing was always beautiful. He animated the sad songs with exaggerated weeping and tears, and the happy ones with clapping and foot stomping. After each song, Ana told us its story, the sad ones, of course, mostly bemoaning lost love. We joined in the clapping, the laughing, and even the tears, amazed at the magical performance while the storm raged outside and our boots and shoes steamed by the fire.

By perhaps 9:30 the rain had stopped. We stepped outside to a nearly full moon bobbing and weaving behind the clouds and throwing its bright silvery light over a dark and soaked world. The scene was so eerily spectacular that Thilo was inspired to set up his tripod and finicky camera with huge telescope lens to give us each a view of lunar seas and mountains and craters while we shivered in a very brisk wind.

We wrapped up our celestial viewing, Ion and George took their leave, and after a very long day we headed for our tents. By now I was exhausted and craving my semi-warm sleeping bag. But just as I stooped through the entrance of my tent, I stuck my hands into my pocket... *Oh no! I have the keys to the Land Rover! Jürgen is locked out!*

While I knew that Jürgen could share the Passat with Cata, his sleeping bag was surely in the Land Rover. Plus he was constantly misplacing the keys, and now he'd be frantic thinking he had lost them for good. I had to return to the pass. I had to give up the idea of sleeping in the semi-dryness that I had so patiently achieved by fire, for me, my clothes, and my shoes. I had to make the long trek back to the pass through water and mud in cold, wind, and dark. *Thank God for the moon*, I thought as I zipped my coat tight to my neck and recalled areas along the road where nothing but a six inch wide bank of semi-solid footing separated deep muddy ruts on one side from a precipitous fall on the other.

At the top of the slope the sound of none-too-friendly barking reminded me of the shepherd dogs patrolling the slopes further above that we had encountered on the way in, which I assumed would be even more diligent and aggressive at night, so I proceeded no further until I had armed myself with a stick. It wasn't long before clouds again obscured the moon, leaving me in pitch dark. *At least the dogs will keep werewolves at bay. Or will they?*

I had to feel my way along, using my headlamp sparingly for fear I would deplete the batteries, using it only where I sensed particularly uncertain footing or a washout or pool that had to be leapt. Fortunately the dogs and all other beasts held off, and by taking one careful step at a time, often along the narrow wobbly bank, I managed to complete the mile-long journey without falling into water or the abyss.

My mud-weighted shoes sloshed as I marched across the dark parking lot and approached the lifeless-looking Passat. I tapped on a fogged-up window, assuming that both Cata and Jürgen were at least trying to sleep within the wind-rocking vehicle. Nothing. I tapped harder. Still nothing. *Where can they be?* There was only one option. I walked around to the front of the A-frame and peered cautiously through a window. There they were, Jürgen and Cata sitting at the table under warm lights, smiling and laughing and tipping a couple of beers! I opened the door to crash the party.

My two friends were having a grand time with the towering proprietor, whose face was beaming under his Tyrolean hat. Somewhere in his fifties, he was formerly a professional folk musician, as Jürgen explained and the man proudly confirmed by pointing to his CDs and the photos from his heydays that lined the walls and hung from the ceiling. Looking more closely, I could indeed see his younger self, clothed in traditional embroidered folk clothing and playing a kind of horn.

I took a while to reveal my embarrassing secret, but when Jürgen saw the keys, he brushed it off with a tip of his bottle. Turned out Peter had left the second set—something he had never done before. So I had abandoned my semi-dry tent and sleeping bag and trudged through the dark, windy, and freezing night for nothing. Well, not for nothing: I accepted the offer of a beer, and Jürgen urged our host to sing. He put on one of his CDs and we clapped along with his song. My second party of the night! When this somewhat more conventional version of Ion (*could they be brothers?*) learned of my American origin, he insisted on seizing and shaking my hand, arm, shoulder, and entire upper body while giving my back a slap.

Though I was enjoying the warmth, camaraderie, and good cheer, after a time the journey back to my tent began to loom. I started yawning and worrying (probably needlessly) that Thilo and Ana would be wondering what happened to me. So as the outlines of my friends began to blur, I reluctantly hoisted myself up and stepped out into the bracing cold. I went first to the car to don dry socks and hiking boots and then got underway. The moon shone brightly now, the wind was with me, the dogs were still, and somehow I made it back, again without a spill.

Not long into my sleeping bag it began to pour, and I fell asleep to the familiar roar of rain on nylon.

Ion's camp. © Jürgen Sauer.

Today the rest of the team remains at Ion's Camp while Jürgen and I drive to Vadu Izei to pick up a group of three new eco-volunteers, Mathias, Göran and Suzann, who are driving from Germany. Arrangements have been made for us all to stay overnight at Mihai's house—the friend of Jürgen's who arranged our rendezvous with Ion— and tomorrow we'll all come back in the Passat to rejoin the team at Ion's camp.

Mihai, a prim man in his mid-thirties, of medium height with a shock of dark hair and eyebrows and neatly trimmed mustache below a prominent nose, is a border patrol officer and entrepreneur, utilizing his yard to dabble in the tourism business. He has built a very small and very quaint log cabin behind his house, which he lets for tourists. The little cottage is vacant now, and some of us will sleep in it tonight (it sleeps only two; maybe three if the floor is used). The rest will bunk in the main house.

Jürgen and I grab warm showers in the cold cabin before Mihai gives us a tour of his large yard in the ubiquitous rain and mud. A determined businessman with the humility of a monk, our host carries his shoulders softly and deliberately, and he speaks likewise as he discusses his plans for building another cabin.

Back in the house, the rooms of which are softened by floral tapestries with black backgrounds ringing the walls and an assortment of patterned rugs covering the floors, Mihai's wife Ilena—about the same age and stature as her husband, with dark hair pulled back from her round, olive face—insists on giving my clothes a washing. Ducking into the bathroom to disrobe, I'm uncertain whether she's motivated by fastidiousness or pity. In any case, hoping to give her machine a fighting chance, I rinse and wring the worst of it down the sink before handing them over.

While my clothes agitate and we await the new eco-volunteers, Ilena lays out an incredible three-course dinner—(1) pork-based cold cuts, cucumbers, tomatoes, and eggs; (2) mashed potatoes and roasted pork; (3) and cabbage soup—all washed down with a shot or two of plum schnapps. Jürgen has brought gifts across hundreds of wild kilometers for the family's two children, a boy of twelve and a girl of five, and they romp about with delight at his thoughtfulness.

Mathias, Göran, and Suzann arrive late, but they get the same treatment of food and drink before we all retire to our quarters—the eco-volunteers to the cabin, and Jürgen and I to rooms in the house. Reluctant to disrupt their neat and clean guest bed, I take the floor, unfurling my thin pad over a thicker rug.

Friday, April 22. Snow camp. Prislop Pass, Romania

During the tour of Mihai's yard yesterday I pointed to our host's rubber boots and used gestures to summarize the obvious: His feet were dry and mine were not. This morning I discover that someone has moved my mud-caked boots into the clean entryway for the night, while all other footgear has remained outside. Someone has also laid out a splendid breakfast of bread, warm milk, eggs, cucumber, tomatoes, and cold pork. Mihai and Ilena are giving Ion a run for his title.

The pervasive mud is finally defeated. It has given way to ice and snow.

As we drive back up the Setref Pass to join the team, pelting rain morphs into soft flakes and the hills gradually change from green to white. When we arrive at the pass, the others have just hiked out from Ion's after a reportedly frigid night. We all join in tossing their gear into our vehicles, our faces and hands and anything exposed stung by the horizontal blast.

After everything is in, Sandra and Klaus take shelter in the Passat with Peter, who will take them to Bistriţa to catch a bus back home to Germany. With no way to squeeze nine into the Land Rover, Ana, Markus, and Thilo must secure their hats, hoods, and zippers and set out for Sacel on foot. Sacel is the small village at the bottom of the pass, where Peter will pick them up on his way back to our next camp (and where they end up getting a tour of a 600-year-old ceramic factory). The rest of us will set up the camp somewhere near the next pass called the Prislop. We stop first at an open market on the outskirts of Sacel to buy fresh produce, joining a throng of other shoppers taking shelter under tarps and umbrellas.

We then wind up the hills into a world of white, knowing we're going to have to camp in the snow, but hoping at least for something flat. Finally a small clearing at the end of a short turnoff seems our best bet. I resurrect my tent on the snow and begin unfurling inside, only to discover that I left my cheap foam pad at Mihai's. I'll have to make do with only Peter's spare (I've been doubling them up whenever I can).

While we prepare potato soup in the fading light, our little gas stoves struggling mightily against the wind, snow, and cold, I realize just in time that my toes are about to go numb. They are soaked and freezing and I must keep them moving vigorously. (Given their subsequent sensitivity to cold, I think this is when my toes came closest to frostbite.)

Snow camp. © Jürgen Sauer.

Saturday, April 23. Snow camp. Prislop Pass

Last night dipped to -6° C (21° F) and Peter's spare pad stood no chance. I shivered and tossed and turned on the icepack throughout the night. Everyone had a cold night, at least everyone who was not in a car. But Mathias, in his flimsy fly-less little green tent, must have positively froze. After we are up and about, he stomps and hugs himself and shivers and asks for advice on how to survive another night. Yesterday afternoon I joined him for a short hike, and as we plowed through the soggy snow up a modest slope, the slightly overweight man sweated and struggled for air, and I also wondered how he was going to handle extreme power hiking.

"Wear your winter clothes inside your bag," I suggest. He hunches and shivers even more, clutching his steaming cup of tea. "I ddddid. I was still very ccccold."

The only other suggestion I can think of is to put some green spruce boughs under the tent, which Mathias thinks is a good idea. In fact, after Jürgen leaves to bring the hiking team to the top of the pass, I decide to try this myself. I'm a little uneasy about wounding a tree or two, but another sleepless night won't do me much good, and Mathias, a forester in Germany, just endorsed the concept. So I find a small spruce sapling that is growing sideways out of a dense clump, mostly buried in snow. Its deformed orientation gives it no chance, I reason; it might even be a blow down. So I dig and pull and yank it free from the crusted snow, cut off a few soft boughs, unpin my tent, and spread them over the impression left by my sleeping pad that is now mostly frozen mud. Just as I finish re-staking my tent, Cata looks at me from where he is sitting at the fire smoking a cigarette, looking fairly rested after his night in the Passat. "That's not eco," he offers.

"Well, the tree had no chance," I rationalize.

"Still, it's not eco. If everyone cut, we'd have no trees in Romania."

"Mathias, who is a forester in Germany, thinks it's ok," is my retort. But I do feel guilty. Perhaps my mistake is more social than ecological, but I feel we foreigners should set as good an example as possible. After all, I'm never happy with the way everyone else washes dishes with soap in the streams and rivers.

I'm now alone at "Snow Camp," performing guard and fire-keeping duties. Jürgen, Cata, and Ana have departed for Borsa to seek repairs for the Land Rover (a suspension problem of some kind) and food. As I search through the snow and mud for deadwood to burn, breaks in the clouds brighten the world, melt the snow, and reveal panoramas of brilliant white peaks. My apologies for a familiar theme: I want to hike, I think my knees are ready—but now my boots are not. I simply cannot use them on a long hike in these wet-snow conditions. My feet are constantly wet and cold as it is.

By early evening no one has shown up. I have no phone, so no word. Clouds darken the sky and snow starts to fly in heavy squalls, sticking to everything. I figure I better start cooking. Just as the rice starts to boil, the Land Rover pulls up and Ana and Cata jump out. Jürgen, however, surprisingly backs up the vehicle and continues up the pass.

There was a problem, and Jürgen must pick up the hiking team. It's now nearly dark, so Cata and I erect the other tents on higher ground while the wind drives frozen needles into our face and hands. Then we sit around the sputtering fire and wait. I was preparing only enough food for four, but hope that with lots of bread we can stretch it out for nine. When they return, we get the story: The new eco-volunteers were not prepared for the deep snow conditions so they had to abort.

Once we're all gathered around the fire and eating, Jürgen announces it is my birthday. Apparently he remembered a conversation I had long forgotten. Yet another example of his thoughtfulness, he breaks out cheesecake, licorice-like sweets (Cata says they are called "excrement" in Romanian), and beer he had bought in Borsa. As we all partake, I'm serenaded with the universal "Happy Birthday" song made very special by German and Romanian accents.

This celebration around our fire against wind, snow, and dark will surely be one of my most memorable birthdays. Romanians, though, may have dreams of more worldly gifts on this night. For today also marks the Feast of St. George, which according to Romanian folklore— despite Bram Stoker's warnings of evil doings—is the most favorable time for finding buried treasure. For only on this night do the gems, jewelry, and silver and gold coins that were buried under the roots of trees or tucked under rocks or stashed in caverns by many a fleeing or fallen king, noble, knight, or bandit—be they Darius of Persia, or Decebalus of Dacia, or even Attila the Hun himself (there are legends for them all)—emit a bluish flame. The glow is discernible only to favored treasure hunters, but if they follow particular protocols, and overcome monstrous guardians, and contend with threatening curses, they may be set for life. Such lucrative legends, widespread throughout the Carpathians, have been reinforced by real discoveries from time to time[103]; but my bedtime wish is only for warmth, which comes as a much-appreciated gift from a deformed spruce sapling.

Honoring St. George. © Jürgen Sauer.

Sunday, April 24. Snow Camp. Prislop Pass

Thilo is upset. He just crawled out of our tent into a mush of slush and cow shit. Turns out we set up in a pasture, and he thinks we should have found something better.

After a hurried breakfast in the cold, Jürgen and I take Mathias, Göran, and Suzann back to Vadu Izei. They have decided to bail completely. Mathias, who speaks English very well, expresses regret that he won't get to spend more time with us. At my prompting he describes forestry practices in Germany, explaining how it is only a slight exaggeration to say that in some forests almost every tree is managed as an individual. He invites me to come visit him any time and he'll show me firsthand. Göran, who cannot speak a word of English, conveys through Mathias that he regrets he cannot speak with me as he feels a connection. He has the V-shape physique of a weightlifter and maybe senses I'm also a gym rat in my other life (alas, with more the shape of an H). Suzann is mostly quiet or speaks only with Göran. It's sad to have only spent a couple of days with these nice people. How many more poignant goodbyes will we have?

Back at Mihai and Ilene's, after the eco-volunteers have left, Jürgen and I are served a delicious lunch of soup and bread. Then another tour of the premises. Guiding us along a small river that borders the far edge of his yard, Mihai, moustache twitching as he talks, presents a plan to build a "traditional washing machine"—some kind of device that uses rocks and the power of flowing water—by diverting part of the stream. It will be interesting for tourists, he says, but I wonder whether my dirty clothes had inspired a goal to preserve their more modern machine.

On our drive back to the Prislop Pass, we pass folks gathered in groups, standing or sitting in front of tall wooden fences carved with patterns of twisted rope, grapevines, crosses, sun rays, and animals. In the yards of some of the houses are trees adorned with brightly colored pots stuck to the ends of branches; once the sign of a marriageable girl inside, these days it usually just means someone wants to spruce up the yard.

The afternoon is dry and warm, and the people are dressed in their Sunday best. Nevertheless, most heads are prepared for the usual conditions—male versions covered with felt or straw fedoras, or tall black woolly cones, and female with dark kerchiefs—while the footwear of the elders looks particularly impervious: pointy-toed moccasins held up by leather thongs lashed to calves around white padded uppers. The older folks throw a few gruff looks when we stop to take photos, but warm up quickly when they see we are harmless; the girls, meanwhile, stay shy, while the boys ham it up from the get go.

Sunday Best. © Jürgen Sauer.

Monday, April 25. Poienile de Sub Munte, Romania.

Yesterday I greased my hiking boots, confident my knees are ready. But Ana also wants to hike, and this will be her last opportunity, and there aren't enough snowshoes for us both, so I defer. I have three more months (although she has had the last three weeks!). So we drop the hiking party off atop the Prislop Pass once again, and then Jürgen, Cata, and I make for Vişeu de Sus. We haven't been able to find hiking maps of this region, so we search the shops of the bustling little town for a place to print our downloads. We succeed, but our most prized find is a collapsible spade that stays uncollapsed when we want it to.

Highway 18 then brings us northwestward to a gravel road that aims for our destination: the snowy Maramureş Mountains on our right. The road is anchored by a little town called Ruscova, which seems dreary, although in a mud season like this, surely even Beverly Hills would lose its luster. Still, poverty seems more rampant in these northern reaches of Romania. *Is this indicative of Ukraine, just to the far side of those cloud-making peaks?* The next country on our tour looms as a mystery.

Rodna Mountains. © Jürgen Sauer.

Hamming it up. © Jürgen Sauer.

Last night around the campfire we were joined by a Mr. Pop from a local nature protection organization and a Mr. Costel from the Maramureş Mountains Nature Park, both of whom also joined the hiking team today. As the obligatory bottle of rotgut was passed around, our discussion came around to Ukraine. The Romanians—Ana, Cata, Mr. Pop, and Mr. Costel—all think we are crazy to go there, warning us of the many dangers, such as roving gangs of mafia types just waiting to prey on foreigners, and roads far worse than in Romania. As we jar along another mogul-filled, rutted, muddy track—this time towards a village called Poienile de Sub Munte ("The Meadow under the Mountains"), where we have arranged to stay at National Park headquarters—how Ukrainian roads can be worse is a mystery to me.

At least there was no mention of a new and menacing species of wolf.

Poienile de Sub Munte hides at the end of a long shallow valley, and, although lacking pavement of any kind to stave off the mud, the square wood houses with dull metallic hipped roofs and stacks of firewood along the exterior walls appear neat, sturdy, and warm. Brightly colored clothes flap on lines, bucking the bleak grayness of the day, but getting no drier in the pouring rain. The park headquarters is at the end of the line: the last building before the gated road ascends a steep rocky ravine into the mountains, alongside the tumultuous path of the Ruscova River.

Having become numb to the rain, mud, and cold, surprisingly I'm not especially keen on indoor accommodations. Once inside, however, and sitting next to a blazing woodstove, I warm up to the idea. Until now, I hadn't realized how slowed by the constant cold my handwriting had indeed become.

We pretty much have the large rustic building to ourselves, and it even has a kitchen. What luxury for our Romanian finale!

Tuesday, April 26. Poienile de Sub Munte, Romania

The hiking team is due late today, and we had made an appointment for the Land Rover to be repaired in Vişeu de Sus this morning. We also expect enough spare time to catch up with friends at an internet café and for Jürgen to get a tooth repaired. But as soon as we get phone reception on our drive out to the highway, we receive a text from Peter: "Come to Borsa to get us. We had problems." Our hearts sink when we realize it was sent last night.

After the team spills out in Vişeu de Sus, we get the story: Yesterday they climbed from the Prislop pass to an altitude of about 1,700 meters, along a trail partially broken by two wolves. After the wolves gave up, the snow deepened—to a meter and a half in places—slowing progress and further obscuring the trail. Fortunately, Mr. Pop was familiar with the path and guided their way. Nevertheless, by early evening, then in heavy rain, the cabana where they had intended to spend the night was out of the question. Peter, Markus, and Thilo were prepared for camping outdoors, but Ana, Mr. Pop, and Mr. Castel were not; they had no tents, tarps, sleeping bags, or pads. So they all retreated back to a glen that dove down the slopes towards Borsa. They made it out to a forestry administration building where they spent the night, though not before Thilo fell off a log into a creek.

Following the way of wolves on the Prislop Pass. © Thilo Brunner

Descending the Prislop Pass. © Thilo Brunner.

In the early afternoon Jürgen and I leave the comfort of our indoor sanctuary to explore the village on foot. After all the rain, the road is basically an avenue of mud. We start down the valley, past the single row of tottering picket fences and steep-roofed houses that line one side of the road and a green pasture that shoots up the slopes on the other. A flock of sheep comes by, bleating, muddy-legged, and racing forward in tentative surges under the stick of a surprisingly well-dressed woman. We next come to a quaint, ancient sawmill, where a determined old reciprocating blade, borne by a clunky wooden carriage and driven by a chaos of belts and cables, toils slowly but deliberately on its latest victim above mounds of sawdust. This machine would be an antique west of the Danube, and its dawdling rhythm seems to belie its probable role in the bread-and-butter of Poienile de Sub Munte: wood harvesting and processing.

Then, further down the road and before the next cluster of houses, we come to what must be the true pride and joy of the village: a silver-roofed log building with a trinity of gleaming onion-shaped, tri-bar-tipped domes reaching to the sky in glorious semblance of the trees and hills behind. The modesty of the church's wooden frame contrasts sharply with the majesty of its shiny top, without which it could be just another unassuming log house, and at first we have no idea what we're about to behold.

A pile of boards and a locked door impede the entrance, but as we're peering in the windows a workman opens the door and invites us in. The scale and intricacy of the world we enter halts our breaths. The iconostasis—panel upon panel of glimmering sacred images stacked between ornately carved wooden frames and columns—soars into starred and angeled heavens. The walls are lined with processions of haloed saints, and immense scenes of contemplation and glory animate the lower reaches of the vaulted ceiling. All bursts with color—not a square centimeter of wall, ceiling, or door goes unadorned—and all seems to be lit with an internal glow.

Our heads tilt back in awe as we try to take it all in. *Can this be the same humble log church we saw from without?* A painter is at work, balancing on scaffolding above construction debris and delicately touching up one of the icons under the glare of a spotlight. The workmen speak not our language, but they admire us admiring their church, occasionally pointing to something we may have missed. They are obviously very proud of what this otherwise unpretentious village possesses.

I later learn that this is a well-known church: the "New" Ukrainian Wood Church of Poienile de Sub Munte, which has taken over the services of the even more famous "Old" Ukrainian Wood Church, originally devoted to the Transfiguration but now devoted to tradition and tourism. This venerable church, like most here where East meets West in the Eastern Carpathians, must have experienced several transfigurations of its own. When it was first built sometime in the 1700s[104], most of the residents of Maramureş were Vlachs or Ruthenians (East Slavic dwellers in the northeastern Carpathians; see next chapter)—long disadvantaged Orthodox then living within the Catholic Habsburg Monarchy of Austria—who were facing intense pressure to join that bridge over the Great Schism, Greek Catholicism. In fact, the Orthodox Church no longer officially existed in Maramureş, or anywhere else in the Carpathians.

The Greek Catholic churches had formed as a series of "Unions" between the Orthodox and Catholic churches, starting in the late sixteenth century north of the Carpathian divide, in what was then Poland-Lithuania (which included most of what is now Ukraine), and cascading southward through the mountains into Hungary and Transylvania (see Appendix C). Finding themselves on the western fringes of their faith and within Catholic realms being swept by the Counter Reformation—or in the case of Transylvania, within a Protestant Principality being swept by the Catholic Austrian Habsburgs[105]—and finding themselves as disadvantaged ethnic minorities as well[106], certain Orthodox clergy sought to preserve as much of their religion as possible, and to gain at least a modicum of respect, through acts of compromise: In return for acknowledging the administrative and jurisdictional authority of the Pope and accepting a few key principles consistent with the Catholic Church[107], they could keep their Eastern (Byzantine) rites, as well as the rights to elect their own bishops[108] and to marry. They also shed the lowly status of being feudal vassals, or in some cases even serfs[109], and secured the legal rights and authorities enjoyed by Catholic clergy, at least in theory. And in Transylvania, they shed being required to teach certain Protestant doctrines and to adhere to certain Protestant customs (an influence from Protestantism willingly accepted by the Orthodox clergy that was certainly positive from the point of view of the congregations was the use of the local vernacular for sermons and prayers). The mostly impoverished Eastern clergy and their flocks were relieved of paying tithes to other churches, and they could now hold previously forbidden public posts. They became *Uniat* (also spelled *Uniate*), as the new faith was initially called (changed to "Greek Catholic" in the 1770s to shed derogatory connotations), and as soon as some had done so, the rest were forced to follow: In the territories of the Unions, the Orthodox Church—the church of the Vlachs for well over a thousand years[110] and of the Ruthenians only somewhat less—was legally dissolved[111].

Not all Orthodox complied. Ever since Christian missionaries brought their faith, and probably since long before, religion has been the most vital, personal, reassuring, and unifying aspect of life in and around the Carpathians. The laity was especially loyal to traditions they had been taught from birth is not only the Truth but is also the Good and the Beautiful—is what gives their hard lives meaning—and many believers viewed the compromise as apostasy. Clashes broke out between those who converted and those who did not, with especially violent battles fought over churches and other property being transferred to the new religion[112], and in Transylvania the pot was further stirred by the pushing and pulling of Protestant and Roman Catholic forces[113].

Witnessing the pain, violence, and futility associated with forced conversions, over the next hundred years the Habsburgs gradually relented. But whether the congregation of the Ukrainian Wood Church of Poienile de Sub Munte took advantage of the slow legal revival of

Orthodoxy[114] before Communist regimes brutally made it a requirement seems to be undocumented, at least in English; they may have done so as part of the Ruthenian resistance to Hungarian assimilation during the second half of the nineteenth century. In any case, when the Soviet Union and Stalin's proxies in Poland, Czechoslovakia, and Romania took over at the end of World War II, Greek Catholicism was banned throughout most of the Carpathian region, and those of its hierarchy who refused to convert, to either Orthodoxy or the state religion of atheism, were imprisoned or executed[115].

Faith proved stubborn once again, however, and when the thumb lifted with the fall of the Communist regimes (and earlier, in the case of Slovakia[116]), the subvertly loyal returned to the Greek Catholicism by the hundreds of thousands. Greek Catholic churches were resurrected in Belarus, Slovakia, Ukraine, Carpathian Ruthenia, Romania, and Russia.

Throughout it all, whether Orthodox or Greek Catholic in spirit or by law, the Carpathian highlanders maintained the skill of building their churches with readily available logs, and today nearly a hundred Orthodox and Greek Catholic congregations can still worship in wooden churches built throughout the mountains of Maramureș. The craft is dying, however, and to preserve the rustic yet majestic icons of a way of life that was once widespread throughout a larger region of Europe, thirty-three of The Wooden Churches of the Carpathians—with their weathered horizontal log walls, soaring bell towers and steeples (some over 50 meters high), and steep wooden-shingle roofs—have been designated World Heritage Sites by UNESCO: eight in Poland, nine in Slovakia, eight in Ukraine, and eight in Maramureș. In the way of unique, inspiring, and beautiful religious monuments they complement the Painted Monasteries of Bukovina (Orthodox, also called the Churches of Moldavia, located in today's Suceava County)—also World Heritage sites that lie just to the east of Maramureș. But alas, the Way of the Wolf will not take us to those.

Poienile de Sub Munte and the neighboring villages of Repedea and Ruscova comprise one of the largest enclaves of Ukrainians (or "Ruthenians") in Romania, the region having been most recently settled by a mountain people known as the *Hutsuls*. It is thought the Hutsuls came from the north mostly during the eighteenth century. Since the area is so isolated, most people living in these villages still speak the Hutsul dialect of Ukrainian[117].

Poienile de Sub Munte farmer. © Jürgen Sauer.

New Ukrainian Wood Church of Poienile
de Sub Munte, outside. © Alan Sparks.

New Ukrainian Wood Church of Poienile
de Sub Munte, inside. © Jürgen Sauer.

Old Ukrainian Wood Church of Poienile
de Sub Munte. ©Horia Dinca.

Later in the afternoon Peter, Jürgen, Ana, Thilo, Markus, and I trek for a few hours in the hills above the village in the inevitable weather. It is the first time that "team Romania" (except Cata) has been able to hike together, and although not a through hike, I am thrilled to be able to join! A gravel road now doubling as a stream takes us up to where the trees are still naked, gray, and brown, although splashes of reddish-green are touching the tangles of branches and splashes of green the lower bushes and clumps of grasses. On the side of a slope, Peter pauses to howl and we all pause to listen, but not even echoes can make it through the muffling matrix of fog and rain.

Back at the lodge on this dark, rainy, late afternoon, we have access to the best cooking facilities since we began—a stove, pots and pans, and a sink—yet no one feels inclined to start a meal. I certainly don't, and neither apparently does Ana. Maybe we both feel a bit taken for granted. Maybe also eating a warm meal is not as necessary now that we have warm and dry lodgings. In any case, no one broaches the subject, probably for fear they will be held responsible; so we all just nibble on cold provisions—bread, salami, cheese, chocolate, and wormy but tasty apples.

Wednesday, April 27.
Poienile de Sub Munte, Romania

We are staying put for another day before we head for Ukraine, so today I hike solo. I take on the road that climbs the ravine alongside the gushing river. I'm expecting heart-pumping exercise and the wild jumbled beauty that is the essence of mountainous terrain, but I also come upon two mysteries. The first is a level platform of grass about the size of a basketball court poking into the forest that is lined with two rows of weathered, crumbling, log-siding shacks, perhaps a dozen all told, some of which are in pieces. Was this once the site of a hut factory, abandoned for some tragic reason in mid-production? The second is another of the spruce-bough "tents" that have been cropping up recently, this one filled with bundles of green sticks. Much smaller than cabins and not abandoned—on the contrary, still green and new—what are they for? This one, I suppose, could be for drying kindling.

Leaving valley puzzles behind, I take an old trail up the sheer side of the ravine, switchbacking through thick woods and then across broad, exposed ledges, up to heights where snow and ice still cling. Through brief breaks in a thick, white fog come tantalizing glimpses of jagged black ramparts floating in the clouds.

On the way back down by a circuitous route I encounter fox tracks in mud and snow; the bones of a horse splayed on the ground, like the skeleton of a diminutive Tyrannosaurus Rex staring from out of the swirling mists; and a very fresh and loose pile of scat. I think the latter might be from a bear, since it is not the usual twisted, hairy cylinders typical of wolves. Nor is it brown—it is greenish-grey—although small bits of bone indicate a predator. I rummage through my pack for the sealed vials and sanitized wooden "popsicle" sticks we use for collecting scat, but my search is in vain, so a stick from the ground and a used sandwich baggy make do. Not exactly uncontaminated, I know.

Upon my return Peter takes a whiff and confirms it is wolf. He also confirms my technique was flawed, but declines my offer to lead him back on the two-hour trek for a better sample.

The Mountains of Maramureş. © Jürgen Sauer.

Thursday, April 28. "Windy crow camp"
near Livada, Romania.

We awake at the park headquarters to the usual dark, rainy day, and cram ourselves into our vehicles to head to Mihai's by way of Sighetu Marmatiei.

Once the capital of the Hungarian province of Maramureș, Sighetu Marmatiei is now a city of about 40,000 people set along the left bank of the Tisza River (and consequently the Ukrainian border), which is famous for its infamous prisons. Here is where, in the early nineteenth century, hundreds of Orthodox clergy and their Ruthenian flock were imprisoned and tortured for sticking with their church rather than converting to Uniate (which also led to suspicions of Russian rather than Hungarian secular sympathies). The confining legacy of Sighetu Marmatiei grew even more during the Second World War, when thousands of people of Jewish faith were rounded up and stored in the city's ghetto before their deportment to Auschwitz—including Eliezer "Elie" Wiesel, the famous Holocaust survivor and author[118]. And it grew still more after the war, when hundreds of politicians, clergy, and intelligentsia were imprisoned and tortured, many of them to death, by the Securitate (Communist Romania's secret police)—treatment so brutal and recent that their chambers have since become a museum, a part of the "Memorial for the Victims of Communism."

Ana and Cata point out the three-story, stucco, block-long, rather innocent-looking building of the Sighet Memorial Museum, but provide no details, so barely aware of its inglorious past, Peter and I disembark into an internet café while the others tour, shop, or continue on to Mihai's. The café has only one functional PC, so while Peter checks his email, I grab lunch in a smoky grill.

Weary of team schedules and uninspired by the prospect of another jam in the car with fogged-up windows to see through, when the others come to pick us up, I decide to stay. I'll take over the PC, catch up with the outside world at my own pace, and then walk the seven or so kilometers to Mihai's. Actually, I have only a vague notion of where Mihai's is, recalling that it is tucked away down some nondescript side street, but I assume the village isn't so big that I can't eventually find it.

Once underway, I revel in my rare independence. But I also feel exposed, away from mountains and woods, and vulnerable, having no phone. If I can't find Mihai's, how will I ever reconnect with the Way of the Wolf? I don't even know Mihai's last name.

Hoofing along the road, I find myself in a downpour. I needn't repeat that I love to walk in the rain, but this is a wind-driven deluge. Cold wet pellets plaster my back and legs and drench my ancient, now permeable, overstuffed daypack, which, I remember with horror, contains my journal. Truck after truck splashes me mercilessly as I plod along the shoulder-less road and tip-toe along the small mud bank to get out of the way, until finally, soaked and shivering, I arrive at a recognized street of a village.

Mihai rushes me into his warm house and then rushes a "*tsweeger*" into my cold hands. The Romanian elixir lives up to expectations, warming and loosening my bones while my concerned host helps me out of my water-logged "raincoat" and shirt, puts them on radiator, and hands me a dry t-shirt. The others have already eaten, but a plate of warm soup and hearty bread is quickly served up.

While I eat, Jürgen tells me about a tour they made in and around Sighetu Marmatiei, visiting a wooden church with the tallest steeple in Romania, a woodcarving shop, and a very memorable cemetery. Known as the "Merry Cemetery of Sapanta," its tombstones famously celebrate life rather than grieve death. Sprouting at the heads of planted rectangles, which themselves lift from fields of polished flagstones, the headstones are sheltered by little peaked roofs and are painted and inscribed with folksy pictures and poems depicting the triumphs, tragedies, comedies, indiscretions, and even banalities that made up the lives of those now gone—and of course that symbolize the lives of us all.

Just as I finish dining and am beginning to contemplate the appealing prospect of a convivial evening with the entire team in the warm, dry comfort of Mihai and Ilena's cozy home—our last evening together—I learn that Jürgen and I are scheduled to depart at midnight to bring Markus to the train station in Satu Mare for a 3:00 a.m. departure. We will miss the final parting of Cata and Ana, so we say our goodbyes just before trying to catch a couple of hours of sleep. The happiness provoked by visions of clean, dry warmth and native-speaking company is not entirely obscured by misty eyes and sad faces, while the emotions of those of us still committed are less conflicted. Goodbye, my Romanian friends!

Merry Cemetery of Sapanta. © Jürgen Sauer.

Friday, April 29. "Windy crow camp"
near Livada, Romania.

Images of our nocturnal journey unfold as in a dream.

Our headlights lit only fog, so we began at a crawl with hopes of avoiding the craters that popped unexpectedly out of the blackness. We hit a few, raising deep sympathies for the tires and suspension of our trusty Passat, but we risked being late, and since we had no idea where the train station would be once we got to the unknown city, and since the road lacked mileposts of any kind, Jürgen had to speed up. He hunched intently over the wheel peering into nothingness while I hunched intently over the dashboard trying to help.

We hit the outskirts about an hour before the train's departure. Driving along otherwise deserted streets, we spotted two men walking the sidewalk. We pulled up and I asked for directions to the "*gara.*" They spoke broken English, and I sort of understood their answer, but couldn't really remember what they said, or what I thought they said, after two or three lefts and rights, so we pulled into a gas stop for clarification. Turned out we were already quite near, so after a couple more rights and lefts we arrived.

The terminal was dark, desolate, and Gothic, like something out of a Batman movie. The ticket agent was curt as Markus tried to explain he wanted a ticket for a 3:00 a.m. train that was supposedly aimed for Switzerland. She impatiently declared that the train is "personal," with a tone suggesting that Markus could not possibly take it. When I asked what "personal" meant, thinking maybe it just meant frequent stops, she was exasperated to have to explain in English—which she fluently explained she spoke little of—that the train made frequent stops.

I explained that the critical point was the destination, and after she confirmed the train would indeed head in the right direction, Markus paid for the ticket. We exited the echoing structure and moved our vehicles from among the taxis to a parking lot to wait, where, while trying to doze in our seats, we got solicited by two rather attractive women. Our declination produced no sleep, however, as we were fascinated by the comings and goings of men between cars and taxis and a sort of restaurant at the base of a sort of motel. One of our rejected solicitors was even there, standing on a porch and throwing stares our way.

With about ten minutes to go, Jürgen and Markus made for the terminal while I guarded the car. Just as they reached the door, a woman, whom we had seen earlier accosting a drunken man at a taxi, bumped her nearly spherical body into Jürgen. Startled at first, Jürgen quickly recovered and ushered Markus along.

About fifteen minutes later, Jürgen came springing out of the terminal with the corpulent woman and a companion on his heels. Jumping into the car, Jürgen gave me the story: As he and Markus had approached the train, these two women knocked into them while spewing the alluring words "fucky, fucky" and grabbing for Markus's camera. Jürgen shuttled Markus onto the train while warding off their fans, who pursued without much improvement in their vocabulary. After Markus had found his cabin, the women followed Jürgen off the train, pestering him like a swarm of flies.

Our next goal was to find a place to sleep. We were supposed to hook up with Peter and Thilo later in the day somewhere near the city, after they had gathered our two new eco-volunteers, so we didn't want to go far. Driving thus too long through city and suburb looking for a place sheltered from morning traffic, the buildings finally thinned, and a dirt track finally shot off into a field, where cornstalks and thick fog finally gave promise of peace.

A long driveway brought us to a small, darkened house and barn hidden amid last year's stalks. We turned around, hoping that our headlights hadn't woken anyone, and drove about half way back out. Off with the engine and headlights, back with our seatbacks, and into our sleeping bags, we tried to sleep. We must have succeeded, because when a tapping on our window brought us nearly to our senses it was nearly dawn.

A peasant woman from out of the nineteenth century materialized outside the fogged-up windows. She scowled while we stirred, but as I rolled down my window, her expression gradually morphed into a semi-toothless smile. She gestured for a cigarette, but we were out, so we tried to explain we'd be on our way. At the sound of "Satu Mare" she waved us frantically towards her house, as though the city were poison and her abode the antidote. But the dusky fog was too eerie, and visions of Hansel and Gretel and our responsibilities ahead haunted our sleepy heads, so we started the engine, rolled forward, and waved a happy goodbye.

This is our last full day in Romania, and it's a sunny one at that, although with a cold north wind. Perhaps the rare brightness is a good omen for national transitions. Jürgen and I are sitting in a cornfield near a small village called Livada. We are waiting for Peter and Thilo to arrive after they've dropped off Cata and Ana at a bus station in Baia Mare.

A crow is drinking water from one of many puddles. This European variety of corvid looks like an American crow, except for the grey nape and sides of the neck that give it a masked appearance (the Eurasian Jackdaw, *Corvus monedula*). Jürgen just asked me for the name of this camp, and suggests "Wind Camp." The flat contour and rustling cornstalks suggest "Camp Nebraska" to me, but I doubt my European friends would get it. Lots of crows vigorously debating strategies produce a synthesis: "Windy Crow Camp" it is.

After Peter and Thilo return, Jürgen and I spend a relaxed day in the city. While Jürgen goes off to find a post office to mail postcards, I walk around the centre, buy a pastry, and eat in a park. Once the site of a medieval citadel that helped protect the city's citizens and salt carriers from raiders and invaders such as Magyars (until the Magyars seized it from the semi-mythical and possibly Dacian holdout Menumoret[119] in 895 A.D.), Ottoman Turks, Habsburgs, and even uppity Hungarian nobles (after the city had become "royal free"[120]), Satu Mare is now a city of about 110,000[121] residents, with lots of streets, buildings, churches, and high rises crowded around the central square. Like most modern cities the world over, it is busy on this final day of the work week, with smartly dressed people rushing about their business and lots of cars and buses speeding by and pigeons pecking the ground.

But just as I'm thinking how far removed this bustling cosmopolitan center is from the third-world-like, rural regions that comprise the majority of this beautiful country, and musing about the tremendous gap between the few rich and the many poor in Romania, a wild-eyed sheep comes running full bore from under an archway, followed by a yelling and waving shepherd decked in full shepherd attire. The sheep leaps a couple of benches while the shepherd gains not a meter on his charge. As the dashing pair exit under an archway on the other side of the plaza, three or four spiffy city girls who had been stopped in their tracks sneak embarrassed "did-you-see-that?" glances at me and hold their hands to their mouths trying to stifle giggles.

Saturday, April 30, Near the Ukraine border.

Last night I didn't bother to set up a tent. I slept in the Passat and slept well, catching up. Peter and Thilo made do under a tarp attached to the side of the Land Rover. Only the new eco-volunteers, a couple, Stephan and Kathrin from northern Germany, slept in a tent, which they brought with them (which means I'll have my own tent in Ukraine!).

Stephan is quite tall (around 6'3", I guess) and Kathrin is quite quiet, at least around me, as she knows very little English. They seem nice enough, but there is this feeling that our old friends are gone and these new folks are strangers. I suppose this is typical in this situation, and will surely happen more and more during the coming weeks. After Ukraine, we expect nearly weekly changes of eco-volunteers.

We awake to fog, but here in the lowlands, at least, the days are getting warmer. Just before the border we stop at a roadside shop in a small town called Halmeu to stock up. While Peter does the buying, Thilo and Jürgen photograph a white stork. Harbingers of good fortune in Romania, could this be a male, tidying its huge, ancestral bundle of sticks after its epic flight from Africa, and awaiting its mate, which it hasn't seen for two-thirds of a year?

I stand on the sidewalk, as usual wearing my sunglasses, which, if nothing else does, makes me stand out. Suddenly a smartly dressed man approaches me, says "hi," hands me an "Easter cake" (as the others call it)—not a piece of a cake, but the whole sweet and spongy disk—and reaches out for a shake, all before I have time to realize this is unusual. I shake his hand and manage a "*Multsemesc*" before he disappears.

UKRAINE

April 30, Rakhiv, Ukraine.

Wow! The world is basking in the loving warm bright yellow glory of the sun! And the earth and everything on it is offering its steamy moisture to the whisking breezes. We truly enter a new season as we enter Ukraine.

The border is defended by fences and gates and armed guards peering from dark green pill boxes perched atop soaring steel towers, while a white stork supervises all from its nest of sticks on top of a searchlight spire. Our crossing goes smoother than expected, although the presence of an American does hold things up a bit. Given the precarious history of Ukraine, human guards, if not storks, have reason to be diligent.

A fecund land of profound transitions, where the great forests of one continent give way to the great steppes of another[122], Ukraine "... [lies] astride the main routes between Europe and Asia, [and thus has been] repeatedly exposed to various frequently competing cultures"[123]. In other words, Ukraine has often been ravaged by war. The country's fertile black soil—among the richest in the world, capable not only of feeding a continent but of sprouting momentous human seeds: the

Proto-Indo-Europeans (those original horsemen and extroverted spreaders of language), the Proto-Slavs (those concealed dwellers of forest and fen), the Rus' (those Scandinavian-swayed East Slavic tribes), and the Cossacks (those independent, magnificently-mustachioed, fleece-hatted, and saber-waving cavaliers) all got their start here—this fertile black soil has been too frequently enriched with the blood of humans. Like winds sweeping the grasses first in one direction and then the other, invaders and the invaded have charged back and forth across Ukraine's fields so often that one can reasonably wonder how people living in this "breadbasket of Europe" ever had the time to raise livestock, pursue families, and plant fields rather than raise armies, pursue enemies, and plant spears.

In fact, it's no small miracle that today there is an independent nation called "Ukraine" spanning the geographical center of Europe, bounded by the Black Sea to the south, the arid steppes of Asia to the east, and the Carpathian Mountains and wooded plain of northern Europe to the west. When the term was first coined in the twelfth century, "Ukraine" had the meaning of "borderlands" (or, in more archaic terms, "march")[124], referring to the periphery of what was then the center of the most dominant political entity of northeastern Europe: the stronghold of Kyiv[125]. The fact the appellation has persisted ever since is a clue that most of the people holding most of the power over most of Ukraine most of the time were not the people living here: a conglomeration of Eastern Slavic tribes arising by at least the sixth century A.D. who acquired a Scandinavian elite and evolved into the ethno-culture we know today as Ukrainian. And the fact that the country is still often called "THE Ukraine" speaks to the enduring strength of the perception that Ukraine is a remote land, marginal to the interests of outsiders at best and perilous at worst. Prior to our arrival we were often warned not to come here: "Are you crazy? Ukraine is dangerous. You will be killed."

Thankfully, wolves pay no attention to such prejudices, and neither have we. This is our way.

Apparently my visa is in order (shortly after the expedition, visa requirements for Americans staying less than ninety days in Ukraine were dropped), and the guards wave us through. Now we're driving along a river gushing with spring melt. This is the Tisza, that long liquid course that drains the inner side of half the Carpathians, whose waters have separated Dacians from Celts, brought forth the Huns, floated the commerce of Avars and Magyars, and isolated the Rusyns. The river has floated fallen Carpathian giants from the mountains to the plains for ages, and here forms a part of the modern border between Romania and Ukraine.

We are entering a region of Ukraine known as "Transcarpathia," which includes the southwestern slopes of the Ukrainian Carpathians down to the banks of the Tisza. From the point of view of Kyiv and the rest of Ukraine, we are "beyond the Carpathians" (thus "trans"): in a perennial frontier region long a part of Hungary, very briefly an independent nation, and changing political status at least seventeen times[126] and states six times during the twentieth century alone (see Appendix D). The homeland of an east Slavic population since at least the fifth century A.D.; located at the oft-disputed junction of five nations (today's Poland, Hungary, Slovakia, Romania, and Ukraine, all with varied historical antecedents); and always the most remote and impoverished region of whichever state managed to seize and hold its claim, today Transcarpathia is an *oblast*[127] of Ukraine, "as far from Kyiv as it is from God," as a local saying has it[128] (the transliterated name of the oblast is *Zakarpattia*).

Lush green meadows, resplendent with yellow, white, pink, and purple flowers and dappled with blooming apple trees march down to the roiling waters. Sharp hills rise behind, whose slopes are covered by manes of spindly gray trunks with feathered crowns just beginning to go green. Here and there large cinderblock boxes with dark, gaping holes pop from the fields; later we learn these are the homestead dreams of "rich" Romanians drawn by the lower prices of Ukraine.

The sun dazzles from an infinite blue sky generously stippled with brilliant white fair-weather clouds. Small cemeteries shoot profusions of colors from the midst of the fields: flowers, garlands, wreaths, streaming ribbons, and rows of staggering black and white stones and crosses, all guarded by planar icons of Christ tacked high on crosses surmounted by gleaming sliver halos.

We come to one such graveyard quite unlike the others. It is next to the road, just before a collection of houses hiding on the other side of the street, and is cast in shadow, as though springtime has neglected the condemned ground and always will. A thick labyrinth of branches— black and barren and lifting multitudes of dark, bushy crow's nests, where legions of black crows congregate and squawk—shades the forlorn plot. An isolated, autonomous breeze stirs swarms of dead leaves around the headstones, which climb out of a tangled jungle of undergrowth dotted with bright orange poppies. The stones are surprisingly straight, sturdy, and elegant, however, earnestly holding the images of their honored deceased in their upper corners.

When we stop to take photos of the Poe-esque scene, while my friends are snapping away and I'm trying to capture everything with my eyes, brain, and heart, a man comes rushing out of a house across the street. He's coming to say hello, I think. Short and with an unruly shock of thick dark hair just beginning to go gray, the man appears very excited. As soon as I say "hi," he becomes even more animated, reaching out to vigorously shake my hand. "American boy! American boy!" he declares. Apparently this is about the extent of his English, but we manage to exchange names in the universal fashion.

Crow cemetery. © Jürgen Sauer.

Pavel then grabs my hand and leads me across the street and rushes me around the small village, apparently looking for someone, whom he soon finds: a shy girl of about twelve who can speak a little English. From the cemetery Jürgen catches what is going on and jogs over to join us, camera in hand. Apparently not as interested in fellow Europeans, Pavel shakes Jürgen's hand curtly and then brushes us into his house to meet his family: a wife of around forty and a boy of eight or nine. We line up for photos—me with Pavel, me with Pavel and his wife, me with Pavel and his wife and his boy, and me with Pavel and his wife and his boy and our translator.

After the shoot my new friend insists on food and drink. Jürgen escapes with the excuse that the team is probably waiting and he'll try to hold them off, but I'm trapped as eggs and bread and pastries are quickly laid out on a table and a couple of dirty shot glasses are filled with a clear fluid. "Yushchenko!" Pavel shouts, raising and emptying his glass in one swift motion. "America! Ooo-kra-eene! Bush! Friends!" he repeats several times, expanding my impression of his English vocabulary while urging me to follow with my glass.

If you think American (or Western) politics are divisive, consider those of Ukraine, where fistfights occasionally break out in the parliament and prominent politicians have been imprisoned and poisoned. A long history has established a distinct identity for Ukrainians, but the most recent in the long list of dominating foreign powers was their powerful eastern neighbor, in the form of the Russian-centric Soviet Union, and due to settlement patterns both ancient and modern, and forced and unforced, and boosted by war and famine, a significant minority of people living in the eastern region of the country today are of Russian heritage, and even more—a majority in some areas—speak Russian as their first language[129]. And with many Ukrainians eager to escape their recently subservient past, while contemporary Russian political leaders are intent on pulling Ukraine eastward for political inspiration and closer social and economic ties, the schizophrenic politics of Ukraine should come as no surprise[130].

Consider for example the presidential election of 2004, only a few months before The Way of the Wolf:

By early fall, after a contentious prelude in which preliminary alliances were settled, two leading candidates remained: Viktor

Yanukovych—the eastern-leaning and Russian-backed Prime Minister serving under the presidency of Leonid Kuchma; and Viktor Yushchenko—a former Prime Minister and leader of a coalition of opposition parties (including the party of the irrepressible Yulia Tymoshenko). Yushchenko's party, known as "Our Ukraine," chose orange for its color, and its public events became known for orange-clad crowds vigorously waving orange flags and releasing flurries of orange balloons.

Yanukovich was not expected to win. Although economic growth had been robust under Kuchma (who couldn't run again because of term limits), the administration was unpopular outside its political base in the south and east. It was suspected of being corrupt, especially after Kuchma was implicated in the abduction and murder of a journalist[131]. It also didn't help that Yanukovych could not speak proper Ukrainian. But there had been shenanigans in earlier local elections[132], and Yushchenko supporters were prepared, training for protests and hoarding tents and other supplies[133].

The politicking leading up to the first round of the election was intense, and Yanukovych's party, known as "The Party of Regions," was not reluctant to leverage its ruling power. Opposition activists were arrested, critical media outlets were shut down, and journalists were stifled by statutes dictating what they could and could not report. A more sinister plot unfolded when explosives were surreptitiously stashed in the offices of an NGO working to support a fair election; upon discovery of the munitions, the NGO's Ukrainian volunteers, who were perceived to be mostly opposition supporters, were accused of being terrorists.

Then things got even worse. Yushchenko, savvy leader in a body politic known for danger, somehow ingested an amount of dioxin (a very toxic and trace byproduct of certain industrial processes) that should have killed him. He survived, but was seriously sickened and his ample charisma seriously dampened by a newly pockmarked face. Nevertheless, and in spite of suspected fraud, the initial contest ended in a non-majority tie. It was on to a second round.

Yushchenko was now widely expected to win. He was expected to garner most of the non-Yanukovych voters of the first round, and exit polls suggested he had a nine-point lead. The official results: Yanukovych by a slim margin. Election observers, both foreign and domestic, reported significant fraud in favor of Yanukovych. Ballots went up in flames in Yushchenko-majority districts and appeared from out of nowhere in Yanukovych districts, and some voters were physically intimidated into seeing the Yanukovych way.

Yushchenko did not take it sitting down. He declared the election stolen and called for protests. The age of social media had not yet arrived, but word spread anyway, boosted by a supportive cable TV station and a web-based newspaper. Crowds gathered in Kyiv's Independence Square (*Maidan Nezalezhnosti* in Ukrainian, now more famously known as "The Maidan"), a half million showing up within two days. The protestors blocked government buildings and marched on Parliament, which may have helped encourage the legislators to refuse to ratify the election. The councils of several cities, including Kyiv, followed suit, while foreign observers declared that the election did not meet international standards[134]. U.S. Senator Richard Lugar, observing for the United States, had this to say: "It is now apparent that a concerted and forceful program of election-day fraud and abuse was enacted with either the leadership or cooperation of government authorities."

Yushchenko continued agitating protestors and even took a symbolic presidential oath in the hopes of legitimizing himself as the commander-in-chief should security forces or the military become involved. (In fact, internal ministry troops were mobilized, but the dissention of other security forces prevented martial action[135]). Drawing inspiration as well as organizational skills from other recently successful, nonviolent, anti-fraudulent-election movements in the former Eastern-bloc nations of Serbia (the 2001 ousting of Slobodan Milošević in what was called the "Bulldozer Revolution") and Georgia (the 2003 ousting of Eduard Shevardnadzethe in the "Rose Revolution"), and with activists and consultants funded by various NGOs and foreign governments (including the United States), the protests continued even through the weather of a very frigid winter. Protestors stayed warm by waving orange flags, eating oranges, dancing to the music of popular musicians, and according to reports, even making love[136].

Nor were Yanukovych forces impotent. They staged protests of their own in the south and east, while Party of Regions officials proposed unconstitutionally federalizing the nation or even splitting it. Some Yanukovych demonstrators even made it to Kyiv, though they were overwhelmed by the more than one million in orange who had by then shown up.

Negotiations were attempted—mediated by representatives from

Poland, Lithuania, Russia, and the EU—but these broke down, and on November 24th the Central Election Commission (itself accused of fraudulent vote counting) declared Yanukovych the winner once again. Yushchenko upped the ante, calling for sit-ins and a nationwide strike, and the orange faithful rallied. The Parliament passed a vote of no-confidence in the Cabinet of Ministers, technically requiring the government to resign but with no power of enforcement. Finally, on December 3rd, the Ukrainian Supreme Court invalidated the election and ordered a new one to be held.

Fear of bloodshed had motivated the opposing parties in Parliament to negotiate a change to the constitution, reducing the power of the presidency (favored by the Yanukovych side, which probably expected to lose the new election) and changed election laws to reduce the possibility of fraud (favored by the Yushchenko side), and both candidates vowed to abide by the results of the new election. Under the close scrutiny of domestic and international observers[137], the new election, held on December 26, went smoothly, and it went to Yushchenko: 52% to 44%. Yanukovych attempted a final legal challenge, but the observers declared the election fair and the Supreme Court validated it. On January 10, 2005, the Central Election Commission declared Yushchenko the winner. The Orange Revolution had succeeded. For then[138].

So why did my new friend Pavel in this tiny village across from this eerie cemetery in southwest Ukraine invoke the name of the President of the United States? The Bush administration had been a supporter of free and fair elections in Ukraine—vocally, financially, organizationally, and observationally—and "free and fair" in the Ukrainian presidential election of 2004 basically meant support for Yushchenko. Of course, the United States also had policy reasons for preferring a victory by Yushchenko[139], although in condemning a stolen election it needn't really take sides. In any case, when it was all over, the Bush administration supported the new government with more than just words, asking Congress for a modest increase in foreign aid to Ukraine. George Bush had won more than a few hearts and minds in Ukraine, at least in the west.

I know Peter doesn't generally like unplanned interruptions, but I'm having trouble extracting myself from Pavel's enthusiastic hospitality. I also believe this fits the charter of our mission: improving relations between West and East. Maybe I'm even the first American to visit this village, although judging from the scowl on Pavel's wife's face, I can guess another reason why my new friend savors the distraction.

Nevertheless, I know it's time to go. I keep explaining I must leave and moving towards the door, while Pavel keeps waving it off ("it" being the general direction of my friends outside), pouring me another shot, and handing me another pastry. "*Momento*," he says, "*Momento*." The pastries are good, and I do feel honored by the attention, and thus my creeping departure is delayed a few more times. Between bites I try to answer questions about why we are in Ukraine, and I keep trying to explain why I must be going, but it seems to not matter. Gradually, however, I get to the door and make it clear I'm leaving.

Finally acknowledging the inevitable, Pavel grabs my hand and shakes it vigorously and pats me on the back. I think I even detect moistness in his eyes. I feel a bond in kind as I exit the door and cross the street and see the whole team waiting in our vehicles, Peter's face without a smile.

We pass children sweeping sidewalks and a man spraying crops from a cylinder on his back. I had naively thought such agro-technology hadn't made it here, where the nineteenth century seems otherwise to be still hanging on, and resolve to more carefully wash our vegetables from now on. As we drive along, I supplement my munchings at Pavel's with a couple slices of bread. We are destined for a town called Rakhiv, where the Carpathian Biosphere Reserve[140] headquarters is located, and where Peter will arrange for various permissions, and where we will spend the night.

Maria is a woman of eighteen years, with very blond, wavy hair cropped above the shoulders, high cheekbones, and a hint of the steppes in her sky-blue eyes. She stands nervously in our little circle in the parking lot of the headquarters of the Reserve, listening to Jürgen, Thilo, and I cracking bad jokes as we semiconsciously try to make the newer folks amongst us feel at ease in what for them must be a very intimidating circumstance: the prospect of living for three weeks in the Ukrainian Carpathian wilds under the guidance of people whom they have never met and who have never been here themselves. Especially for Maria, who is not only young but will start out with no familiar companion. She learned of the opportunity to be our interpreter through a family friendship with Yaroslav Dovhanych, the chief of the Zoological Laboratory of the Reserve. Peter is with Yaroslav now in the stucco-walled administration building, discussing our plans and arranging official permissions to hike and camp in the Reserve.

A couple of large military-style vehicles watch over us as we shuffle our feet and laugh at the jokes or at least smile at the efforts. Here, higher up than the lowlands near the border, the trees are still mostly bare and a chill is falling with the lowering sun. While I knew Maria would be joining us, I am surprised by her age, and think she must be very brave. At least she bravely tolerates our sense of humor, which is surely strained by our month on the road.

We'll sleep tonight inside the administration building. As dusk approaches, Maria leaves to spend one last safe night at home, while we others bustle about the hallway and rooms, picking cots, unfurling sleeping bags, and assigning and executing food preparation chores.

The Tisza's spring surge separates Ukraine and Romania. © Jürgen Sauer.

Monday, May 2. The Camp of Small Flies, near Luhy, Ukraine.

In the morning we, or at least I, feel refreshed after a sound sleep inside, off the ground and out of the damp night air of this cold Eastern

European spring. I also reorganize my packs, moving some of my heavier winter gear into my suitcase, which I will now store in Thilo's large aluminum box atop the Land Rover, hopefully for good. After another indoor breakfast on chairs, we complete our packing and head into town to pick up Maria and buy some food.

A collection of modest but trim houses and small shops strung along the Tisza River just below the confluence of the river's "Black" and "White" tributaries, Rakhiv offers a secluded and lively setting for its 15,000 residents. Mountains surround the city and a river rushes through its heart, the waters raucously celebrating their escape from the icy grip of Hoverla, the highest mountain in Ukraine (2061 meters/6762 feet), and the rest of the Chornohora ("Black") Range to the northeast, as well as the Gorgany Range to the north. The encirclement of Rakhiv is completed by the Svidovec Range to the northwest, the Krasna Range to the west, and the Rakhiv Range to the south[141], and at 430 meters the city is the highest in Ukraine. With nearby mineral springs, a ski area (Dragobrat)[142], glacial lakes of mysterious repute[143], several patches of the Carpathian Biosphere Reserve, and the Carpathian National Park, Rakhiv is, or should be, a choice destination for outdoor enthusiasts. And as I steady myself on a footbridge swaying above the raging Tisza, I see that Rakhivians, like people in most of the cities, towns, and villages of the Carpathian Mountains—and throughout Central and Eastern Europe for that matter—like to be out and about. Out and about on foot, that is.

This strikes me as a sharp contrast to most small towns in America. About as many people live in Rakhiv as in my hometown of Westbrook, Maine, and the business districts of both lie along roughly one-kilometer stretches of main drag, each following a river. Yet, while the smooth sidewalks of my hometown are unlikely to guide the destinies of more than one or two pair of human feet at a time— and those usually on short, transverse dashes between a car and an apartment, or one of the few stores, banks, or restaurants that have yet to migrate to the regional mall—the broken sidewalks of Rakhiv are almost always hopping with pedestrians.

Along the chestnut and spruce-shaded main street they stroll, browsing the continuous walls of small shops, banks, and cafés that line each side, or visiting the school, the hotel, or the Orthodox or

Greek Catholic churches that share a tiled plaza. They dally in a small park along the river, or explore the residential neighborhoods either side, where more shops pop up unexpectedly and open markets offer shoes, clothing, produce, and innumerable odds-and-ends on tables or hangars crammed in small shacks or under blue tarps.

Throughout the day and well into evening men rush past toting briefcases; women prance by in heels, platforms, pumps, and sneakers; mothers stroll along pushing strollers; teenage girls glide by hand-in-hand or with mobile phones plastered to their ears, while their male counterparts in backward baseball caps swagger and frolic with feigned nonchalance on the other side of the street. Policemen march by on patrol, their wide-round-flat-topped hats rocking with talk, and even an occasional dog trots by on its way.

The adventurous (or the homebound) might continue up the longer side streets, which gradually steepen into rock-and-mud tracks that swerve past tottering woven hovels as well as big, new, stucco houses, with cobblestone driveways and ornate gates, perhaps financed by employers in the Czech Republic or Poland where the breadwinner has gone to work[144]. Here they encounter the sights, sounds, and scents of cows, sheep, chickens, and dogs, densely packed until the path finally transcends the capabilities of mere motorized vehicles and neighbors aren't found until the next hill. And behind it all, climbing the unclimbable slopes, stands the impenetrable forest, watching and waiting...

Back along the river, the shops of Rakhiv are small, some just a few trays of spices and seeds offered by hopeful old women. But taken all together, they seem to meet the daily needs and maybe even much of the ambition of the people of Rakhiv (and its few visitors)—from bubble gum and shoelaces to mobile phones and laptops. If you add them all up, I doubt you'd get a Walmart, but the essentials are all there, and they keep people out. All together and all over town, maybe one or two thousand people—around one tenth of the town's population—are walking the streets of Rakhiv during the busiest part of the day.

Or would they be out regardless of the shops? With a per capita GDP of $7,600 (U.S), not many of Ukraine's 47 million people[145] can afford a car. And as they walk, people can hear birds and children proclaiming their exuberant young existence. They can smell food cooking. They can feel refreshed by the breeze and hypnotized by water tumbling over rocks. They can rest and dine under the awnings of cafés, where they can survey the greening slopes and watch clouds sail by in a deep blue sky and smell flowers blossoming after a nighttime shower.

Some walk with a purpose, upright and eager for the next event in their lives, while others shuffle along with a stoop, having seen enough already. But they are out—and they know each other! They greet their neighbors, and their aunts and uncles and cousins, and maybe the person they had a crush on in high school. The whole town is a community, and very few are obese.

We drive eastward up the valley of the White Tisza, which is rushing wildly from the spring melt. A few bone-jarring kilometers along the rough, muddy road brings us past two or three clusters of houses strung along the road. A map will tell you these are hamlets with names such as "Roztoky" and "Bohdan," only one of which has a shiny metallic cupola lifting from one of its roofs and thus, having a church, can properly be called a "village."

Along the riverbank where several tents are pitched, we come upon a group of helmeted folks appearing ready to plunge a trio of jury-rigged contraptions into the raging waters. As soon as they spot us, they seem happy to delay their impending thrills—which, in addition to the usual, seems likely to include the kick of wondering whether their boats will hold up—and wave us over.

Their apparent leader, a slim, bearded man with graying hair, is friendly to the extreme, continually smiling and shaking my hand and even putting his arm around my back. He proudly explains they are from "the city" and built the boats themselves. As Maria translates this revelation, my informant's compatriots prepare their crafts anew while a few local teenagers gather to witness the results. This audience doesn't bother getting off their rickety bikes, perhaps not expecting the entertainment to last long, and probably wondering at the mentality of city folk who go out of their way to encourage disaster here in this unpredictable and impoverished backdrop of Ukraine, where it is likely common enough. We foreigners have our own adventures to get to, so we stay just long enough to see one of the boats get hung up on rocks as it's teased into the torrent.

A few more kilometers brings us to a flat, green pasture maybe forty meters wide tucked between the road and the river and wrapped by a motley fence with alternating intervals of rail and picket. Two cows are grazing outside the fence, showing more interest in the tall weeds along the roadside than the shorter grass of the pasture. A partially fenced-off area is claimed by three or four horses, but the rest of the field looks safe, so I pull over. Maria and I get out to set up camp while Jürgen takes the hiking team further up the road to start a two-day trek; they will skirt the southwestern slopes of the Chornohora ridge, which through dark conical spruce trees can be seen lifting the lofty, grey-green and snow-patched Hoverla.

Across the road the land shoots almost straight up. A spring is bubbling crystal-clear from out of the bank, and after filling our bottles we raid the brushy slope for firewood, dragging down a fallen evergreen whose reddish-brown needles offer promise of flame. While we're at it, a man comes hobbling along, talking to himself and gesturing to invisible companions. This apparition is followed throughout the afternoon by a sporadic parade of boys and young men; I noticed similar groups of males hanging out in Rakhiv and along the roadside of the small villages we passed, but this is a phenomenon we hadn't generally seen in Romania. Is it because we are closer to settlements? Or is it spring break? (After all, Maria is taking these three weeks off.) In the afternoon a more gender diverse group of backpackers from Poland comes striding by, students on break who explain they are trekking heights in Ukraine because it's cheaper.

Our evening is quiet, with just Jürgen, Maria, and me—our smallest group yet—huddling around the campfire. This is also Maria's first night out, and she chooses to share a tent with me rather than face the dark outdoor night alone, with at least one strange man and who knows what other strange beasts about. We, or at least I, fall asleep to the patter of light rain.

In times not long past we might have heard the long haunting wail of the *trembita*—the alpenhorn of the Carpathians—echoing off the hills. These radically long horns would have been sounded by Hutsul shepherds, calling in sheep and dogs from out of the evening mists, or Hutsul heralds, announcing funerals, weddings, or attacks [146]. The Hutsuls (sometimes transliterated as "Huculs") are the wild and wooly mountain people who have long called these hills of southeastern Transcarpathia home. They have traditionally dwelt in the highlands on both sides of the upper Tisza and its tributaries, roughly from the eastern Gorgany Range eastward across the Carpathian divide and southward as far as the Maramureş region of northern Romania.

With similarities in culture, lifestyle, and dialect, the Hutsuls may be considered part of a larger group of East Slavic-speaking northern Carpathian highlanders known as *Rusyns* that also includes the *Boykos* (or "Boikos")—who traditionally lived to the west, from the western Gorgany range through the central and western Ukrainian Carpathians into areas now in southeastern Poland and northeastern Slovakia—and the *Lemkos*, who originally lived west of the Boykos, along the Slovakia-Poland border (the Boykos, and Lemkos north of the border, are now mostly gone, for causes we will encounter in Slovakia). The Hutsul, Boyko, and Lemko Rusyns sometimes refer to themselves as *Verkhovyntsi* ("Highlanders"), while the fourth and largest group of Rusyns, who began settling the bottoms of the valleys of the Tisza and its tributaries as early as the thirteenth century A.D., coming over the mountains from Polesia and Podolia via Transylvania where they seem to have spent time with the Szeklers[147], are known as the *Dolyniane* ("Lowlanders").

The terms *Rusyn* (which, along with *Rusnak*, is how they have referred to themselves) and *Ruthenian* (which is how outsiders have referred to them) have a complex and charged history, originally referring to all the descendants of Kievan Rus' (see below), but eventually applying only to those who hung on to ancient East Slavic ways—including especially the language—by virtue of living in or just beyond (from the point of view of Kyiv and the rest of Ukraine) the intimidating slopes of the Carpathians; they are sometimes more descriptively called "*Carpatho-Rusyn*," "*Carpatho-Ruthenian*," or *Carpatho-Ruthene*." The homeland of the Rusyns spans four modern countries, including all of Transcarpathia and adjacent mountainous areas in Romania, Slovakia, and Poland, and covers some 18,000 square miles. While it has always been divided politically (though not by choice), it has been variously designated "Carpathian Ruthenia," "Carpatho-Ukraine," and "Carpathian Rus'" (among other names). See Appendix E for more about the geography of the Carpatho-Rusyns.

Aspects of a distinctive northern Carpathian Mountain culture can also be recognized among the West Slavic-speaking Gorals living still further west, traditionally in northern Slovakia, northern Czech Republic, and southern Poland as far west as the Sudet Mountains of Silesia (which we will get to).

Hutsuls, Boykos, Lemkos, and Gorals: bedecked with vibrant embroidery, whirling to wistful music, reaping from forest, field, and pasture—a consonant cultural milieu painted from an Eastern and Central European palette textured into longitudinal variety by the rippled canvas of the Carpathians. The colorful style of their arts and crafts is matched by the gaiety of their celebrations, which are spiced with earthy cuisine, enlivened with home-brewed spirits, and quickened with windy, fast-paced songs and dances that often build to crescendos, played on fiddles, accordions, and local versions of fifes, bagpipes, jaw harps, and *tsymbalies* (hammered dulcimers). (One style of Hutsul dance is famously known as *arkan*, for which more than one musical band has been named.) Taking full advantage of too-rare breaks in hard lives, the festivities tend to be long and rambunctious, although they have mellowed somewhat in recent years. I'm told that weddings, for example, though still wild enough, used to go on for three days (and in the "old days," seven), with communal cooking, parades through the village, mock battles over the bride between the bride's men and the groom's, and the groom dancing till he drops.

The Northern Carpathian cultural milieu continues: Nearly every mountain village proclaims its piety with a wayside cross planted along its approach, while ancient folklore still influences rituals and beliefs. Thus vampires and werewolves may still be dreaded, and soothsayers and witches blamed, thanked, or asked for bad luck (for others) or good (for self). Until recently (at least), no traditional male highlander would have been caught without his *bartok* (or *bartka*)[148]—a wooden handled axe about four feet long with a smallish iron head. The *bartok* traditionally served as machete, tree chopper, throwing weapon, game dispatcher, confidence builder, dispute resolver, wedding adornment, walking stick, and perhaps, after the wielder's rambunctious days were over (or mostly so), cane; the style and intricacy of its engravings, which emblemized the clan to which it belonged, was a source of pride and prestige.[149]

Today some 26,000 people in this corner of the Carpathians consider themselves Hutsul, although most will officially identify themselves as "Rusyn" or "Ukrainian" (the terms *Hutsul*, *Boyko*, and *Lemko* were all originally nicknames given by neighbors—particularly each other—not usually taken and sometimes even despised by the peoples themselves.) They can be distinguished by their traditional clothing when they are so inclined to wear it (nowadays, mostly on festive occasions), which has been described as the most "distinctive and lavish" in all of Ukraine: brilliant white linen shirts, blouses, and dresses that disport like flowers-on-snow with intricate patterns embroidered in thread and glass beads;

red, maroon, orange, yellow, green, and black are emphasized though all colors may be found, the designs varying from village to village. Traditional men's shirts are long, reaching down to mid-thigh, and are bound with belts of cloth or studded and stamped leather, often dark red and ranging from narrow to very wide (up to a foot), which in times past may have kept knives, pistols, and money within quick reach. Men's pants are usually white or scarlet, of linen when warm and wool when cold. Women's skirts flow to the ankles and are often white and covered by two long front-and-back homespun woolen aprons with fine horizontal- or vertical-striped patterns often in red or orange.

Men shade their crowns with narrow-brimmed or fancy broad-brimmed hats with plumes of feather or string, and warm them with cones of wooly black fleece, while women usually wrap their heads modestly with headbands or kerchiefs—the latter always after they are married. On special occasions Hutsul women may also sport elaborate ribbon headdresses or necklaces bursting with embroidered flowers and webs of beads.

Cool weather brings out sheepskin jerkins, richly embroidered and adorned with strips of leather, metal rings, small mirrors, coins, lace, and brightly colored pompons, and worn wooly-side out when not too cold and smooth-side out when colder. Even colder weather finds black or dark red wool coats or capes draped over all.

Hutsul architecture, woodwork, metalwork, carpets, ceramics, and decorated eggs all display similar geometrical and floral patterns to the clothes, whether etched, carved, embroidered, or painted. Decorating eggs with colorful folk images and patterns has been a springtime passion among Slavic, Romanian, Hungarian, and Lithuanian peoples in Central and Eastern Europe since pagan times. The eggs are called *pysanky* in Ukrainian, and as attested by archeology, the designs have been "written" on wood, clay, stone, and bone models as well as the seeds of fowl since ancient times (*pysanky* derives from the Slavic root "to write"). A tradition celebrating rebirth naturally transferred to Easter when it came along, certain colors and patterns may have once been intended to ward off evil powers or entrap them in spiral patterns, while others, such as heart symbols on those created and given to young men by hopeful young maidens, were designed for positive magic. Hutsul versions of *pysanky* are especially well known for the intricacy of their patterns, religious and animal themes, and colors of red, yellow, green, and white.

Hutsul houses follow a traditional Rusyn model that can still be found perched on high mountain slopes or nestled at the bottom of narrow mountain valleys throughout all of Carpathian Ruthenia: built of beech or oak logs with wood shingle roofs (many formerly of straw, and some now of metal or clay tile), clay whitewashed interior walls, a porch supported by carved posts along the front and side, a few small windows, no chimney, and a brick oven that was also a bed for the oldest and youngest. Some Hutsul homesteads, called *grazhda*, are larger, traditionally sheltering multi-generational families and extending the basic Rusyn domestic architecture with courtyards enclosed by farm buildings and log walls or fences, the house usually situated along the northern side.

Having been historically tugged between churches not always of their own free will (like all Rusyns), most Hutsuls have belonged to the Ukrainian Greek Catholic Church since it was founded and when it was allowed (when it was not allowed, most were members of the Ukrainian Orthodox Church of the Kyivian Patriarchate Church). Their villages usually feature a small, rustic wooden church with soaring wooden-shingled towers and super-steep gable roofs sometimes of metal and sometimes of wood, ornately decorated interiors, and floors covered by beautiful handmade wool rugs—instances of the famous "wooden churches of Maramureş" described previously.

Like many micro-ethno-cultural groups in Europe, the Hutsuls acquired distinction from mountainous isolation, which also obscured their origins. There are several theories involving descents from and mixings with both Slavic and non-Slavic peoples, such as Thracians, Dacians, and Goths; White Croats[150], Tivercians[151], Ulichs[152], and other tribes of Kievan Rus'; and eastern nomads such as Pechenegs and Cumans. Some may descend from legally sanctioned residents—landowners, their serfs, and imported laborers who settled frontier mountain estates awarded by Hungarian kings for the protection of the realm—but a common theme is that the Hutsuls (like the other Rusyns) largely descend from whoever managed to find refuge in the mountains (first on the northern side)—those escaping the Mongol invasions of the thirteenth century, for example, and peasants seeking to evade serfdom, Tartar raids, conscription, or prison[153]. It's likely that the Hutsuls of today descend from all of them, but whatever their origins, the Hutsuls were identifiable on the northern slopes of the Ukrainian Carpathians by the fifteenth century, and they expanded southward as far as the Maramureş region of northern Romania during the eighteenth century, with migration continuing from north of the mountains until well into the mid-nineteenth century. According to Bonkalo, the first Hutsul settlement on the southern slopes of the mountains was Rakhiv, where by 1598 fourteen Rusyn shepherds had built year-round huts along the rushing Tisza waters and were paying taxes ("one-tenth of their sheep, 14 wildcat pelts, and 1000 trout"[154]). Bonkalo writes:

"According to a Hutsul legend, the shepherds had bragged in Galicia and Bukovina [on the northern side of the mountains] about the rich pastures, the healthy air, and the springwater with healing power at the two headwaters of the Tisza. Consequently, more and more Galician and Bukovinian peasants packed up all they had and moved in." [155]

While constantly subject to political dominance by more numerous neighbors, the Hutsuls were hard to subdue, inspired as they were by legendary folk heroes—rascally, Robin Hood-like brigands called *opryshky* ("rebels") in the Carpathian region[156]—especially one Oleksa Dovbosz. In fact, one theory ascribes *Hutsul* as deriving from the Romanian word for "the brigand"—*hoțul*—and it is said that Rakhiv got its name from being the site where Dovbosz counted his booty ("to count" is *rakhuvaty* in Rusyn). (When one hears of the exploits of sylvan, legend-boosted characters like Robin Hood, and Dovbosz, who led his gang from 1738 until 1744, and Andrij Savka, a seventeenth century robber and rebel we will meet along the Slovak-Poland border, it is easy to conclude that something universally thievish yet just lived in the dense forests of the medieval European imagination, if not in the hearts of real woodland souls.)

The Hutsuls frequently participated in peasant revolts and uprisings against castled nobles, whether of Polish, Hungarian, or Austrian extraction, and when the Cossacks were actively fighting for Ukrainian autonomy—off-and-on from the seventeenth into the early twentieth century—the Hutsuls could usually be found on their side. Particularly noteworthy was the early eighteenth century (failed) rebellion led by the Transylvania (Protestant) Prince Francis II Rákóczi against (Catholic) Habsburg rule in Hungary. The aid given to Rákóczi by the Carpathian Rusyns—many armed only with scythes, hoes, and pitchforks—so impressed Hungarians that they became respectfully labeled "the people of Rákócziz" or "the faithful people" in Hungarian literature.

Nevertheless, the Hutsuls were quick to throw off a Hungarian yoke at the end of World War I, "almost as soon as the guns fell silent"[157].

Hutsul partisans, fighting in the hodgepodge of uniforms they happened to possess—from modern and staid Austro-Hungarian threads to ancient and flamboyant hussar regalia—overthrew the local Hungarian gendarmes in Rakhiv and set up a state. The "Hutsul Republic" lasted only about four months, from February 1919 until Romanian troops marched in and handed the ephemeral state to Czechoslovakia, along with the rest of Transcarpathia and parts of Bukovina.

During the next global conflagration it was the Hutsuls who provided the largest percentage of fighters for the Ukrainian Insurgent Army (known as the "UPA" from its transcribed initials), which fought from forest hideouts, especially in the Carpathians, against Nazi, Soviet, Czechoslovakian, and Polish armies in turn[158], and whose dirt and debris-filled trenches and bunkers can still be stumbled upon (or into) today. (The UPA also conducted an incredibly brutal ethnic cleansing of Polish civilians, in which as many as 100,000 Poles may have been slaughtered—one terrible example in a long history of Ukrainians and Poles treating each other badly, hopefully now past[159].)

The Hutsul's independent spirit may have been enhanced by their rugged landscape. Unlike most other peasants in Europe, Carpathian highlanders had little experience of being enserfed. Large-scale farming was not practical on the steep slopes, where labor was also scarce, so medieval lords (who in Ukraine were mostly Polish and Lithuanian) never much bothered trying to enforce feudal restrictions on the remote and valued land "improvers"—farmers, shepherds, lumbermen, raftsmen, and hunters[160]—who, incidentally, were aided in their productivity by a short, compact but strong and hardy horse adept at pulling logs and carts across slanted terrain, famously known as the Hucul pony.

Modern celebrants of Hutsul culture.
© Stanislaw Tokarski / Shutterstock.com

(These days, modern physical and psychic mobility are obscuring ethno-cultural lines, even in the remote Carpathians. Embroidery, for example, might be seen as being more Ukrainian, Slovakian, or Polish rather than Hutsul, Boyko, or Lemko, although local themes still shine through. In any case, having attended a wedding in Rakhiv some eight years after the expedition, and seen the cheerful twirling, and heard the haunting melodies and frenzied rhythms, and tasted the sumptuous dishes, and watched the hilarious games until dawn was reflected in happy, sleepy eyes, I can testify that celebrants of Ukrainian weddings in the land of the Hutsul know how to have a great time, whether specifically Hutsul or not. The wedding was Maria's.)

Today, since we are staying until early afternoon, we spend a leisurely morning at this site, which as the day warms up we gradually become persuaded to designate "The Camp of *Small* Flies." We have yet to encounter a new and intimidating species of wolf, but the flies of Ukraine, though smaller than the ones we left behind in Romania, are unusually fierce. Meanwhile, on a long walk further up the road, we are happy to confirm that healthy populations of amphibians extend across the border. Here multitudes of endangered Carpathian newts (*Triturus montandoni*) squirm in the puddles, "oblivious to the impending doom that might arrive with the next thundering truck"[161].

Carpathian newt (*Triturus montandoni*). © Jürgen Sauer.

After lunch Jürgen heads down the valley seeking a phone connection, food, and some kind of road that allegedly will carry us northward along a tributary of the White Tisza, to somewhere near our next hookup with the hiking team. Maria and I pack up the rest of our camp and follow, but our way down is blocked by a double-hung gate stretched across the road. Did the passing of Jürgen raise an alarm? There is a gatehouse, so Maria goes in to see about getting us through.

After a few moments staring at the inert little log building, I head over and arrive just as Maria is stepping out the door. "He's asleep," she whispers. I peek inside to see for myself. He is indeed asleep. Very asleep, judging by his snore... and clutching a set of keys in his meaty hands.

Maria and I look at each other and back at the guardian and reach a plan without a word. Rather than startling and then having to explain to this dissipated official why an American man and a young Ukrainian woman are trying to escape this apparently valuable valley, I hold open the door while Maria—surely the more nimble of us two—tiptoes over and gently liberates the keys. We freeze to allow the snorts and writhes and wiggling fingers to run their course, then make for it, stifling laughs as we rush out the door. We get to the gate, find it unlocked, and fling it open. I run back to the gatehouse, tiptoe across the floor, place the superfluous keys on a table next to the still oblivious guard, and dash back to the car. Once we're through, Maria hops out, closes the gate, hops back in, and with unrestrained laughs we're on our way.

Jürgen is waiting in a tiny shop in a tiny village where our bill for some bread and a few snacks is tallied on an abacus. Then we follow a rough track up along the rushing tributary of the White Tisza until drivability ends in a gravelly circle. A flat grassy shelf lies to the left next to the stream—a natural campsite overlooked by a small wooden gazebo up a gentle slope to the right. After a lunch of bread, cheese, cold sausage, and apples, Maria and I continue on foot, exploring the overgrown path that hugs the dashing waters.

The ravine steepens and the water is forced into a narrow surging channel, where ferns sprinkled with wild germaniums soften and color the wet, slippery trail. Our voices stand no chance against the roar, so we climb without speaking until the tumult is tamed by a brief leveling and old cement walls. We duck under branches and dance to keep

Transcarpathian cash register. © Jürgen Sauer.

our balance along the narrow, crumbling edges, below which rusted axels and gears stick out of the concrete. Could these frozen relics have once driven a generator for the Arpad Line of World War II? These living green slopes are almost impenetrable now, how much more with 3,000 hydro-powered volts strung across?

The Arpad Line was a chain of defensive positions along the Carpathian Mountains designed to protect Hungary during World War II ("Arpad" is the name of the founding dynasty of Hungarian kings). Located where heavy weapons such as machine guns and mine throwers could be transported effectively only by pack animals, and heavier artillery and tanks were limited to the few roads, only passable when dry, the Line was comprised of steep slopes, rushing waters, concrete pill boxes, trenches, barbed wire, and electrified wire running between concrete towers. As the Soviet Red Army advanced into Poland in 1944, it needed to protect its southern flank, and thus the densely Wooded Carpathians (as the Ukrainian Carpathians are sometimes called) became the scene of intense, continually shifting, inconclusive mountain warfare between the Russians and dug-in German and Hungarian forces. In fact, largely because of the Arpad Line, the Axis defenders could not be completely dislodged before the war ended.

One can almost hear these gears squeaking, giving wires a hum while shells burst, rocks split, trees splinter, and bones shatter, until remembering that all violent echoes have long since faded into the placidity of rustling leaves, rippling water, singing insects, and chirping birds.

Tuesday, May 3. "The Party Campground," near the hamlet of Luhy, Ukraine.

Youths that came to hang out at the gazebo late yesterday afternoon have inspired the name of our camp. They revved their motorcycles and drank bad wine and horsed around throughout the darkening evening. Jürgen went over first to photograph and discuss bikes, and Maria and I soon followed. A couple of young men sat on their bikes proudly posing while Jürgen snapped away, and Jürgen's interest and artistic direction seemed to thaw the ice; they became friendly enough, although with a rough edge. They certainly weren't shy about asking whether they could drive the Land Rover. But we couldn't be as generous with our vehicle as they were with their wine, which they passed around in the bottle.

At our time to retire, the festivities across the way were picking up, so Maria again chose to share a tent. Although there was no rain, the air next to the river was damp, cold, and foggy, and my sleep was delayed by sympathy for Maria, whose sleeping bag is of the cotton variety—basically a blanket roll of the sort I had when I was a child back in the '60s. I lent her my pad and settled myself for a folded-up tarp, but I know from experience that the thin sheet of foam would do little to hinder frigid claws from reaching out of the wet ground. Yet I was the one cold and restless—Maria seemed to dose off quickly—with sleep further thwarted by bright headlights, gunning engines, and screeching wheels.

Now it is warm and sunny, and still humid, and we are waiting, absorbing the sun like the European Green Lizard (*Lacerta viridis*) that shares our campsite. This squiggly little fellow (I know it's a male because the females are brown)—about eight inches long head to tail— is well camouflaged amidst the green grass and brown mud. Green lizards can grow twice as big as these, and insects especially, but also mice and the avian guardians of eggs and hatchlings, had best be wary when these cold-blooded dragons are about.

European Green Lizard (*Lacerta viridis*) © Jürgen Sauer.

Now that it is well into spring, and we are amongst slightly less lofty mountains, we expect the hiking team will be gone for more overnight treks, so the backup team should have more free time. Outdoor life in the center of Europe seems normal to me now, and somehow Maria's presence also brings a sense of peace. I'm no longer counting the number of days finished and remaining. Maria herself seems generally serene, taking things such as nocturnal gunning engines in stride. And it's nice having someone who speaks English when the others keep to German. I am less lonely.

Around midmorning a group of four or five boys show up on beat-up, small-wheeled mountain bikes. Perhaps eleven or twelve years old, they gather around the gazebo and start drinking bottles of beer, apparently determined to pick up where their elders left off the night before. "Bad kids," Maria remarks as they eye us from across the road. They come marching over as if on cue, boisterous and aggressive, peering into our vehicles and tent and firing questions at Maria. But our interpreter meets their attitude with one of her own, holding them pretty much at bay. I remember some candies we picked up somewhere so I make a peace offering. They accept the probably stale sweets as though it's their right, and I wonder if I'm setting a bad precedent.

Once they figure out no more offerings are forthcoming, the boys regroup back at the gazebo, returning to their antics and their beer. Meanwhile, we decide that Jürgen should drive back down the road to where he can get a phone connection to check for news from the hiking team. Maria will go with him in case there are any issues, and to help with shopping if they find food in one of the villages.

As soon as my friends are gone, I lock the Land Rover, just as the boys are stomping back over. I had anticipated the invasion, but they are only boys, and not very big ones, and though they emanate mischief I figure I can hold them off with my larger size and single word of Russian. On the other hand, there are four or five of them, and after I've managed to keep them out of my tent and off the roof of the Land Rover for a while, they start to mock my "*nyets*" and take turns attacking from behind. While I chase the others away, one of them, the tallest and biggest, suddenly makes a stand. Tossing an unruly bang aside, from under his coat he brandishes an enormous knife. Curiosity getting the better of greed, the others ignore our suddenly vulnerable goods and gather round.

As we square off, this future Ukrainian politician discovers with a devious grin that the shiny blade poses a dual threat: By rotating it back and forth he can reflect the sun into my eyes. While I squint against the flashes, the scene from *Crocodile Dundee* pops into my mind: "*That ain't a knife. This is a knife...*"

But here I'm the one with the pathetic blade (located somewhere in my backpack, I think), so I decide my best strategy is to use what I believe I still have to my advantage—larger size and greater experience. I cease the *nyets* and all traces of a smile, draw myself up, and stare into the little man's eyes. A formidable step forward and I hope I'm effectively projecting what I'm thinking: that even though these are just kids, I'm ready to kick and claw and bite and throw whoever jumps me from behind (*do they have knives also?*) while I seize the boy's arm. I try to ignore the embarrassing prospect of being found seriously injured or killed by a group of pre-teens, or whether I can be sued here as I would in America if it goes the other way.

I realize I've won as soon as a look of doubt creeps across the young face. My opponent slowly lowers the knife and slinks back to the gazebo as nonchalantly as possible, with the others in tow.

So I've taken the first round, but when will Jürgen and Maria return? Will another bottle of liquid courage motivate these miniature delinquents to go further? I keep a wary eye as I hang about our camp, trying to hide my discomfort with a veneer of confident indifference. Ere long, as I had guessed, they collect into a huddle; then, just as my nemesis begins leading a group-strut back over, the Passat comes bounding up the road.

Turns out the hiking team cannot make it down to this camp. Stephan has a problem with his knee, and they're also having trouble finding a trail. So we'll retreat to our previous campsite for the night.

As we break camp, the kids hang about on our periphery, apparently still craving booty, if not blood, and I'm a little embarrassed as I briefly summarize our interaction. I just can't feel like much of a hero in thwarting a bunch of eleven-year-olds. But Maria makes a couple of knowing remarks that help me feel better.

When we get into our vehicles and drive off, the enemy launches a final assault. They hurl rocks, a couple of which ding off the Passat. I slam on the breaks, shrouding the car and the kids in a cloud of dust. I hesitate for a moment, then put my ego in check; mostly: as I race off I can't prevent the tires from hurling a few pebbles of their own.

In the tiny village of Luhy (pronounced "Lugy"), at the intersection with the road that will bring us back up to our former campsite, I wait while Jürgen and Maria go down to a bigger village in search of bread and hopefully some vegetables. I'm sitting on the dusty steps of a small building that with a tiny shop offering a few tools, shoes, socks, gloves, hats, and sunflower seeds seems to comprise the center of town. No trees shield the hot sunshine, so although the air is humid, the earth has already dried. As I watch the village life, which on this sleepy day is practically nonexistent, a rush of liquid comes pouring out from the bottom of the building and hurries to the weedy path lining the single street of the village, which is now hard-packed mud. Someone has flushed a toilet.

After my companions return, Jürgen continues on. He will drive as far as possible to pick up the hiking team, but we want to be sure we will really stay at our former camp before following with the Passat. Maria and I take the steps, ignoring the ghost of the effluent and bowing our heads to the muggy heat. A trio of girls around eleven or twelve gathers across the street, looking much more benign than their male comrades; in fact, they look pretty much like typical American girls, clad in blue jeans and clutching mobile phones—albeit first-generation giants, like Maria's.

Maria is bright and quick to smile, but she's also a little shy, and so am I, so we are often silent. I suggest we play the "initials game" to fill our wait, wherein one of us chooses a famous character—real or fictional, dead or alive—and the other tries to guess who it is by asking yes-no questions. Whoever guesses with the fewest questions wins the round. Maybe not the profoundest of activities, but for two shy people from different cultures who barely know each other, it can fill some silences that might otherwise go on too long. One of the rules of course is that the character must be known to each person, and since Maria has lived her entire life of far fewer years than mine in Ukraine, I must give care to my choices. While we are at it, the young terrors from our previous campsite suddenly come flying by on their low-riders, pulling wheelies on the bumps and smiling and waving like we are long lost friends.

Seems we've been waiting a lot lately. Is waiting an inevitable corollary to adventure? Probably, at least for those involving more than one person. How many times did Shackleton's or Scott's crews have to wait around for things to happen? Many, for sure, although not likely in such stifling heat as this. Our game melts, and time convinces me that we must indeed be staying at the Camp of Small Flies. I drive up the road, concentrating on avoiding craters, and just as I'm beginning to wonder how I could have made a wrong turn where there are no turns, we come upon Shira tugging Peter down the road with Kathrin in pursuit. I assume they left the others at the campsite and decided to walk down to the village, so we wave and continue on. The road gets rougher and steeper than I remember, and after bouncing along for another fifteen minutes or so, I finally realize that I somehow missed the gentle pasture alongside the river with a fence and possibly a cow or horse or two and a Land Rover. I push on a little further with a scrape or two before I can find a place wide enough to turn.

About a kilometer back down and there is the pasture, and the Land Rover parked under a tree, and our companions, busy setting up tents and hanging clothes to dry on the fence. I internally scratch my head. *Where was my mind? Or 'our' minds; Maria didn't notice either. Did the heat and the bumps rock us to sleep? Well, so much for saving gas.* I'm prepared for ridicule, but everyone is so busy that I'm let off the hook.

With others around, Maria now prefers her own tent, so I help her get started and then assist Thilo with ours. The air is heavy and still, and the sky is darkening with a rumble or two, and just as we get the tents up, the downpour begins, with a flash of lightning and clap of thunder. We wait it out in our tents, but I've had enough of waiting recently, so as soon as the rain eases, I go out to gather firewood. The wood is wet, but the sooner we get it under cover, the better chance we'll have, although by now we've become quite adept at soggy ignitions. And a shower can't hurt either; according to Slavic folklore, spring showers ensure health and beauty.

Once the rain stops, I invite Maria on a walk up the familiar road. Her English is pretty good, but still I tease her about her pronunciation of "willage". She asks me about American traditions, and after some thought I give her a quick rundown of Thanksgiving.

"What about a Ukrainian tradition?" I ask.

Maria thinks for a while, then describes a "special" day each year when the girls of the village make garlands of flowers and throw them into a river. The boys wait downstream, hoping to fetch the one made by their sweetheart, or perhaps trusting to chance, because the girl who made the garland retrieved will become the retriever's bride. Marriages may have actually once been arranged this way, but no longer, Maria assures me.

The special day is called "Ivan Kupala Day." Originally a pre-Christian Slavic summer solstice celebration, it has since been pegged to the calendar (now beginning regularly at sunset on June 23rd) and to St. John the Baptist. It is a favorite of Central and Eastern European youth, especially in Russia, Ukraine, Belarus, Latvia, and Poland, to whom it gives an excuse for what is supposed to be some good-natured mischief. A relatively innocent example is the pouring of water by boys over girls' heads. In fact, many of the original rituals of Ivan Kupala involved water, which was believed to be imbued with special powers by the sun at its high point in the sky. Celebrants would bathe in open waters such as rivers and lakes (usually after sunset, with clothing optional), and this is probably why—combined with a pious hope to temper some of the more lascivious activities of the irrepressible holiday—the festival was eventually linked to St. John ("Ivan" is the Slavic version of "John").

"Kupala" derives from the Slavic word for "bathing," although some sources say it was also the name of a pagan goddess of water, herbs and sex. Others say that "she" was a "he"—a god of love, harvest, and fertility[162]—but in any case the day was originally intended to honor and encourage the summer's productivity[163]. Bathing can be considered purifying—recommended for those who till the soil and harvest the crops—and if water doesn't cut it, then fire will. So after dark, bonfires were lit on riverbanks or hills, around which the drenched celebrants dried and sang and danced, and over which the courageous jumped hand-in-hand. Straw effigies were burned—perhaps symbolizing the temporary suspension of Death—and flaming straw-laced wheels rolled down slopes—perhaps symbolizing the impending decline of the sun.

Fertility being the theme, there are reports, or at least rumors, of rather free-spirited sexual activity, particularly before the Church got involved. In fact, Kupala Night may have been the one night when pre- or extra-marital sex was socially sanctioned or at least overlooked. Some contemporary writers (especially of the sixteenth century) also associated the fire dancing with worship of the devil, and the fire jumping with symbolic self-sacrifice to the same, although this interpretation was likely influenced by the Church[164]. Some werewolf folklore has lupine transformations peaking on Ivan Kupala Day (along with Christmas: essentially the summer and winter solstices).

Primal elements these: water, fire, and sex. Modern anthropologists try to interpret the rituals of Kupala by assigning meanings like honoring the role of water in fertility and productivity to the bathing; and honoring the role of the gods (i.e., fate or luck) in fertility and productivity to the incineration (i.e., symbolic purification and human sacrifice); and honoring the role of sex in fertility and productivity to the sex. Maybe. Or maybe it was just an excuse to have fun.

In any case, the garland tradition may have originated both from the belief that garlands (also known as "Ukrainian wreaths") protected girls from evil spirits[165] and the belief that the summer solstice is the only time that "fern flowers" bloom. To find the magical flower of a fern—the flower of the Slavic thunder-god Perun, which shines so brightly on Kupala Night that human eyes cannot look directly upon it—brings very good luck indeed[166]. Thus around midnight, after the bathing and fire-jumping and frolicking, the partiers would enter the forest in search of the fern flower, as well as other magical herbs. The women would go first—the unmarried ones usually wearing garlands, both for protection and to identify their status—and the guys would follow, some of the singles (at least) surely hoping for romances to blossom amidst the trees—which might even be caught ambulating or speaking on this special night.

Regardless of what other magic might transpire under the sylvan canopy, any herbs gathered before the Kupala dawn with dew still upon them were believed to have special powers, or to have their natural medicinal powers magnified[167] (the dew was believed to be tears of the goddess of dawn and beauty, Zaria)—a belief the Church eventually sanctioned with blessings from the local priest.

And the next day, preferably after washing with goddess tears, nervous girls would go down to the river to float their garlands, and nervous boys would go downstream to wait.

On our walk I ask Maria to start teaching me some Ukrainian words. I set a goal of three a day, and I deem that "yes" (*tak*), "no" (*nie*), and "thank you" (*spacibo* or *dzenku*) are the most important to start with. I also ask her the word for "you" (*ti*), as I have a plan.

As Maria pronounces the words and I repeat them, then after a few minutes repeat them again, trying to copy them from my very short-term memory into my slightly longer-term memory, the words are not impossible to pronounce and remember, which should be a clue that as strange as Ukrainian sounds to me—and as strange as Romanian sounded and probably as strange as the other languages I will encounter along the way will sound—they are not as strange as they could be. Not as strange as all the random vocalizations that are possible for human beings to make.

Etymologists speculate that not far from here, just beyond the Carpathian foothills to the east—perhaps somewhere in Ukraine's forest-steppe zone—is where a Neolithic tribe first began enunciating and arranging their vocalizations in a general way that would spread across the vast Eurasian continent, from Ireland to India, as their language diverged into the Indo-European family of languages[168]. Thus somewhere below is probably where children first learned to close their lips to form an "m" sound to attract the attention of the one who fed them milk and held them most; and where they learned to inflect the ends of words for objects to signal their socially perceived masculine, feminine, or androgynous nature and whether those objects were the actor or the acted upon; and where they learned to inflect the middle or ends of words for actions to indicate when the actions were performed[169] and whether by one or more actors.

They learned that the abrupt short sound starting with "n" was meant to stop whatever mischief they were up to, and they learned names for the flora and fauna around them (clues which help historians locate their homeland): words for beaver, bee (and honey), beech, boar, cow (and milk), crane, dog, duck, eagle, goose, hare, hedgehog, horse, lynx, mouse, oak, ox, pig, pine tree, red deer, salmon, sheep (and wool), steer, and wolf (*wḷqos* or *wailós*, the latter, paradoxically, also meaning "humble"). Known as the Proto-Indo-European (PIE) language, it had probably evolved by about 6,500 years ago[170], and today about three billion people speak one of its descendent language or dialects[171].

The spread of a language and culture can mean the expansion of one people at the expense of others, but it doesn't have to. After all, things like iPhones and the words that describe them now rapidly spread more or less peacefully from one end of the planet to the other. While objects and words were not always so mercurial, if things like axes and arrows and amber could be hurled and shot and exchanged from one clan to the next, then how much easier words and ideas and ways of doing things.

Given how widely PIE and its daughters spread—across not only a vast region but a multiplicity of cultures and ethnicities—more than fire and arrow must have been involved. There must have been something particularly mobile and prestigious about the people who spoke it, something that made them worth emulating. Based on both linguistic and archeological evidence, Proto-Indo-European speakers were probably patriarchal (ruled by men), patrilineal (inherited property through the male line), and patrilocal (brides went to their husbands' households). They herded cattle, sheep, and horses (often with the help of dogs); they worshipped sky gods[172] to whom they sacrificed livestock; they stratified into priestly, warrior, and peasant classes; they buried their deceased elites under huge mounds of earth (called *kurgans*); and they may have been the original cannabis heads. But several additional attributes may have been more important for scattering their language: They were among the first, maybe *the* first, to ride horses (probably after they had been eating them for a while); they were either inventors or early adopters of wheels, wagons[173], and chariots; they were ecological generalists, raising livestock as well as cultivating modest plots of grain; they traded goods far and wide; and they liked to raid. Their effective and varied agricultural methods, including the relatively new practices of wool shearing, dairy farming, and plowing, led to an accumulation of livestock and land, which led to an elite class, which developed cosmopolitan attitudes. (Another side effect of their mobility and efficiency was probably the earliest example of suburban sprawl in Eastern Europe: the first single-family farms, as opposed to exclusively collective settlements.)

With a generosity that wealth allows, the PIE elite became adroit at plugging themselves into the society of "others." Rather than exclusively attacking their neighbors, for example (which they certainly did), they also won them over with huge feasts, where poetry, song, prayer, sacrificial meat, and mead added to the charm. In other words, the Proto-Indo-European elite knew how to throw a great party.

Thus, enabled by mobility and prestige, starting around 4,200 BC, PIE speakers, or at least the language they spoke, began to spread far and wide, interacting with indigenous peoples and tongues and diverging[174]. To the south, they skirted the Caucasus Mountains, circled the Black Sea, and settled in Anatolia (Turkey), where Hittite descendants were the first to write something down in an Indo-European language (around 1,600 BC)[175]. To the east, they made it to northwestern China, where their language evolved into what we call "Tochaian"[176], which eventually died out.

To the west the Carpathian Mountains caused a major split. In the dense forests north of the mountains, PIE evolved towards Proto-Balto-Slavic[177] in the east and Germanic[178] in the west. To the more open south, PIE fanned into a virtual rainbow of languages: Celtic to the west, Italic to the southwest[179], and—with the Balkans producing their usual fracturing effect—Ilyrian, Albanian, Greek, Thracian, and Phrygian to the south and southeast[180]. Dacian arose in the Carpathians themselves—maybe or maybe not a tongue distinct from Thracian[181].

Meanwhile, from the central homeland east of the Carpathians, PIE waves continued sallying forth. They hurdled the Caucasus, expanding south and east across the Iranian plateau and the Hindu Kush, reaching the banks of the Indus and Ganges (where some who called themselves Aryans wrote the Vedas and invented yoga) and sowing Armenian[182] and the many daughters of Proto-Indo-Iranian[183] along the way.

The condensing lens of time can make the spread and splintering of PIE seem a swift and turbulent process, but in fact it required more than two thousand years. While later mounted invasions from the east that swept up to, through, and around the Carpathians were fast, furious, and overwhelming, the early PIE herders and farmers, though not shy about attacking and raiding, had not yet organized themselves into the large militarized armies that were to come. And in the west, at least, some scattered Indo-European speaking communities remained isolated for long periods of time.

Threatening patches of cloud cling to the dark green hillsides as Maria and I walk and sometimes talk, and puddles fill all depressions as the earth gradually recovers from the deluge. Darkness is falling when we return, and the others have chopped and cut the dead trees and have a fire going and dinner ready, and it feels nice to have taken this one off. We are low on vegetables so it isn't much—noodles with dehydrated soup powder and lots of carrots—but it satisfies empty stomachs and warms against the chill night air.

A rustling during the night raises me from my sleep and out of my tent, where several flashlight beams reveal horses poking around near the tarp that stretches from the side of the Land Rover. Once spotted they pretend to be grazing, but unconvinced, we shoo the immense thespians away. After I've crawled back into my sleeping bag, images of horses thundering and stomping through our fabric walls gradually dissolve into the roar of a downpour, which slowly recedes into the oblivion of sleep.

The White Tisza flows past the Camp of Small Flies. © Jürgen Sauer.

Thursday, May 5. Near Krasna, Ukraine.

Yesterday we awoke to another soggy morning, broke camp, and started the long ponderous drive back down to Rakhiv for some business at the park administration headquarters and to restock our food supply. The Land Rover needed some work—the brakes, I think. My ignorance of German still often shrouds the details of our plans, especially when I don't have to appear at a particular place and time, although I'm not sure any one person ever knows them all.

Peter drove the Passat while I rode shotgun and Maria took the back. After an hour or so of bumping along, Peter suddenly tensed up and asked me if I had packed Shira's leash.

"No," I answered.

"Did you see it?"

"I think so. I think it was hanging on the fence. I thought you'd take it."

Peter cringed.

"It was Djanga's."

Djanga was Peter's previous canine companion, who—among many other poignant memories for Peter, I'm sure—accompanied him on countless treks through the mountains of Transylvania during many years of tracking wolves for the Carpathian Large Carnivore Project. I had been lucky enough to join them near the end, and I shared Peter's horror at my unintended mistake. The car came to an abrupt stop.

"You should make sure NOTHING is left behind when we break camp!"

I was about to defend myself with the insights that I am not always the last to leave and I cannot always anticipate which items that I happen to see lying around will be forgotten as I'm scrambling around during the usual morning rush, but Peter suddenly released a resigned sigh. Maria and I took the hint, hopped out, and squeezed into the Land Rover while Peter spun the car around and started the long drive back up to the Camp of Small Flies. So much for saving gas.

Jürgen deposited Maria, Thilo, and me at the center of Rakhiv to shop for food while he went off to search for a repair shop, taking Stephan and Kathrin with him. We had no problem finding the usual potatoes, onions, and carrots, but we were desperate for more variety and were especially on the lookout for tomatoes. The first shop we visited had just sold the last one, and they suggested another we might try. Same story there. We went from shop to shop without ever catching the last fresh tomato in town.

Back at park headquarters, Peter returned with the leash, and we waited in the yard while he dealt with officials. Apparently there was a problem because we waited a long time. This gave me the chance for my next word.

"How do you say 'have' in Ukrainian? As in 'You have'"?

"*Miesh*."

Finally Peter came out and said there was a problem, but the officials had offered to open the park museum for us while things were worked out.

The museum of the Carpathian Biosphere Reserve displays the symptoms of underfunding so common in Ukraine, giving it the feel of a century past to someone from the West. But it is well done, and without it I may never have been able to visualize the truly deep colors of traditional Hutsul life.

Through stunning murals and half-life-sized paper-mâché models, one can almost hear the roar of a raging white river as it tosses a log raft, steered with epic oars by crouching mustachioed rafters in red-banded fedoras and white tunics and red trousers; and one can almost hear the blast of *trembitas* and the ring of *tsymbalies* announcing the arrival of a plume-hatted and *bartok*-emboldened wedding party, decked out in a blaze of white, red, orange, and black. Richly embroidered sheepskin jerkins hang from stands over billowing white sleeves, and traditional axes, saws, stone grinding wheels, *trembitas*, and *bartoks* give three-dimensional life to the displays. The Stone Age isn't forgotten, nor is nature, with a walk-though cave of sparkling stalagmites and stalactites and forest dioramas with stuffed denizens such as boars and badgers. Down in the rather cold and dank basement, rows of terrariums and aquariums line the walls, some containing living samples of their labeled fauna, such as snakes, lizards, and fish.

Hutsul river rafters on display in the museum of the
Carpathian Biosphere Reserve. © Jürgen Sauer.

By late afternoon business was finally settled, and we packed into our vehicles, left Rakhiv, and headed back south and west along the Tisza, on the road that had brought us from Romania. Like a kid on a family vacation, I didn't know exactly where we were headed—only that it would be new and interesting—and enjoyed passively taking in the fresh spring scenery.

Not far out of Rakhiv, a military checkpoint required even Maria to show her passport. I wondered what the young armed guards thought of a young Ukrainian woman traveling with four German men, one German woman, and an American man. Can roadblocks thwart the serious problem of enslavement in Ukraine?

As Ukraine's economy teeters, organized criminals have taken advantage, luring and forcing women and children into prostitution and labor. The country is a source, destination, and transit for trafficked human beings, and while some are coerced within its borders, most are delivered to Western Europe, the Middle East, or South America. A 2006 International Organization for Migration survey reported that 117,000 Ukrainians had been "forced into exploitative situations in Europe, the Middle East, and Russia" since 1991[184]. Ukraine is classified by the United States government as a "Tier 2" country, which means it does "... not fully comply with the TVPA's minimum standards, but [is] making significant efforts to bring [itself] into compliance with those standards." Although a U.S. Department of State report concluded that Ukraine's laws against human trafficking are "sufficiently stringent," the same report cited complicity of government officials, lax enforcement, and weak witness protection programs as serious obstacles to their effectiveness. In 2006, for example, while 83 convictions of 95 prosecutions were achieved, in 59 of these cases the perpetrators received probation instead of imprisonment[185].

In 2007, the Prosecutor General of Ukraine issued a directive for more aggressive prosecution, including the appeal of previous probation sentences, and better training of enforcement officers, judges, and prosecutors, and there were some modest attempts at improved witness protection. As a result, 44% of convicted perpetrators were jailed in the latter half of the year, although this still does not seem like much for forcing women to have sex with dozens of men a night, typically under threat of beatings or the murder of their families.

But the increased pressure, along with education programs, has helped. It is believed that the enslavement of women in Ukraine peaked around 2006, and these days, while still a bitter problem for thousands of disadvantaged women, and still illegal, and still greased by corruption, most sex workers now supposedly participate "voluntarily"[186], although such reports do not generally consider economic desperation to be a coercive factor. Still, Ukraine remains a popular destination for foreign men seeking sex or brides, and probably not coincidently the country now has one of the highest rates of HIV in Europe[187]—in spite of FEMEN's topless protests[188].

Our papers and Maria's explanation apparently dispelled whatever curiosity the guards may have had and we were waved through.

A roadside monument marks the geographical center of Europe, located just west of Rakhiv (officially by the Viennese Geographical Society in 1911) because someone decided that Europe starts at the Ural Mountains. From a gray stone platform wrapped by a curvy white wall shoots a shiny double metallic spire—sort of an upside-down cross, or a sword—high into the canopy of the lush green deciduous forest that marches up the steep slope behind. The woods, hills, and rivers take no notice of this milestone, however, and neither did we linger, driving through what otherwise might be dinnertime as the skies thickened with clouds. The delays at the park headquarters and checkpoint had set us back, and there was no good place to camp along this settled and steep-banked stretch of river.

The clouds began to lift by the time we turned onto a paved road that wound northwards like a black ribbon over greening foothills, but they were just gathering their forces against a higher tier of hills. About where the pavement changed to gravel, we were compelled into near cringing by an angry darkening sky and sought refuge on a green sward lying between the road and a churning river that was somehow still semi-luminous. Of a size and smoothness of a soccer field, the turf was wrapped by a tottering rail fence and protected by an icon of Christ pinned to a towering, freshly-hewn wooden cross. The image was reverently framed by a shiny metallic arch and a chain of flowered evergreen wreaths, and ominously underscored by a skull-and-crossbones. Although I wondered whether camping beneath the crucified figure might be seen as sacrilege, the threatening night left little choice.

The barrage began just as we were raising a tarp between the cars. Stephan—all six-foot-three of him—towered under the tarp like the thunder-god Perun, holding the center aloft with raised arm while the edges flapped wildly and the rest of us rushed about unstrapping the poles and getting them up. After we finally managed to replace Stephan with a center pole and get the edges secured, we gathered underneath the pathetic shelter to wait out the wind-driven downpour. While we huddled, each of the four slanted pitches of roof repeatedly sagged with water before dumping its collection over the edge with a splash. By now none of us, except possibly Stephan, were what you could call dry.

The gloom darkened further, and although there were brief respites, there was no sign the rain would stop anytime soon. So rather than stand under the tarp or sit in our foggy vehicles like sardines until who knows when and then have to set up in complete darkness, Thilo and I unpacked a tent and raised it under the tarp. At a slight let-up we splashed across the field and staked our abode at the least soggy spot in sight and returned before the next downpour began. Stephan and Kathrin followed our example; Jürgen would take his usual place in the Land Rover; and Maria would take refuge in the Passat.

At the next lull, Thilo and I dashed to our flapping and whipping abode and hopefully tossed in our anchors: backpacks, sleeping bags, pads, and clothing. While the Marmot tents with their "waterproof" floors have done an amazing job so far, I wasn't sure any mere fabric could keep out the flood we'd be facing that night. But we crawled into our only option and unrolled our pads and bags and arranged our things and then returned to the tarp where Jürgen had a stove going. Wind, misery, and darkness limited our cooking to drink, and we settled for a cold meal of cheese, sausage, and soggy bread. Since I was sick of cheese, sausage, and bread, soggy or not, I ate very little. By now I was calorie-deficient and thoroughly chilled by the wind and rain.

By the time we finished nibbling, the storm took a pause and we heard some voices. Two boys, in their late teens maybe, came walking from out of the suddenly still blackness like shimmering ghosts. They approached each of us in turn to shake our hands, and as the first extended his hand to me, I offered my best "dobra dane" ("good day," a common greeting in Ukraine, as I pronounced it). He smiled and shook my hand vigorously, and I was thankful for my lessons from Maria. Then he handed me a large bag of potatoes.

Where exactly these boys came from and how they knew we were there, as I saw no houses nearby, and why they would think to bring us potatoes during this brief reprieve from the tempest, was a mystery. How many small town folks in America would in the darkness of a stormy night approach a group of strangers speaking a strange tongue who show up on the outskirts of their town and set up camp on their sacred field? And how many would bring a gift to boot? From what I had seen of the few domiciles scattered in these hills, it was no small gift.

Maria translated our thanks and a little small talk, but the conversation soon lagged. No one seemed to know what to say. There should have been plenty to say, but cold dampness suppressed the gregarious mood our gracious new friends—our hosts, really—deserved.

We awake to a gray day and brief showers. The river is seriously swelled and hints of flooding its banks—i.e., the field on which we are camped. At least we managed to avoid planting our tents in the previously indiscernible depressions that were already under water. Or in the case of Peter, his tarp, which was all he bothered to set up. During breakfast and breaking camp, Shira uncharacteristically remains curled up snoozing on the tarp. Apparently expedition life is taking its toll on our four-legged member.

I thought the day would be a hiking day, but plans change. I guess expedition life, or at least the rain, is taking its toll on all of us: the hiking team decides to take another day off. So after we break the "Rain Camp," we pile into the cars and drive further into the mountains until we're halted by a small string of houses along the road called *Krasna*. A makeshift market is underway, offering goods such as grains, dried mushrooms, cheeses, slabs of cold processed meats, and a few packaged products, all on display in cardboard boxes on tables sheltered under blue tarps. There isn't much in the way of fresh vegetables, just the usual staples: a few apples, onions, carrots, and potatoes that have seen better days, available at negotiable prices. The apples, which look nothing like the shiny, spotless versions we have back home, but which I crave, are succulent, tart, and delicious.

In fact, our meals of late have been brief, meager, and sporadic, with sometimes only a few cookies for lunch, and we are cheered to see that the hamlet has a small restaurant. Jürgen, Stephan, Kathrin, and I enter and worm our way through a packed and smoke-filled room. The patrons are exclusively male, many dressed in camouflaged military fatigues, and all vigorously drinking beer. We find a table and try to fit in as best we can.

A dirt road breaks from the village and darts up a narrow valley to the west, following the course of a churning stream that tumbles down from a long ridge of mountains. A kilometer or so up, a small level patch of ground is squeezed between the road and the river, just big enough for two vehicles and three tents. Setting up next to the incessant roar presages plenty of white noise to lull us to sleep come nightfall.

Maria and I traipse down the road to a house opposite a small dam thoroughly swamped by the flood, where three or four white geese defend the yard, the driveway, and the road, waddling and splashing in the puddles until duty requires a rushing, hissing and beating of wings. More farm animals out back suggest the possibility of milk, so we knock on the door. Sheep milk—cold no less—can be had for one *hrvnia* (only a few cents), and if we come by later, we can get the milk of a cow.

Two boys around ten or eleven in rubber boots and a baseball cap follow us back, with two dogs slinking in the rear. Once in camp, the boys proudly pose with the dogs for Jürgen's camera.

Young visitors. © Jürgen Sauer.

While our hiking team takes the day off, this afternoon Jürgen, Maria, and I make it a hiking day for ourselves. We start up the road that climbs the valley, which at our campsite is narrowed to a gorge. After crossing the river via a wooden bridge of log beams, the road levels off and the valley floor broadens into lush, soaked fields that are feeding a few cows. The road itself has become a small river that parallels the main stream, and as we leap from muddy hump to muddy hump and tiptoe along the narrow bank on either side of the road, I wonder how Maria can manage. Her feet are clad not in hiking boots but black leathery calf-high boots with rounded fronts and smooth soles and inch-high heels that might be appropriate for a day at the mall. These stylish boots cannot have been a trivial investment for her, but she never complains as we continue on, leaping trenches carved from the road by brand new tributaries of the river. Although logs have been set at a few such channels, the flood makes most irrelevant now.

The road eventually claws to firmer ground as it wends its way past greening meadows and woods. In a verdant pasture guarded by a broken-down old fence are a couple of small, rough-hewn shacks where an old woman is picking up storm debris from the yard. I can't imagine anyone dwelling long in these huts, especially during the winter, since they are built of thin boards rather than thick logs. When we stop for Jürgen to take photos, a large, brown horse comes lumbering along, dragging through the mud a flatbed cart on which jiggle a large sack and several implements. Three men follow on foot, bearing axes and clad in the ubiquitous calf-high rubber boots.

Where the road turns a corner and cuts up a steep wooded slope, the river, now a smaller and faster cascade, shoots through a narrow cleft, and behind some brush is a small waterfall with a small pool underneath. I've already worked up a sweat in the muggy air, and opportunities being limited, I urge my companions to continue on. The water is so strong and cold that it hurts my head, not to mention my feet, so I make it brief, but after my clothes are back on and I have scrambled up to the road to join the others, I'm renewed and already re-warmed.

Up the slope the light yellowish-green of newly adorned ash and wild cherry in the clearings, and maple, elm, oak, beech, and an occasional white birch and larch in the thicker stands, gradually yield to the abiding darkness of fir and spruce. A multitude of little streamlets spring from the leafy floors of these hillsides and trickle down and collude in increasingly boisterous ranks, until in a mad flood they rush past our campsite towards their destiny with the Teresva and the Tisza and finally the Danube, where they join a placid pilgrimage to the Black Sea. On their journey through the heartland of Central Europe these waters will nourish field and forest, cool the feet of storks, quench the thirst of deer, refresh the spirits of splashing farm children, float the hulls of boats, serenade the lonely, reflect the lofty towers of cathedrals, and scour the refuse of villages, cities, and factories.

Such springs of life and hope were once sacred, yet when was the last time a human being even saw these important little headwaters? They deserve names. *Hydronyms*, the words we attach to waters, are among the most durable of human labels, often remaining after the people who gave them have gone, and thereby informing the reconstructions of historians. Thus we name three tiny trickles that merge a little ways down the slope. We solemnly designate them *The Maria*, *The Jürgen*, and *The Alan*.

Had we known it, we were labeling the stuff of exorcism. The folklorist Bogatyrev, writing of Transcarpathia in the early twentieth century, reports that water from the confluence of three springs, when poured before dawn over the body "from top to bottom," was believed to drive demons from out of the possessed—more effective magic, in fact, than that expected from doctors of modern medicine, who were to be avoided at all costs, even when sent by the government to administer vaccinations[189]. Tri-spring healing power seems to be widespread in the Carpathians, being also a characteristic of Romanian folklore[190].

River road. © Jürgen Sauer.

Forest keelback slug (*Bielzia coerulans*) © Jürgen Sau

Rushing to the Danube. © Kathrin Merkel.

For the rest of the afternoon we romp through the forests and meadows of the slopes, finding lots of mushrooms, stunning iridescent slugs (forest keelback slugs—*Bielzia coerulans*), an isolated log cabin, a couple of grizzled yet dignified men, and spectacular views of rugged green-brown hills and jagged snow-speckled mountains that seem to stretch forever.

"How does one say 'beautiful' in Ukrainian?"

"Depends. Is it like a man or a woman?"

"A woman."

"*Kraseva.*"

Appropriate, here near the village of Krasna.

A Carpathian mountain man contemplates spring. © Jürgen Sauer.

As we explore, I feel an ancient presence in these mountains. I feel it in the moss-covered trunks and lichen-crusted stones, in the rick-scattered pastures and the warped-log huts. We are at the very heart of Europe. *How long have people lived here? Where did they come from?* Few Latin-speakers here: it started when we crossed the Prislop Pass, and certainly since we crossed the Tisza, we've been fully in Slavic land. It turns out more than waters and languages have gotten their start in this "unexpected" country (as Ukraine has been called[191]) anchored by the Carpathians.

Archeological evidence suggests that anatomically modern humans first appeared in the area of today's Ukraine around 32,000 years ago[192], as the relatively tall and solid "Cro-Magnons" (now more technically called "European Early Modern Humans") spread north and westward into Europe, gradually eroding the 200,000-year tenure of the even solider Neanderthals[193]. Another 24,000 years and people with true modern fragility (no "early" qualifier required) began to supplement hunting, gathering, and fishing with planting, harvesting, and herding as they carried the Criş culture over the Carpathian Mountain passes from Transylvania (the eastern branch of the Starčevo-Criş mentioned in the last chapter).

A thousand years more and people living near the high mountain passes of the eastern Carpathian slopes became notable innovators and lovers of sanitation and fashion, crafting fired-clay floors, elegant pottery, ceramic female figurines, copper ornaments, and fine fabrics with the most advanced technologies of the day. They must have had leisure, yet were also no sloths, hunting roe deer, red deer, wild boar, aurochs, and maybe a horse now and then, and clearing large patches of woods to grow wheat, oats, barley, millet, rye, hemp, peas, beans, apricots, plums, and grapes, and to graze cattle, sheep, and goats.

Archeologists call their culture Cucuteni-Trypillian, which they gradually took down the slopes and river valleys eastward, down to the gentler lands below (the Podolian Upland of Ukraine). A social and devout folk, they arranged their log huts in clusters around larger community centers, where they cooked and worshipped female deities, eventually creating some of the largest settlements in the world at the time (sheltering up to 15,000 people)[194]. But they were also a somehow dissatisfied folk (or perhaps especially fastidious), burning their villages to the ground every four or five generations or so.

Another 800 years (around 4,200 B.C.) and the Proto-Indo-Europeans came marching their herds, masculine deities[195], and language across the fields from the east. They (or at least their ways) dallied—requiring some 900 years to traverse central and western Ukraine and reach the Carpathian foothills—even as their young men initiated themselves into warrior brotherhoods and gained the hoofed capital required for brides[196] by riding horses to the edges of Cucuteni-Trypillian settlements, donning wolf skins, and creeping up to stockades to steal cattle. Archeology reveals that PIE and Cucuteni-Trypillian interactions in fact spanned the gamut from violent to cooperative[197]; in any case, within another half a millennium the Cucuteni-Trypillian were extinct (by around 2,800 B.C.).

Cultures now came and went with quickening pace, the Carpathian Mountains largely directing the flow—although by 2,000 B.C. most everyone was speaking a version of Proto-Indo-European. The mountains also largely fed the new technologies, as magicians—crazed ones who stood in smoke pumping their bellows—learned to how to turn Carpathian rocks first into copper, then bronze, and then, by about 800 B.C., iron[198].

By then the hills were settled by "Thracians," early keepers of the Eleusinian Mysteries and allies of the Trojans in their legendary war with the Greeks. A collection of tribes ranging from the northern Carpathian Mountains to the Balkan Mountains in the south, the Thracians began to diverge, those to the north beyond the Danube becoming known as *"Getae"* by the Greeks and as "Dacians" by themselves (see endnote 41). After the invention of the saddle and the mass-production of arrows enabled the first true mounted armies from the east, it was the Dacians who pretty much fended them off until the arrival of the Romans.

Several nevertheless made it to the eastern foothills. The first were the Cimmerians, about whom so little is known that Robert E. Howard decided his hero Conan could feasibly be counted among them. Next came the Scythians, those cone-hatted, arrow-shooting, javelin-throwing, scalp-taking, blood-drinking, mixed-gender warriors who stormed their way to the Carpathians by 600 B.C., their female heroes inspiring Amazonian legends along the way. Then the Sarmatians[199] (by about 100 B.C., after the Scythians had taken glancing blows from the Macedonians under Philip II and his son Alexander the Great)), those horse-hoof-armored Scythian relatives whose female warriors so idolized the Scythian example that, according to Hippocrates, they remained virgins until they had taken the lives of at least three enemies[200].

Tribes showed up from other directions as well, drawn by rumors of a better life along the frontier of a developing empire. Between the third-century B.C. and the third-century A.D., metalworking westerners called Celts[201] and Germanic-speaking northerners called

Bastarnae and Vandals (whom we met in the last chapter) hauled their households through forests by wagon into the northern Carpathian foothills, while the mysterious Costoboci[202] also popped up, from where is not clear.

Then came the Goths. Beginning around 200 A.D., members of this rambunctious Germanic tribe began leaving their Baltic homeland, sweeping assorted kin with them (Gepids, Vandals, Taifali, Rugi, and Heruli) and bringing iron, amber, and slaves around the eastern arc of the Carpathians to trade with the Romans. They found that plundering also paid off, and seizing all of Dacia, and even performing mercenary service in the imperial army, until they were pretty much kicked out (or absorbed) by the Huns some two centuries later.

And then arose the Slavs.

With the usual limited views taken of (or allowed by) ancient peripheries, our earliest accounts of Ukraine offer only myopic perspectives from neighbors who could write: first the Greeks, then the Romans, then the East Romans (later called Byzantines) and Arabs. Thus, from the first millennium B.C. until the early Middle Ages, our view is biased towards what happened in the south. But while the dramas we know most about were unfolding east and south of the Carpathians, deep in the woods just to the north a people were arising who would become known as "Slavic"[203]—a label that may derive from their own word for "word" (*slovo*). A common tribal tendency, to call ourselves "The People who can speak"—to each other, of course. (An alternative theory posits derivation from the Slavic word for "glory"—*slava*—as in the "glorious ones" or the "ones who give glory to God"—i.e., the "true worshippers"—another common form of tribal self-identification.)

Exactly when and where the "Proto-Slavs" first began to diverge from their common ancestors with the Balts is uncertain, but the split was complete by the fourth century A.D. at the latest, and most evidence suggests it occurred somewhere in the forests just north or northeast of the Carpathians, somewhere between the Vistula and the Dnieper Rivers (see Appendix F). It may have even happened *in* the northern Carpathian foothills—a viewpoint certainly promoted by some who live here[204]. In any case, by the late fifth century A.D., a group of Slavic people was living along the outer Carpathian foothills, and they were on the move[205]. Drawn into vacuums created by the great swirl of humanity known as the "Great Migration"—itself stirred by the collapse of the Roman and Hunnic empires—these sylvan drifters were likely propelled by intrinsic motives as well: subsistent farmers and pastoralists, they were already used to pulling up and moving a few kilometers every generation or so, to carve fresh and fertile plots from the forest[206].

Now the wild and wooded arc of the Carpathians provided an ideal path for the Slavs[207], and they began to move faster and further. Woodsmen (and women) to the core, they hunted the forests for meat, fur, honey, and wax (and the lakes and rivers for fish and fowl), and they girdled, burned, and cut trees, growing wheat and millet in the small clearings and grazing cattle, sheep, and goats on the pastures. From the logs they built small huts—which they typically sank a few feet in the ground and clustered into hamlets of up to ten or so—and carved canoes—which they typically used to navigate rivers—until by the early sixth century A.D., Slavic settlers could be found standing on doorsteps, the heat of stone ovens warming their backs, gazing at the rolling hills of Moravia at one end of the Carpathians or the steamy plains of Wallachia at the other[208].

Then they began to leave the familiar mountains. Over the next two hundred years Slavic pioneers flowed down from the Carpathians in all directions:

- Northward along the Vistula and Oder Rivers and through the forests of Poland to the Baltic[209].

- Southward across the lower Danubian Plain and into the Balkans.
- Westward-southwestward across the Middle Danubian Basin (i.e., Transdanubia and the Little Hungarian Plain) as far as the eastern slopes of the Alps and western shores of the Adriatic (parts of yesterday's Pannonia, Carinthia, and Dalmatia; today's western Hungary, eastern Austria, Slovenia, Croatia, and Bosnia and Herzegovina)[210].
- Westward-northwestward across the Moravian Gate and along the Sudete and Ore hills into Silesia, Moravia, and Bohemia (today's southwestern Poland, southwestern Slovakia, and the eastern Czech Republic), and then northward along the eastern Elbe basin also to the Baltic (today's northeastern Germany and northwestern Poland)[211].

- Eastward along wooded river valleys such as the Dniester, the Southern Bug, the Sluch, the Horyn, the Pripet, and the Dnieper into today's western, northern, and central Ukraine[212].
- West-southwestward over Eastern Carpathian passes and down onto the Transylvanian Plateau.[213]
- Onto the Great Hungarian Plain from the entire mountainous arc[214].

At first they didn't make many waves, assimilating whoever they may have encountered[215], but as time went on and they left the hills, things got dicey for the Slavs. To the west, Germanic tribes blocked the way; to the east, Sarmatians, Khazars, and arid plains; to the south and southwest, wealthy and powerful East Romans and Avars. So they built strongholds to cope (in the forests of the north) and coalesced into larger tribes (in the more open south), and they finally got into history when two tribal collections known as the *Sclaveni* and the *Antes* put their squabbles aside to face the Romans together. Described by their civilized prey as exceptionally tall and strong, of neither fair nor dark but "slightly ruddy"[216] complexion, and with democratic[217], egalitarian, independent, and hospitable tendencies (though patriarchal, with wives so "sensitive" they willingly followed their deceased husbands to the grave[218]), these rather materially challenged barbarians were believed to come from lands of impenetrable forests, fetid swamps, raging rivers, and fierce beasts (with "swamps and forests for their cities"): the Sclaveni from just north-northeast of the Carpathians and the Antes from more to the east[219].

By the early sixth century, after advancing southward along the eastern edge of the mountains and clawing their way through the nomad-infested Danubian plain, the Antes and Sclaveni were terrorizing imperial domains. They started small, led only by petty chiefs and raiding from whatever woods were available[220], and they fought mostly on foot—some half naked[221] to the amazement of their enemies—making good use of short javelins and short arrows with poisoned tips. But they soon entered into a complex and shifting web of alliances, subjugations, contracts, and conflicts between Avars[222], Bulgars, Sarmatians, and the Romans themselves, and whipped up their own recruits—female as well as male—until they were storming East Roman fortresses by the thousands. Taking advantage of aquatic skills they had probably learned in the Carpathians, Slavic raiders even attacked Aegean coasts from flotillas of dugout canoes.

After a hundred years of relative Slavic unity, the Romans managed to renew a former split and win (or bribe) the Antes to their side, provoking the Antes' destruction under the thrusts of Avar lances (602 A.D.). The Avars, ranks swelled with Slavic warriors, willing and not, went on to dominate most of the Central European lowlands (the area wrapped by the Carpathian Mountains, the Balkan Mountains, and the Alps).

And so not only by invasion but also invitation, and not only by Avar pushing but also Avar pulling, by the end of the seventh century A.D., Slavic settlers were scattered across the Carpathian Basin and the Balkans, from Transylvania in the northeast, to Dalmatia in the northwest (see endnote 150), to the Peloponnese in the south. Linguistically (at least), they eventually overwhelmed their Avar and Bulgar overlords, allies, enemies, and neighbors, making Slavs of them all.

With progress halted in nearly all directions by seas, aridity, or particularly intimidating holdouts, by late eight century A.D. only one path remained open to the Slavs: The deep, dark forests to the north and northeast. The way was rather flat, but perhaps only sparsely populated, and only by the related and perhaps less obstinate Balts, or even other Slavs, so once they got started the pace was just as fast: by mid-ninth century, Slavic axes could be heard ringing as far north as the southern shores of Lake Ladoga and the banks of the upper Volga River. As they approached the cold-stunted taiga of the north, the Slavs began colliding with Finno-Ugric tribes, as well as a new threat from the sea. They built ever larger strongholds, but were finally halted, perhaps as much by the clime and their own disputes as by any foreign enemy[223].

(From the northeastern rim of the Carpathians, the distance to Lake Ladoga—about 1300 kilometers/800 miles—is almost exactly the same as the distance southward to the Peloponnese. Both spans were covered by Slavic culture in about the same amount of time: a century or so. Given the difference in the physical and human landscapes, this equivalent pace is rather remarkable.)

By the time they claimed most of Central and Eastern Europe, Slavic settlers had been successful enough, and rooted enough to the land, that some of each generation stayed put. With a territory so vast, diversification was inevitable; Slavic speech split into three main branches: West Slavic (which evolved into Polish, Czech, Slovak, and Sorbian); South Slavic (Bulgarian, Macedonian, Serbo-Croatian, Slovene, and Church Slavonic[224]); and East Slavic (Belorussian, Russian, Ukrainian, and Rusyn)—languages (with a few additional subgroups) spoken today by more than 420 million people.

(Legend offers a more poetic explanation for the split of the northern Slavic nations. A collection of thirteenth and fourteenth century West Slavic myths describe the Moses-like adventures of three noble brothers: Lech, Czech, and Rus'— according to one source[225], sons of Javan, son of Japheth, son of Noah —who founded the nations of the *Lechites* (the Poles), the Czechs, and the *Rus'* (East Slavs).)

In the evening Stephan volunteers to run our group meal. While others cut vegetables, Jürgen and I seek firewood, which is not readily available in this scoured-out gorge. We gather what we can—small twigs and a few branches and a log half buried along the roadside— and prepare a spot on the flat rocks and sand adjacent the river. While Jürgen stands on the log and I saw, a boy who looks to be about twelve comes riding up on a bicycle, hops off, and struts over. I straighten to welcome both the boy and the break.

"Dobra dane," I attempt.

The boy stares at me and mutters some reply. He does not smile, and as he scans us I recall my last encounter with local youths. But as soon as Jürgen hops off the log to construct a tent of twigs over a small pile of dead grass, the boy hops on to take his place.

"*Spacibo.*"

No reply, and again no smile.

I cut several more pieces while the boy stabilizes the log and then Jürgen and I alternate blowing into the sputtering and smoking pile as we've done many times before. But this one is difficult, maybe the most difficult yet. The twigs are green and the grass damp not only from the recent rain but also from the mist of the torrent nearby. The boy watches for a few minutes and then adds his breath too, but all we produce is more smoke.

Jürgen and I look at each other. We've never had this much trouble. But while we catch our breaths and our wits, the boy starts gathering dead stems that are scattered about, mere hollow stalks from last year's weeds. I hadn't considered them substantial enough and dry enough to be much good, but the boy keeps piling them on, so I start adding twigs and soon we have a very promising pile. Jürgen has gone off to other chores and I take a secondary role, curious to see what this young man can do. There is evidence of other fires here. Maybe he is the fire-king of this ever moist site.

Working together silently, manipulating the tiny stalks into strategic positions methodically, and blowing carefully, the boy and I finally succeed in getting a small blaze going. My new associate stands staring into the flames while I go get a piece of chocolate. He takes a small piece, but no more. Nor, after the fire is going strong and I'm eating Stephan's delicious stir-fry of potatoes, eggs, onions, and strategic spices, does this solemn boy accept my invitation to join our dinner. He does, however, brighten significantly when Maria strolls over to chat.

The Fire-king. © Jürgen Sauer.

Friday, May 6. Near Krasna, Ukraine.

This morning Maria and I are the only ones in camp. The others have all started the next sojourn up the valley and into the mountains. Stephan, Kathrin, and Jürgen will return this afternoon (Stephan's knee is still troubling him), while Peter and Thilo continue over night. Maria and I take this opportunity to tidy up the camp and wash a lot of clothes. As always, I'm careful to pour the soapy water some distance from the river, in this case on the other side of the road. As the morning begins to warm, we construct a shower and hang Jürgen's camp shower bag hopefully in the sun. After an hour or so the cold edge is off, so Maria gives it a try. For me there is no hope.

Later in the morning we walk down the road. One of the geese bites me.

"How do you say 'smile' in Ukrainian?"

"Verb or noun?"

"Noun."

"*Ushmiska*".

Slowly I put my words together. "*Te miesh kraseva ushmiska.*" ("You have a beautiful smile.") I suppose it is flirtatious, but Maria does indeed have a beautiful smile, and I see no harm in telling her, and in her own tongue at that. Her response is a smile.

We return for a lunch of bread and cheese (yeah!), and about when we're finished, our young friend and a couple of older teenage boys stop by. We chat a bit, mostly through Maria, and once they learn about the expedition, they relate that they sometimes hear stories in the village about "wolfmen." The boys invite me to watch a football (soccer) game going on somewhere up the road. Strange, since we haven't seen anyone pass by.

I'm reluctant to leave Maria alone at camp, but she assures me it's okay.

"Sometimes I'm alone in my country."

A little embarrassed by this truism, I depart with the boys. As we stride up the road, the two older boys are excited to try their English unaided, and although their skill is rudimentary we manage to cover the basics, like names, and whether we have brothers and sisters, and what are their names, and what is my job, and do I play football. I demonstrate via mock dribbling that I play basketball. They ask questions about Maria, obviously intrigued, and through some rather crude gestures they ask whether I'm sleeping with her. I shake my head and try to explain that we are just friends, but this abstraction is too much for mere hand signals.

We come to the football game, with a dozen or so boys running and kicking and yelling on a verdant field that has drained since yesterday. My companions join the fray while I sit with those taking breaks on a bank overlooking the field. A very large dog approaches, with bared teeth and raised tail, but I win him over with some pets, which plopping down and offering his back he immediately claims as his right.

It has become a gorgeous spring day under an endless blue sky and brilliant golden sun, and caressed by a warm breeze that sways the branches and flutters the grasses, with birds chirping and the boys chattering, I drift into drowsy surreality. *Is this really an unfamiliar land?* The springtime scent of newly liberated humidity and sprouting life is the same as I'd smell back home, and this moment and everything in it seems as natural and inevitable and beautiful as life itself.

Soon I inspire more interest than the game, and the ball is abandoned and the gang gathers round. They tell me of a lake some fifteen kilometers away. Maybe there is something special about it, or its prospect is especially spectacular. Could it be one of the crystalline alpine lakes of which legends are told? Perhaps Lake *Vorozheska*, for example, where two shepherd brothers once drowned when a sudden tempest arose as they were swimming across in contest for the heart of the girl they both loved. Or maybe Lake *Maricheyka*, which sprung into existence during a thunderstorm-earthquake, fortuitously swallowing a band of Tartar raiders led astray by their Hutsul prisoner, a peasant girl named Maria. In any case, the boys convey the idea that I should check it out, as well as a statue of Christ on the Cross somewhere nearby.

After our meager vocabulary runs dry, we drift towards the road, the dog prancing ahead with drooping tongue once our path is clear. As we approach the camp and our separation, the boys invite me to a disco dance that will be held this night—and they advise me to be sure to bring Maria.

After Jürgen, Stephan, and Kathrin return later in the afternoon, all but Kathrin walk down to the village for a meal. At the main road three or four small boys are spraying passing vehicles with a hose and then shrieking with hilarity. Their motivation is evidently not altruistic, but no one seems to take offense, and a few passers-by even join in the laughs, a few maybe even getting slightly cleaner cars.

In a tiny diner Jürgen and Stephan go for a beer, Maria gets tea, and I try a mug of kvass. The national drink of Ukraine, kvass is a low-alcohol brew (usually not more than 1%) made indirectly from the bounty of Ukraine's fields—wheat bread—that has quenched Ukrainian thirsts since the time of the Rurik princes. Hearty and refreshing, it tastes something like a stout, only sweeter.

Most early Slavic villages were clustered in groups of three or four, often arrayed alongside rivers or around small central strongholds. But by the ninth century A.D., some settlements north and east of the Carpathians had grown into large fortified centers of craft and trade, such as Kyiv[226], along the Dnieper River, and Novgorod[227] near the northern shore of Lake Ilmen, far to the north. As these centers grew, they began to attract the attention of adventurers, traders, pirates, and opportunists from Scandinavia who were exploring the rivers emptying into the Baltic. These were the Vikings, and the ones who traded ships for riverboats and poled and oared their way into the forests of northeastern Europe were called *Varangians*. And the Varangians who began to lord it over the area around Novgorod were also called the *Rus'*[228] (pronounced "Roosh").

The Rus' crossed the watershed of the Valdai Hills to the south and east and found the headwaters of great waterways—the Volga and Dnieper Rivers—that could take them to lucrative markets on or beyond the Black and Caspian Seas: the great empires of the Byzantines, Khazars, Samanids, and Abbasids[229]. With better weaponry and military retinues funded by raiding and trading, these eastern Vikings found they could supplement their product mix by exploiting the indigenous Slavs, Balts, and Finno-Ugrians. So they rounded up weapons, handicrafts, timber, flax, honey, wax, Baltic amber, and especially furs and human beings, and piled them on boats, which they floated down the rivers to trade for wine, spices, jewelry, silk, icons, books (!), precious metals, and coins. The trade in slaves was particularly lucrative, starting a plague on Slavic peoples that was to last through medieval times. (And thus a people's word for "word" would become the universal label for captive human beings[230]).

The stronghold of Kyiv was strategically located on the route to the Byzantine Empire—a natural and defendable warehouse about midway down the Dnieper—and within 140 years of its legendary takeover by Varangian princes known as the Rurik dynasty, the city had become the center of the largest political and economic entity in Europe: The early pseudo-state known as Kievan Rus'. (See Appendix G for more about the founding, the life, the zenith, and the decline of Kievan Rus'.)

Kievan Rus' was not a state in the modern sense. Its early rulers were more ruthless businessmen (and businesswomen, in the case of Olga—see Appendix G) than noble statesmen, and as the realm expanded and dynastic descendants proliferated, it became organized as a loose federation of principalities rather than a kingdom. During fall and winter, the princes would roam their territories with well-armed retinues, holding court in the various stronghold-trading centers, extorting taxes and tariffs from lesser traders, and collecting tribute—mostly furs such as sable, ermine, and squirrel—from the locals. They would also raid the countryside for conscripts and slaves (some evidence suggests that most slave raiding took place beyond the borders) and squeeze in the recreational hunting of animals on the side.

Once the rivers thawed, the entrepreneurs would float their goods to Kyiv, often on boats carved from trees by local Slavic craftsmen, and then set out for Constantinople in great flotillas of larger boats, where, if they made it past rapids and nomadic raiders, they would trade with the Byzantines under favorable terms previously extorted[231]. The reigning Grand Prince—essentially the CEO of Kievan Rus'—reaped the most, reportedly ten percent of all profits[232]; but nobles and minor princes also got their cut or ran smaller independent operations on the fringes.

Operating something like a medieval version of the Hudson Bay Company (a comparison not unique to this writer), such was the primary enterprise of the early Rurik dynasty, which together with expanding and defending their territory and fighting amongst themselves comprised their most conspicuous activity. But the Scandinavian elite did establish order, and with the help of local Slavic, Baltic, and Finnic might, voluntarily or otherwise, they kept nomadic invaders (especially the Pechenegs) and other oppressors (especially the Khazar Khanate) at bay. In these the interests of the rulers and the ruled were aligned, although the fact that some of the latter were among the objects of trade must have been a serious point of dispute.

The cooperation between the Scandinavians and the Slavs, as forced as it might have been, allowed for peace and prosperity, and as time went on, the Scandinavians, who were always greatly outnumbered[233], became more and more Slavicized. By the third generation of rulers they had taken Slavic names[234], and archeological evidence of grave goods and burial methods confirms there was considerable mixing of Scandinavians, Slavs, Balts, and Finns.

Their lust for wealth and power never satisfied, the Rurikids continued leading (or forcing) warriors into battle, until, under the reign of Volodymyr the Great (*Vladimir* in Russian), who came to power in 980[235], Kievan Rus' became the largest polity in Europe, covering some 800,000 square kilometers. With the help of an able general named "Wolf's Tail," Volodymyr fought in the east against Volga Bulgars, in the southeast against Byzantines, and in the west against Poles. He annexed what is now western Ukraine and eastern Poland, and forced an understanding with the other dynasties rising around the Carpathians: the Piasts of Poland, the Premyslids of Bohemia, and the Arpads of Hungary. Volodymyr's conquests unified the White Croats of the northern Carpathians with the rest of the East Slavic family, and began the Carpathians' enduring role as the anchor of a wiggly corner between West Slavic, East Slavic, Magyar, and (eventually) Vlach domains—and just as importantly, between Orthodox, Catholic, and (eventually) Protestant Churches. In fact, for more than a century following Volodymyr the Carpathians were an officially designated "No Man's Land" (*Terra Indagines*) separating Hungary, Poland, and the Kievan Rus' principality of Galicia, where the few people living off the slanted earth did so without the rule of country and at their own risk.

A realm this large required a leap in administration and infrastructure, so—starting a dynastic plunge—Volodymyr put his twelve legitimate sons in charge of scattered towns and districts. (They were probably a minority of Volodymyr's issue, since in addition to five wives, he reportedly kept some eight hundred concubines[236].) He built new towns, bridges, and roads, rebuilt the wall around Kyiv, and constructed a system of fortifications south of the city. The latter were linked by so-called "snake walls" that towered up to four meters above twelve-meter-wide ditches, effectively defending against that constant terror from the steppes and those cavorters with wolves, the Pechenegs.

In 988 the busy prince took the step that would prove most influential in the lives and destiny of the East Slavic people: He converted to Christianity (of the Byzantine form)[237]. In those days, when the ruler publically converted, so did the people, whether they wanted to or not. Thus the populace of Kyiv was herded into the river and baptized en masse, and to seal their devotion, Volodymyr ordered the pagan statues he had previously raised toppled into the river[238]— even his heretofore favorite, the thunder god Perun—and replaced cult centers with churches. Volodymyr's pious activity ensured sainthood for himself, and an enduring Byzantine influence for Ruthenians (as the unified peoples throughout the realm of Kievan Rus' could now be called by the ever more wary civilizations to the south) in art, architecture, ideology, law, literacy, literature, science, and religion[239].

The rule of Kievan Rus' over the vast forestland spread out beyond the northeastern rim of the Carpathian Mountains was to last two and a half more centuries, rising then gradually declining (see Appendix G) until finally falling under the hooves of Mongol horses. The mounted terrors, who had already pillaged, raped, murdered, and slaved their way through China, Persia, and most of Central Asia, reached Kyiv in 1240. Their leader Batu—grandson of the "Great Wolf" himself, Ghengis Khan—didn't generally need any prodding, but when Mykhailo, the reigning prince of Kyiv, had Batu's envoys murdered and hung above the city gate, the Golden Horde (as the western contingent of Mongols was eventually called) didn't hold back.

Although Mykhailo fled the storm, the soldiers and citizens did not, fighting valiantly from house to house after the walls were breached[240]. But the frenzied attackers prevailed, destroyed the city, killed or enslaved those who did not escape, and ravaged the countryside, sending most of the populace fleeing into the Carpathian forests or the forests to the north. The Rurik princes, meanwhile, shifted their base to the remote, up-and-coming trading post of Moscow, where they bided their time as Mongol vassals.

Thus ended the legendary and glorious roots of a national identification[241]. Or actually four national identifications. Given its position in space (large), time (preceding the rise of Moscow), and status (semi-mythical roots and a distinctive East Slavic culture), Russians, Belarusians, Ukrainians, and the Carpatho-Rusyns have all laid claim to the heritage of Kievan Rus'. This needn't be a problem, and in fact it is very likely they all do descend from the multi-ethnic stock of Kievan Rus' (themselves with multi-tribal roots[242]). But when one nation or another claims exclusive heritage, relegating the others to non-distinct status—nationalities not entitled to their own identity and without the right to determine their own destiny—more than feelings can be hurt.

Back in camp we settle on a long label: "The Camp Where It is Difficult to Find a Place for a Toilet" (in its less crude version). Privacy is minimal here where the cliffs squeeze the river and road and leave room for only a few trees and bushes.

During our evening meal around the fire, I ask if anyone is interested in searching for the dance. But it just doesn't fit; we haven't the threads and we must rise early besides. We have a long drive tomorrow.

Hiking team sets out from Krasna... © Jürgen Sauer.

...and reaches the Krasna Ridge. © Jürgen Sauer.

Shop in Krasna ("Produkti"). © Jürgen Sauer.

Sunday, May 8. The "Children's Camp," near Nehrovets, Ukraine.

And a long drive it was, bouncing along from ten till seven on the roughest road yet. Our plan was to continue further up the valley of the Teresva River along the same road that brought us to Krasna—a solid yellow line on our map continuing all the way to Kolochava, just beyond the ridge of mountains flanking the western side of this valley—the *Chrebet Kasna* ("Beautiful Ridge", sometimes labeled *Polonyna Krasna*)—where we expected to meet the hiking team some three days hence.

This ridge is one of a group of ridges called the *Polonynskyj Chrebet* ("Polonyna Ridge"), which extends northwestward from Rakhiv and includes the *Chornohora*, the *Svydovets*, the *Krasna*, the *Polonyna Kuk*, the *Polonyna Borzhava*, and the *Polonyna Rivna* ("Smooth Polonyna"). "*Polonyna*" is one of those wonderful words to be found like gems in other languages that don't translate to a single word in English. It refers to the alpine meadows on the high slopes and rolling ridgetops typical of the Carpathians, opened by shepherds and their livestock since at least the fifteenth century, and embroidered with wildflowers such as buttercups, gentians, wild pansies, and the endemic and very purple Carpathian snowbell (*Soldanella carpatica*) and Carpathian bellflower (*Campanula carpatica*), and enlivened with animals such as alpine shrews (*Sorex alpinus*), Tatra pine voles (*Microtus tatricus*), and beautiful (and increasingly rare) Apollo butterflies (*Parnassius apollo*), and still used as pasture when the snow is gone.

Apollo butterfly (*Parnassius apollo*).

Spring arrives late on the *polonyny* of Transcarpathia. © Thilo Brunner

Thus the sheep seem to have it pretty good. Sent up the slopes along with their tenders around the Day of Saint George, traditionally with feasting and magic in a celebration called *Mishania* (or *Mira*) to elicit a safe and productive season[243], in return for suffering milking and shearing they get to graze and lounge about these magnificent meadows for the snow-free season under the (sometimes) watchful protection of dogs. Most of them make it. (The CLCP found that shepherd dogs that are fed only the cheap, grain-based diet common in the Eastern Carpathians sometimes shirk their guard duties in order to hunt extra protein.)

Easing the Passat carefully around or over moguls and occasionally stopping to wait out herds of goats, progress was slow. Here and there small wooden houses lined the road, with steep and rippled metallic roofs and dark brown or gray painted log siding and matching green or white window frames, louvered shutters, and swirling trim hanging from gables that faced the road. A few surprisingly substantial villages with contorted names such as Ust'-Chorna, Rus'ka Mokra, and Komsomol's'k also lined the dubious path, where food was offered at open markets and religion in stately stone or brick churches capped with shiny, metallic, onion-shaped cupolas. When we tentatively poked our heads through the heavy wooden doorway of one such church where a service was underway, curious heads turned and we were waved in. Worshippers—women in kerchiefs and everyone in coats—filled the pews and overflowed the back, and after the adults had dutifully returned their attention to the cloaked priest in the front, only the children paid us much mind.

Just outside one of the villages, devotion long past could be sensed in a venerable old building standing alone and silent amidst ancient gnarled trees on a small hill. This relic of squared, weathered, and warped timbers, which interlocked at the corners, sagged under the weight of its steep, soaring double-tiered gable roof and square tower. Small as a one-room schoolhouse except for the mountainous top, with only one or two small holes for windows and its weathered gray fish-scale roof shingles overrun with moss, the ghost building's rustic elegance nevertheless showed through—especially in the ornately carved wooden arches that supported the eaves over its double-decker front porch. I didn't refer to my compass, but if this Hutsul church was typical, it would be oriented on an east-west axis; women would have entered the weathered, double-hung wooden front door from the west, while men, taking off their caps, would have stepped through the inconspicuous side door from the south.

Ghost church. © Jürgen Sauer.

After another interminable haul, somewhere after the village of Komsomol's'k, the track took a sudden turn and plunged directly into the river. A mere wooden footbridge—two logs topped with a layer of transverse planks and with a single handrail—spanned the roiling waters, to where a double-line of crushed rock continued on the far side. We stared at the solid yellow line on our map and then at the river, but none of our exclamations could repair the map's broken promise. We had no choice: We'd have to drive all the way back to Teresva—back down to the Tisza and the main highway from Rakhiv—a route we had spent the better part of two days negotiating—before we could continue westward to the next road that would take us north to Kolochava. Or at least, that's what the map showed, although it too was merely another yellow line.

We mitigated our frustration by stopping in one of the villages to eat at a small café. At Maria's suggestion we ordered *varenyky*, which she explained was something like the national dish of Ukraine. While we were waiting I asked if there was a restroom. Yes, out back.

About fifty yards up the hill I found a small shack with a concrete floor in which two holes were overflowing with excrement and odor. No stall walls, no doors, no toilet paper, and no sink; I longed for one of my hurried excavations at "the Camp Where It is Difficult to Find a Place for a Toilet."

The portions of *varenyky* were small, but the square dumplings stuffed with potato, cheese, meat, and cabbage were tasty and surprisingly filling. After our stomachs were more than satisfied, we were drawn to a shiny bust perched on a pedestal across the street. It looked much more important than the drab municipal building in front of which it stood, and as we got closer, the face of the silvery head became high-foreheaded, amply mustachioed, and slightly frowning, and Maria answered our unspoken question. "Taras Shevchenko," she said with obvious respect.

While the national poet of Ukraine surveyed the road with an intent but kindly gaze, his dignity seemed only enhanced by small brownish patches of missing paint on his face and collar.

While seeds of an independent Ukrainian nation can be found in the attitude and actions of seventeenth century Cossacks, who ranged the "wild east" of the Polish-Lithuanian Commonwealth challenging the political, social, economic, and religious domination of kings, clerics, and magnates (especially one Bohdan Khmelnytsky, a rotund and originally rather placid noble, who in a plot out of a Hollywood western lost his property and his wife to the invasions of a Polish magnate, and so flamboyantly led a bloody and nearly successful peasant revolt), a case can be made that it was more the exploits of a poet than those of a soldier that crucially fertilized the nation that would sprout from the fields, forests, and mountains of Ukraine.

By the time Shevchenko was born in 1814, in a small village on the forest steppes, the people inhabiting the future Ukraine had been governed by nothing resembling a unified and autonomous state since the fall of Kievan Rus'. Although they possessed a distinct culture (or at least an affinitive set of cultures), a distinct language (or at least an affinitive set of dialects), and a distinct label (see Appendix E), during most of their history the Ukrainians had been divided and ruled by varying external powers, and for several centuries (off and on), the peasantry had been oppressed by the state-enforced institution of serfdom[244].

In the early nineteenth century, it was the Russian Empire doing most of the ruling and oppressing (except for the far west and the Carpathians, where it was the Austrian Empire), and under the absolute authority of the Tsar, Alexander I, the only way the stateless "Little Russians" (as they were called) could express their national character and unity was through art, music, and language[245].

Born a serf and orphaned at age twelve, the young Shevchenko had a difficult childhood. But he also had a propensity for drawing, and though the village teacher[246] discouraged such a useless pastime, the boy's master must have recognized talent when he saw it, because when he took Taras with him to the city, he apprenticed his young servant to some rather well known artists. And after a few years (in 1938), Shevchenko's mentors and colleagues must have recognized not only his talent but his qualities as a friend, because they organized a lottery to buy his freedom. A famous painter and professor (Karl Bryullov) painted the prize, and after Shevchenko's freedom was secured, the budding artist enrolled in the Imperial Academy of Arts in Saint Petersburg, where he could study under the tutelage of his benefactor. Then began a life of rebellious productivity and struggle that many Ukrainians feel symbolizes the tragic course of their nation.

Shevchenko didn't limit his art to the visual. He began producing notable works of both painting and poetry, including a collection of poems called *Kobzar* ("The Bard"). Acclaimed as the most important work in the history of Ukrainian literature[247], *Kobzar* integrated Ukrainian dialects with Church Slavonic and the colloquialisms of peasants and townsfolk to express romantic and historical themes. The young poet had put to rest a prevailing perception that the Ukrainian language was merely a "peasant language," incapable of elegantly expressing the deepest and subtlest human thoughts and feelings[248].

During the early 1840s, Shevchenko continued writing influential literature. His epic poem, *Haidamaky*, with its powerful portrayal of a historical Ukrainian peasant revolt, earned its author status as a sort of Ukrainian national hero, even though there was as yet no unified Ukrainian nation. Shevchenko's Romantic[249] poetry portrayed the sorry history of the Ukrainian people through personalized allegories (such as the seduction and betrayal of a Ukrainian girl by a Russian soldier) and mythological parallels (such as the periodic and eternal torment of Prometheus). The writing, some of which adapts the style of Ukrainian folksongs, and some of which *became* Ukrainian folksongs, is considered structurally innovative; but more importantly

Taras Shevchenko. © Jürgen Sauer.

it is considered "indescribably beautiful and inspiring"[250]—certainly by readers of Ukrainian, and from what I have read, by readers of English translations as well.

Yet Shevchenko's impact arose from more than just the grace and power of his art. On trips to his native country to document its architecture and folklore for the Kyiv Archaeographic Commission, he became reacquainted with the oppressed conditions of his countrymen—including his still enserfed siblings—and he met fellow artists and writers and activists trying to do something about it. He hooked up with the Brotherhood of Saints Cyril and Methodius (named for the two "Apostles of the Slavs" who first brought writing into the Slavic world)[251], an organization with revolutionary goals, although the only thing it really did was publish literature suggesting that society be free, equal, and just, and that Slavic people be allowed to express their cultures, and, if they so choose, to form a federation of nations with democratic institutions. This was a viewpoint known as Pan-Slavism, and the Brotherhood specifically mentioned the United States of America as a source of inspiration.

Shevchenko's writings now became more political, and he began to get into trouble. His arrest during a crackdown on the Brotherhood in 1847 exposed a collection of unpublished poems that movingly portrayed the oppression of the Ukrainian people, justified a Pan-Slavic solution, criticized the ruling powers, and called for proactive measures. His sarcastic political commentary was bad enough, but his poem *Son* ("The Dream") included personal barbs directed at the Tsar, Nicholas I—and even worse, at the Tsar's wife, Alexandra Feodorovna. The story goes that Nicholas laughed when he read about himself, but he got seriously pissed when he read the mocking portrayal of certain physical traits of his wife. Thus, after Shevchenko's initial confinement in a Saint Petersburg prison, the Tsar took a personal interest in extending the poet's punishment. Shevchenko was exiled to a remote post on the steppes and was forbidden to write, draw, or paint.

Apparently, however, even the word of a Tsar loses power at remote outposts. Or maybe such places are simply where practicality trumps policy. For Shevchenko's guards decided that the artist could best serve as the official sketcher on a military survey around the Aral Sea. Shevchenko did as he was told, and thus licitly created an illustrious set of paintings depicting the lives of indigenous nineteenth-century Kazakhs.

After the tour the Tsar's directive was more strictly enforced. Nevertheless, during his ten years of exile, Shevchenko managed to surreptitiously produce more than a hundred drawings, numerous poems, and several novellas (the latter in Russian). This more personal and philosophic work included musings on the fate of persecuted activists, exhortations to Ukrainians to stay the course, portrayals of the harshness of peasant life (especially that of women, in part as a metaphorical reference to Ukraine), and prophetic views of a just and triumphant future.

After his return from exile (1857), Shevchenko continued to write, paint, and etch, but his movements were restricted and activities watched. He was granted a visit to his native land, but was soon arrested (for blasphemy) and ordered back to Saint Petersburg, where he died two years later. He was 47 years old.

Shevchenko's life and work served as a vital warming flame during the long cold struggle for Ukrainian nationhood. Language was perhaps the single most integrating factor in the life of the Ukrainian people, and during the late nineteenth century—when it was banned from publications, stages, and schools—Ukrainians, especially young Ukrainians, sought to preserve their heritage by coalescing around the example of their national poet. The Shevchenko Literary Society, for example, founded in L'viv in 1873 to develop and disseminate Ukrainian art and science, was key to preserving Ukrainian national identity throughout the trauma of the twentieth century[252].

During the Soviet era, Shevchenko's work was filtered to suppress its nationalistic content and allow only its anti-Tsarist and class struggle aspects to reach the light of day, but Ukrainian national consciousness survived, and Ukrainians finally got their independent nation when the Soviet Union collapsed in 1991.

Back down the valley of the Teresva, then a dash west along the rushing Tisza to Bushtyno, then northward on the road that hugs the Tereblia—a long roundabout loop of some 130 kilometers by the time we intercepted the road we had abandoned. But the new road was a highway compared to the old, and we made much better time. Beyond the village of Vil'shany the river is dammed into a lake, which is surrounded by the thick green billows of a lush deciduous forest tumbling down the slopes to the rocky shores. On a warm sunny day, which this was not, I'm sure the waters would have been inviting, but now, swollen as they were, they were content to thunder down the dam unswum.

On break at the lake we received word from the hiking team. The going had been tough and the trail not well marked, but they had already reached the end of the Krasna Ridge and were coming down a day early. They were on the other side of the river, so either they or we had to find a place to cross. Hopping in the cars and driving on, we soon found a solution: a footbridge spanning the river.

As we got closer, "footbridge" became a generous term for the precarious contraption spanning the torrent, and I decided I had better give it try. Supported by two parallel steel cables attached to rusting, tilted posts, the bridge sagged parabolically across its length of about fifty meters. The floor—an airy hodgepodge of thin, lengthwise wooden planks—was supported by transverse logs spaced about four feet apart that were somehow attached to the cables. Two thinner cables ran along one side pretending to be rails, held aloft from the floor by a single post in the middle, while dangling cables on the other side gave evidence of former partners. As I tiptoed across, boards slid and sagged and bounced, some more rotten than others and some not at all attached. Waters roiled below my feet while the whole rig twisted and wobbled this way and that. Although I'm a strong swimmer and was fairly confident I wouldn't drown if a board gave way, I was wrapped in layers of winter clothing to ward off the stiff cold wind, and I imagined that water, which had recently lie frozen on the mountains, wasn't any warmer than the air. I continued stepping from board to board, willing myself lighter and offering a prayer near the depressed center of each one, never letting go the skittish cable, which sagged so much I had to crouch to retain my hold, until pride and providence finally propelled me onto the firm green earth at the far side.

With a residual wobble I walked gratefully along the solid bank, reveling in views of the valley and the slopes and the snow-patched mountains beyond, and then I stared in rapt fascination at the turbulent river. At least I knew the boards would support my return, if I could remember which ones I had stepped on.

Soon after my slightly more confident re-crossing, Peter, Thilo, and, not inconsequently, Shira, arrived at the far bank. A few local men had also gathered, some standing and some sitting on a big log, smoking, chatting, laughing, and apparently eager to watch how these foreigners outfitted with modernity would fare crossing their local span. If they have inherited the skills of their forebears, they would be worthy judges: a sixth-century Roman chronicler known as Maurice declared that the early Slavs were the best river-crossers in the world, and added that they were so at home in the water that they were wont to escape danger underneath it, breathing air through snorkels of reeds[253].

I didn't assume my friends were so adept, either above the water or under it, so I waited downstream, removing my shoes and a few layers of clothing while reviewing the major points of my lifesaving training. Thilo went first, stepping gingerly but hastily along, trying to out-quick any boards that might break and clutching the flimsy lifeline with one hand and his hiking poles in the other. I'd say that Thilo and I, and Peter for that matter, do not differ much in weight, but Thilo was carrying his large pack full of camping gear, photography equipment, and at least one day's worth of food, which surely tested not only the strength of the boards but also his balance. Yet make it he did, even a bit more gracefully than I had, I think. Then, after shedding his pack, he immediately turned and went back for more. My first guess of adrenaline addiction was belied when Thilo got to the other side and hoisted Peter's backpack while Peter removed Shira's leash. Of course! No way a sane dog would willingly tackle such an insane jumble of boards spanning a moving chasm.

After Thilo got Peter's backpack across, Peter carried his dejected friend tucked under one arm while grasping his hiking poles with his other hand. I stood ready on the bank with the water rushing past my feet and feeling stupid that I hadn't anticipated Shira's dilemma and waited to lend a hand.

Local river crossing. © Kathrin Merkel

While we detoured, the hiking team toured, and they got to sample one of the natural wonders of Ukraine: the primeval beech forest of the Uholsko-Shyrokoluzhanskyi unit (or "massif") of the Carpathian Biosphere Reserve. At around 8,000 hectares (and part of 29,278 hectares in Ukraine and Slovakia included on UNESCO's World Heritage List as the "Primeval Beech Forests of the Carpathians"), this is the largest contiguous old-growth European beech forest still in existence; very few others cover more than a thousand hectares.

In summertime not much sunlight makes it to the soft floors of the great wooded cathedrals, whose green vaults are lifted by living columns up to 46 meters high (150 feet) and a meter-and-a-half (five feet) in diameter, so there is little undergrowth. But now, before the leafy canopy has fully unfurled, slanting sunbeams bring forth bursts of color from out of the forest floor: yellow wood anemones (*Anemone ranunculoids*), lavender honesty (*Lunaria rediviva*), reddish-violet fumewort (*Corydalis solida*), and white bittercress (*Cardamine glanduligera*), snowdrops (*Galanthus nivalis*), and bedstraw (*Galium transcarpaticum*). The trunks of forest giants are scattered about, lying stretched across the ground or held aloft at angles by living neighbors, cloaked with carpets of moss, shelves of fungi, and beards of lichen. The long rotting cylinders release their centuries of stored solar labor gradually and pungently, nourishing bacteria, fungi, and plants, which nourish insects, rodents, and deer, which nourish birds, martens, and wolves. Since this forest is "unmanaged," about fifteen percent of its wood is being recycled into other life forms at any given time—a process quickened by noisy woodpeckers.

Shade-tolerant beech trees are so efficient that few other species can compete in the conditions that prevail on this sloping landscape. But local variations in moisture, temperature, minerals, and sunlight, caused by vagaries of altitude, contour, geology, and tree-fall, sustain scattered stands of sessile oak (warmer), hornbeam (warmer), sycamore (higher and wetter), grey alder (along rivers), ash, elm, lime (or *linden*), juniper, and the toxic and diminishing yew (*Taxus baccata*). The latter, which grows best on limestone slopes, can live for more than 3,000 years and used to be common in the Carpathians—the Tisza River is named for it—until it was over-harvested for things like lutes and longbows between about 1,400 and 1,700 A.D.; today it is threatened by disease and its utility for pharmaceuticals.

And splendid woods are not the only attraction of Uholsko-Shyrokoluzhanskyi. Stunning cliffs and deep caves have been sculpted in the limestone substrate by the ceaseless action of water, including thirty or so "karst" caves—popular in the distant past with cave bears (who left their bones) and Paleolithic humans (who left tools and fireplaces)[254]—and a mysterious void cut clear through the bottom of a tree-capped rock hill called the Karst Bridge—popular in the recent past with human pagans.

We arrived yesterday afternoon on this flat, grassy shelf, about an acre in extent and cut into the southern side of a line of foothills overlooking a broad shallow valley. A stream carrying its waters westward to join the Tereblia wiggles like a snake along the rock-strewn bottom of the valley, and a string of metal-roofed houses lines the far side of the stream, which can be reached by several short footbridges—solid ones made entirely of wood. After we set up our tents and arranged a circle of stones and gathered wood, I strolled down the muddy road to the village, joining a scattered parade of well-dressed young people looking for Saturday afternoon action, heels and all clicking the dust.

This terrace and the lower slopes are mostly treeless and covered with the burgeoning grass of spring. Cows are currently grazing, perhaps with annoyance that we've taken the choicest spot. Our vehicles are parked about fifteen meters below, along a dirt track that follows the brook upstream and eastward into the mountains. With an expansive prospect of the valley to the west, and of the foothills and ridges that stack up to the snowcapped peaks of the Eastern Beskids to the east, this shelf seems an ideal spot for a stronghold—common in these parts, when peopled by wild tribesmen still.

Before there was a Kievan Rus', there were strongholds: politically independent encampments of a hectare or so surrounded by ramparts. They started appearing in Central and Eastern Europe by the seventh century A.D. and were ubiquitous within two hundred years. They were so common, in fact, that the Scandinavians called the region along and to the north of the Carpathians "*Gardariki*"—"the country of strongholds"—before they began to invade it.

As Slavic tribes settled the land, most people chose to live near strongholds, not only immediately outside but also in clusters of small villages spaced two or three miles around, and comprised of between four to seventy log houses. Thus strongholds became the primary organizing theme for early medieval life in Central and Eastern Europe. They were usually situated near water, and often in defendable locations such as terraces, hilltops, or scarps overlooking valleys, or in the middle of swamps or bogs.

The ramparts consisted of double walls of horizontal logs held in place by vertical posts and notched crossbeams and filled with earth, and a ditch often ran along the bottom of the outer wall. Although early strongholds were likely built by consent rather than forced labor, the effort required to construct them provides the earliest evidence of an evolving social organization beyond simple clans, made possible by surplus. They also provide evidence of increasing social conflict, as they sheltered people and livestock from attack—including, when necessary, companies of warriors—and were defended by marksmen who could shoot arrows and sling rocks from atop the walls.

Most of the earliest strongholds were small, only big enough for a single homestead, perhaps the home of a chieftain. Or, they housed no one at all, being reserved for temporary refuge, meetings, or cultic rituals. But as time went by they grew in size and sophistication, and by the tenth century some ramparts towered four or five meters high, had gabled roofs, were anchored by underground caissons (pyramids of horizontal timbers buried under a sloping wall of earth), enclosed several hectares, and contained several buildings, often arranged in a ring along the walls. Some of the largest strongholds were even guarded by more than one ring of walls.

Since political organization was initially decentralized, consisting of clans ruled by communal (though patriarchal) assembly, the positioning of the first strongholds was haphazard, depending mostly on landscape. But as society coalesced first into tribes and then into larger alliances, eventually culminating in what might be called states, the organization and placement of strongholds evolved. Strongholds in central locations were expanded to house the political elite—the chiefs, leading boyars, princes, and administrators (tax and tribute collectors)—of local extraction or from external dominate polities such as the Khazar Khanate to the east, while smaller and more defensive military enclosures were built along the peripheries. Thus rings of strongholds appeared around important centers such as Kyiv in the ninth century and Prague in the tenth, and later along the borders of the first states: Bohemia, Moravia, Polabia, Pomerania, Poland, and Kievan Rus' (there being around 500 strongholds in early Poland alone).

As strongholds evolved into political-administrative centers, they also became centers of production and commerce. Craftspeople and merchants settled in and around them, initiating a process of urbanization. In fact, one of the words for town or city in Polish, Russian, and Belarusian (*gród, gorod, gorad,* respectively) derive from the early Slavic label for strongholds: "enclosure." And while some strongholds were eventually abandoned, others evolved into cities of today. Examples—where rings of piled earth, rotted wood, and troughs can still be found in their hearts —include Kyiv, Vyshhorod, Chernihiv, Pereiaslav-Khmelnytskyi, Liubech, and Bilhorod-Dnistrovskyi in Ukraine; Prague, Levý Hradec, Libice nad Cidlinou, and Mikulčice in the Czech Republic; and Krakow, Poznań, Gniezno, Wroclaw, Opole, Lublin, and Przemyśl in Poland.

This morning we named this site the "Camp of the Barking Dogs," but now I think "The Children's Camp" is more appropriate. Although we were definitely a hit with the village's canine residents last night, we're an even bigger hit with its young human residents today.

While Jürgen is down in the Land Rover using the laptop, and the others have gone down to the village for food, I've remained on this barren shelf to guard our tents. But if there was ever a rampart here to discourage errant children, there is no longer, and they've come romping into our camp. Lots of them. At least a half dozen at first, ranging in age from perhaps four to nine. They are bold and curious, especially about what might be in the tents. Some try speaking to me while others run around the campsite, but my vocabulary is too meager to hold their interest for long. There is no way I can keep all of them away from our tents and items hanging around the fire, and while these younger children are smaller in size and lighter in attitude than the heavies back near Rakhiv, I need a distraction. While trying to recall words I've learned from Maria that might draw them in, I stumble upon an idea. I grab my notebook to prove my sincerity, and then start pointing and gesturing. First to my hat.

"Hat... Hat."

"*Schlepa!*" they finally cry, getting the game.

After I give "*schlepa*" a try, they are thrilled to repeat the English. "Hat."

"House."

"*Boudenok! Boudenok!*"

"River."

"*Rika!*"

The children giggle and laugh at my pronunciations, hopping up and down and stomping their feet in delight. But of course kids are ever impatient for something new, and as more show up, the game loses its power. For some reason, however, just as I'm about to totally lose control, they decide to give me a break. They teach me to say "goodbye" as they scamper down the slope. "*Do pobachennya!*"

Then suddenly a little girl stops. A thought seems to have turned her round, and with gestures she makes her question clear: Do I have any candy?

Like a school of fish they all pivot at once and rush back up the slope. *Yes; do you have any candy?* At first I indicate with empty hands that I have none, but then I remember we might have some cookies in the Land Rover. Though a bit wild, these children seem basically good, and I want to be a generous emissary of the outside world. So I trounce down the slope with the flock at my heels. Not wanting to reveal our treasure's likely location on top of the Land Rover, Jürgen suggests I lead them back up the hill and he will bring what he can find.

Just as Jürgen and I start handing out the chocolate and semi-stale crackers, our companions arrive. I give Maria the scoop, and the children hop and scream when she starts translating and lessons renew. With no more goodies, however, and with more guards to keep them from our booty, the kids gradually drift off to other adventures.

Or so I thought. Later, in early afternoon, four or five children return; I guess we are after all the most interesting diversion around. They huddle together at a distance and then call Maria and me over to show us something. After we've joined their secret club, two of the children open their hands with wide-eyed wonder to reveal dozens of transparent crystals glittering on their small palms. The gems are tiny, most not more than a couple millimeters, but they are sharply cut and as clear as glass. Or as clear as diamonds. *Could they be?* The children give a few to Maria and me with pride, and I stash the little sparkles away with visions of having them checked and returning to make these poor children rich.

(A professor of geology at the University of Colorado in Boulder later identified them as quartz. A gift from such proud, happy, and poor children as these, however, they *are* diamonds in my heart.)

Maria and Kathrin in Children's Camp. © Jürgen Sauer.

Although it is now almost mid-May, the winds blow strong and cold off the mountains and they bring intermittent rain. We must dress in our full winter coats, both this morning when we arose and now in mid-afternoon. I go for a walk along the road further up the valley to get some exercise and generate some warmth.

Tributary of the Tereblia. © Kathrin Merkel

Not far up the road I pick up a friend. Or she picks up me: a black short-haired dog, about mid-sized as dogs go. At first she tags along nonchalantly, looking away or pretending to investigate something whenever I look her way. But as we continue up the valley to where the hills start crowding the road and the stream starts tumbling, and after we pass an open gate, the ruse is over. The dog has definitely thrown in with me.

When we reach a few cows blocking the road, Blackie, as I silently call her, herds them out of the way, keeping between me and them. Not only do I have a friend, but a guardian. When I call her over for a grateful pat, however, she remains aloof. Such was the attitude of the wolves Poiana and Crai, and as a "village dog" of indistinct breed, Blackie may in fact be more closely related to wolves than most dogs in America[255].

The road becomes a jagged path along the cascading waters, and I divert onto a trail that cuts away from the ravine and ascends a wall on the right, up what is now a mountain. The way becomes a very steep stairway betwixt boulders, and as I climb and Blackie follows a few steps behind, I wonder what will be the limits of her loyalty. Surely by now she must be wondering where we are going, and why. She is looking at me a lot, and each time I stop and turn my head to survey our progress, her tail wags. If I make a slight shift downward, she starts to bound back down, until, with a turn of her head at my own steps upward, she comes leaping back up to join me; and then I feel guilty for all the extra effort my unintended change in posture put her through.

I know that I must somehow leave her, or drive her off, before I return to camp, because, understandably, Peter does not want local dogs cavorting with Shira. He made that clear when we tried to befriend the dog back in Romania. So I continue up, even though it is getting late and beginning to darken beneath the few stubborn trees on this north-facing slope. The way becomes so gloomy that the yellow spots on the shiny black body of a fire salamander (*Salamandra salamandra*) seem to flash from a void between the rocks.

After we've climbed about half way up the mountain, I stop to eat a bit of chocolate, which of course I cannot offer to Blackie. This time, when I continue on, she does not follow. Maybe she is put off by my stinginess, or maybe this reprieve was her last hope that I would give up my foolish ascent. Either way, I'm relieved but saddened. Given how high we've climbed, and how steep is the trail, Blackie's loyalty went well beyond what I had any right to expect, and I imagine it is she who now feels betrayed.

I climb a bit higher in a light rain that now slickens the rocks, to ensure our bond is well broken. Then I turn and start down, forlorn in my hope that this loyal companion is not waiting for me somewhere in the darkness of the valley below.

Monday, May 9. Mizghiria, Ukraine.

It was nearly dark when I returned last evening, and raining lightly. No one was at the sputtering campfire, not even Blackie, and no one had taken any steps to prepare a dinner. Peter was in the Passat updating the diary, and only Maria's boots under her tent fly gave hint of her presence. I didn't know where the others were, and I didn't feel like cooking myself, so I grabbed a little of our semi-stale bread and cheese and salami and took it into my tent. We have no communal shelter up here on the terrace, as we had not bothered to set up a tarp since our usual vehicular wall (the Land Rover) was down below. After eating, I was feeling very down, what with the boring, cold food and no one around, and during a pause in the rain I went out and fed the fire. I took a seat on a rock and stared into the flames, while a cold wind flapped the tents and blew the warmth away.

Gradually, people started to show. First Peter, who reported that the children had kept him company by peering in the Passat's windows most of the afternoon as he wrote. Then Jürgen and Stephan, who came climbing up the slope carrying bundles of dry firewood in their arms. Where did they get *dry* wood? While searching for the same, they got invited into the home of the man who had been letting us get water from a constantly spouting pipe in his yard, at a house across the stream. I can imagine how it went: In Ukraine, a man (or boy) comes up to you and glares at you like he wants to cut your throat. Then (if he is not a certain kid near Rakhiv) he reaches out his hand for a shake and tells you where to get drinking water and gives you dry wood and maybe even helps you get a blaze going. And in this case, even more: Jürgen and Stephan had been well fed, at a table and under a roof no less, and had not been able to refuse a round or two of vodka to boot.

I regretted missing the party with the father-and-son woodworkers and house builders, and the warm meal, and a tour of local churches and cemeteries that Jürgen and Stephan had taken earlier, but as they stoked our pathetic fire with the dry wood, we all warmed up. At least those of us around the fire warmed up. Thilo had arrived from somewhere, but Kathrin kept to her tent—and had anyone seen Maria? I was a little worried that her boots might not prove her presence, but no, in this muddy terrain she could not possibly be without her inappropriate footwear. I guess it would be just a Boy's Night Out.

Maria had indeed been in her tent, and slept until about 9:00 this morning. Fourteen hours! After she stretches and yawns and brushes her teeth and assures me she is not ill, I'm not above giving her a little flak.

"Never slept fourteen hours in my life."

"I had to catch up," she admits with a smile.

The hiking team—today Peter, Stephan, and Kathrin—start out with light packs. Jürgen will meet them on the other side of a ridge, drop off Thilo, food, and equipment for a three- or four-day excursion, pick up Stephan if his knee hasn't held up, and then join Maria and me in Mizghiria, a town of about 9,000 residents towards the northwest. There, among other probable diversions, we hope to restock our meager supply of vegetables. The hikers, meanwhile, will be trekking through the National Nature Park Synevir—according to local highlanders, the wolf capital of Transcarpathia[256].

Scenes around the Children's Camp. © Jürgen Sauer.

Irena K. has had a long day. Up at five to milk the cow and mollify the noisy roosters with a few grains of corn, Irena finds it impossible to keep the mud from invading her doorstep with her homemade broom of sticks. A spring thaw has come early to Transcarpathia, where her house sits perched precariously above the edge of an upland valley. She lost one of her dogs to wolves last month, her husband is away in the Czech Republic—he sends back money when he can find work—and the kids are off seeking modern lives. The fate of their small farmstead, and the livestock, now depends entirely on her—with the help of her one remaining canine guard.

Nighttime brings impenetrable darkness and a silencing light snow. The day's work is done. Irena has finished her prayers, and just after she's extinguished the last candle beneath the household icon, her dog starts jumping and scratching frantically outside the door. The latch gives way and in rushes a pandemonium of canine, snow, and cold.

"*Out! You know you're not allowed in the house,*" Irena scolds. She chases the animal into the kitchen, grabs it by the scruff, drags it scratching across the floor, and throws it out. She locks the door, but then has a tinge of doubt: *What if I lose this one as well?*

Well, he is fierce, the descendent of generations of dogs that can take care of themselves. He'll be okay. He'll protect the sheep and will bark up a storm if there's trouble.

The crowing of roosters announces the dawn. A blanket of fresh snow covers the ground, and when Irena goes out she sees canine tracks everywhere. But where is her dog? She plows a path to the drafty barn. The dog is nowhere to be seen.

After she resignedly milks the cow and returns to the house, Irena discovers her protector cowering under her eldest's empty bed.

Her dog had not been alone. Irena had thrown out a wolf.

This is a story related by Yaroslav Dovhanych, the Carpathian Biosphere biologist back in Rakhiv. I've added details descriptive of local customs and conditions, and while no one confirmed the animal was a wolf, the story is accepted as plausible by Ukrainian wildlife experts, illustrating the proximity of wolves and people that has been common in the Carpathians for millennia.

Yaroslav tells another tale circulating in the Carpathians, this one with a more folkloric quality: A man is walking home from a wedding celebration—where he had performed as a musician and had a few too many—when he falls into a pit that was made to trap wolves. After dusting himself off, he sees a dark shape in a corner of the pit, glaring and growling at him with teeth bared. The musician removes his violin from the case and begins to play, charming the wolf until he is rescued.

✸

At a large, open-air market in the heart of Mizghiria, horse carts and pickup trucks dispense mountains of potatoes and booths burst forth with flowers, hub caps, bolts of cloth, boots, clothing, and the best selection of fresh vegetables we've seen in Ukraine—even some that are green. Throngs mull about, inspecting the stalls and making bargains while the sun makes tentative appearances and briefly defeats the chill. Coming from the wilds, we find the festivity and abundance almost overwhelming. So we are soon on our way, continuing northwest through intervals of gloom and rain.

Winding up the valley of the Rika River ("River River"), after a few kilometers of woods we come upon an incongruous sight: a brand spanking new building set back from the road amidst an opening in the trees and next to piles of recently scraped earth. It looks something like a hotel, and having just been corrupted by civilization, and it being cold, wet, and late, we cannot bear the thought of stopping at some pathetic wet patch along the roadside to pitch tents and fire up stoves and spend an hour or so heating up water in the cold night air just to cook for the three of us. So in we pull.

It is indeed a hotel, and a clean and modern one at that, though not completely finished, and very inexpensive by Western standards. The hallway is empty, cold, and echoey. Our room is no warmer, and the heating system either isn't working or is off for the season. So we solicit an electric space heater from the staff and turn on the water heater, and when I'm finally standing under a stream of hot water, I'm able to wash off not only accumulated dirt and grime but also the guilt of abandoning our friends to the indifferent outdoors. *Well,* I rationalize, *since one of the support team's roles is scoping out tourism infrastructure along The Way of the Wolf, what better way than to sample the industry of whatever pioneering entrepreneur risked his or her fortune on this remote oasis?*

At the moment we seem to be the only takers.

Later, from our laptop Bob Marley serenades our vegetable chopping and arranging of bread and cheeses and salami, and we even have something green: cucumbers from Mizghiria. Sitting on chairs at a table under a roof, warmed by a space heater, eating our fresh food with clean bodies and hair, wearing dry clothes, and listening to music—it all seems excessively opulent and sterile, and I cannot say I do not miss a campfire, a clean breeze, and the sound of a rushing river.

Tuesday May 10. Richka, Ukraine.

I slept very well, although I did awake once and felt too warm under the multitude of blankets. In the moonlight filtering through the window Maria looked cold under hers, so I threw one of my extras over her and went back to sleep.

Today is cloudy and cool, with sprinkles and rain mixed with short bursts of sunshine. I'm feeling the lethargy that sometime follows a good night's sleep and wonder if it would be better to keep to the outdoors after all. The hiking team should be continuing along the crest of the ridge that frames the southwestern side of the Rika valley, and today one of us is to bring them up some food. I want to go, but so does Jürgen, and since his cellphone provides our only hope for their GPS coordinates, Jürgen it will be.

Richka (or *Ricka*) is a peaceful little village of a few trim and stuccoed houses collected along a stream next to a small pond formed by a small dam, at the end of a long side road that shifts to gravel and crosses the dam and continues winding up into the foothills below the ridge where the hiking team should be. Unlike most of the villages we've seen, which are mere lines along the road, this one is two-dimensional, with a couple of mud lanes extending its sides. (The typical linear layout of most early Slavic villages infuriated the ancient Romans, who were forced to split into two narrow, and vulnerable, columns in order to pillage from both ends.)

We park our vehicles on a shoulder next to the dam and with Jürgen's binoculars scope out the ridge up which the supplies must go. It is tall and steep and I can see that Jürgen could use my help. I'm itching to give it, but I'm also reluctant to leave Maria by herself for most of the day in this isolated hamlet. So I offer to carry some of the supplies, but only as far as I can get in an hour or so.

The ridge is further away than the binoculars revealed. It takes about twenty minutes just to get to the bottom of the hills, and as we begin climbing the wooded slope, along what used to be a forest road but is now merely a sequence of washed-out gullies, I can see that an hour is not going to get us anywhere near the top. I pick up the pace, wanting to be as helpful as possible, even hoping to reach the hiking team (I admit to a faint hope that my contribution will not go unnoticed), but I also crave the exercise and higher views of the freshly washed, nova-green hills. As my temperature rises and forehead moistens, I wonder: *Are we climbing a Boyko path, once used by village emissaries to fetch milk and cheese from shepherds camped high up on the polonyny? Following the springtime Feast of Mishania—the festive and magical sendoff of the flocks and their tenders up the slopes—they would have brought village news to the eager exiles, and returned with the dairy carried in wooden vessels on horseback or shoulders.* For with a shift no less subtle in culture than in landscape, we have reached the heart of *Verkhovyna* ("Highlands")[257], the land of the Boykos[258].

Like the Hutsuls and Lemkos to their east and west, the Boykos traditionally spoke an East Slavic Rusyn dialect. But they spiced their language with a distinct blend of indigenous elements, words from their midland neighbors—Polish, Slovakian, Romanian, and Hungarian— and a southern influence from Old Church Slavonic, and Boyko roots may predate even the earliest Slavic presence in the northeastern Carpathians[259]. Like the Hutsuls they also absorbed miscellaneous refugees over the years, probably including Magyars fleeing Ottomans and migrants from the Urals fleeing poverty[260]. A southern cultural influence, which extends to dress and music, may have begun before the Magyars came and split the Slavs in half during the tenth century A.D.[261]. The origin legend of the Serbs has their ancestors coming from "White Serbia," which, like "White Croatia" that it was allegedly next to, was located somewhere along the northern Carpathians, and which, according to the tenth century Byzantine Emperor Constantine VII, was called by them "Boiki" (see endnote 150.) In any case, whatever southern cultural embers lay smoldering among the Boyko were stoked by the arrival of Vlachs from the Balkans and Wallachia about five hundred years later.

Traditional Boyko clothing generally seems less flamboyant than that of the Hutsul, typically (though not always) embroidered with simpler patterns and fewer colors: usually only one—black or red—or two—red and black, or red and blue. The embroidered panels of vests and dresses are often dark or black instead of white, and the woolen coats and overcoats are usually brown or gray. It is understandable if Boykos were less prone to flaunt: According to nineteenth and early twentieth century reports, of all the northern Carpathian Mountain peoples, the Boykos were the most materially challenged. Boyko huts, for example, were almost universally (and sympathetically) described as straw-thatched hovels[262] wherein multiple families[263], hay, tools, and animals all resided under the same straw-thatched roof: the humans in one room and the animals in the other, all contributing their warmth.

Nevertheless, the Boykos gave their best to their churches, which are so rustically charming that a few have been purchased and shipped to America and Canada by successful Boyko emigrants. Boyko churches extend the general Rusyn roof-dominated wooden church tradition, with most consisting of three rectangular log-frame sections oriented on an east-west line, each section topped by a soaring, multi-tiered pyramidal, hexagonal, or octagonal wooden-shingled roof or tower narrowing to a hipped cap that lifts in sequence a cupola, a spire, and a Greek cross. The central nave is often the largest and its tower the tallest, but not always. Most serve Ukrainian Greek Catholic congregations, while a few are Ukrainian Orthodox.

Traditionally, most Boykos were livestock breeders and herders, famously specializing in the husbandry of oxen that are white. Given the climate and the infertility and rockiness of their land, plant cultivation contributed only a small and unreliable supplement to their table—mostly potatoes, oats, and barley. Some of the young would go down to the Hungarian plain, seeking farm work and pay in grain. They also harvested mushrooms and berries from the forest, provided middlemen services on the main trade routes over the mountain passes between Galicia to the northeast and Hungary to the southwest, and for a time were renowned carriers of salt.

Bonkalo cites a legend that shows how one Boyko woman put the Carpathian *trembita* to good use:

In olden times, when all Boykos had flocks grazing in the alpine slopes, the richest farmer had a beautiful daughter who could play the trembita *with such artistry that she expressed not only her feelings but also her thoughts. It so happened that at times robbers from Galicia attacked and drove away the flocks. One day the robbers came across the rich man's flocks and tied up the shepherds. Besides taking the sheep, they wanted to take the girl also. The girl pleaded with the robbers: "Permit me to say good-bye to the mountains and let me play once more my* trembita.*" The robbers agreed. They were so fascinated with her sounds that nobody realized that she was warning her father about the danger. The rich man understood his daughter's call, and accompanied by the men of the village, rushed to the hills. He captured the robbers, saved his daughter, and retrieved his flocks too.*[264]

Around 50,000 Boykos lived in Ukraine after the First World War, but most were urged or forced out after the next global conflagration (more about the forced deportations of Boykos and Lemkos when we get to Slovakia), and among those who remained, the designation of Boyko is not much used: in the most recent censuses, only 131 in Ukraine and 258 in Poland. The term may have originated from the distinctive regional affirmation "bo-ye" ("because it is so"), but today most people of this heritage consider themselves simply Rusyn, *Verkhovyntsi* ("highlander"), or Ukrainian, and some reject the term "Boyko" as derogatory.

Yet unique and ancient cultural traces remain in their dress, music, fast dances, and festivals, with those who have stayed close to their traditional lives still working as farmers, harvesters of trees, milk, or oil, and gatherers of mushrooms and berries.

The skies throw rain and hail in between sunshine. Where the track peters out, Jürgen and I bushwhack straight up the slope, and though a stiff cold breeze has arisen, I become drenched with sweat. At one of the sporadic locations with a phone connection, I text Maria that I'll be delayed another hour. Guilt and pride push me on, scrambling up one slope only to find another, until patches of sky poking through the trunks give hint of the top. When Jürgen catches up, we unload my pack into his, I help him shoulder his now bulging pack, and wish him the best. With lighter step but heavier heart, I now bound back down the slopes as fast as I can. Although it was surely meant to refer to the difficulties associated with a lack of provisions, a Rusyn proverb seems appropriate: "Heavy is the loaded backpack, but the empty one is even heavier."[265] I feel that, forced to abandon either Jürgen or Maria, I've abandoned both.

When I arrive back at the village it is late afternoon and Maria is relaxing in the Passat. Having no connection, she never received my message, but is waiting unperturbed. I apologize for leaving her alone for so long, but she brushes it off and says she was perfectly content hanging about the village. "I'm sometimes alone in my country."

We lean on the rail that spans the dam and watch the ducks swim contentedly around the pond. The weather has settled, and a background buzz of insects cheers the warmth of the late day sun. I have never been here before, and after a few more hours, likely never will be again. But I feel at home. When we have peace, does it matter that we ever have not?

Three or four children come skipping along. They exchange a few words with Maria and then hang around, making sure we see how well they can skim rocks over the water. After a while Maria and I stroll along the road, past the houses and into the fields beyond, closer to where Jürgen should come down. We continue dallying about, sometimes talking and sometimes not. I begin to wonder about Jürgen. At least three hours have passed since I left him, and it seems he should have reached the top of the ridge not long after, and although we weren't sure exactly where the hiking team was, they should have been less than an hour away.

Another hour puts the sun well below the western ridge. Without a connection we have no way to know what's up. I'm used to uncertainty by now, so I keep my concern in check, but once stars begin popping out of the blue-black twilight, I begin to seriously worry. Then, just as I'm contemplating a drive back towards the main road to find a connection, Jürgen comes strolling out of the darkness, looking a little stiff. Turns out the ridgetop was much further than we had guessed, and after a two-hour wait there, he still had to hike far along the *polonyna* to meet the team.

Jürgen lets go a deep sigh with his pack. This has actually been his first major self-propelled, load-bearing excursion of the expedition.

"Alan, we are old men."

"No. No, Jürgen. If we were old men, we'd be sitting at home watching TV."

After a thoughtful pause, "You're right," he replies, with a grateful smile.

(Jürgen was to recall this exchange many times during the ensuing years of our friendship.)

It is fully dark by the time we pull out, so about halfway back down the road we simply pull over, make a quick meal of pasta, and Maria and I sleep in the Passat rather than taking the time to set up a tent. The village of Richka must indeed be a quiescent place, as only one or two cars disturb our sleep; no one stops to investigate why a couple of vehicles with German plates are parked on this lonely access to their idyllic world.

Timeless work. © Jürgen Sauer.

Wednesday May 11. Volovec, Ukraine.

We awake to the sound of rain pattering on the roof of the car and an SMS alert: We are to wait in the village. Thilo and Kathrin "may" come down. On the way back, a prior century seems to materialize out of the mists in the form of two men wearing flat caps and knee-high rubber boots who are harnessing two lean, sway-backed horses to warped log traces; the unenthusiastic beasts are about to pull some kind of ancient mower under the guidance of two enthusiastic dogs, but are delaying with grazing their eternal task.

Once at the pond we receive another message simply stating, "I come down." We're not sure who "I" is until Thilo comes sauntering out of the fog, bent forward by the weight of his photography gear and the obfuscation of this so-familiar weather. Our disgusted photographer hops into the Land Rover and we continue to the town of Volovec (pronounced "Volovets"), a collection of houses, shops, and a few factories and office buildings filling the valley of a small river, with more houses dotting picturesque farmlands on the rolling hillsides around. A restaurant near the center of town brightens our day with fantastically good food, in my case, baked fish and French fries.

Rain keeps us hanging around the town throughout the afternoon, where we gather vegetables, chocolate, and other supplies. Thilo, who apparently has had enough of camping in wild lands with photographically fuzzy weather, opts for a hotel near the center of town, without hiding his enthusiasm for a hot shower. The rest of us head back out of town along the way we came. We thought we had passed some likely camping sites, but nothing appeals in the downpour, so we return to town defeated and find a roof much less elegant than Thilo's.

Thursday, May 12. Camp Pleasant.
Near Pidpolozzya, Ukraine.

This morning a few patches of blue sky allow the sun to brighten the edges of the gray clouds to a radiant white. Still, the hilltops remain enshrouded, and more rain threatens. After breakfast we retrieve Thilo and some money, and then depart towards the northwest. Green-brown slopes dappled with white fields of snow float in the clouds to our right, and we are feeling the approach of Slovakia. (According to Bonkalo, since Mizghiria we are following almost exactly the line traditionally marking the nebulous transition between the Verkhovyntsi highlanders and the Dolyniane lowlanders, and will be doing so all the way to Humenne in Slovakia.) After a few zigs and zags the road curves westward in the direction of Uzhgorod—our final destination in Ukraine, though still a few days off. A gravel road branches left that we hope leads to Abranka, a tiny dot on our map that marks our next appointment with the hiking team.

The dusty track conspires with a stream to penetrate a mile or so of brush before the first houses of the village. Just before the houses, where the two forsaken ruts of a side path veer into the stream and reappear on the other side and cut up a thickly wooded hill, a concrete beam about a foot wide spans the waters. An old woman is walking across the beam, balancing with a stick in one hand and a bright yellow plastic bag in the other, while a dozen cows take the lower route through the water.

The village in fact seems dominated by cows. . . and chickens, both species having free run of the place. And both the cows and chickens of Abranka seem especially splendid creatures. The bovines, which amble about with a placid, intelligent look in their great limpid eyes, have fine black, brown, or taupe coats, small wide-set horns, and ears that twitch at flies and every sound. Their flightless little companions are bright, multicolored dandies that lounge about in the sun or strut around pecking the dust with showy confidence.

Cows of Abranka. © Jürgen Sauer.

Humans, on the other hand, are scarce—at first. But as we hang around and talk outside our vehicles, people start popping out of their houses. Most keep their distance, talking among themselves while throwing sly glances our way, but a few approach for a chat. After a little small talk through Maria, a woman offers fresh milk and eggs for purchase. She invites us into her home, where her son, a slim, dark-haired man perhaps around twenty, is visiting, and they take us to their barn to see where our milk will come from. Fresh indeed, the woman grabs a bucket, takes a stool and tugs away, white squirts ringing the tin.

Back in the house and around the kitchen table, I take a few tentative sips. But Thilo grimaces and cannot manage to down a drop of the warm fluid that was so recently in the udder of a cow, let alone an unsterilized bucket. This brings a few stifled smiles from our hosts, but they quickly cover by offering up some coffee and chocolate and then a tour of their home. They show off the walls softened almost floor-to-ceiling with tapestries and paintings of mountain scenes and local flora and fauna, and, with special pride, a large cupboard full of elegant dishes, glasswork, and wooden knickknacks carved by the husband and father. The woman unfurls beautiful examples of Ukrainian embroidered *servetki* (napery), and as I admire the colors and intricate designs, I am made to understand they are for sale. Maria says I should negotiate, but when I'm told the opening price I negotiate up, not down, much to my vendor's chagrin. After the deal is closed, she compensates with more chocolate.

(With hindsight I wonder whether any of the wall coverings included images of Rákóczi. Bonkalo, writing in the 1930s, states that Rusyns of Verkhovyna (the Highlands) at that time still honored his memory as a not-quite-finished savior, hanging his picture on their walls and telling tales of him staying in every village, pointing to an oak tree under which he rested or a table on which he slept, and even developing a proverb of resignation: *Bude, jak Rakotsi priide* ("things will be better when Rákóczi will return")—i.e., "never.)

Once outside I climb an open slope across the road, making for a house where we were told a *magazine* can be found. One can indeed, if you're willing to knock and wait a few minutes before being allowed in by a weathered and stooped old woman. The shop consists of a small room with a few packaged items lining the shelves behind a table. Not much appeals to me, but I ask for some rather expired looking packages of noodles and sunflower seeds (the latter very small, still in the shell, and very popular in Ukraine), primarily to reward the storekeeper for her trouble—both for me now and for the hamlet as long as she can.

After touring the village, we cannot find any flat ground that isn't occupied by houses, livestock, or tall poky weeds, so Maria and I drive back to the main road and find another lonely dirt road that leads right down into a thick copse. After a kilometer or so, the bumpy road dips down to the left bank of a wide river, perhaps thirty meters across, and after another kilometer upstream, we come out of the woods and alongside a broad, flat grassy field lying between the road and the river. No houses are in sight, and although the ground is damp, as any ground will be after the recent rains, this is about as ideal a spot for a campsite as we can imagine. We'll again be isolated and serenaded by flowing waters.

The gentleness of this valley belies a fierce and momentous past. For this river is the Latorysta (also transliterated *Latorica*), which is born on the slopes of Veretsky (also transliterated *Verecke*) Pass to the northeast, where the Magyars are believed to have crossed the Carpathian divide in 895 A.D. So it is down this little dale, which they called the *Havas wood*, that the main body of Magyar warriors stormed[266], borne on horses and weighted down with swords, shields, and stuffed quivers as they made for the great plain they would shape into the Kingdom of Hungary. They took first the town they called Munkács (Mukacheve), and "rested there for forty days and they loved the land more than can be said,"[267] then they seized the Castle of Ungvár (at today's Uzhgorod)—despite the defense of one Prince Laborets', whose feats may or may not have been valiant, but whom legend has made into the first great Carpathian-Rusyn hero[268]—and then they raided from the security of the castle and other settlements along the upper Tisza valley for the next five years (before moving on to Pannonia), thus acquiring from the castle their new moniker: "Hungarians."

And that was probably not the end of this peaceful valley's fateful role. Some 345 years later, after they were finished with Kyiv, the Mongols also crossed the Veretsky Pass. So it was likely along these same sparkling and hypnotic Latorysta waters that the next invaders of Central Europe also came[269].

Maria and I get out and walk the green grass, disturbed now only by a gusty wind, trying to find the highest, driest, and flattest area for our tents. The others soon arrive, and we begin settling on the field, which is dappled with daffodils (*Narcissus angustifolius*). Although beautiful and welcoming, these scattered white and yellow lights are a mere hint of the hordes that can be seen this time of year covering the nearby Narcissus Valley like a blanket of snow (located back near the Tisza, near the city of Khust).

The cold wind chills, periods of sunshine warm, and foggy billows of rain dance over the mountains. After the tents are up and we've constructed a circle of stones and logs on a flat rock outcropping overlooking the river's edge—we plan to be here a couple of days, so we put extra work into it—and after Jürgen has hauled in the hiking team, who are looking very weary—we are attacked by the rain and wind, which batter and whip our tents and tarps.

By the time we've finished our evening meal, the rain has ceased, and we have a calm twilight, celebrated by the singing of retiring birds. While the others gather round the orange flames to welcome the dusk, I naively march over to the river to rinse my dinnerware. Just as I'm swishing my shiny pan under the rippling waters, I see her. Green-blond tresses wavering beneath the ripples, white teeth flashing amongst broken reflections of the fading blue-pink glow of the sky, slender body undulating in the current... I hear a subtle, crystalline voice singing with the murmur of the water, and I see pale, bottomless eyes reflecting the first few stars. Her arms are inviting, her smiles are enticing, her eyes are pleading... she is wavering, wavering... *If I can just get a little closer. If I just ease myself into the water, surely I can grasp her, save her, hold her... and feel eternal love in those welcoming arms, and discern eternal truths in that faultless voice...*

At the crucial moment, I divert my attention.

In folklore that may have originated in Western Ukraine, perhaps even here in the northern Carpathians (like the early Slavic people who first created them), *rusalki* are female spirits haunting springs, bogs, lakes, and fast-running streams and rivers just waiting to drag down their victims (not unlike the Carpathian lamprey (*Eudontomyzon danfordi*) also inhabiting these waters, although the victims of this much less attractive, eel-like predator are usually other fish). Vengeful souls of tragedy—the spirits of young women who died by violence, drowning, or suicide before knowing the love and security of matrimony (perhaps taking their own lives to avoid the shame of unwed motherhood), or of children who died before knowing the love and salvation of baptism (perhaps out-of-wedlock infants drowned by their mothers), *rusalki* originally may have been benevolent: nymphs or mermaids or water goddesses responsible for bringing forth clean, life-giving water, especially from the earth in springs. Succumbing to the defamation of new religions, or simply the whims of human imaginations, most eventually took on an evil bent[270].

Regardless of character, most *rusalki* are irresistibly alluring (the exception being decidedly ugly ones inhabiting the northern realms of Russia). With greenish-blond hair flowing past their waists, pale bottomless eyes that plead for rescue[271], and lithe bodies covered not at all or with only transparent (being ever wet) white shifts, when the beautiful *rusalki* arise from the waters and dance erotically, coyly throwing inviting smiles and singing with siren voices, voyeuristic mortals are doomed.

On moonlit nights, *rusalki* might leave the water entirely, unfolding themselves on rocks or riverbanks where they seductively comb or weave flowers into their hair. In late spring and early summer[272], when the waters are celebrating their freedom and the earth is greening, they might stray still further, dripping and dancing naked on the shores, or climbing into trees to rock and swing on branches (birches being their favorite). With the courage of numbers, they might even venture to a nearby wood or meadow to dance in a circle under the stars, the site of their revelry marked the next day by a ring of lush, watered verdure.

Thus *rusalki* occupy themselves and revel in their vanity. But the true passion of these spirits fatale is to spread their misfortune, with (usually futile) hope of shedding it[273]. So if clueless mortals should happen along, with promise of unlimited pleasure and freedom for men, and erotic mojo or feigned sympathy for women, the apparitions lure their weak-kneed victims into the waters, and tease them with riddles and tickle them with fingers until their wannabe saviors, lovers, or beneficiaries cannot swim. Then they drag their aching victims down to crystal palaces below.

But *rusalki* can be appeased. They might even be convinced to pass along their unused fertility to hopeful young brides. So week-long festivals were once held in their honor (and in some places still are), usually in late spring when the aqua-spirits were believed to be most active out of water (sometimes held during Trinity Week or Green Week, also called "*Semik*": the seventh week after Easter). Another excuse for a party (although contrary to Ivan Kupala Day, swimming was understandably banned), the *Rusal'naya* (or *Rusalye*, *Rusaliia*, or *Rusalki*) celebrations ended with a solemn ritualized funeral: the violent dispatching of a previously honored *rusalka* effigy into the earth or a river. In some cases the effigy doubled as a representation of the "unclean" deaths of the past year, i.e., those that could not, or should not, be honored by full Christian funerals: the unbaptized (which usually meant babies or very young children), drunkards, suicides, witches, sorcerers, and those whose bodies were never found.

One of many supernatural beings enlivening the Slavic world, the *rusalki* have had a notable influence on the Ukrainian imagination, spicing the nation's folklore, literature, music, drama, painting, and cinema with mystical eroticism. Indeed, so distinctive and sexy an image can be found playing many a varied role in Slavic folklore, and they are making a comeback today—particularly in the form of *Berehynia*, a recently invented neo-pagan goddess of home, homeland, and women[274].

The hiking team retires early, but Maria, Jürgen, and I stay up, talking around the campfire. Maria notes that she thinks the English words she hears us use most often are "a little bit," "maybe," and "but."

In other words, on an expedition such as this, anyway, the world is best taken in small portions, nothing is certain, and there are always exceptions.

Friday May 13, 2005, "Pleasant Camp,"
near Pidpolozzya, Ukraine.

The sun is shining. And this is a rest day for the hiking team. So in midmorning I decide to take full advantage of both these singularities and head out of camp with my backpack stuffed with food, water, and appropriate clothes in case of usual weather.

I'm drawn to the top of a rounded mountaintop the other side of the river, maybe 1,500 feet high, where a few gray cliffs poke out from a freshly adorned deciduous forest. I must first cross the river, so I start down the road, passing a wide flat of land as level as a pool table sandwiched between the road and the water. The field's fertility, which must be periodically recharged by floods, has been partitioned into a quilt of different purposes: huge rectangles of green grass, yellow dandelions or rapeseed (I can't tell which), and brown earth where kerchiefed women are bent over working the furrows.

Not far past the fields, a path cuts towards the river that takes me to a footbridge—a new, solid, and wide footbridge, with a floor of thick planks supported by sturdy crossbeams hanging from thick steel cables spanning the fifty or so meters from bank to bank. This superhighway of Ukrainian footbridges feels refreshingly safe to tread, although it ends rather ingloriously at an overgrown footpath, barely detectable between the water's edge and the steep wooded slope that starts the mountain.

The wall of tree and shrub is thickening by the minute, and I can only gain entrance where a small stream tumbles out of the jungle. Once under the canopy, a dim trail takes me slithering with the stream up a steep and narrow ravine, climbing rock to rock while the water drops pool to pool. The heavy deciduous roof gradually lifts to a higher but darker vault of conifer, where the undergrowth thins. But the trail peters out, so I scramble straight up the cascade, hopping side to side until I'm finally forced away from the waterfall and up a bank slick with needles and leaves. An occasional step gives way, but the slant slowly eases and a speckled deciduous light returns and then even brighter grassy openings where runners tug my feet (these small meadows in the forest are called *poianas* in Romanian, a beautiful word I shall take advantage of). Up another steep slope, northwards now, through a stately beech forest, and I finally hoist myself onto a saddle running between two higher domes, the western one my original destination.

And what kind of Elven hall is this!? A wide gap in the trunks runs the quarter-mile length of the saddle, from one rounded mountaintop to the other. And although the leaves are less unfurled up here and let in a bit more variegated light, the corridor is still fairly enclosed by a lofty canopy, like a great sylvan hall. Wider and smoother than a typical forest path—broad enough for four or five people or a couple of horses to walk comfortably abreast—each side is lined by a colonnade of stately beech trunks and its floor is softened by an unbroken bed of leaves.

Why such an elegant passage up here? Could it once have served a martial purpose? These high Transcarpathian ridges have often served as fronts, not only during the Second World War, for example, but also the First, when they formed one of the most persistent and brutal lines between Russian and Austro-Hungarian forces. Early in the war, a battle memorable for Ukrainians occurred as a division of their riflemen held off a much larger Russian force at Mount Makivka, just across the lower chain of ridges to the northeast, now commemorated by a military cemetery and memorial. Thus, did teams of horses once plow through the deep snows that buried this aisle, during the "Carpathian Winter Campaign of 1915," dragging artillery pieces defiant and squeaking from hilltop to hilltop as strategy demanded? Like the hydroelectric relic back near Rakhiv, this way is peaceful now, with only roe and red deer leaving any trail—and a fox, which non-deferentially deposited its scat atop a rock along the shallow embankment.

The eastern peak is capped with a large rock that exposes magnificent views. Hills and mountains recede towards the hazy blue rolling contours of the Skole Beskyds. A land of bounty unfolds, so green and prodigiously photosynthesizing that I can almost smell the oxygen rising from the lush forests, fecund pastures, and planted fields below. Bountiful yes, although contorted and rocky and difficult to work. An even greater and easier bounty unfurls just beyond the hills, where lies among the most productive ground on earth. So why did the people living in these mountains largely escape the scythe of starvation that once reaped its harvest across the fertile and compliant lowlands below?

Of the entire Eurasian steppe—at about 6,500 kilometers (4,000 miles), the longest flatland on earth—it is the western end, the end leeward of the Carpathian Mountains, the end that rises gradually in a series of rolling uplands and gets watered by moisture swept up from the Mediterranean and Black Seas by winds channeled by the mountains—that is most fertile. This is where eons of accumulated solar energy combined with wet decay has produced a blanket of rich, black soil called *chernozem* that reaches a depth of a meter and a half in places. Hence the common nickname of Ukraine: "The breadbasket"— of whichever region or state it happens to be most connected to or controlled by. When eastern powers ruled, Ukraine was the breadbasket of Russia or the Soviet Union. When western powers dominated, or when Ukraine is independent as now, it is labelled the breadbasket of Europe. The nation's flag signifies this vital role: a yellow stripe (field of grain) lying beneath a blue stripe (the sky). Today, while Ukraine is only the forty-sixth largest country in the world, it is ninth in the production of grain (2013) and third in grain exports (2011)[275]. (Poland and Romania are also very agriculturally productive: Poland: 70th in area, 13th in grain production; Romania: 83rd in area, 27th in grain production.)

Yet during the early 1930s, when Ukraine was the breadbasket of the Soviet Union[276], it most definitely was not the breadbasket of itself. Somewhere between 2.4 and 7.5 million Ukrainians—somewhere between 7% and 23% of the population[277]—are believed to have died of starvation or of diseases exacerbated by starvation in a famine now officially called the *Holodomor* ("Murder by starvation").

Joseph Stalin, General Secretary of the Central Committee of the Communist Party of the Soviet Union—the man calling the shots throughout the USSR at the time—hated peasants. The reasons for the veracity of his antipathy may have gone with him to his grave, but the fact that peasants, at least in theory, were more self-sufficient than the wage-earning factory workers of the urban industrial economy—the primary focus of the Soviet interpretation of Marxist economic theory— probably had something to do with it. After all, even if deprived of legal title to the plots on which they toiled, peasants can still control what happens on the land. They can decide when it is plowed and with what it is sown and how it is tended—at least they should if they are to be efficient—and they can feed themselves regardless of the manipulations of the state—at least they can if there is any humanity in their overlords.

Stalin especially hated "*kulaks*": those peasants who had risen from the ashes of serfdom in the nineteenth century and had shown enough initiative and ingenuity to accumulate a bit more land and livestock than some of their neighbors. In fact, Stalin hated *kulaks* so much that he decided to get rid of them.

Most *kulaks* living in the Soviet Union at the time lived in Ukraine. Thus, in the late 1920s—when they represented about five percent of the peasantry—more than a million of the most efficient producers of food in Ukraine (including their families) were either executed or shipped by train to Siberia[278], where they were either dumped onto the frozen ground to fend for themselves or worked to death in labor camps.

Yet this was not the end of Stalin's "silent war" on Ukraine. Under Marxist theory, private ownership of productive property was considered theft. It turned out that peasants in Ukraine, rich or poor, were traditionally more likely to own and work their own plots than those in colder and rockier Russia, where a more communal approach to farming had long since taken hold. Naturally (or unnaturally) paranoid, Stalin was also suspicious of the nationalistic tendencies he perceived among the Ukrainian intelligentsia, who advocated private agriculture as the key to national independence. So the intelligentsia was to be eliminated along with the *kulaks*. The ruthless dictator even had it out for the blind Ukrainian minstrels who preserved Ukrainian heritage by traveling about the country singing epic folksongs[279].

Thus the purges and forced "collectivization" of farms throughout the Soviet Union that got underway during the 1920s[280] hit Ukrainians the hardest, and they resisted the most. Unruly peasants suffered the fate of *kulaks* regardless of their means, and many of the rest killed their animals rather than surrender them to the collectives. As a result, between 1928 and 1932, Ukrainian livestock shrank by half. Meanwhile, those peasants who were poor and passive enough to be spared continued to work the farms they no longer owned, but often grudgingly, and at the direction of bureaucrats who didn't know much about what they were doing (party activists recruited from the cities, for example). So inappropriate crops were planted, and crops weren't properly rotated and fertilized, and it didn't help that the peasants were paid less than any other class in the society. The central planners hadn't arranged for, or the factories couldn't produce, enough tractors to compensate for the shortage of draft animals, or enough train cars to transport the grain, or enough silos to store it, so much of the harvest—almost a third in 1931—was lost to rot and rats.

And then came the drought.

Even as fields dried up, Stalin didn't let up. In 1932 he raised the quota on Ukraine by more than forty percent, so that even seed grain was seized. Farmers in Ukraine specifically were forced to surrender any extra grain they may have earned for meeting or exceeding their quota the year before, and if they weren't currently meeting their quota, their livestock plus fifteen times their quota of grain were seized (if they had it), and the offending collective was not allowed to receive any deliverables of food or supplies. As people began to starve, anyone caught trying to escape Ukraine was returned or shot.

Meanwhile, the government encouraged the rest of Soviet society, especially the laborers in the cities, to view peasants with disdain. Any peasants might be *kulaks*, and *kulaks* were enemies of the people, if not as individuals then as a class. Thus farmers had to endure abuse, possibly including the rape of their wives and daughters, by brigades of urban youths who assisted in the confiscation of grain, and who had been convinced by state propaganda that peasants were subhuman. They deserved to be robbed even if they were obviously starving to death; in fact, if they weren't starving, then they were likely hiding grain. So they had to be constantly watched, from watchtowers for example, and anyone, including children, caught hiding even a handful of grain could receive ten years of hard labor if they were not executed on the spot.

Whether Stalin deliberately exacerbated difficult conditions in order to eradicate Ukrainian nationalism and resistance to the Soviet economic principles of production, distribution, and ownership—in other words, whether it was an intentional act of genocide—or whether it was more a matter of incompetence—the natural inefficiencies of a planned economy along the Soviet model—is still a matter of debate. Those who oppose the genocidal label point to the millions who also suffered or died outside the borders of Ukraine, and to similarities with the Russian famine of 1921 (occurring in the Ural-Volga region), although the latter was pretty clearly caused by an ideological rather than an ethnic motivation for likewise robbing peasants of their produce.

But the intent in the mind of their dictator mattered little to the millions of Ukrainian peasants who had their grain forcibly confiscated to the point where some, after failing to subsist on rats, bark, leaves, and their pets, fed on the corpses of neighbors or relatives[281]. And while the famine was not limited to Ukraine, many of the state actions that exacerbated it were. While swollen-bellied, twig-limbed children starved to death, the Soviet regime did not import grain from abroad— it even diverted enough grain from Ukraine to feed five million people— it prevented emigration, and it tried to hide the conditions from the rest of the world.

Thus a joint declaration honoring the memory of those who perished—issued by Ukraine at the United Nations in 2003 and signed by twenty-five nations (including the United States and Russia)—uses the term *Holodomor* (though parenthetically)[282], and in 2008 the European Parliament passed a resolution designating the *Holodomor* as a crime against humanity. It has been claimed that as few as nine and as many as nineteen modern governments have officially recognized the *Holodomor* as an act of genocide (due to ambiguities of language, even which countries have and have not is a matter of dispute).

Just as its peaks float above the clouds, the province of Transcarpathia floated above the worst of this human tragedy. Nearly 400,000 ethnic Ukrainians (i.e., "Rusyns," "Ruthenians," "Carpatho-Ukrainians") lived in Transcarpathia at the time, economically the poorest of their countrymen and the least politically organized. The early 1930s were a difficult time everywhere, and Bonkalo, writing in 1939, reports that Rusyns living in the Carpathians did suffer famine[283]. But it seems to have been chronic rather than acute, part of life in impoverished regions of Europe for centuries, and not an enforced state policy. For after the First World War, as a former province of Hungary and as the result of machinations by influential Rusyns living in America, Transcarpathia was incorporated into Czechoslovakia instead of the Soviet Union (see Appendix D). And not only did the Stalin not rule here, but the governments of Czechoslovakia and Poland did not much bother enforcing Communist collectivization on the remote farmers eking a living from the mountainous landscape[284]. Thus, like many an Eastern invader, the grim reaper of early 1930s Ukraine largely passed on scaling the Carpathian ridges.

(Nevertheless, the *Holodomor* and Stalin's attitude about Ukrainians caused reactions that spread into the Carpathians and fed the flame of Ukrainian nationalism, and during the next global conflagration, as two devils battled it out across their homeland, some chose to side with the new devil rather than the old—at first.)

On my way down, I come to a *poiana* with a gnarled old oak tree standing in the middle. Its huge trunk has a long horizontal bend, like an enormous crooked arm. I take a seat and dangle my legs and eat my usual trekking lunch of bread, cheese, nuts, chocolate, and apples. The afternoon is warm and the birds are singing and insects buzzing, so I start feeling my usual post-lunch crash and stretch out on the natural (though hard) hammock where I feel almost safe from ticks and other crawling creatures.

When I wake the sun is lowering, and although I have no timepiece I realize I must have dozed for some time. So I waste no time getting underway, sidestepping down the final steep ravine while trying to shake off drowsiness. A solution arrives where the ground finally levels: a small pool in the stream beneath a tiny waterfall. Too diminutive and shallow for *rusalki*, I hope, I chuck my clothes and step into the icy water. The spout slaps me awake. It also gives me a momentary brain freeze, but nevertheless, with a clean change of clothes I arrive back at camp a new man. The others are busy cutting vegetables, tending the fire, and drying clothes in the early evening sun, and they honor my break by not even throwing me a come-help-us glance.

Later, after we have eaten and darkness has fallen, we stoke the campfire into a strong blaze and sit around throwing song into the night air, all but Peter and Maria quenched by a beer. Since we can only read Peter's well-worn songbook by headlamp, Peter passes it around with the request we each pick a song and let the others join in as best they can. This is our first songfest for our Ukrainian team, and most of us are shy about starting off alone, and our knowledge of the lyrics is so sporadic that after a while most of us just gather behind the book-holder and join in as best we can.

The little book blazes with headlamps. I choose "Morning Has Broken" by Cat Stevens, which seems a popular choice. When a German classic is chosen, Maria and I fall back to listen.

No moon shines on this field. There is no glow from any dwelling, nor reflection from any tree. From a few steps back, there are no other sounds except the trickling of the river and the stirring of the breeze. Our little crackling circle, its fiery glow and sounds of song and laughter, are swallowed by the immense night.

Planting along the path of invaders, the Latorysta valley. © Jürgen Sauer.

Saturday May 14. "Pleasant Camp."

Another rare day of sunshine, dryness, and leisure for the entire team. A tiny restaurant sits back along the highway, and Stephan, Kathrin, Jürgen, and I replace our usual bland midday diet with professionally prepared dishes such as fried fish, "salad" (the shreddings of cabbage and varieties of root vegetables such as beets), and of course delicious Eastern European French fries. We have to eat in shifts of two, since there is only one small table.

Peter reports fewer traces of wild animals here in Transcarpathian

Ukraine than in Romania, and in the morning he decides to survey the forest in the vicinity of our camp—more of a concentrated inspection than usual. Bushwhacking woods from new growth to old, and from the level valley floor to high, steep slopes, including recent small clear-cuts, he finds only trace spoor of deer and fox. There is no sign of large carnivores, and we wonder if this apparent paucity of wolves and other wildlife results from marginal protection in Ukraine.

As in Romania, wolves in Ukraine likely thrived when humans were preoccupied with killing each other during World War II, although it's unlikely anyone was counting. Also as in Romania, wolves in Ukraine suffered greatly after the war, when Communist leaders included the contumacious, four-legged opportunists in their purges. Unlike Romania, however, Ukraine never experienced a bear-hunting autocrat the likes of Nicolae Ceaușescu, so by the 1970s the predators had been brought precariously low, to perhaps as few as a couple of dozen surviving only in the deepest recesses of the Carpathians.

Then the wolves of Ukraine got a reprieve. The break was due more to lack of attention, exacerbated by the throes of nation-building, then by any intent to coddle; nevertheless, after the fall of the Soviet regime in 1991, wolves began to recover. By the time of our expedition, they could be found throughout the entire country, and by the time off this writing (2015), there are officially 2,500 in Ukraine. Most experts believe there are actually far fewer—half as many, perhaps, or as few as a thousand. Wolf counting—conducted annually by district game managers in Ukraine—is not easy to begin with, and numbers are likely inflated by several factors: Counting in December before winter and hunting have taken their full toll; multi-counting wolves that wander between districts; and by politically-motivated exaggeration. In any case, wildlife managers of the Carpathian Biosphere Reserve are fairly confident there are between 350 and 400 wolves roaming the Ukrainian Carpathians, the wildest habitat in the country (excepting the Chernobyl Exclusion Zone, where there are almost no people and wolves are doing remarkably well[285]).

The expansion of wolves in Ukraine has brought the usual conflicts and stirred the usual passions. The latter range pro and con, but negative attitudes are prevailing. Reports of attacks on livestock and people; hysterical warnings from hunting and forestry officials about wolves running amuck; and maybe even old memories of wolves scavenging the barely-buried corpses of war, all add to the image.

Thus, while a few advocates are calling for greater protections, and while Ukraine officially accepts EU goals for ensuring a viable wolf population, calls for greater control are increasing. In fact, humans are probably already killing at least half of the wolves in Ukraine annually (research estimates range from 30 to 70 percent)—a rate difficult for wolf populations to tolerate[286]—despite a law passed in 2010 that eliminated bounties and restricts wolf hunting to run from early November to late March (but with no bag limit).

Ukraine is a cash-strapped country with limited resources for conservation (made worse, of course, by its current war). So enforcement is lax and poaching high: Wolf pelts can fetch more than a hundred dollars in Ukraine, a very lucrative incentive[287]. The poaching of wild ungulates is also high, which sets wolves on livestock, which sets farmers and shepherds on wolves, regardless of season (often with the illegal use of strychnine). Meanwhile, development and resource extraction, legal and otherwise, is fragmenting the large tracts of habitat that are required for viable populations of all the large carnivores of the Carpathians: wolves, bears, and lynx[288]. For example, large clear-cuts are supposed to be illegal in Ukraine, but they happen anyway in remote Carpathian highlands where few are looking.

Yet there is also opportunity. In a legacy from Communist times, most undeveloped forest areas in Ukraine are owned by the state. There can be room for wolves and other predators if Ukraine can come up with the funds and the will to implement the proven strategies of livestock protection (using new methods such as electric fences, fladry, and motion-triggered hazing, as well as old methods such as well-trained and nourished dogs), compensation for livestock losses, the protection of wild habitat, public education, and creating economic incentives via ecotourism.

(Although the protection of wildlife in Ukraine is often considered marginal, it was the Ukrainian government that initiated the formation of "The Framework Convention on the Protection and Sustainable Development of the Carpathians," otherwise known as the Carpathian Convention, signed by the Czech Republic, Hungary, Poland, Romania, Serbia, Slovak Republic, and Ukraine in 2003 and ratified in 2006, with the intent to provide a "multi-level governance mechanism" to protect and guide the sustainable development of the Carpathian region[289].

A Convention assessment completed in 2009 concluded that the

Ukrainian highlands are a key component of the entire Carpathian bio-region, being located at the "corner" of the mountain chain and thereby linking east with west and north with south. The Carpathians themselves were designated as "globally important" for conservation, with traditional uses such as agriculture and forestry and the "mosaic landscape" that results being "enormously important" for maintaining the rich and unique biodiversity of the Carpathians—provided they are performed sustainably and complimentarily to protected core areas and corridors.

As of 2009, 14% of the area of the Ukrainian Carpathians is officially protected. "In general, [however] the existing protected areas have very low levels of financial and political support for protection and management activities."[290])

Throughout the afternoon most of us lounge around in the sun. Jürgen sets up a hammock and naps. Stephan takes a splash in the river. Thilo drives off somewhere to snap photos, taking Maria along for interpretation. I sit on rocks alongside the river, succumbing again to the ceaseless, chaotically flowing water.

A rare black stork (*Ciconia nigra*) lands amidst the ripples and wades about on its gangly legs, avoiding sprites and catching fish. Back in Romania I had picked up some fishing line and hooks with the same idea in mind. Now, hoping to land some free protein and maybe even some praise, I fashion a pole from a stick, dig up an earthworm, and give it a try, but the stork has better luck than me.

Black stork (*Ciconia nigra*)
fishing the Latorysta.
© Jürgen Sauer.

After Thilo and Maria return, Maria informs me that Thilo was enthusiastic in his violation of Peter's driving speed guidelines.

"What did you think about it?" I ask.

"It was fun. I like going fast."

Sunday, May 15. "Fire Calamander Camp,"
probably near Tur'ya Polyana, Ukraine.

We break camp in light rain, drive for several hours, and drop off Peter and Stephan around noon. They will be the only hikers today, as it is Kathrin's knee that is now acting up, and Thilo has spiritually already begun his departure. They will meet up with us in the evening.

We others continue driving, more westward now, towards Uzhgorod. The Passat is very low on gas but the only station we find is closed. It is Sunday, so maybe tomorrow. Several kilometers up a forest road, in deep, dark woods along a stream, just about when the gauge touches red, we find a place to camp.

Fog enshrouds and the dank forest drips from every needle. After setting up our tents on a small platform next to roaring water, Maria and I take a long walk further up the road, which switchbacks up a ridge. We, or at least I (Maria doesn't seem greatly affected) swelter in the humidity, but the views are gorgeous after we meet a mountain meadow and the fog eases and the sun almost shines. Along the way we leave three fire salamanders and one of those incredibly beautiful blue iridescent slugs to their imperceptible progress (who ever thought a slug could be so beautiful?), and we catch glimpses of a loquacious but coy cuckoo. Upon our return I refresh under a frigid waterfall just downstream from our tents.

Fire salamanders in fact abound around this camp, thus its name. But we could just as well call it "The Camp of Two Fires." Stephan built the first in late afternoon, on a point jutting above the stream just over the waterfall, on the other side of a small thicket of fir trees from our camp. Thilo built the second in early evening, quite close to our tents, for reasons that neither Jürgen nor I could fathom. So after an excellent dinner of fried potatoes, eggs, onions, greens, and spices—designed meticulously and cheerfully by Stephan without a hint of autocracy—we have a choice as to where to warm our feet and dry our clothes. For a team that has been living relatively harmoniously for almost three weeks now—with a quartet going on a bit less smoothly for seven—two fires present a dilemma.

At first, Thilo's fire illumes only its creator. But after a while I notice Maria has abandoned our more social flame—I assume to give Thilo some company—and I feel a twinge of jealousy. *Does Maria prefer Thilo's company to mine? She definitely prefers his driving style. I* wander over nonchalantly, and see that Maria is drying her shoes at the fire. *Maybe Thilo's fire is more convenient. But what is happening to me, that I am jealous?*

Due to the paucity of level ground, our tents are crowded next to the water, and the water is rushing uproariously, making conversation difficult, so we all retire early. Though we are crammed tight on this little patch of rock, the dampness and noise send us each into our own dreamy worlds.

Scenes from the Fire Salamander Camp. © Jürgen Sauer.

Monday, May 16. "Flower and Mosquito Camp," near Simerky, Ukraine.

In the morning we awake to garbage strewn around our campsite. A fox raided our trash bag, which we forgot to stow on one of the rooftops. We seem to have monthly amnesia when it comes to the pilfering tendencies of foxes.

Our first priority is to get gasoline for the Passat, so after the hikers (today including Kathrin) shoulder their packs and get underway, Maria and I depart for Uzhgorod with high hopes, but four or five stations on the outskirts of town fail us. They are all out. Once in town and needle long since bottomed, we ask for suggestions from people who have the sense to get around on foot. A possibility is alleged across town, which we manage to find with our car fueled by prayers, but it too is out. Apparently southwestern Ukraine is dry. Could all the бензин ("benzin") have disappeared across the border? Reportedly, entrepreneurial Ukrainians such as teachers can double their income simply by filling their tanks with cheap gasoline and siphoning it into the tanks of grateful motorists waiting across the border "two or three times a month"[291].

I step out next to the useless pump to spurn our imminently useless car and to call Jürgen for rescue. While I'm listening to the ringback, another station up the road drifts into my awareness. This one with a queue! A trot over confirms we're saved.

Uzhgorod has served as an oasis for more than just thirsty engines. In 1646, sixty-three Rusyn Orthodox priests from "Subcarpathia" met at the local castle, the Castle of Ungvár (*Ungvár* was the Hungarian name for the city), to save their Eastern liturgy. (Subcarpathia is that part of Carpathian Ruthenia lying on the southern slopes of the Carpathians—"under" the Carpathians from the point of view of southwestern nations to which the region sometimes belonged: the Kingdom of Hungary and the Austrian Empire.) Succumbing to pressure from their Catholic worldly rulers—the Habsburgs of Austria—they did in the Union of Uzhgorod what their fellow priests in the Polish-Lithuanian Commonwealth north of the Carpathian divide had done in the Union of Brest fifty years earlier, and what more Orthodox bishops and priests would do throughout the Eastern Carpathians over the next fifty years: accept the Pope as spiritual leader and join the Uniat fold (see Appendix C). Later called the Ruthenian Greek Catholic Church, the church these priests formed became the only legal institution for Eastern rite practitioners in Carpathian Ruthenia—until the Soviets forced them all back to Orthodoxy—or atheism —after World War II.

With relief and a full tank, we return northeastward to meet Jürgen and Thilo in a town called Perechyn, where at an open market supplied by horse carts and pickup trucks we buy vegetables and bread and even succumb to the allure of a roasted chicken. The prepared little carcass is spiced with a touch of guilt as we devour most of it at a roadside stop.

A quiet, barely paved road takes us next along the lazy curves of the Turia River, where we are halted for an hour or so by men clearing the trees of a washout. Then a left onto an even lesser track directs us northward to a sleepy little village surrounded by dense rising forests that probably goes by the name of Simerky, where on the dusty, empty main street we are stopped by more men. Less busy but sterner folks than the lumberjacks, and attired in military-style uniforms, they tell us that we cannot breach national park territory without permits, and the papers that Peter had secured will not do.

Camouflaged fatigues and firearms seem to contradict the reputation for lax protection of Ukrainian nature, and I wonder whether something else is going on in the wooded hills beyond the small collection of quiescent houses. In any case we are given only one option: a gravel track escaping eastward from the village. This eventually brings us to a prolific green field nestled in the ninety-degree crook of a tree-lined river. Some kind of miscommunication delays our locating Peter and Stephan, but by late afternoon we are all settled in.

After our tents are duly raised in a circle, the battle-weary sun comes out and steams the meadow. *What an idyllic spot!* The tall grass is soft and inviting, and a grove of alders provides shade along the water—as good a site as we can imagine to wind down our Ukrainian experience. The warm sunshine seems to presage other momentous changes as well: the more populated, affluent, and westernized countries of Central Europe; the departure of Thilo, Stephan, and Kathrin; the arrival of new eco-volunteers; and maybe even the advent of a milder season.

Socks, shirts, pants, raincoats, boots, and tent-flies are thrown onto the tops of tents, cars, bushes, and branches to steam in the sun—as well a shirtless and silent Thilo, draped nearly horizontal on the portable chair. Stephan gobbles down what is left of the chicken, but Peter refuses the offering with a hint of disdain: The delicacy is likely guilty of violating not only the spirit of our adventure but the limits of our finances, since he probably doesn't know that Jürgen, Thilo, and I paid for it ourselves.

While the others lounge about, I opt for solitude and a dip in the river. I meander across the blooming meadow, butterflies fluttering off wildflowers and grasshoppers leaping from my path. Near the edge, alongside a small thicket lining the river just after its turn, Maria is kneeling half hidden amidst tall grass and the flittering sparks of insects. She is picking flowers, and as I get closer I see she is making something. She does not look up.

"Are you making a garland?"

"Yes," she answers with a smile, but still without a look.

A memory surfaces from ages ago, back at the beginning of Ukraine. "Is it the garland that girls throw into the river?"

"Yes."

"Then I will go downstream to wait," I say casually, so she can easily ask me not.

I pause for a reply, but Maria just keeps at her work, her radiant blue eyes and golden hair harmonious with the blue sky and yellow sunshine. So down the river I go, thrashing through a dense thicket of alders and looking for a strategic location where I might have the best chance of seizing whatever might float by. The river is maybe ten meters wide and swollen from the recent rains, and I know a snag won't be easy.

I find a likely spot and sit on a rock, the water swirling and tumbling and singing by with springtime joy. After I come to my senses, I guess at least thirty minutes have passed. I conclude that Maria isn't going to throw her meticulously crafted handiwork into the river, so I plop off the rock and take a roundabout path back to our camp. I expect Maria to be there, but she is nowhere to be seen. I can't imagine she's still at the garland, so I traipse back through the meadow towards the river, my plan to bathe revived.

As I approach the clearing, Maria is still there and still crafting the garland. And what a garland it is! Leafy, and resplendent with yellow, violet, white, blue, and crimson flowers, some tiny and some large, woven amidst a matrix of dandelion and woodier stems.

"I waited a long time."

No response but another smile as she weaves in another blossom.

"Okay. I'll wait again."

Again I wait for a reply, but Maria is lost in another world. I turn and return to my spot, and this time I find the long, straight, body of a sapling that has been swept into the alders and fashion it into a pole. Not long enough to reach across the river, I know, but maybe it'll help.

I sit on the rock and gaze upstream, analyzing the turbulent waters, trying to determine a likely route a garland would take. *Will she really throw that beautiful creation into the river?* I know this is a game, but as I drift again into the hypnotic world of this opulent, ringing, wood-and-water fairyland, I start to feel like a Ukrainian boy of times past, waiting downstream with pounding heart. Maria is intelligent, mature, brave, and—perhaps most impressive to me—serene. She certainly is more serene than me, who is still too often swept by passionate tides. She has read Tolstoy, Kafka, Mann, and Shakespeare. She knows who Vishnu, Shiva, and Brahma are. She possesses a sophisticated wisdom and an engaging sense of humor. She will make someone a great companion. *But me? Fighting off bears and bandits, perhaps, but getting hitched is not something I signed on with this crazy adventure. And anyway, I'm far from being a Ukrainian boy! Come to your senses...*

If she throws it in, I know the garland will be coming fast. My first opportunity will surely be my last, so I cease daydreaming and focus on the river. *Something is floating far upstream!* It looks yellowish, and is bobbing in the waves and approaching fast. My heart races as I pick up the pole... *It's a garland! She really threw it in!*

The wreath drifts towards the far side... *I don't have a chance!*

It gets caught in an eddy and spins round and round on the other side of the river... *Will it stay there forever?*

The waters are too strong for me to cross. I wonder if there is a bridge somewhere... *It's breaking free!*

It's carried into the main torrent... *I must be quick, it's rushing by!*

The garland shoots past beyond the reach of the pole, so at the last moment I plunge into the water, snag the flowery ring with the long stick, and wade back to the bank before the slippery rocks and forceful waters can conspire to topple me over.

Feeling at once triumphant and abashed, I take my time removing my boots and wringing my socks. Back in the clearing, the tall grass, wildflowers, and butterflies are undisturbed, as though Maria was never there.

When I get back to camp, the others are hanging around doing their things. Except Maria. *Maybe she's in her tent. If she is, we won't have much privacy.* I hide the garland under my hat.

"Are you there?" I softly call into the flap of the tent.

"Yes."

Ducking into the tent, I pause a moment for suspense and then uncover the garland. I am feeling very shy. *What is the power of Ukrainian folklore deep in this remote Carpathian forest? Can it defeat different ages and different countries and social acceptance and all else practical? Are our fates sealed?*

And can the others hear? My tongue freezes into an awkward moment. Then Maria smiles and offers a greeting familiar between us. "So?"

"So?" I reply, stalling.

"Do you know what this means?" she asks.

"Do I know what it means?" Still stalling. "Y. . . yes. . . It means we will be married?"

"Yes." She smiles. "We must find a church."

"Today?"

Maria laughs. Suddenly, I realize I'm standing in wet pants. I ask if she wants to get married in Ukraine or America.

"Do you want to live in Ukraine?" she replies.

Actually given the beauty of this place, I wouldn't mind. But with thoughts of visa and such, I give the more practical answer, for me at least. "Maybe we should try America first."

"Okay."

"Okay."

Finally turning serious, Maria adds that she is surprised that I really managed to get the garland. We make a little small talk, and I let my place as a happily engaged Ukrainian lad dissolve into the steamy haze that still covers our campsite with a golden glow.

Later that evening, Maria designs a borscht soup, "As best I can," she says, "but we are lacking many ingredients." Everyone declares its excellence, but Maria is adamant. "It is not really borscht." She and I are nonchalant, though I wonder if anyone else overheard our conversation in the tent or saw me carrying the garland.

After dinner, I set off alone up the dirt road. The air is still. The only sounds arise from a few insects in the meadows and birds in the trees. I finally get my dip in the river, at an eddy near the shoreline where I needn't fight the swift current. Debris has taken shelter here, but nothing unnatural so I pay it no mind.

Upon my return, walking into the lowering sun, I pass a meadow sloping easily down to the road on my right, framed by tall, darkening woods. In the middle of the clearing, two apple trees stand like sentinels, silhouetted in golden haloes that scintillate with millions of swirling flecks. Rolling cricket swells are punctuated by the trills of birds. A cool shadow is spreading from the soaring slope of evergreens on the left side of the road. A sudden breath of air carries a scent of flowers. I see nothing more than the usual abundance of wood blossoms on one side and field blossoms on the other, but for a moment, synchronized with a crescendo of crickets, the sweet fragrance becomes very strong. *I'm without human company, but everything is alive. I'm not alone at all. I'm part of the perfection of this place and this moment. (If only I could realize this everywhere and always.)*

It is nearly dark when I arrive back at our campsite. The river is loud and the mosquitoes are serious, and everyone has already escaped to their tents. I speak with Maria through her screened entrance. I want to describe the idyllic scene I have just witnessed, but realize this is impossible. So I just tell her that I'm very happy.

"Why?"

Fearful of breaking the spell, and too shy to tell her that I feel how someone should feel about being "engaged" to her, even if a game, I only manage to say, "I just am."

Later, after it is completely dark, restlessness pushes me from my tent. As I'm looking at the stars, which fill the vast black dome untouched by any earthly light, I seem to hear, just barely, the sound of a female voice singing with the river. For some reason it reminds me of the perfume I scented along the meadow. *Are rusalki about?*

Tuesday May 17. "Flower and Mosquito Camp"

Later during the night Perun paid us a visit, as though to see us off from Ukraine. Or was the Slavic God of Thunder merely blessing the day's events? In any case, being shielded from the fury of a violent thunderstorm during the blackness of night by nothing but a couple of sheets of fabric drives home why thunder and lightning were deified by the ancients. The winds force the trees to bow, the rain and hail batter the air, brilliant white flashes strike every which way, and the earth trembles to the monstrous booms of cracks rent in the very fabric of the world. *Something* is angry, or at least violently enthusiastic—and it is something of terrible power.

As god of thunder and lightning, Perun ruled the rain, storms in general, fire, weapons, war—in other words, all the most violently powerful forces in the lives of the ancient Slavs. As liberator of water from the grasp of clouds, and the sun from the grasp of winter, Perun was also guarantor of the earth's fertility[292]. Vital roles these, which probably explains why he receives the most press in the sparse written record of Slavic mythology[293], at least in the East. Perun was the god most invoked by pagan Riurik princes to add heavenly legitimacy to their rule and metaphysical gravity to their word, and he led the pantheon promoted by Volodymyr the Great before his Christian conversion. His precise role and rank likely varied from place to place and time to time[294], but for some, especially in the east, Perun may have been the ruler (or at least progenitor) of all the gods, or the supreme Creator, or Absolute Lord of the Universe, or even the One[295].

Like his brothers in the Indo-European thunder-god fraternity[296], Perun manifested as a very large and robust man—Volodymyr's otherwise wooden statue gave him a head of sliver and mustache of gold—who hurled lightning from the clouds, shot arrows with the rainbow, and traveled by chariot—characteristics that eventually got him converted into St. Elijah[297]. He was especially akin to his divine neighbor to the north: like Thor, he enforced his will with an unusually heavy and loyal weapon (though usually an axe instead of a hammer) and shared an affinity for oak trees. Imprisoned annually in cloud caves by demons, when Perun freed himself come springtime, everyone knew it[298]. A mountain man through and through, of both celestial and terrestrial scope, it's not unreasonable to suppose that the Carpathian Mountains gave Perun his start, along with Slavic expansion and spectacular spring thunderstorms.

Our understanding of pagan Slavic pantheons (there was more than one) is speculative, reconstructive, varied, and controversial, but Perun definitely had company[299]. *Volos* (also spelled *Veles*), a diverse if not schizophrenic deity—at a minimum, the god of herds (i.e., cattle) and perhaps abundance in general, but also probable lord of the underworld and the dead within it[300]—was usually included with Perun in princely oaths. Volos's annual glory was the winter solstice—the darkest day and Day of the Dead—celebrated in the festival of *Koliada* with feasting, singing and dancing, and plenty of fire and blood of goats[301]. Durable in Russian folklore, Volos was likely a trickster god, and maybe even a primary antagonist to Perun. A speculative tale reconstructed from an analysis of Indo-European myths and Slavic folklore has the two gods facing off in a good-versus-evil, order-versus-chaos, fertility-versus-barrenness, thunder god-versus-dragon cosmological struggle; Perun eventually triumphs—and important natural cycles get explained[302].

Yet the evolving history and variegated world of the Slavs spawned more than cosmic dualism. An ancient god of the sky (or more generally, light, in the form of daylight or "White Light") named *Svarog* may have once topped the pantheon, possibly even birthing Perun and the other gods, and all of creation for that matter, but he abdicated early on, leaving the fate of the universe to others and becoming satisfied with the earthly responsibilities of terrestrial fire, blacksmithing, and the hearth[303]. In some versions of this possibly earlier (or more westerly) tradition, Svarog is given two primary sons—*Dazhbog*, who remained aloft with the sun[304] —and *Svarožič* (or *Svarozhich*) —who rather than his father was the one who fell[305], with Perun and Volos playing secondary roles[306].

Besides Perun and Dazhbog, Volodymyr's idols in Kiev (the ones he had erected and then destroyed to the chagrin of devotees) included *Hors* (sometimes transliterated as *Khors*), *Stribog*, *Simargl*, and *Mokosh*. These must have been important deities, but of all but the last we know little. Hors may have been yet another sun god of Scythian origin; Stribog may have been god of the winds; and all we know about Simargl was that he may have arrived from Persia and had the head of a dog and the body of a bird[307].

Mokosh (or Mokosha), however, is ubiquitous in Slavic folklore. Apparently the only female deity to impress Volodymyr, she may have been a holdover from pre-Slavic matriarchal times, evolving from an older fertility goddess, perhaps from Moist Mother Earth (*Mat Zemlya*) herself[308], whom she came to serve. A common figure in folk art to this day, Mokosh is still honored as a patron of vital (and tedious) female tasks such as spinning, weaving, and washing, as well as a deliverer of drought-relieving rain (in folklore she is sometimes mentioned as Perun's consort). Mokosh made occasional nighttime appearances as a wool-spinning apparition as recently as the twentieth century.

More Slavic deities pop up scantily in ancient references or survive in folklore. *Zaria* has already been mentioned as a goddess of beauty and dawn[309]. *Rod* (or *Rog*) and his consort *Rozanica* (sometimes manifesting as two or more consorts, or daughters, called the *Rozhdenytsia*) appear as sponsors of kinship and birth; making the written record in Old Church Slavonic anti-pagan literature, their roles may have extended to fertility and creativity in general. Accepting only bloodless offerings (to ensure healthy births and destinies), and possibly among the oldest and most indigenous Slavic deities, Rod and Rozanica have become favorites of Slavic Neo-pagans[310].

Early West-Slavic pagans had their own favorites. *Svetovid* (also called *Svantovit*) was top god for the Elbe Slavs (also called Polabian Slavs) of northeastern Germany. Sometimes considered a local version of either Perun or Svarog, Svetovid was given the unusual honor of an enclosed temple, complete with a huge four-faced wooden statue, a sacred white horse, and an oracle[311].

Fertility in the west had more than one sponsor, as *Jarilo* (also called *Jarovit*)[312], god of vegetation and springtime, also joined in. *Morana* (also *Marzanna* or *Morena*) was a goddess of winter, death, and nightmares who is still burned and drowned in effigy in certain West Slavic rivers on the first day of spring. In the Czech Republic, *Radegast*, a possible god of hospitality, welcomes beer drinkers to this day[313]. And a three-headed god called *Triglav* may have combined Svarog, Perun, and Dazhbog into a Pomeranian lord of the three universal realms: heaven, earth, and the underworld.

(There are more: A search of the literature and the internet yields a seemingly endless list of Slavic gods and goddesses with a rich variety of roles and attributes, which may teach more about what the human imagination can create out of a sparse mythological record than it does about who and what the ancient Slavs actually worshipped and feared.)

Volodymyr's statues were made of wood, and with few exceptions wood was the preferred substance for expressing the intangible for the ancient Slavs. Durable temples were also rare[314], so Perun's wooden totem poles typically stood under the open sky, towering at the center (or edge) of levelled circular (or oval) glades within stake-fenced oak groves, or on flat hilltops or riverbanks, where they could receive the honor of sacrificed food, drink, domestic animals, and maybe occasionally people[315]. Sacrifices were especially offered by those who had recently escaped death from sickness or war, in accordance with prior deals made with Perun. Devout throngs danced wildly around, lit and fumigated by the smoke of fires kept perpetually burning along the outer edge; reportedly, some female zealots even danced themselves to death. Yet the ceremonies were probably exclusively led by males, priests known as *volkhvy* who were believed to be capable of divination and who perhaps doubled as chiefs. Cults were strictly local however— no centralized or hierarchical priesthood administered the early Slavic world.

Wood in the form of trees could also be sacred: Certain oaks, or trees touched by the bolts of Perun, serving as the focus of ceremonies. In fact, in a Slavic version of an Indo-European theme, the cosmos itself may have been envisioned as an enormous oak tree, whose top lifted the light-and-life-giving heavens and whose roots drew sustenance from the dark, decaying underworld[316]. Since fire was considered purifying, and a mediator with the gods, ashes from trees struck by lightning were used to heal and protect, and throughout the pre-Christian era, the deceased were sent on their way by cremation.

Closer to the home and daily lives of traditional Slavic people, even before there were gods, were the many spirits, sprites, nymphs, fairies, and demons that animated the rivers, lakes, springs, forests, and meadows[317]. It was believed that almost nothing occurred without their influence. Some were good and helpful to mortals, while others were malicious: the cause of the many maladies and tragedies of lives so tied to the whims of nature. Some were beautiful—nymphs and *rusalki*, for example—while others were not—small, hairy, red or dark-colored naked gnomes with oversized heads and brushy eyebrows that could avoid visibility, kindle troublesome fires, and cause illness or death.

Water—which quenches as well as purifies, and which separated the world of the living from the realm of the dead—was vital in Slavic folklore and was especially favored by spirits. There were the *rusalki*, of course, and their southern cousins the *vily*, and the volatile *vodyanoy*—fat, frog-like male beings, fond of carousing, and causing mischief for fishermen, beekeepers, and millers, and even floods if not paid enough tribute. But there were also benevolent spirits of water, especially of springs—sources of clean, life-sustaining water—whose favor could be enhanced with offerings. Indeed, spring water splashed onto children and cattle could protect them from unclean forces[318], and certain springs are considered unusually healing to this day. (In folktales the restorative power of water often required two forms, which to save a fallen hero must be retrieved from far or guarded places, sometimes by animal helpers such as wolves or ravens: the "Water of Death," which re-stitched broken corpses, and the "Water of Life," which reanimated the restored bodies.)

A mischievous, windy, and territorial demon called the *leshy* (or *lesovik*) ruled the forest and all manner of unknown and untamed beings within (including werewolves, called "*volkodlak*" or similar in Slavic languages). In his normalized form the *leshy* was a pale, blue-blooded, green-eyed, male spirit, with hair and beard of grass and vine, who could grow as tall as the trees or shrink to the height of grass, but could also take the form of trees, whirlwinds, friends (of the lost or soon to be lost), or animals: favorites being the wolf and the owl. The *leshy* might punish woodcutters who cut too much, or hunters who killed too many, but he might also harass according to whim, unless paid off with goods like tobacco, food, or personal crosses. He might mimic people's calls with echoes, luring them deep into the forest (wearing shoes on the wrong feet was said to defeat this ill guidance); or steal their axes; or, like the *rusalki*, tickle them to death. But the *leshy* also protected and guided animals —including the animals of man if paid the proper respect—and was especially a friend of bears and wolves.

(The fields had their spirits as well: the female *poludnitsa* and male *polovoi*; more about these when we get to Poland.)

Even closer to the Slavic home were the spirits of ancestors, or the recently deceased[319], or simply the spirit of a particular house (or barn), who, like the spirits out in the wilds, could be benevolent or not. If they were the spirits of sorcerers or people who had died "prematurely"—before enjoying such natural human pleasures as marriage and raising children, or the spiritual pleasure of baptism, and especially if they were suicides—they were likely not, and were especially feared in the Ukrainian Carpathians. The best might help with household and farming tasks, and be a friend of livestock and pets, and offer protection from unclean forces, but the worst might drag neighbors, relatives, or livestock with them into the realm of the undead[320].

The ancestor or house spirit was known as the *domovyk* (a possible successor of Rod[321]), and it was in the flames of the hearth or under the stove that the *domovyk* most commonly chose to reside (possibly with a female companion or "wife": a *kikimora*, who insists on a clean house or else[322]. . .). The hearth was the center of the spiritual life of the family, and the household fire—a source of warmth physically and abundance symbolically—was treated with deep respect; in some homes it was never allowed to expire. In the shepherd huts of the Carpathians, the new fires each season had to be lit by friction instead of flint or match. Called "living fire," the flames so lit symbolized the rebirth of the upland camp, and were tended diligently from spring until the camps were vacated in the fall.

Whether a supernatural being was a god, local demon, or spirit, and whether benevolent or not, it was wise to practice some devotion. So offerings were made and rites and rituals performed—according to both personal and communal schedules[323]—to discourage or appease negative forces and encourage or beseech the positive (such as asking for an abundant harvest). Witches, wizards, magicians, fortune tellers, seers, spiritual healers, and sorcerers—known as *kolduny* or *volkhvy* (the latter derived from the word for pagan priest)—might be retained, or might take it upon themselves, to influence or divine the powers of the otherworld, or merely each other[324]. Protective patterns and power symbols of gods, goddesses (especially Mokosh), and special or mythical animals and plants, such as the Tree of Life, were embroidered, carved, or painted on clothes, houses, and tools.

As the people converted—or were converted—to Christianity, all unsanctioned entities of the other world, regardless of personality, appearance, or domain, were deemed manifestations of the "unclean force," to which relations were discouraged. Yet the suppression of cherished rituals, music, dances, arts, and superstitions—long believed to have practical impact on the sometimes cruel natural forces that dominated daily life—was resisted, and pagan ways persisted[325]. Some were absorbed into the newly adopted religion[326]—through reluctant acceptance by ecclesiastical authorities provided they could be reconciled with the beliefs of the Church—while others survived independently in a sort of merger known as *dvoeverie* (double-faith), wherein people sincerely practiced both the old and new religions simultaneously[327].

Ancient pagan beliefs especially persisted in the hinterlands; especially in the wilds of the Carpathian Mountains, where fertility, the harvest, and the forest remain of primal importance, and where even today, nymphs still sing at springs, sprites still cavort in woods, and vampires still rise from graves.

In the very early morning, before first light, above the sound of heavy rain comes the hoots, hollers, and whistles of a man. *What now?* I'm too sleepy and it's raining too hard to find out. But I don't hear anyone else stirring, and the man has obviously come into our camp, so I finally force myself up and start donning my wet socks. Then I hear a car door closing, and I think Jürgen's voice above the din of the wind, rain, and river, and then definitely the stranger, speaking about three times louder. *Are we camping somewhere we shouldn't?* Thilo isn't budging. I lay back down and leave it to Jürgen or Peter or whoever to figure it out.

When I awake to some light and crawl from my tent, a small, thin, grizzled man perhaps in his late fifties is sitting contentedly on our camp chair under the tarp, legs crossed and sporting a friendly, semi-toothless smile. Jürgen is with him, and tells me the man is drunk, but not as drunk as he wants. Jürgen has stayed up with him for nearly two hours, deflecting his pleas for vodka and any other mischief. As the rest of us finally start stirring about the camp, the man shuffles dejectedly up the road.

Maria's impending departure hangs over me like a cloud, and I want a private moment with her. But no opportunity comes in camp, so after we've eaten I ask her to join me for a walk. But ("always 'but'") Peter has already asked her to help him with the expedition notes, sort of a debriefing of our Ukraine experience, I guess, so I say goodbye to the verdant fields and forests of Ukraine alone.

The rain has ceased, but it is still very muggy, and when the sun manages to find holes in the thick clouds, it is sweltering. I return midmorning to find Maria sitting alone at the fire, which heat unneeded provides a refreshing dryness. Peter is still in the Passat, and the others have all left to shop for food, fuel, and other supplies, since everything is presumably cheaper in Ukraine than it will be in Slovakia.

We exchange smiles.

"I heard someone singing last night. A girl. Sounded like it could have been from your tent."

"No. It was not me," she replies, poking at the embers.

"Hmmm. Strange. Who else could it have been?"

I throw on some deadwood and stir the embers. I'm not sure whether I'm relieved or disappointed. Did I really miss another encounter with a *rusalka*?

Just then comes a flash of lightning, a clap of thunder, and a downpour. We take cover under the tarp. The storm is short, and after it's over we prepare and eat lunch, Maria using the camp chair and me a small log that stayed dry under the tarp. Everything else is drenched. The sun pierces the clouds, liberating heat and steam. We talk little.

Finally Maria says she hopes we will depart very early the next morning at the latest: She has to catch a bus from the border town that will get her to Uzhgorod in time for a bus to Rakhiv, and she has no idea about schedules. We guess there will be little enthusiasm about dropping her off in the maze of Uzhgorod ourselves during our busy country-crossing day. So why don't I bring her to Uzhgorod myself today? It would be a lot easier and certain.

Feeling a little annoyed that Maria's return is so unplanned, I suggest our idea to Peter. "We shouldn't really need her translation at the border," I add. "And I can refuel the Passat today, and we won't have to figure out how to get Maria to a bus when we'll probably have plenty of other things to deal with." I present these arguments knowing that we're always trying to minimize, but I think Peter also senses that

I'm determined to not essentially abandon Maria at the border. Maybe he also senses that I'd like a more personal goodbye. He agrees with a simple "Okay."

Living outside and traveling together almost 24/7 for three weeks through the wild terrain and weather of Ukraine creates bonds that transcend mythical engagements, and as I help Maria pack I'm feeling very sad. After the others return, Maria exchanges emotional goodbyes with them all. I'm looking forward to a final private talk and goodbye myself, but then, just as we're getting in the car, Thilo rushes over and says he wants to come. He "needs to take some photos." *What? Didn't he just come that way with the others?*

We drive in pretty much awkward silence all the way to Uzhgorod, stopping a couple of times to allow Thilo to quickly jump out and snap a few photos at the side of the road. Each time he gets out and takes the pictures and gets back in without a word. When we arrive in Uzhgorod, we have no idea where the central bus station is, so we stop to ask a taxi driver. The directions are complex, so finally he motions for me to follow. We pull into the parking lot, and a posted schedule reveals that an appropriate bus is departing immediately. I run with Maria to the crowded bus and see her on board.

I wave farewell as the bus pulls out.

On the drive back I notice for the first time that the vegetation of the countryside is now that of full summer. But it is not yet the solstice. It is not yet Ivan Kupala Day.

TO BE CONTINUED

APPENDIX A:

Geography, Subdivisions, and Nomenclatures of the Carpathian Mountains

At their northwestern tip the Carpathian Mountains begin as a two-prong fork taking a southwestward stab at the Danube River. The westernmost prong gives Lower Austria a very slight Carpathian taste as a set of hills rising from the banks of the Danube, about fifteen kilometers upstream from Vienna, while the eastern (and higher) prong rises from the left-bank riverfront of Bratislava. From this fork the Carpathian Mountain chain unravels northeastward, starting a long, gentle arc, the convex side to the north. The peaks fairly quickly climb to their greatest heights—as the sharp, showy, High Tatras—and spread to their greatest breadth—as a series of declining ridges stretching across Slovakia and northernmost Hungary.

The main Carpathian spine also quickly gets to its political task, lifting Slovakia's borders, first with the Czech Republic and then with Poland. After the Tatras it falls into a broad line of rolling hills, continuing an easy curve and continuing the divide of Poland and Slovakia until it crosses into Ukraine and climbs again to carve out Transcarpathia. Aiming southeastward now, it rises to the high, windy slopes of the Chornohora and Hoverla, beginning the lift of Maramureş on the inner (concave, southwestern) side and Bukovina on the outer (convex, northeastern). After leaping the valleys of the Tisza and the

Prut (the *Yablonitsky* or *Jablonica* Pass, also called the Tartar Pass), the mountains penetrate three-quarters of Romania before taking a sharp turn west, serving to separate the historical provinces of Transylvania, Moldavia, and Wallachia.

In their span across south-central Romania, Carpathian peaks return to nearly the heights of the Tatras, before the chain bends southward again and tumbles back down to the Danube. Carpathian rock not easily yielding to the waters, the great river only manages to carve out the narrow gorge of the Iron Gates, at the border between Romania and Serbia, before hills rise again on the other side. They gradually return to the height of mountains, elevating the boundary between Serbia and Bulgaria before finally merging into the Balkan Mountains. (Some human conventions stop the Carpathians at the Danube, considering the Serbian Carpathians to be Balkan rather than Carpathian. This decision is somewhat arbitrary. In fact, from above the Carpathian/Balkan complex can be seen as a unified structure, looking like a giant inverted "S," or like a giant question mark with a horizontal line running through it, depending on how much of the Balkan Mountains, the Dinaric Alps, and the Peloponnese the eye chooses to include.)

Viewed from above in the usual north-is-top perspective, the Carpathian Mountain chain (north of the Danube) can also be seen as a bent right arm as seen from behind, held aloft with elbow pointing southeastward from central Romania towards the Black Sea. Sort of where the thumb would be, in western Romania, there *is* a thumb, a rather large one, formed by a cluster of mountains that break off to the north beyond the Mureş River. Known as the Apuseni Mountains, this thumb reaches almost back to the upper arm in northern Romania, completing the enclosure of the roughly triangular Transylvanian Plateau.

From Danube-to-Danube (i.e., not counting the Serbian Carpathians) the Carpathian Mountain chain stretches some 1500 kilometers (930 miles), second only to the Scandinavian Mountain chain in Europe. It spans between 12 and 350 kilometers (7–217 miles) in breadth[328], and covers about 200,000 square kilometers (77,220 square miles) in area, second only to the Alps in Europe.

Like the rest of the Alpide belt[329], the Carpathian Mountains are relatively young, having begun forming when various tectonic plates started colliding some 100 million years ago. Thus only moderately high, they are relatively sharp. They also receive a significant amount of precipitation, falling as snow for a good part of the year, so the peaks and ridges of the Carpathian Mountains are impressive, both to the casual viewer and to the adventurous climber. A northward gaze from the lush green fields near Poprad, Slovakia on a clear spring day, for example, offers a panoramic view no less spectacular than that of the Teton Range offered by the dusty sagebrush fields near Jackson, Wyoming.

The Highest Heights by Country.

Slovakia: *Gerlachovský štít* (Gerlach Peak)—2655 meters (8710 feet); Tatra Range; the highest peak in the Carpathians.

Romania: *Vârful Moldoveanu* (Moldoveanu Peak)—2,544 meters (8,346 feet); Făgăraș Range.

Poland: *Rysy* (Mount Rysy)—2503 meters (8212 feet); Tatra Range.

Ukraine: *Говерла* (Mount Hoverla)—2,061 meters (6,762 feet); Chornohora (Black) Range.

Serbia: Depends on a somewhat arbitrary division between the Serbian Carpathians and the Balkan Mountains: either *Beljanica* Mountain—1,339 meters (4,393 feet); or *Šiljak* Peak—1,565 meters (5,135 feet), one of the peaks of the Rtanj Mountain massif (the latter is sometimes considered a Balkan rather than a Serbian Carpathian mountain).

Czech Republic: *Lysá hora* (Bald Mountain)—1323 meters (4341 feet); Moravian–Silesian Beskid Range.

Hungary: *Kékes* (Blue Mountain)—1014 meters (3327 feet); Mátra Range.

Carpathian Woods.

There is no more compelling feature of the Carpathian landscape than the immense, lush forests that carpet the rippled terrain right up to the feet of the sheerest cliffs and peaks. More than a third of the plant species of Europe can be found in these woods and the meadows they enshrine, and more than a hundred of the higher plant species are endemic to the Carpathian region.

The lowest and gentlest slopes are now largely cleared, with oak (genus *Quercus*) dominating the remaining stands of woods, with sprinklings of lime (genus *Tilia, also called linden)* and hornbeam (*Carpinus betulus*) in the north; chestnut (genus *Castanea*) and walnut (genus *Juglans*) on south-facing slopes; and maple (genus *Acer*), elm (genus *Ulmus*), birch (genus *Betula*), and pine (genus *Pinus*) throughout.

European beech (*Fagus sylvatica*) and silver fir (*Abies alba*) dominate the middle heights, with scatterings of sycamore maple (*Acer pseudoplatanus*), birch, mountain ash (*Sorbus aucuparia,* also called rowan), larch (*Larix decidua*), and yew (*Taxus baccata*).

Still higher and steeper, Norway spruce (*Picea abies*) prevails, with dashes of stone pine (*Pinus cembra*) and larch, especially at the approach of tree line (larch especially in the Tatras). Above tree line, the rocky meadows may sport shrub-like coats of mountain pine (*Pinus mugo*), dwarf juniper (*Juniperus communis*), green alder (*Alnus viridis*), and rhododendron. (Stone and mountain pine are rare and legally protected).

Subdivisions and Nomenclature.

The Carpathian Mountains are convoluted, not only as individuals but as ranges. The entire glorious bow consists of collections of peaks of greater and lesser heights and of greater and lesser breadths separated by depressions of varying intensity, generally aligned along spines oriented in varied directions—though with a tendency to follow the line of the transcendent arc of the chain like metal filings under the guidance of a magnet. On a larger scale there are several regions of distinct geological composition[330].

Consistent with the human need to categorize and make discrete what might otherwise appear continuous, nomenclatures have evolved to designate the various regions and ranges of the Carpathians, based on vertical distinctions or horizontal distinctions (cardinal orientations) or both. These nomenclatures cannot match the fractacality of the rippled landscape itself, of course, but after trying to learn them, one might conclude that an attempt was made. There are names, and sometimes multiple names, for ranges, ridges, massifs, peaks, and hills, and collections of such, and for collections of collections (collections of Carpathian ranges are sometimes called "groups"), and in multiple languages. One can become almost as lost in Carpathian nomenclatures as in Carpathian landscapes.

At the highest level, the Carpathians are usually divided into three main divisions:

- The Western Carpathians—spanning eastern Czech Republic, all of central Slovakia, southern Poland, and northern Hungary.
- The Eastern Carpathians—spanning southeastern Poland, northeastern Slovakia, southwestern Ukraine, and north-central Romania.
- The Southern Carpathians—spanning south-central Romania and eastern Serbia (when the Serbian Carpathians are included).

This scheme is oversimplified and ignores, for example, the fact that to Romanians the "Eastern Carpathians" mean the mountains in the northern and central-eastern part of the country, the "Southern Carpathians" mean the branch that extends from the Predeal Pass near Brasov westward across the country (also known as the "Transylvanian Alps"), and the "Western Carpathians" mean the Apuseni Mountains to the north of the "Southern Carpathians." For Ukrainians on the other hand, "Eastern Carpathians" means only the eastern half of the mountains that lie within their borders (which they may call the "Ukrainian Carpathians" or the "Wooded Carpathians").

The terms "Inner" and "Outer" are sometimes overlaid on this highest level nomenclature, referring to the concave and convex sides of the arcing Carpathian divide, respectively, for the northern half of the chain. Thus we have the "Inner" and "Outer" Western and Eastern Carpathians. In addition, the western half of the Southern Carpathians and the Apuseni are also sometimes collectively called the "Western Romanian Carpathians," and we also have, of course, the Serbian Carpathians.

Other naming conventions achieve more detail, down several levels of resolution and often with national or local variations that may differ, conflict, or contradict the larger schema (the "*Polonynskyj chrebet*" (Polonyna Ridge), for example, is sometimes called the "Inner Ukrainian Carpathians" in Ukraine, even though they are part of the "Outer Eastern Carpathians" of the higher level schema). Many ranges have names completely independent of the label "Carpathian" (e.g., *Tatras, Beskids, Maramureş, Rodnei, Călimani, Bucegi, Făgăraş,* and *Apuseni,* to name a few). Indeed, one can become dizzy trying to understand the varied application of the term *Beskid* and its variants (*Beskids, Beskidian, Beskyd, Beskydy, Bieszczady*) and qualifiers (*Eastern, Western, High, Low, Middle, Central, Little, Sub, Czech, Slovak, Polish, Ukrainian, Moravian, Silesian, Wooded,* and others linked to more local political regions) to various ranges and collections of ranges along the northern, mostly "outer," rim of the Carpathians. For those who are interested, the tireless writers of Wikipedia have made an attempt (http://en.wikipedia.org/wiki/ Divisions_of_the_Carpathians), as well as those of the World Heritage Encyclopedia (http://www.worldheritage.org/articles/Divisions_of_ the_Carpathians).

There are various theories concerning the name "Carpathian" itself. As discussed in the narrative, it may have derived from the name of the tribe who seriously harassed the Roman Empire in its Balkan provinces during the third and early fourth century A.D. Or it may derive from the Proto-Indo-European word for "rock" (*kárrēkā*), from which also are derived the Albanian word *karpë* and the Slavic word *skála.* A Polish modifier that signifies a rough or irregular surface, *karpa,* and the Polish word for "cliff" (or "escarpment"), *skarpa,* also derive from this root, and it seems likely that these words were used to refer to the mountains in the south of the country. The Greek word for "wrist," καρπό, has also been suggested as a possible antecedent to "Carpathian", possibly relating to the shape of the mountain chain in Romania. Perhaps the universal appellation "Carpathian" evolved as a coincidental confluence of all these roots, wherein each was applied to the highlands of Central and Eastern Europe at one place or another at one time or another in one language or another. In any case, the first known written reference to the mountains using the name Carpathians (*Carpates*) was provided by Ptolemy in his *Geographia,* written in the second century A.D., referring specifically to the Western Carpathians.

APPENDIX B:

The Geography of the
Ancient Kingdom of Dacia

Transylvania and its ring of mountains formed the core of the ancient Dacian kingdom, which probably typically extended to the Tisza River in the west, the upper Tisza and Dniester Rivers in the north, the Siret and Black Sea in the east, and the Danube in the south. These were the boundaries described by Ptolemy. Thus in addition to Transylvania, the area occupied by Dacian people often included the rest of today's Romania, the eastern area of Hungary between the Apuseni Mountains and the Tisza, and parts of Moldova and southwestern Ukraine. At its max (probably during the first century B.C. under King Burebista), the Dacian kingdom may have extended a bit further in all directions, possibly to as far as Bohemia in the west (the "Hercynian Forest" in ancient sources), the Bug River in the east, the upper Vistula in the north (where Dacian presence is indicated by a few toponyms), and the Haemus (Balkan) Mountains in the south, thereby including the entire Carpathian Mountain chain (including Slovakia and southern Poland), most of Hungary, far eastern Austria and the Czech Republic, northeastern Croatia, northern Serbia, northern Bulgaria, and more of western Ukraine. Of these, the western boundaries—the areas in Austria, the Czech Republic, Croatia, and Hungary west of the Danube, where they were blocked from further expansion first by the Celtic Boii and later by the Sarmation Iazygi (who sometimes pushed the Dacians eastward back across the Tisza to the Apuseni Mountain border of Transylvania)—are the most speculative.

The Roman Empire never controlled the entire region inhabited by Dacians. Judging by the location of the Roman limes (the Limes Alutanus along the Olt River, the Limes Transalutanus several kilometers east of the Olt River extending 250 kilometers from the Danube northward to Râşnov, and the Limes Porolissensis in northern Romania), the suspected location of Constantine's Wall (along the southern Carpathians) and Upper Trajan's Wall (from near the Prut River in northeastern Romania across Moldova to the Dniester River), and the location of other Roman castri (military camps or forts), Dacia Traiana (also called Dacia Felix), as the Roman province was called, seems to have not included (or at least did not control) most of the eastern Carpathian Mountain highlands (the home of "Free Dacians") east of the Olt River (which cuts through the Southern Carpathians roughly at their midpoint). It did include the Apuseni Mountains and other valuable highlands where mines were located and the lower elevations of the central Transylvanian plateau probably not further north than the southern border of Maramureş (although there were a few Roman settlements in Maramureş); Banat west of the Southern Carpathians to the Tisza River; Wallachia north of the Danube and south of the mountains; and Moldavia east of the mountains to perhaps the Siret River.

For administrative purposes, in 119 the emperor Hadrian subdivided Dacia Felix into *Dacia Apulensis* ("Superior": the northern half including the Southern Carpathians northward, which included Transylvania) and *Dacia Malvensis* ("Inferior": the southern half which included Banat and Wallachia west of the Olt–also known as Oltenia), and then in 124 he split the former into *Dacia Apulensis* in the south and *Dacia Porolissensis* in the north.

APPENDIX C:

The Acts of Union Forming the Uniat/Greek Catholic Church of Eastern Europe

The Unions in Eastern Europe between the Orthodox and Catholic Churches, which formed the Uniat Church, later called Greek Catholic Church, were as follows:

- The Union of Brest (1596). Confirmed by the Pope and accepted by most (but not all) the Orthodox bishops within the Polish-Lithuanian Commonwealth (i.e., the Metropolia of Kyiv/Halych and all the Rus') in the eastern regions of the Commonwealth north of the Carpathian divide. This Union along with subsequent actions of enforcement triggered vigorous resistance by many of the Orthodox priests and laity, stimulating the cause of the Cossacks as defenders of the Orthodox faith and instigators of independence for Ukrainians. The Ukrainian and Belarusian Greek Catholic Churches of today descend from this Union.

- The Union of Uzhgorod (1646). Proposed by 63 Orthodox priests in four Hungarian counties (Szepes, Sáros, Zemplén, and Ung) south of the Carpathian divide in what is today far western Ukraine and eastern Slovakia and confirmed by a council of Hungary's Catholic bishops in 1648. This Union gradually spread southeastward along the Carpathians as control by the Protestant princes of Transylvania waned. It was joined in 1664 by the Orthodox priests in the western and central part of the Eparchy of Mukacheve, bringing the Hungarian counties of Bereg and Ugocsa into the fold, and about 50 years later by most of the remaining priests in the Eparchy, bringing in the county of Maramureş and thus the rest of today's Transcarpathia and extreme northern Romania. The Slovak, Ruthenian, and Hungarian Greek Catholic Churches of today descend from this Union.

- The Transylvanian Act of Union (1698). Accepted in 1700 by a synod of Transylvania Orthodox bishops under pressure from the Catholic ruler of Transylvania (the Habsburg Emperor Leopold I), who wanted to reduce the influence of both Orthodoxy, which was becoming widespread in Transylvania due to an influx of Vlach immigrants, and the Protestant Reformation. As a benefit, Vlachs who converted to the new faith regained rights similar to those enjoyed by the other Three Nations of Transylvania (the Hungarian nobility, Szeklers, and Saxons). Ultimately, however, most Romanians defiantly remained Orthodox. This Union formed the Romanian Greek Catholic Church (formally called The Romanian Church United with Rome, Greek-Catholic).

APPENDIX D:

The Political History of Transcarpathia during the Twentieth Century: A Hundred Years, Seven States

1. **Hungary (until November, 1918).** At the turn of the century, Transcarpathia had been part of the Kingdom of Hungary since around the late twelfth century.

2. **West Ukrainian National Republic (November, 1918–July, 1919).** When the Austro-Hungarian Empire got carved up at the end of World War I, most of Transcarpathia first became part of the very ephemeral West Ukrainian National Republic, which itself united very briefly with the eastern Ukrainian People's Republic (January 1919). Given the interests of much more powerful neighbors (especially Poland and Russia), the West Ukrainian National Republic was not sustainable, and a conflict known as the Polish-Ukrainian War of 1918-1919 sent its government into exile after only eight months.

3. **Czechoslovakia (September, 1919–March, 1939).** Living ever on the mountainous frontiers of nations, the small population of Transcarpathia continued to be pushed and pulled by additional neighboring powers—Romania,

Hungary, and the newly formed state of Czechoslovakia— sometimes with guns, until an elected council chose to endorse a referendum formulated by expat Transcarpathian leaders living in the United States to become an autonomous region within Czechoslovakia (May 1919). The move became official when it was endorsed internationally on September 10, 1919 in the Treaty of St. Germain (one of the treaties of the Paris Peace Conference ending World War I), which also provided the first international recognition of the East Slavic people living in the Carpathians as a distinct nationality known as "Rusyn" by themselves (actually, by the common folk) and "Ruthenian" by others (and their own intelligentsia) (see Appendix E).

Czechoslovakia assigned to the new province the historical term that had been used by Hungary and Austria to refer to all the lands inhibited by East Slavic people that from their southwestern point of view lie "under" the Carpathian divide: Subcarpathian Rus' (sometimes shortened to "Subcarpathia"). In addition to Transcarpathia, these lands also included the Prešov Region of today's eastern Slovakia. (Interestingly, the governor of Subcarpathian Rus' from April 1920 until April 1921 was a Pennsylvanian lawyer named Gregory Zhatkovych—the only American citizen to ever govern what would become a province of the Soviet Union.)

The autonomy promised by the Treaty of St. Germain was never quite realized to the satisfaction of many Rusyns, however, and when Hitler began carving up Czechoslovakia in the late 1930s, and with Germany threatening on one side and its ally Hungary on the other, Prague had no choice but to accept Rusyn (as well as Slovak) demands for more autonomy. Thus, on October 11, 1938, with the acquiescence of the Nazis, Subcarpathian Rus' received (on paper) self-governing status within Czechoslovakia: the Subcarpathian Autonomous Region. It established a militia called the Carpathian Sich[331], and, signifying its cultural link with its neighbor east of the divide, it subsequently changed its name to Carpatho-Ukraine.

But such small fry in the turbulent waters of Central

Europe during the late 1930s stood no chance. In yet another move to undo the treaties of the Paris Peace Conference, Germany and Italy "arbitrated" agreements to return more territory to Hungary, including, in the First Vienna Award (November 2, 1938), the southern portion of Carpatho-Ukraine: that is, the lowland region of Transcarpathia southwest of the Carpathian foothills down to the Tisza valley (the land of the *Dolyniane* Rusyns). This transfer included the province's capital and two largest cities, Uzhgorod and Mukacheve (as well as most of the railway depots connecting the province to the rest of Czechoslovakia), so the Carpatho-Ukraine government was forced to move to Khust. The Czechoslovak parliament, meanwhile (November 22, 1938), in a last ditch effort to save the country, modified the constitution to federalize its Czech, Slovak, and Carpatho-Ukraine components (politically independent except for a common president, foreign relations, and monetary system).

4. **Republic of Carpatho-Ukraine (March 15, 1939– March 17, 1939).** For his future plans, Hitler wanted loyal allies along Poland's southern (and Carpathian) border. That would be, at least for a while, nations or peoples whose nationalistic ambitions he could stroke, such as long disadvantaged Slovakians, Ukrainians, and Rusyns. Thus, on March 14, at Germany's insistence and with promises of support, Slovakia declared its independence. On March 15, Germany seized Bohemia and Moravia. In a desperate and symbolic act, on March 15, 1939 the diet of the Autonomous Region of Carpatho-Ukraine proclaimed itself an independent Republic. (This spark in the Carpathians was to last only two days, but it lit a flame of independence in the hearts of not only Carpatho-Rusyns but of Ukrainians in general that burned for the rest of the century.)

5. **Hungary (March, 1939–June, 1945).** The Kingdom of Hungary, again with German approval, invaded its former frontier mountain province immediately. By March 17th, the Hungarian army had mopped up the Carpathian Sich and sent the government of Carpatho-Ukraine packing (to Romania). Transcarpathia was once again a part of

Hungary.

6. **Ukrainian Soviet Socialist Republic (June, 1945–December, 1991).** After the Red Army liberated Transcarpathia from Axis domination, Stalin reneged on agreements made during the war to make Subcarpathia (Transcarpathia and the Prešov Region) part of a restored Czechoslovakia and dictated that Czechoslovakia cede Transcarpathia to the USSR. This made Transcarpathia into a province (oblast) within the Ukrainian Soviet Socialist Republic, transliterated as *Zakarpattia*. Although some Transcarpathians welcomed the closer link with their Ukrainian kinsfolk, the Prešov region was not included (nor, of course, was the Lemko region north of the Carpathian divide in Galicia and Poland), so the Carpathian Rusyns were split once again. The Soviets strove to erase any distinctions between Transcarpathian Rusyns and their East Slavic neighbors the Ukrainians or Russians, via forced deportations, deceitfully encouraged migrations, banning of the Greek Catholic Church, and the teaching of only Ukrainian or Russian in the schools. (In the mountains to the west, in the Prešov Region of Czechoslovakia south of the divide and Lemko Land in Poland north of the divide, the Soviet proxy governments took similar actions to either assimilate Carpathian Rusyns or send them east.)

7. **Ukraine (December, 1991–present).** When the Soviet Union crashed in 1991, 93% of Transcarpathian voters approved the December, 1991 referendum for Ukrainian independence, and Transcarpathia became a province within an independent Ukraine: the *Zakarpattia* Oblast.

APPENDIX E:

An Ethnography of the Carpatho-Rusyns

The term.

The term "Rusyn" derives from *Rus'* (pronounced "roosh"), the Viking name that eventually referred to the entire, mostly East-Slavic populace of the state of Kievan Rus', which formed during the tenth century A.D. This state was called "Ruthenia" in Romance languages, and so the people living in it were called "Ruthenians" by most outsiders in Europe, as well as, eventually, by those Ruthenians wanting to be seen as "European"—that is, their own intelligentsia.

Kievan Rus' was vast—the largest state in Europe at the time—so there was regional variation from the beginning, and as the descendants of Kievan Rus' diverged further into three main groups known as "Russian," "Belarusian," and "Ukrainian," the terms "Rusyn" and "Ruthenian" were gradually dropped until they applied only to the East Slavic peoples living in and just beyond (from the point of view of Kyiv) the remote Carpathian Mountains.

It happened like this (roughly):

"Russian": After the fall of Kievan Rus' to the Mongols in the thirteenth century, Ruthenian power shifted to the northern Grand Duchy of Muscovy. Being Orthodox, the early Muscovites took their name from the Greek transcription of *Rus'* and thus early on became *russkii* ("Russians" in English).

"Belarusian": There are various theories regarding the origin of "white" implied in "Belarus" (literally, "White Russia"), but the term was commonly used by the seventeenth century to refer to the northwestern part of the Kievan Rus' state that avoided Mongol control.

"Ukrainian": "Rusyn" and "Ruthenian" held on longer in the territory of today's Ukraine—the original center of Kievan Rus'—most of which came under the control of western powers by the sixteenth century: The Poland-Lithuania Commonwealth (most of Ukraine) and the Kingdom of Hungary (the Carpathian region, most often that part south and west of the divide—also called Subcarpathia).

Beginning with the Truce of Andrusovo between Poland and Russia in 1667 and finishing with the partition of Poland (in three stages) between Russia, Prussia, and Austria near the end of the eighteenth century, all but far western Ukraine was taken by the Russian Empire. The Russian imperial authorities and bureaucrats considered this region to be a restored part of Russia, which they called "Little Russia," and the people living there, "Little Russians". This might be considered a put down, and such it became for some, but the initial meaning came from the fact that of the two main descendent states of Kievan Rus', Galicia-Volhynia in today's western Ukraine and Moscovy in the northeast, the former was the smaller. In fact, the qualifier "little" could have been taken as a compliment, referring to the original, central, non-colonial area of Kievan Rus', as opposed to the "greater" area that also included Moscow (as in "Denver" versus "the greater Denver area").

In any case, by the late nineteenth century most of the people living in "Little Russia," at least most of the elite (nationalist conceptions being primarily elite phenomena, not much the concern of people struggling in the fields), considered themselves as something other than "Russian", and the label of "little" had become perceived as pejorative. So they adopted the label "Ukrainian," using another ancient label for their homeland, referring to the "borderlands" around the city of Kyiv. (Ironic that "borderlands" could also be associated with something like "marginal"—i.e., something the opposite of central and even something like "little." But "borderlands" can also imply "independent," or "wild," and this indeed is the meaning most Ukrainians wanted to take, an inheritance from their Cossack heritage.)

Meanwhile the partition of Poland sent far western Ukraine,

including Transcarpathia and western Galicia, to the Austro-Hungarian Empire rather than the Russian Empire, so there the terms "Rusyn" and "Ruthenian" hung on, referring to the East-Slavic peoples living in the eastern extremes of the realm. "Ukrainian" nevertheless crept westward, and by the time Austria-Hungary was disintegrated at the end of World War I, it had supplanted "Rusyn" everywhere except in the remote mountain villages of the Carpathians and the small sliver of lowland down to the Tisza where isolated East Slavic-speaking peoples still lived.

During the nineteenth and early twentieth centuries, "Rusyn" as a distinct national identity was sometimes discouraged and sometimes encouraged by the powers that politically dominated the northeastern Carpathian region, depending on whether they viewed it as an aid or a hindrance to controlling and assimilating the population. Austro-Hungary, due to increasing strife with Russia, banned the use of "Rusyn" in official business, considering it a seditious term used by their restless and rebellious East-Slavic subjects to psychologically, spiritually, and culturally align themselves with their East-Slavic neighbor, competitor, and enemy, Russia. This was consistent with established Hungarian policies forbidding the use of the Rusyn language in official business, schools, and publications. They preferred Rusyns consider themselves, if not loyal Austrians or Hungarians, then at least Ukrainian. Under Hungarian and Czechoslovakian rule later in the twentieth century, however, "Rusyn" identification was encouraged as a tool for psychologically splitting the "tiny separate" Carpathian people from both their larger East-Slavic Ukrainian and Russian cousins. "Russian" identification was sometimes encouraged (better the more distant Russian threat than the nearby Ukrainian), and at still other times, Russian and Ukrainian identification were encouraged simultaneously as a strategy of division.

Thus, as political struggles for the hearts and minds (and land and homes, in the case of forced deportations and tricked migrations) of the irrepressibly independent Transcarpathian highlanders continued during the twentieth century, so did the controversy about whether they should be viewed, or should view themselves as, primarily "Rusyn," "Ukrainian," or "Russian" (i.e., loyal members of the larger East Slavic family). (And a parallel controversy went on for their kinsfolk west of the Ukrainian border: "Rusyn," "Lemko," "Rusnak," "Slovakian," or, north of the divide, "Polish"?) It continued: When the Soviets took control of Transcarpathia after World War II, they banned the term "Rusyn," towards the more manageable goal of making the comrades all be Ukrainians. And when the Soviet Union collapsed, Rusyn identity revived.

Today the terms "Rusyn" and "Ruthenian" usually apply exclusively to the mountain peoples of the northeastern Carpathians—the Hutsuls, Boykos, and Lemkos—and the Dolyniane lowlanders of East Slavic heritage just "beyond," as well as pockets of their diaspora located in other areas of Central Europe (including the Czech Republic, Serbia, Croatia, and Hungary), the United States, and Canada. "Carpatho-Rusyn" or "Carpatho-Ruthenian" is used when clarification between this modern usage and the formerly more general usage is desired.

In fact the exonym "Ruthenian" has become the official designation of this national minority within European countries containing significant populations (see below). According to Magocsi, today there may be as many as one million people in Europe and several hundred thousand in the Western Hemisphere with Carpatho-Rusyn heritage. Like many stateless minorities, however, many are either reluctant to identify as such, consider it a private matter, or no longer consider themselves a separate ethnicity (Magocsi 2006). Younger people especially tend to identify with their larger national group (Ukrainian, Slovak, or Polish), although a recent revival is going on (see below).

The language.

Some linguists define the Rusyn vernacular spoken in the Carpathian region today as a distinct language with regional dialects (also called Ruthenian or Ruthene), and some define it as a set of dialects of the Ukrainian language; each interpretation carries with it controversial implications as to where the Rusyns belong historically and politically: i.e., whether they should be considered a people distinct from Ukrainians. As with Ukrainian, there was a struggle for Rusyn to be considered something more than an informal peasant tongue (or collection of tongues), with the additional twist of being something distinct from Ukrainian and the role of Taras Shevchenko being played by the Rusyn "national poet," Alexander Dukhnovych (1803-1865).

In any case, Rusyn is recognizably an East-Slavic language closely related to Ukrainian, although it features an east/west division. In Eastern Rusyn dialects (i.e., Hutsul and Boyko), the syllable of words receiving the accent varies (like all the other East Slavic languages), and most borrowed words are from the neighboring languages of

Hungarian or Romanian; in Western Rusyn dialects (i.e., Lemko/ Rusnak), the penultimate syllable almost always receives the stress, as in Polish, and more words are borrowed from Polish and Slovakian in addition to Hungarian.

Polianskii (Best, et.al 2012) claims that the Rusyn dialects are closer to the earliest language of the Slavs (which may be explained by their possible proximity to the original Slavic homeland and their mountainous isolation from external influence) and are therefore the most universally understandable modern Slavic dialects.

The land.

With the caveat that what is meant by the term "Carpathian Ruthenia" has varied and its full extent is not and has never been a geopolitically precise region with definite borders (although some of its boundaries as defined by ethnologists do or have corresponded to political boundaries), the region to which the term may currently be applied is a roughly oval shaped territory following the arc of the Carpathian Mountains, with the long axis spanning some 375 kilometers in a southeast to northwest direction, from the Prislop Pass in Romania at its southeastern end to the eastern edge of the High Tatra Range in the northwest. In terms of today's national borders (with other historical political or traditional associations in parentheses), it includes northern Romania (Maramureș and parts of Bukovina), southwestern Ukraine (Transcarpathia and Maramureș south of the Carpathian divide and parts of Galicia and Bukovina north of the divide), northeastern Slovakia (the Prešov Region), and southeastern Poland (part of Galicia, also traditionally called "Lemko Land"—*Lemkivshchyna* in Ukrainian, *Łemkowszczyzna* in Polish, *Lemkovyna* in Lemko).

The southeastern two-thirds of Carpathian Ruthenia (i.e., that part which lies east of the western Ukraine border, roughly) is bounded by the high Carpathian divide on its northeastern edge and roughly by the upper Tisza River and its Iza River tributary along its southwestern edge, and thus is generally considered to include only the southern slopes of the Carpathians. Since at least the eighteenth century, it has been the home of Hutsuls (in the southeastern portion) and Boykos (in the northwestern portion), although populations of both also live or have lived on the northern slopes in today's Ivano-Frankivs'k and L'viv oblasts of Ukraine. To the west of the Ukrainian border, where the Carpathian divide is lower and crossing easier, Carpathian Ruthenia spills across the divide to include both the northern and southern slopes of the Carpathians, and this is the land of the Lemkos (who are often called *Rusnaks* in Slovakia). (Note that Carpathian ethnic borders are fuzzy and fluid, and one can find references to Lemkos living in far western Ukraine—especially after deportations following World War II—and to Boykos living in northeastern Slovakia.)

That part of Carpathian Ruthenia that is south of the Carpathian divide—Maramureş, Transcarpathia, and the Prešov Region—was long a part of the Kingdom of Hungary and from that side of the mountains was traditionally called *Subcarpathian Rus'* (the Land of the Rus' Under the Carpathians") or just "Subcarpathia". (The political province of Subcarpathian Rus' within Czechoslovakia during the early twentieth century corresponded only to Transcarpathia, however.) The lowland areas lying between the foothills and Tisza, including the tributary river valleys beginning with the Teresva and continuing downstream (which also corresponds to the far northeastern corner of the Great Hungarian Plain), is the traditional home of the Dolyniane Rusyns, who probably began to be separated from their East Slavic relatives the other side of the mountains as early as the ninth century.

Carpatho-Rusyns could also be found living beyond the fringes of these fuzzy borders, where ethnic majorities were found on a village-by-village basis, especially before the upheavals of World War II and the forced deportations that followed. Some of these villages contained a majority of Rusyns, while others contained mostly the neighboring ethnic majority: Romanian, Hungarian, Slovak, or Polish. There were also a few villages with a majority of Germans, most of whom were invited and given special privileges to work in mines and forests by a German landlord during the period of Austrian Habsburg rule during the latter half of the eighteenth century. Most villages throughout these northeastern Carpathians also contained small minorities of Czechs, Russians, Bulgarians, and—before the war and it holocausts—Jews, and a few Roma mostly living on the outskirts.

The last available census of Transcarpathia before the war (1930) lists 451,000 Ukrainians and Rusyns (62%); 116,000 Hungarians (16%); 95,000 Jews (13%); 35,000 "Czechs and Slovaks" (5%); 14,000 Germans (2%); and 13,000 Romanians (2%).

The most recent Ukrainian census (2001) lists 1,000,000 Ukrainians (81%); 151,500 Hungarians (12%); 32,000 Romanians (2.6%); 31,000 Russians (2.5%); 14,000 Roma (1%); 10,000 Rusyns (1%); 5,600 Slovaks (0.5%); and 3,500 Germans (0.3%). Note that today, most Ukrainian citizens of Rusyn heritage are likely to self-identify as Ukrainian.

A few majority Rusyn villages were (and still are) found even further from the core area of Carpathian Ruthenia, for example in northeastern Hungary and Serbia, where many Rusyns immigrated during the eighteenth century. Today, as a result of historical emigration both forced and voluntary, about three-quarters of the people who may be considered Rusyn living in the Carpathian region are found in Transcarpathia.

Needless to say, this is a complicated array of names for the Land of the Carpatho-Rusyns and its various parts, each label providing historical connotations related to which state the people found themselves, or saw themselves, or others saw them as belonging to: Kievan Rus', Galicia, Hungary, Transylvania, Poland, Austria, Czechoslovakia, Slovakia, Romania, Ukraine, and, very briefly, and never as a whole, their own autonomous or independent nations.

The dispersal.

Today not all Rusyns live in the Carpathians. The turmoils of the nineteenth and twentieth centuries tossed them far and wide, including hundreds of thousands to the Americas and Australia. These days, Rusyns are joining in a revival of ethnic identification, and the countries of Poland, Slovakia, Romania, Hungary, the Czech Republic, Serbia, and Croatia all formally recognize Rusyn as a national minority (using the designation "Ruthenian"). In Romania, one seat in the Chamber of Deputies is reserved for an ethnic Carpathian Rusyn.

Politics.

The political sympathies of Carpatho-Rusyns have long been split between Hungarian, Slovakian (or Czechoslovakian), Russian, Ukrainian, and independent orientations, with varying degrees of passion. Most recently, Ukrainian, Russian, and autonomous trends have dominated. Some highlights:

- Although 93% of Transcarpathian voters approved the December, 1991 referendum for Ukrainian independence, 78% also approved a simultaneous referendum to have a special status as a self-governing administrative district. This proposal for a semi-autonomous Transcarpathia, an opportunity for Subcarpathian Rusyn mountainfolk to finally be considered their own nation or people (*narod*), rather than Hungarian, Czechoslovakian, Slovakian, Russian, or Ukrainian as they had been historically by controlling powers, was not accepted by the Ukrainian government.

- In May of 1993, some Rusyn patriots set up "a Provisional Government of Sub-Carpathian Ruthenia, appealed for Russian support, and declared their intention to join the Commonwealth of Independent States independently of Ukraine." (Batt and Wolczuk 2002.)

- Ironically, Ukraine, where the majority of Rusyns live, in response to the ambitions of independent-minded, politically active Carpathian highlanders, and perhaps justifiably paranoid about the country's territorial integrity, especially given the recent conflict with their powerful neighbor to the east, has not designated *Rusyn* as a national minority, thus far preferring that Rusyns consider themselves Ukrainian. On March 7, 2007, however, the Zakarpattia Oblast Council "officially recognized the Rusyn people as an indigenous nationality of the region" [332].

- The current dispute between Ukraine and Russia (2013–) has raised concerns among some of the minorities in ethnically diverse Transcarpathia, including some Rusyns and Hungarians, that the Ukraine government, in their zeal to maintain Ukraine's national integrity and to preempt Russian-inspired agitation, might step on their rights. Thus there have been new calls for Transcarpathian autonomy, and even a call among Hungarian activists to return Transcarpathia to Hungary[333].

- In April, 2014, The World Academy of Rusyn Culture in North America joined in an appeal to the Ukrainian Parliament to restore a minority language law that was hastily repealed by the new government in Kyiv after the Maidan uprising and the fleeing of Yanukovych (Carpatho-Rusyn Society, 2014). The law was restored.

APPENDIX F:

The Slavic Homeland:
In the Shadow of the Carpathians?

Since there are no written records, the very early history of the Slavic people is shrouded by uncertainties and controversies. Theories regarding the location of the original Slavic homeland are influenced by psychology and politics, as evidenced by a strong correlation between locations proposed and the locations of the proposers, and a tendency for modern political states, many with tenuous histories, to lay claim to the original Slavic homeland in order to (as they see it) enhance their prestige and legitimacy.

Nevertheless, based on archeological and linguistic evidence—such as the current distribution of languages, place names, and the local names of flora, fauna, and geographic features such as rivers—the most widely accepted theories posit that the Slavs arose as an identifiable ethno-linguistic-culture somewhere in the forests just north of the Carpathian Mountains and east of the Vistula River, by *at least* the fourth century A.D. (Proto-Baltic-Slavic roots may date as far back as the third millennium B.C., with Slavic-Baltic divergence beginning perhaps as early as the second millennium B.C.—see endnote 177.)

The earliest written references to people living in this region, written by Greek and Roman historians during the first century and second centuries A.D., refer to them as *Venedi*. These historians include Strabo, Pliny, Tacitus, and Ptolemy. All but Strabo located the Venedi on the northern side of the Carpathians, to the east of the Germanic tribes, roughly between the Elbe and Vistula Rivers and between the German and Sarmatian peoples (and north and west of Dacia). Tacitus (in *The Germania*, written around 98 A.D.) placed them east of the Vistula between the Fenni (Finns) to the north and the Carpathians in the south, and he described their land, or at least the land they plundered over, as "wooded and mountainous," which would seem to imply the Carpathian Mountains themselves.

Whether the Venedi at that time were Slavic cannot be determined from what the earliest writers had to say. Tacitus classified them as Germanic based on the fact that they lived in permanent houses, carried shields, and got about mostly on foot—as opposed to the horse-bound nomadic "Sarmatians" further east—but he knew nothing about what language they spoke. *Venedi* was probably an exonym, and whether Slavic or not, by the time the Slavs and their language were established north of the Carpathians, they had inherited *Venedi* as a general label, at least by the early Romans. In western regions adjacent to the Germanic tribes, *Venedi* evolved into *Wends*, a term that held on into the Middle Ages in the area of today's Poland. In the east, later Byzantine writers such as Jordanes (sixth century A.D.) believed that the Antes and Scalveni were types of Venedi, all descended from "a common stock" (Jordanes, translated 1908); but the stubborn resistance of the Sclaveni may be why their name came to replace *Venedi* as a collective term for all Slavic tribes.

There are many proponents for a more specific Slavic homeland just to the north and/or east of the Eastern Outer Carpathians (perhaps the same area from where they started rapidly spreading at the end of the fifth century A.D.), including: (1) The pine-oak and deciduous forests and Pripet marshes of southern Belarus and northwest Ukraine (an area known as *Polissia*, also spelled *Polesia*). (2) The deciduous forests and forest-steppes of western Ukraine between the mountains and the upper Southern Bug River and/or the Black Sea (an area known as *Podolia*). (3) The forest-steppe zone between the Southern Bug and the Dnieper. (4) The forested foothills of the Carpathians Mountains.

Anthony proposes that the pre-Slavic language evolved between the upper Dniester and middle Dnieper Rivers as a dialect among those proto-Balto-Slavs who remained in this area, while the people who went on to speak Baltic continued migrating northwards (see endnote 177).

In any case, recent genetic evidence seems to confirm that people we may classify as Slavic first appeared in the area of modern Ukraine to the north and east of the Carpathians. It is interesting to note that this area also happens to correspond to that part of northeastern Europe where the foraging livelihoods supported by the colder north and east (i.e., hunting, gathering, and fishing) give way to the agricultural possibilities of the warmer south and west

Other candidates for a Slavic homeland include areas in Poland, Bohemia, north-central Ukraine, the northwest Balkans, and the lower Danubian Plain just southeast of the Carpathians (southern Moldavia and eastern Wallachia; see (Curta 2001)). The author(s) of the Russian Primary Chronicle claim the latter, but this may derive from a desire to give the Slavs a homeland closer to Biblical origins than the forests of Ukraine (the Chronicle also claims that the Slavs are descended from Japheth, son of Noah).

APPENDIX G:

The Founding, the Life, the Zenith, and the Decline of Kievan Rus'

The Founding.

The tale of how Kyiv came to be ruled by Viking princes is an engrossing mix of fact and legend. The story goes that sometime around 860 A.D., fractious Slavic and Finnic tribes living in the region south of Lake Ladoga had a case of remorse after having driven the Varangians, who had been imposing tribute on them, westward back to the sea. They couldn't seem to get along without their Scandinavian overlords, so they sent envoys westward across the Baltic to seek the return of proper princes. A Rus' chieftain by the name of Rurik[334] (also spelled Riurik) and his two younger brothers passed muster, accepted the invitation, and claimed their regal seats on the shores of three lakes: Rurik in the middle at Novgorod on Lake Ilmen; Truvor to the west at Izborsk on Lake Peipus; and Sineus to the east at Belozersk on Lake Beloye. When his two younger brothers somehow perished two years later, Rurik inherited it all and became the first exclusive ruler of the "Land of the Rus'."

Two years later, two Rus' nobles by the names of Askold and Dir (there are lots of "twos" in this story) set out down the Dnieper, heading for Constantinople to seek their fortunes. Upon reaching the bustling settlement of Kyiv—which, they were told, had been built in the distant past by three distinguished brothers (and a few "threes"), the eldest named Kiv, but not, we are told (by the chronicler), before the site had been specially sanctified in the even more distant past by Saint Andrew the Apostle—they noticed the city's ideal prospect on high banks overlooking what was surely destined to become a major trade route, and they decided to seize it for themselves. With what must have been a sizable military retinue, they also imposed tribute on the local Slavic tribal union, the Polianians ("People of the field"), and they traded with Constantinople—even raiding it once to establish their credentials[335]—and prospered.

But Askold and Dir were not of regal blood, and while Rurik had endorsed their journey, he hadn't sanctioned their conquering, so after the king's death, when Rurik's kinsmen and heir Oleg showed up at Kyiv on a tour of enforcement, he decided to put the renegades in their place. Finding Askold and Dir firmly entrenched behind the walls of the stronghold, Oleg hid his warriors[336] and regalia, besought the hospitality of one anonymous Varangian noble to another, and when they came out to comply, he slaughtered his would-be hosts.

Or so the story goes. No one was writing thereabouts at the time, and this colorful legend was first recorded about two and a half centuries years later in the "Russian Primary Chronicle" (RPC), the earliest known recorded history of the Rus', which was probably compiled by Christian monks in Kyiv sometime around the turn of the twelfth century[337]. Modern scholars doubt many of the specifics, and the tale may have evolved from an attempt to establish a line of descent from the semi-mythical Rurik[338] to promote not only a royal legitimacy, but also a valiant (or at least cunning) heritage and spirit of unity among feuding Rus' princes.

Whatever the details of his ascendency, Oleg steps out of legend and into historical fact in 882 as the first documented Varangian prince in charge of Kyiv. He moved the capital there from Novgorod, and if he did not actually liberate the city from upstart Rus' nobles, he did "liberate" it from paying tribute to the vast and powerful Khazar Khanate (based to the southeast along the Caspian Sea). In other words, the citizens of Kyiv had to pay *him* instead of *them*. Using his ever-growing conscripted army, Oleg went on to "liberate" local Slavic super-tribes as well: the Polianians already mentioned, the Derevlane ("People of the forest"), and the Severiane ("People of the north"), as well as two more distant tribes: the Radimichs to the north and the Ulichs to the southeast. He also eventually subdued the stubborn Tivercians to the southwest, who resisted fiercely from the shelter of Carpathian foothills.

Oleg even raided Constantinople to extract favorable terms of trade, but he died not long after (in 912 A.D.), when, according to the RPC, a poisonous snake slithered from the skull of his former horse and bit him. The legend says he came to the skeleton not to mourn a loyal steed, but to scoff at prophesy: He had long since banished the horse to pasture, to prevent the prediction of a soothsayer that his horse would be his bane.

Though tainted by the political and religious agendas of its authors, the RPC presents fascinating accounts of war, law, politics, love, religion, and life near the end of the first millennium in northeastern Europe. The authors express wonderment at the rituals of Scandinavian saunas (wonderment which they deflect to Saint Andrew in a legendary report after his legendary tour of the land of the Rus'); indignation at Avars so mean they force their female conquered to pull their carts like horses; pride at the resourcefulness of Rus' raiders who launch an amphibious attack on Constantinople from boats sailed across its landed approaches on wheels; and delight at the beauty, brilliance, deviousness, ruthlessness, and the prescient though private conversion of that rarest of medieval rulers: a woman: Olga, daughter-in law of Rurik.

The RPC also lays out the quite reasonable and thorough content of treaties between the Rus' and the Greeks[339]; matter-of-factly describes child sacrifices to "the gods" (Perun and Volos are implied—see below)[340]; offers moral advice; warns against witchcraft; and—presaging Székler cakes to come—describes a Pecheneg siege ended by a sight allowed to besieging envoys: porridge brewing in two large pits, along with the incredible tale that the very earth will feed the city forever; when in fact, the gruel was made from the starving town's final supply of grain and honey.

The Life.

As in all medieval societies, daily life in Kievan Rus' depended on one's legally sanctioned social class, or "estate." There were the princes, of course, and the princes' families, court, and appointees (judicial, administrative, and military)—the ruling elite. There were the nobles (known as *boyars* in Eastern Europe), the urban patricians (the mostly middle class "burghers," consisting of merchants, shopkeepers, and skilled craftsmen), the clerics and people under the protection of the church, the peasants, the indentured laborers, and the slaves. There were also the soldiers, taken from the ranks of the nobles, who served in the militias of princes and towns, and who could move socially upward with cash or land rewards for exemplary military service.

With dynastic candidates constantly vying for towns, and with princes and nobles more focused on the wealth and power offered by commerce than that provided by plows, and with a large and prosperous urban merchant class, the social structure of Kievan Rus' was more fluid than the feudal systems of the west. Boyars were generally not vassals to the princes (they could, for example, more or less freely change their allegiances); the wealthiest burghers could hobnob socially, politically, and matrimonially with the boyars; peasants, though forced to pay tribute of goods and labor, could own land and move about[341]; and slaves could purchase their freedom[342].

The boyars wielded political power in the form of the *duma*, a council that advised the princes; and the burgers likewise had the *viche*, an assembly of all the free male residents of a town, perhaps predating the institution of prince, which could not legislate but could freely express opinions about princely policies and actions such as wars, treaties, and appointments. With a practical power backed by most of the populace as well as wealth and militias, *vichi* would choose between vying princes, swear them to the bounds of traditional authority, and instigate armed revolts—a tradition continuing in Ukraine in 2013 and 2014.

Most non-peasants lived in the urban centers, in one of the three hundred or so strongholds, towns, and cities that existed at the peak of the polity's expanse. Kyiv was by far the largest, with somewhere between 35,000 and 50,000 residents at the time of the Mongol invasion (larger than London at the time); the city recognized as many as sixty guilds, including carpenters, masons, smiths, glaziers, goldsmiths, jewelers, potters, armorers, leather workers, and painters. Smaller cities such as Chernihiv, Pereiaslav, Volodymyr-in-Volhyni, Halych, and L'viv, each housed a few thousand people.

But by far the majority of the people of Kievan Rus'—about 86 percent—were the peasants who lived in the countryside. Known as *smerdy* ("stinky ones"), they worked plots of wheat, millet, oats, rye, hemp, barley, and flax, and gardens of peas, garlic, cabbage, and turnips. They also raised cattle, pigs, sheep, goats, horses, geese, chickens, and pigeons for milk, eggs, work, and meat; they kept bees for wax and honey; they foraged the forests for berries, nuts, mushrooms, and furs; and they cruised the rivers and lakes for fish. They organized into communes known as *verve* to share resources, work, and results, and they adopted new technologies from the west such as iron-shod plowshares and crop rotation to improve productivity.

In the early days, peasants could own land and pass it onto their sons, but as time went by they were forced to yield more and more to the boyars until most became enserfed (excepting those living in the Carpathians). And though emancipated in the nineteenth century—living in small log huts, wearing homemade woolens, linens, and furs, scraping an existence from the land—the lifestyle of most Rus' peasants, especially those living in hinterlands like the Carpathians, didn't much change right up to the twentieth century.

The Zenith.

Kievan Rus' reached its peak with the rule of Volodymyr's son, Iaroslav (or "Yaroslav") the Wise (978–1054), who, after violent struggles amongst his many princely siblings, and fortified with the Slavonic liturgy as well as military might, expanded the realm from the Baltic Sea in the north to the Black Sea in the south, and from the Oka River in the east to the Carpathians in the west: some 990,000 square kilometers and holding something between three and twelve million subjects.

Iaroslav conquered Balts and Finns in the north, repelled Polish competitors in the west, and finally subdued the Pechenegs in the east. He also built or improved a multitude of churches (most notably, the magnificent, marble-built Holy Sophia Cathedral in Kyiv, which stands to this day[343]); systematized and codified the traditional oral laws of the land into a relatively liberal and humane legal code[344]; and promoted literature and literacy.

By the time of Iaroslav's reign (1019), the ruling elite of Kievan Rus' had come a long way from their original warrior-merchant roots, as exemplified not only by their evolving political and social policies but also by their acceptance into the matrimonial machinations of dynastic Europe: Iaroslav married a Swedish princess, his sister married the King of Poland, another sister wedded a Byzantine prince, and three of his daughters married the kings of France, Norway, and Hungary.

The Decline.

After Iaroslav things went downhill for Kievan Rus'. The huge territory proved difficult for one centralized authority to administer, and fratricidal wars among children of Rurik princes—continually infused with the foreign blood of Vikings, Poles, and nomads (the Cumans had by now replaced the Pechenegs), and with the consequent compromises, partitions, treacheries, and usurpations—gradually splintered the ruling dynasty[345]. Citizens were treated like disposable pawns in a bloody game of chess. One particularly contentious prince, a great grandson of Volodymyr—Prince Vseslav of Polotsk, also known as Vseslav the Sorcerer—was even believed to be a werewolf.[346] The decline was economic also, as the value of the Dnieper trade route depreciated from banditry, Mediterranean competition, and the decline of the Byzantine Empire.

And then came the Mongols.

ABOUT THE AUTHOR

Alan E. Sparks is the award-winning author of *Dreaming of Wolves* and *Into the Carpathians*, and has written articles about wolves for *International Wolf Magazine* and other publications. He has bachelor and master's degrees in physics and engineering from the University of Maine and Stanford University, and worked for over twenty years developing advance technologies for one of the world's leading research and development organizations, Bell Telephone Laboratories. A voracious reader and student of the natural and cultural histories of the places he visits, he has supplemented his indoor studies with training in mountaineering from the Colorado Mountain Club, mountain ski touring/expedition leadership from the National Outdoor Leadership School, and winter ecology/animal tracking from renowned animal tracker Dr. James Halfpenny of A Naturalist's World. As a teacher of English as a second language, commercial actor, and web designer – and as an avid walker, hiker, backcountry skier, and animal tracker – he has lived, worked, and trekked extensively in the Carpathian Mountain region of Central and Eastern Europe.

ACKNOWLEDGEMENTS

I would like to thank:

The Way of the Wolf core team—Peter Sürth, Jürgen Sauer, and Thilo Brunner (with more to come in Part 2)—for making possible and unforgettable this exploration of the Carpathian Mountains.

Our guides and interpreters: Ana, Cata, and Maria for their wonderful support and friendship.

The eco-volunteers—Markus, Sandra, Klaus, Mathias, Göran, Suzann, Stephan, and Kathrin (with more to come in Part 2)—for their pleasant company and friendship, temporary though it had to be.

The many Carpathian highlanders who offered welcoming and generous hospitality.

The many people in the Carpathian Mountain countries who provided firsthand knowledge about the history and culture of the region, especially Maria Moldavchuk, Sirhy Adamenko, Oleksandra Miniailo, Bartosz Sokołowski, and Simona Buretea.

Jürgen Sauer, Thilo Brunner, Kathrin Merkel, Maria Moldavchuk, and Horia Dinca for supplying or finding photos.

Elizabeth Zach for her encouragement and perceptive editing at an early stage.

Laura Sparks for creating the map of the Carpathians.

The designers and editors at Köehler Books Publishing: John Koehler, Joe Coccaro, and Doug Pilley, for their invaluable contributions in producing a book both beautiful and readable.

NOTES

ROMANIA

1   The route of The Way of the Wolf expedition in 2005 did not include most of the Southern Carpathians. Peter would walk them on a later expedition.

2   Such was the approximate population of Zarneşti in 2005. By 2011, the population had dropped to about 22,000.

3   Braşov (pronounced "Brashov") is a city of around 228,000 residents (about 336,000 in the metropolitan area) located about thirty kilometers northeast of Zarneşti in southeastern Transylvania. It is the seat of Braşov County.

4   (Sparks 2010, 46).

5   The mostly ethnic German migrants came from throughout the Holy Roman Empire during the twelfth and thirteenth centuries, but the term "Saxon" was eventually used to refer to them collectively. The Transylvania Saxons were given provisional autonomy by King Andrew II of Hungary in 1224, which lasted until 1876.

6   The "seven fortified Saxon cities" in Transylvania are Bistriţa, Braşov, Mediaş, Reghin, Sebeş, Sibiu, and Sighisoara.

7   The defense of Transylvania by the Saxons was not without setbacks. For example, many of their cities were ravaged in the 1280s by a Mongol horde under Nogai Khan.

8   In the census of 1930, about 745,000 Romanian citizens identified themselves as ethnic Germans; in 1977 about 359,000 did so, and by 2011 only about 36,000. About 15,000 were killed or captured during World War II, about 100,000 fled the Soviet Red Army near the end of the war, and about 70,000 were deported to the gulag by the Soviets after the war. More than 100,000

emigrated to Germany between the end of the war and the end of Communist rule in 1989; during the 1980s, Ceauşescu's cash-strapped government charged Germany 10,000 marks for each emigrant. It has been reported that some half million people of German heritage left Romania immediately after the fall of Ceauşescu in 1989 (Jenkins 2009), although this seems to contradict the census figure of 359,000 in 1977.

[9]   The lowest levels of governmental administration in Romania are cities (*municipiu*), towns (*oraşe*), and communes (*comune*), all of which correspond to "local administrative units" (LAU) of the European Union, and all of which have a mayor. Communes are the rural version of towns and consist of a collection of villages (which do not have their own government). There are 2861 communes in the country; most have populations under 10,000.

[10]   Szekely Land lies along the western slopes of the Eastern Carpathian Mountains of eastern Transylvania and includes the Romanian counties of Harghita, Covasna, and parts of Mureş; it is home to around 600,000 Széklers, part of a total population of about 1.2 million ethnic Hungarians living in Romania today (2011 Census).

[11]   The Scythians were a diverse but probably mostly Iranian-speaking pastoral people who made it to the eastern fringes of the Carpathians probably by around 600 B.C. The term "Scythian" became more broadly applied by ancient Greek and later historians until it referred to all peoples living to the north and east of the Black Sea. Graeco-Roman geographers of the classical age used the term "Scythian" as a more generic term to refer to all the varied "barbarian" peoples living to the north and east of the Danube and the Black Sea, from the Vistula River and Carpathians in the west to the Volga River and the Caucasus Mountains in the east.

[12]   The Sarmatians were an Iranian-speaking people who made it into the region just east of the Carpathians by the fifth century B.C. They consisted of tribes such as the Iazygi, Roxolani, and later, the Alans.

[13]   The Avars were probably originally a Turkic group of peoples who became multiethnic as they invaded westward (including, for example, Bulgars and Sabirs), and who eventually adopted the language of the more populous Slavs, among whom they settled in the Carpathian Basin beginning around the mid-sixth century A.D.

[14]   Varied tribes of Bulgars were often forced into being allies, perhaps of Huns and certainly of Avars. They eventually formed an empire of their own (the First Bulgarian Empire) wedged between the Byzantine Empire and the Avar Khaganate, which eventually expanded into Pannonia and Transylvania as it pushed the Avars out of the way, with help from Franks and Slavs.

[15]   The Magyars were a Finno-Ugric people originating in the Urals region of Russia who conquered the Pannonian/Carpathian Plain during the ninth and tenth centuries A.D. They were called "Hungarians" by outsiders.

[16]   The Pechenegs were a Turkic-speaking people who made it to the Carpathians by around the tenth century A.D.

[17] The Cumans were a Turkic-speaking people, closely allied with another tribe called the Kipchak, who forced the Pechenegs from the Carpathian foothills by around the eleventh century A.D. Their label in contemporary German, Hungarian, and Slavic languages meant "blond," which is especially interesting since they are believed to have originated as far east as China.

[18] The term "Tartar" was used in Europe to refer generically to invaders from the east since the time of the Mongols. It was used variously to refer to the Mongols themselves, or more specifically to descendants of the Golden Horde (western branch) of the Mongols who settled in various regions north and west of the Caucasus and who had political centers based in the Crimea and Kazan, or also specifically to descendants of Volga Bulgars (who were conquered by the Mongols).

"Tartar" was originally the name of one of the first tribes conquered by the aspiring young Mongol warrior Temujin, who eventually became the great Khan of the Mongols, Genghis, in the twelfth century A.D. Since the Tartars had been a greater tribe than the Mongols, and since, due to Temujin's relatively novel policy of absorbing rather than simply scattering or slaughtering the vast majority of his defeated enemies (the non-elites), many Tartars became part of his growing army; thus the term Tartar came to be applied to the Mongol–led confederacy. The term became generalized by Europeans to refer to invaders from just about anywhere east of the western shores of the Black Sea, be they Mongolian or Turkic, about which not much was known—certainly not their own tribal distinctions. Europeans also used the term "Tartary" to refer to the great Eurasian steppe itself.

[19] (Maenchen-Heflen 1973).

[20] According to a contemporary Roman soldier and writer, Ammianus Marcellinus, the Huns wore clothing made partly of linen and partly of the skins of "field mice" sewn together "until it falls to pieces." (I can imagine the "skins of field mice sewn together" falling to pieces pretty quickly.) Actually, as reasonably suggested by Fermor (who cites archeological evidence from a 400 B.C site at Katanda in the Altai Mountains), the animals who yielded their skins to the Huns may have included steppe rodents at least a bit larger than field mice, such as jerboas. It seems likely that even larger mammals such as hares would have also been used.

[21] The Huns were reportedly so attached to their horses that they didn't bother to get down from them even when they were negotiating the complexities of treaties with defeated or undefeated opponents.

[22] The "Maeotic Marshes" is the name given by ancient Greco-Roman geographers to the marshes located where the Don River empties into the Sea of Azov, in today's southern Russia; they were a hindrance to many a western-moving nomadic tribe.

[23] The Huns first appeared north of the Black Sea by around 370 A.D., and vanguard bands started earning a living as mercenaries in the Roman Empire soon after. We don't know exactly where they came from. One

contemporary Roman source says they came from "the north," and others placed them northeast of the Black Sea by the second century A.D. Nor do we know how many they were, although they tended to pick up peoples on their way and were likely multi-ethnic by the time they dominated the Great Hungarian Plain. They had a propensity for raping and pillaging, certainly, and they would kill those warriors who resisted them, but they seemed to be not particularly motivated to ethnically cleanse. In fact, by the time Attila took over, the Gothic tongue—not the tongue of the original invading elite—had become the working language of the Hunnic Empire.

[24]   The Alans were a Sarmatian confederation with mysterious roots from somewhere around Persia, reportedly with a lot of tall, blond-haired and blue-eyed folks. They initially resisted the Huns, but then joined them, either by force or by choice or both.

[25]   As they were displaced by the Huns, the Goths first fought against the Roman Empire, and then many of them sought asylum within. A large contingent under the leadership of one Fritigern crossed the Danube in 376 A.D. when they were granted refuge by the Emperor Valens, but they soon revolted under the pressure of famine.

[26]   The Vandals seem to have been one of the most mobile peoples of ancient Europe. Most likely a Gothic-speaking people originally from Scandinavia, they made it into the area of today's Poland by the second century B.C., where they may have merged with a possibly Proto-Slavic people known as the Lugii. By the first century A.D. they had crossed the Carpathians and carved out a space between the Dacians to the east and the Quadi to the west, in the area of today's eastern Slovakia, northern Romania, and Transcarpathian Ukraine. From there the larger part of them continued southward and settled in Pannonia until the arrival of the Huns. Only about fifty years later, along with a contingent of Alans (who seem to be the quintessential allies of the classical era in Europe), the Vandals ended up clear on the other side of the Mediterranean in North Africa—not just the fighting men but their families and all their baggage as well—in what surely was one of the epic migrations in human history. They raided and plundered the length of Western Europe, through Gaul and the Iberian Peninsula before crossing the sea and continuing eastward on the other side—in the process bothering St. Augustine in Hippo Regius, in today's Algeria, where he died—and walking through the gates of a compliant Carthage about ten years after the crossing. From there they completed their epic circuit by raiding northern Mediterranean shores and eventually sacking Rome (455 A.D.).

[27]   Maenchen-Heflen believes the facial scarring of Hun warriors was more likely due to ritualized grieving for dying comrades than for the prevention of beards (Maenchen-Heflen 1973). The latter purpose was proposed by a Roman historian, Ammianus. The extent of artificial cranial deformation among Huns is uncertain.

[28]   In the complex world on the periphery of the Roman Empire, allegiance shifted with the wind, and every combination of alliance and hostility occurred at one time or another between subgroups of Huns, Alans, Goths, Gepids, Vandals, and other tribes on the frontier, as well as with the Romans themselves. Soldiers of fortune from all of these groups hired themselves out to the Roman army regardless of whom they might be engaged to fight. Some Roman armies at times were composed almost entirely of barbarian troops, often fighting barbarian foes. Being perhaps the most capable cavalry soldiers of the time, Hun soldiers could probably be found fighting on the Roman side anywhere in the vast realm, including against other Huns. They were valued for their fighting skills, but there are also reports of Hun auxiliary units in the Roman army being out of control, raiding and pillaging terrified Roman citizens and being more of a threat than the enemy they were supposed to be fighting.

[29]   Other rumors and theories regarding the cause of Attila's demise include: hemorrhaging as a result of too much alcohol; the knife-wielding action of his bride; and East Roman political assassination.

[30]   The modern historian Maenchen-Heflen dismisses Priscus's tale of Honoria and Attila as "Byzantine court gossip" not supported by other sources that were not simply copying Priscus (Maenchen-Heflen 1973, 130).

[31]   Priscus' original report has been lost and all we have is an excerpt copied by Jordanes.

[32]   Ardaric and his Gepid-led alliance decisively defeated the Huns at the Battle of Nedao on the Pannonian plain in 454 A.D.

[33]   During the Middle Ages the nobles of Transylvania, and in some cases the peasants, were assigned privileges, duties, and political representation in the Transylvania Diet according to their ethnic-religious-territorial affiliation. Each group had the status of an "estate" (called a "nation" at the time), and there were always at least three: (1) The upper nobility, consisting mostly of Hungarians and others who took on Hungarian ways; most of the Hungarian nobles eventually became Calvinist. (2) The Széklers, who were given military duties and whose estate privileges were eventually extended to include their non-noble class; most Széklers were Catholic. (3) The Saxons, who were mostly merchants and mostly Lutheran.

The "Vlachs," later called "Romanians," most of whom were Orthodox, were considered lower nobility, and sometimes they were given status as a fourth estate and sometimes not. Their original status began to erode after a royal edict in 1366 required all nobles to be Catholic and it was formerly erased in 1437 after a peasant revolt (most peasants at the time were Vlachs). In 1698, when Transylvania was under Habsburg rule, many rights were restored to Vlach nobles willing to convert to the new "Romanian Church United with Rome, Greek-Catholic" (also called *Uniat*); in 1791 the Transylvanian Diet rejected a petition for Vlachs to be restored as a "fourth nation." The separate estate/nations of Transylvania were dissolved in 1849 when Austria gained control and the Vlachs received full citizenship.

Other groups were also sometimes granted special charters in Transylvania, such as the Teutonic Knights very briefly during the thirteenth century, and a few Armenian settlements that were given special trading privileges.

Regardless of the status of nobles, at any given time most of the populace (usually around 95%), especially of Vlachs, consisted of peasants, shepherds, and serfs belonging to no estate and without special privileges.

[34]   The Teutonic Knights, more formerly called the "Order of Brothers of the German House of Saint Mary in Jerusalem," after their adventures in the Holy Land were invited into southeastern Transylvania, with a center in Brașov, in 1211 by the Hungarian King Andrew II to bolster the Kingdom's southeastern defenses, primarily against Cuman attacks from the other side of the Carpathians, in return for certain rights and privileges. The Order began exercising more power and independence than Andrew could stomach. They claimed more territory and as the final straw, put themselves under the authority of the Pope; thus the king kicked them out fourteen years later. At the invitation of a Polish Duke, the Order went on to convert or slay pagan Prussians on the shores of the Baltic. In the end, it would be understandable if the Hungarians regretted their impatience with the Order: the Mongols devastated Transylvania and most of Hungary only sixteen years after their departure.

[35]   The Edict of Torda granted freedom in preaching without harassment specifically only to the four "received" religions of Eastern Hungary: Roman Catholicism, Lutheranism, Calvinism, and Unitarianism. Orthodoxy (the religion of the majority), Judaism, and Islam were "tolerated" religions—i.e., not banned, but without such legal protections.

[36]   A few finds of chipped stones indicate a possible Acheulean presence in Transylvania, but dating is not yet confirmed. Possessors of the Acheulean technology (primitive stone tools), which lasted from about 1.7 million to about 100,000 years ago, are generally considered to be of the *Home erectus* species which predates both Neanderthals and modern humans.

[37]   The skeletal remains of anatomically modern humans found in a cave system called Peștera cu Oase ("Cave of the Bones") in the mountains near the Romanian town of Anina are among the oldest found in Europe. The anatomy of the bones suggests interbreeding between Neanderthals and modern humans.

[38]   Riel-Salvatore, Julien. 2012. Comment posted to "A Very Remote Period Indeed" blog on March 1, 2012. http://averyremoteperiodindeed. blogspot.com/2012/03/bitumen-used-as-hafting-material-in.html

[39]   "Transylvanian Gold Rush: Ancient Mining Site in Romania May Fall Victim." 20011. *Spiegel Online*, September 4, 2011. http://abcnews.go.com/International/transylvanian-gold-rush-ancient-mining-site-romania-fall/story?id=14421852

[40]   The Criș people, as the eastern version is called, kept mostly to terrain that was at least partially wooded, avoiding the open steppes and penetrating

them only along the forested river valleys of the forest-steppe zone, and not going further east than the Prut-Dniester watershed.

⁴¹   The Dacians and Getae may have been northern and southern varieties, respectively, of essentially the same or closely related people, with the Getae dwelling in the Danubian region closer to the Greeks, and the Dacians dwelling further north in and about the Carpathians. The ancient Greeks, so a theory goes, applied the name Getae to all of them, and considered them part of the Thracian group of peoples who also included people living to the south of the Getae (i.e., between the Greeks and the Getae in the eastern Balkans). There is not much reliable historical information, however, about the degree of distinction between the Dacians, the Getae, and the Thracians, and even contemporary writers were conflicted about or confused them. The modern writer Grumeza disputes that the Dacians were a Thracian subgroup or derivative (Grumeza 2009).

Complicating matters further, later Roman writers also referred to the Germanic-speaking Goths as *Getae*.

⁴²   Zalmoxis (also spelt *Zamolxis*) is referenced by ancient Greek writers from Herodotus to Plato to Strabo as a god of the Getae or more generally of the "Thracians", who was once incarnate as a man, a follower or even a slave of Pythagoras, who achieved god-like status through travel (to Egypt), study (magic and mysteries), preaching (immortality), prognosticating (astrologically), and (according to Herodotus) "resurrecting" (from a three-year underground existence). In Plato's *Charmides*, Socrates quotes a Thracian physician who refers to Zalmoxis as "our king, who is also a god." Some ancient sources imply that Zalmoxis was the one and only god of the "Getae," while others imply otherwise. While the terms "Getae" and "Thracian" can be ambiguous in ancient Greek usage with regard to whether the Dacians of Transylvania are included, Strabo specifically includes them when he writes of their belief in Zalmoxis during the reign of Burebista (a Dacian king in the first century B.C.) and the high priesthood of Decaeneus (who, he notes, continued to promote the Pythagorean doctrine of vegetarianism (Strabo, *Geography*, book 7, chapter 3)).

⁴³   Given its pertinence to the thinking of today when it comes to holistic (or integral) health and so called New-Thought, it is worth quoting Socrates' blurb about Zalmoxis (in *Charmides*, by Plato): "Such, Charmides, I said, is the nature of the charm, which I learned when serving with the army from one of the physicians of the Thracian king Zamolxis, who are to be so skillful that they can even give immortality. This Thracian told me that in these notions of theirs, which I was just now mentioning, the Greek physicians are quite right as far as they go; but Zamolxis, he added, our king, who is also a god, says further, 'that as you ought not to attempt to cure the eyes without the head, or the head without the body, so neither ought you to attempt to cure the body without the soul; and this,' he said, 'is the reason why the cure of many diseases is unknown to the physicians of Hellas, because they are ignorant of the whole, which ought to be studied also; for the part can never be well unless

the whole is well.' For all good and evil, whether in the body or in human nature, originates, as he declared, in the soul, and overflows from thence, as if from the head into the eyes. And therefore if the head and body are to be well, you must begin by curing the soul; that is the first thing. And the cure, my dear youth, has to be effected by the use of certain charms, and these charms are fair words; and by them temperance is implanted in the soul, and where temperance is, there health is speedily imparted, not only to the head, but to the whole body. And he who taught me the cure and the charm at the same time added a special direction: 'Let no one,' he said, 'persuade you to cure the head, until he has first given you his soul to be cured by the charm. For this,' he said, 'is the great error of our day in the treatment of the human body, that physicians separate the soul from the body.'"

44   It has been estimated that the treasure seized by the Romans after they defeated the Dacians contained more than 165 metric tons of gold and 300 metric tons of silver.

45   Cities built by the Romans included Alba Iulia, Cluj-Napoca, Turda, and Ulpia Traiana Sarmizegetusa. The latter was the largest and eventually became the capital of the Roman province of Dacia. It was located in the western Southern Carpathians near a natural passage between the Retezat and Poiana Ruscă Mountains that separates Transylvania from an area of the Pannonian plain known as the Banat. The city is now in ruins, and these include the remains of a forum, an amphitheatre, and several temples.

46   Modern historians apply the term "Free Dacians" to those Dacians who remained beyond the control of Rome, both refugees and already resident Dacians living beyond the borders of the Roman province of Dacia, including the Carpi and Costoboci tribal groups. Contemporary Roman historians called them *Dakoi prosoroi* ("neighboring Dacians"). Their territory was also called "Free Dacia," and consisted mostly of the Eastern Carpathian Mountain highlands and foothills, which stuck like a peninsula into the Roman Empire. According to Grumeza, the Free Dacians kept more than half the metal mines and 90% of the salt mines of Transylvania out of the hands of the Romans (Grumeza 2009, 202).

47   The degree of Slavic presence in Transylvania during the late first millennia is attested to by a preponderance of Slavic names for geographic features such as rivers and mountains.

48   Some Armenians were granted special status in Transylvania. An estimated 15,000 Armenians arrived at the invitation of Prince Mihaly Apafi in 1672; most came from Moldavia, where they had settled after the Armenian Kingdom of Cilicia fell to Egyptian invaders in 1375. The three main Armenian settlements in Transylvania (Dumbrăveni, Gherla, and Gheorgheni) were given charters by Prince Apafi, granting certain trading, political, and judicial rights. Most of their descendants have since left or have assimilated, and only about 1,360 Romanian citizens consider themselves Armenian today (2011 census).

49   Whether the Latin-speaking descendants of the Roman province of Dacia were mostly of Roman or Dacian heritage has been a matter of debate important to the identity of some modern Romanians. Given that the Romans were not in the habit of exterminating the indigenous populations of lands they conquered, and the fact that citizens of the Empire came from all over, it is likely that Transylvania was multi-ethnic when the Roman Empire withdrew its border (defenses) back to the Danube.

50   Transylvania was a province of the Kingdom of Hungary from 896 until 1526, often assigned to the eldest son of the king as a dukedom. After the defeat and death of King Louis II of Hungary and Bohemia by the army of the Ottoman Sultan Suleiman I in the Battle of Mohács in 1526, Transylvania was an independent principality until 1690, although it paid tribute to the Ottoman Empire until 1680. After the defeat of the Ottomans in 1683 in the Battle of Vienna, Transylvania became a Grand Duchy of the Habsburgs (from 1690 to 1848). From 1848 until 1920, Transylvania was a province of Hungary and part of the Dual Monarchy created in 1867. The Treaty of Trianon after World War II made Transylvania a part of Romania in 1920. The Second Vienna Award returned the northern half of Transylvania to Hungary in 1940. The Paris Peace Treaties after World War II restored the northern half of Transylvania to Romania in 1947.

51   Throughout the Middle Ages, though the Romanians eventually comprised the majority of the population in parts of Transylvania, they were generally peasants; most were enserfed to Hungarian and Saxon nobles, except for the leaders of their communities and a few others who climbed their way into a mostly informal nobility.

In most of the province the majority of the ruling class (the nobles and aristocracy) were first Avars, then perhaps Slavs, and then the Hungarians (Magyars), Saxons, and Szeklers. Louis I's Decree of Turda in 1366, required that all nobles in Hungary be Roman Catholic, which forced the few Romanian nobles, who were mostly Orthodox, to convert if they wanted keep their privileges and possessions.

52   After the Ottoman devastations of the late seventeenth century, many Hungarian landowners were forced to take on Vlach/Romanian peasants and laborers.

53   We will see this as a trend: The ethnic caldron in and about the Carpathians often made the universal acceptance of national borders impossible. This gave Hitler, for example, an excuse for more than one act of political and military aggression, and Hungary and Romania provide another example, nearly coming to blows over Transylvania during WWII even though they were, until near the end, Axis allies.

54   (Fermor 1986).

55   After the Communists gained control in Romania after World War II, a process of "Romanization" accelerated in Transylvania, including forced relocations/urbanization and the suppression of minority language education

and minority religions. In 1930, 58 percent of the population of Transylvania was Romanian, 24 percent Hungarian. By 1992, just after Communist rule ended, the percentages were 74 and 21, respectively, and in 2002, 76 and 20. Though these official assimilation policies were terminated when the Communist government fell, there are still claims of discrimination.

[56]   (Gheorhgiu 2013). During the 2000s, proposals for Széklerland autonomy have been submitted to the Romania parliament by minority political parties without success. A minority education rights law was passed in 2010 specifying that higher education in Romania be made available in the Hungarian language.

[57]   (Nowak, R.M. in Mech and Boitani 2003, 242).

[58]   A separate subspecies of gray wolf, *Canis lupus communis*, or "Russian wolf," inhabiting north-central Russia from the Ural Mountains eastward, was identified in 1804 by a Russian scientist of the name Ivan Dwigubski. This would place them between the range of *C. l. lupus* and *C. l. albus* ("Tundra Wolf") of northern Siberia, but whether this wolf is (or was) really a subspecies distinct from *C. l. lupus* is a matter of taxonomic judgment, which itself is complex, controversial, and evolving.

[59]   By the early 2000s, after wolves had begun to recover in Europe, about 45% of the wolves in Europe west of Russia lived in the Carpathian Mountains. At the low point of the wolf population in Europe during the twentieth century, small populations of wolves also survived in forests to the north of the Carpathians (Poland, Belarus, Latvia, Lithuania, and Estonia), Finland, Italy, Spain, Portugal, and the Balkans.

[60]   (Rigg and Findo 2000). See also Kecskes in (Kutal and Rigg 2008).

[61]   On average. A CLCP study in 2002 reported that wolves and bears killed 0.58% of sheep in the shepherd camps under study (Carpathian Large Carnivore Project 2002). A study by Kecskes et al in 2004 found an average flock loss of 1.12% to wolves in shepherd camps where some loss occurred during a season. Another study by the same team in 2007 found an average flock loss of 0.48% over an average period of 46 days (Kecskes, in Kutal and Rigg 2008).

[62]   See (Sparks 2011) for more about the status of wolves and issues of conflict and coexistence in Romania.

[63]   The Caliman Mountains comprise the largest volcanic grouping of mountains in Romania. Many of the peaks are conical and steep, and the highest point is Pietrosul Peak at 2303 meters (7556 feet). The Caliman are part of the Căliman-Harghita group of the Inner Eastern Carpathians.

[64]   Due to environmental stresses and vulnerable skins, amphibians are not doing so well in much of the world. The Global Amphibian Assessment, conducted by researchers in 2004, concluded that at least nine and possibly as many as 122 species of amphibians became extinct during the previous twenty-four year period (such a large range results from the fact that proving a negative is difficult, and a few species thought to be extinct are subsequently

rediscovered). As of 2014 the International Union for Conservation of Nature's (IUCN) "Red List" included 36 recently extinct, 112 possibly extinct, and 518 critically endangered species of amphibians, representing about 10% of all extant and recently extinct species, and at least 30% and perhaps as many as 56% of extant species are in serious trouble (i.e., "threatened"), especially in the Western Hemisphere and Australia. The current rate of amphibian extinctions is estimated to be around 211 times the long-term extinction background rate, and at least 25,000 times the background rate if threatened species are also considered (McCallum 2007).

65   There are various explanations as to the difference between *pricolici* and *vârcolac* in Romanian folklore. They may be different words for the same kind of beings, or alternatively the former may refer to souls who return from death in the form of wolves (or sometimes other animals)—in other words, vampires who take the form of wolves (or other animals)—whereas the latter are living people who take the form of wolves (or other animals).

66   It was generally believed that witches could take the form of, or send out "doubles" in the form of, just about any animal. Those who committed their crimes in the form of wolves, or who believed they did so, were often labeled "werewolves," whether they were also considered a witch or not. Thus the distinction between witches and werewolves could be blurry. In fact, there were generally two basic kinds of werewolves within European folklore: those who changed into wolves bodily, and those who transformed metaphysically or outside the normal body: i.e., those whose "doubles," "shadows," "spirit-bodies," or "astral projections" (as they have been called) took the forms of wolves while they themselves lay in a trance. Whether either kind was something real or only existed in people's minds has perhaps always been a matter of doubt and debate. In any case, in the witch trials of early modern Europe, devil worshippers not accused of shape-shifting into wolves far outnumbered those who were. Interestingly, most (but not all) werewolves were men, while most (but not all) witches were women.

67   According to Douglas, such were the conditions during the late sixteenth century when werewolf activity was peaking (Douglas 1992).

68   Torture was the recommended procedure for soliciting the "truth" from condemned heretics such as witches and werewolves during the trials from the fifteenth to the eighteenth century in Europe. Trial by cold water ordeal, famously used in the witch trials, was also sometimes used for werewolves. Contrary to many modern portrayals, this was not a no-win situation: drown or be condemned. If the accused sank, he or she was usually dragged from the water alive.

69   In the case of Peter Stump, for example (one of the most famous werewolves of medieval Europe), tried and convicted in 1589: "... his body was laid on a wheel, and with red hot burning pincers in ten several places to have the flesh pulled off the bones, after that his legs and arms to be broken by a wooden axe or hatchet, afterward to have his head struck from his body,

then to have his carcass burned to ashes" (Summers 2003, 259).

⁷⁰   (Bogatyrev 1998, 148).

⁷¹   In Europe there were also shape-shifting beliefs associated with the continent's other top predator, the bear. In other parts of the world there have been other were-predators, such as were-tigers and were-jaguars.

⁷²   I have found various numbers for the biting power of wolves. A maximum of 1500 lbs. per square inch is the number provided by the International Wolf Center. Whatever figure they provide, most sources report that wolves can bite with about twice the force of the most powerful domestic dogs.

⁷³   Perhaps these wolf impersonators were the precursors of "werewolves of the first kind"—my label for transformations of one's physical body within the belief system of both the werewolf and its society.

⁷⁴   Perhaps these shamans were precursors of "werewolves of the second kind"—my label for transformations that are metaphysical or out-of-body within the belief system of at least the werewolf. According to Pocs, among many early Indo-European societies just about anyone could go into a trance and create a "double" or "shadow" of many possible forms, but often animal, and send it out into the night animated with one's soul, usually for dark purposes but sometimes good. Whether good or bad, these doubles could outlive the original mortal body. Within European and Slavic folklore such a being is sometimes called a *mora* (or *mare*) (from the Indo-European word for "death"), although sometimes this term applies specifically to a usually female projection that sits atop a sleeping person and causes bad dreams ("night*mares*").

Some scholars of the dark suggest that both witches and werewolves, or at least some of them (and in the case of werewolves, especially those of Eastern Europe), evolved from these double-producing dreamers or shamans, or were simply relabeled versions of them.

An example of such shamanistic belief may have survived among the Csango people in the Moldavian Principality on the eastern slopes of the Carpathians into the seventeenth century, where the practitioners were known as *incantatores*, who would go into trances for up to four hours—shaking and contorting going in and coming out—to divine, heal, or cast or deflect spells on behalf of clients. The Csangos are a Hungarian, mostly Roman Catholic ethnic group living isolated from the majority of Hungarians who live west of the Carpathian divide. Some ethnologists speculate that the *incantatores* represent the survival of ancient shamanistic beliefs brought from Central Asia into Central Europe by the Magyars (Eliade 1972, 191-194).

⁷⁵   Norse gods often shape-shifted into animals—especially bears and wolves—and transformations are prominent in Norse sagas. Odin, leading Norse god and god of war, death, and poetry (among other topics) had a special bond with wolves and had two wolf companions, Geri and Freki. He could travel about outside his body in animal form, but he was also ultimately

killed by a wolf (named Fenrir).

76   The *berserkers* were Scandinavian warriors, both mythical—who got extra power from animals, especially bears and wolves—and real—who donned wolf or bear skins and worked themselves into frenzies (berserk) during battle. According to Summers, not all were noble warriors; some were just bad guys who went about "plundering and terrorizing" the countryside (Summers 2003).

77   Perhaps the most famous case of a benevolent werewolf fighting for good was a certain Theiss in Livonia, who in the late seventeenth century claimed he and his fellow werewolves transformed into the "dogs of God" and journeyed to hell to do battle with whips of iron against devils and sorcerers to gain possession of shoots of grain; success would mean a plentiful harvest for the coming year, while defeat meant otherwise.

Further evidence for similar "warrior werewolves" comes from other sixteenth and seventeenth century trials in Livonia and Latvia (in the Baltic region), as well as from Romanian (i.e., *strigoi* folklore) and Slavic folklore and hero epics (in which they are called *zduhać, vetrovnjak,* or "dragons" in the Balkans**)**. The historian Carlo Ginzburg found evidence of a similar cult that existed in sixteenth and seventeenth century Friuli, the region of northeast Italy at the northern edge of the Adriatic Sea, although these warriors did not take the form of wolves.

From the perspective of the people who believed in these strange episodes—participants while in altered states of consciousness—the battles took place between soul (or dream) projections (or "doubles"), often but not always in the forms of animals (not only wolves), usually at night and on mountaintops or in the clouds. These "werewolves of the second kind" (non-corporeal) served as "soul troops" or "spirit-guardians" fighting on behalf of individuals or communities—villages, cities, or, in times of war, even countries —to prevent bewitchment, to protect the fertility of the fields, to prevent or retrieve stolen crops or milk, to prevent bad weather, or to gain the favor of rain. Their opponents were either demons (symbols of chaos) or competitors of a neighboring community. Some of the participants even saw themselves as serving God, and some reported suffering fatigue and wounds in their real bodies as a result of their struggles in the other world.

Some of these stories come from people being tried and tortured for witchcraft, who saw themselves as doing good and who were strongly motivated to convince their persecutors of such. In any case, the belief system that supported these "night battles" predates the witch trials and may represent traces of widespread early European shamanism or perhaps specifically Nordic warrior shamanism associated with the god Odin. According to one theory, this shamanistic belief system evolved into a "witchcraft" belief system largely to explain calamities, with the fighters/fertility magicians who were mostly males evolving into werewolves (of the second kind) and the seers/healers/diviners who were mostly female evolving into witches (Pocs 1999, 125 and elsewhere, citing Ginzburg).

⁷⁸   St. John the Baptist Day (June 23/24) is very near the summer solstice and St. Lucy's Day (December 13) is very near the winter solstice; the pagan roots of both were almost surely intended to be associated with the actual solstices. The winter solstice, the darkest day of the year, was also traditionally considered a day of return of the dead. Werewolf activity in general was believed to peak on both of the solstices. (Pocs 1999, 130).

⁷⁹   The Swedish bishop and chronicler of the north, Olaus Magnus (1490-1557) and others tell tales of veritable festivals of werewolves in the Baltic region held on Christmas night or over the twelve nights of Christmas, complete with binge drinking from looted casks and sport contests in which the losers are devoured. Whilst these werewolves were devoted to self-destructive partying, they could also be decidedly malicious towards mortals; for example, they would attack isolated houses in the forest, and if they managed to break in they would "devour all the human beings, and every animal..." (Baring-Gould 2008, 30, quoting Olaus Magnus).

⁸⁰   According to Machal, among Slavic peoples, those in most danger of being unwillingly transformed into werewolves (by magic) were brides and bridegrooms on the way to church to be married (Machal 1916). I have not found this in any other source, however.

⁸¹   For example, the belief in lycanthropy was declared heretical in the canon *Episcopi*, possibly written around 900 A.D.

⁸²   The most influential work on demonology was the *Malleus Maleficarum* ("Hammer of the Witches), written in 1486 by Heinrich Kramer, a German Catholic cleric. Other famous demonologist writers and prosecutors included Henri Boguet, Jean Bodin, and Pierre de Lancre.

⁸³   Some unfortunate souls were transformed into werewolves involuntarily, either condemned by nature from birth to transform periodically (often at the full moon), or by the curse of witches or even saints. Legend has it that St. Patrick cursed certain tribes in Ireland that resisted his efforts to convert them, dooming them and their descendants to repeated seven-year cycles of werewolfery (Summers 2003, citing the source as *The Book of the dun Cow*, written by a Norse writer in 1250].

⁸⁴   It is interesting to note that, according to Douglas, in werewolf folklore the most common time for transformations is the month of February, which happens to also be the mating season for wolves.

⁸⁵   This list of possible pre-scientific werewolf explanations is a compendium from several early modern era commentators, including but not limited to: Heinrich Kramer (German, *Malleus Maleficarum*, 1486), Henri Boguet (France, *Discours des sorciers*, 1590), Francesco Maria Guazzo (*Compendium Maleficarum*, 1608), and Rhanaeus (German, Breslauer Sammlung, 1728) (Baring-Gould 2008).

⁸⁶   While rabies can certainly cause deranged and vicious behavior that could be seen as wolf-like, and while one gets rabies by being bitten by another

infected victim, like some folkloric werewolves (much adopted by Hollywood), rabies is unlikely to be the cause of most werewolf stories. The rabid usually drool and foam at the mouth and almost inevitably die within a few days, whereas werewolves tend to be rather dry-mouthed and long-lived.

[87]   Besides such exotic substances as the blood of bats and the fat from children's bodies dug from the grave, recipes given for werewolf ointments often included plants with known hallucinogenic compounds, such as henbane (*Hyoscyamus niger*) and other nightshades (genus *Atropa*), aconitum (genus *Ranunculaceae*, which includes buttercup—also ironically also known as "wolf's bane" since its alkaloid extracts were used to poison wolves), and cinquefoil (*potentilla*). But it is unlikely that enough of these substances could be absorbed through the skin from the ointments to cause wolf-like behavior or even delusions of wolf-like behavior.

[88]   Ergot poisoning, also called "St. Anthony's Fire," causes involuntary muscle contractions, crawling sensations in the skin, delirium, and hallucinations due to an LSD-like chemical found in fungus-infected rye flour. Several communal outbreaks stoked the imaginations of European villagers during medieval and early modern times.

[89]   Though not the cause of werewolfish behavior, certain physical deformities have given werewolves a folkloric boost: congenital porphyria, wherein one's urine, skin, and sometimes even teeth take on a red-brown color; and hypertrichosis, wherein one grows so much hair that one can certainly look like a werewolf (in fact, it has been called "werewolf syndrome").

[90]   For example, a study at McClean Hospital (a Harvard University affiliated psychiatric hospital) in 1988 reported twelve cases of people having episodes of behaving as animals and believing they were or could become as animals. A review of medical literature in 2004 found 32 such cases. Douglas cites a few more (Douglas 1992).

[91]   Bistriţa had about 80,000 residents at the time of our visit. The population declined to about 70,000 by 2011.

[92]   The Bargau is another range in the Căliman-Harghita group of mountains. The highest point is Heniu Mare at 1612 meters (5282 feet).

[93]   Today, the northern half of Bukovina is part of the Chernivtsi Oblast of Ukraine, and the southern half is part of Suceava and Botoşani counties of Romania.

[94]   The origins and speech of the Bastarnae are not known for certain. They may have originally been a Celtic-speaking people, but the most accepted theory is that they were Germanic-speakers who arrived from the north, perhaps from around the lower reaches of the Vistula River (now Poland), and settled between the eastern Carpathian foothills and the Dnieper River, arriving first around 200 B.C. In any case, if they were not already, they had become Germanized by the first century A.D., and they lasted as an identifiable people for about 500 years before being absorbed into neighboring peoples/cultures: the Roman Empire, other Germanic tribes, and the Sarmatians.

[95]   Client states of the Roman Empire were conglomerations of peoples along the imperial borders who attained a special status relative to the Empire but were not its citizens. The Empire sought to control these pseudo-states through a combination of coercion, threat of coercion, enticement (e.g., bribery), and strategic political manipulation (e.g., playing leaders against each other) in an attempt to pacify its borders and provide a buffer against even more hostile groups beyond.

[96]   Parts of Dacia were restored to the Roman Empire for a brief period during the rule of the emperor Constantine the Great, in 336 A.D.

[97]   The lexical similarity of *Carpates* and *Carpi* could itself arise from a common derivation from an ancient Indo-European word for "rock" (kárrēkā).

[98]   Some historians speculate that the term "Dacian" derived from the Phrygian word for "wolf." The Phrygians were an Indo-European people living in the southern Balkans by at least the eight century B.C. Other historians dispute this etymology.

Romanian ex-pat authors Mircea Eliade and Ion Grumeza both speculate that wolves played a central role in Dacian culture. Between them, they propose that the Dacian label originated from the fact that the people called themselves something like "wolf people;" that they worshipped wolves and (according to Grumeza) believed that "the wolf was the only effective power against evil" (Grumeza 2009, 75); that their warriors imitated wolves in their initiations; and that the Dacians believed in the possibility of transformation of men into wolves and had a ritual for doing so.

[99]   The merging of vampires and werewolves was typical in the Balkans, the Carpathians, and other regions of central-Eastern Europe, but dissipated further to the north and east in Russia (Ivanits 1989, 121).

[100]   Perhaps because the Orthodox Church was less dogmatic than the Catholic Church in stamping out folklore, werewolves of the East generally have a more varied personality than werewolves of the West, including witch-fighters and partiers instead of exclusively one-dimensional cannibalistic child-killers. And to become an Eastern werewolf is a more fatalistic affair: to be born with the caul, feet first, or with extra body parts such as fingers, vertebrae, teeth (or to be born *with* teeth), or even hearts, or on Christmas Day (links with the winter solstice and pagan day of return of the dead)—especially if one is generally a bad sort anyway—are dead giveaways of a lycanthropic destiny.

[101]   The historical and ethno-cultural region of Maramureş, which was long a county within the Kingdom of Hungary, includes the "Maramureş depression" and the circle of mountains ranges which surrounds it on its southeastern, northeastern, and northwestern sides. The depression consists of a broad lowland about 80 kilometers wide at the widest point that runs along the valleys of the upper Tisza River and its southeastern tributaries, the Iza and Vişeu Rivers. It is oriented on a southeast-northwest axis and stretches about 150 kilometers from the Prislop Pass in Romania to a narrow

opening between the mountains (through which the Tisza flows) near the city of Khust, Ukraine. Maramureş, and more often its southeastern half south of the Tisza, has sometimes been considered part of Transylvania and sometimes not, but in any case the northwestern half of the region now corresponds to the southeastern corner of the Transcarpathia province (*oblast*) of Ukraine.

[102] Tom Bombadil is a character in J.R.R. Tolkien's *The Lord of the Rings*.

[103] A treasure of several thousands of Dacian gold coins and other objects was found in 1543. According to legend, a "Wallachian fisherman" found it under the roots of a tree that had been uprooted along the banks of the Strei River, a tributary of the Mureş River in the vicinity of Sarmizegetusa, the ancient Dacian capital (Gerard 1888). It is more likely that the riches were found among ancient castle ruins of Sarmizegetusa, but in any case the legend lent support to a report by the classical Roman historian Cassius Dio (c. 155-235 A.D.) that before succumbing to Trajan, the Dacian King Decebalus had "...a large amount of silver and gold and other objects of great value..." buried under the bed of a river called Sargetia after it had been temporarily diverted for the purpose, just as the retainers of Attila did a few centuries later. Unlike the latter, however, the laborers who diverted the Sargetia and buried Decebalus treasure were merely "led away" rather than slaughtered, and the location of the king's treasure, or at least some of it, was revealed by a captured aid of the king and recovered by the Romans. Other treasure may have been hidden in caves throughout the kingdom, and there have been other smaller finds of Dacian gold coins in Transylvania during modern times.

[104] I have found references to the Ukrainian Wood Church of Poienile de Sub Munte being built in 1733, 1788, and 1798.

[105] Maramureş was a part of Transylvania until 1732, and during his reign as Prince of Transylvania from 1648 to 1660, György Rákóczi II tried to enforce Protestantism on the Orthodox population of Maramureş.

[106] The Orthodox populations of Transylvania and the eastern regions of the Polish-Lithuanian Commonwealth were numerical majorities within their respective regions, but they were political, economic, and social minorities within their larger states. In Poland-Lithuania they were Eastern Slavs living within a West Slavic state, and in Transylvania they were Vlach and Ruthenians living within a Hungarian or (later) Austro-Hungarian state (and without the status of being one of the "three nations" of Transylvania).

Any individuals who did manage to climb the socio-economic ladder usually had to forfeit their culture, often including their religion, becoming Polonized in the north or Magyaraized or Saxonized in the south. This, together with the fact that most schools were provided by the churches, which most Orthodox churches could not afford, made it even more difficult for the Orthodox Vlach and Ruthenian minorities to climb out of poverty and ignorance.

[107] In addition to accepting the Pope as the head of the Church, the Act

of Union in Transylvania required that Uniats accept three "articles of faith" consistent with the Catholic Church: the existence of purgatory; the use of unleavened bread in the liturgy; and the doctrine of Filioque (the Holy Spirit emanates from both the Father and the Son).

[108]   In Transylvania, prior to the banning of the Orthodox Church, the right of its clergy to elect bishops was subject to the veto power of the Transylvanian prince.

[109]   In Transylvania most Orthodox clergy, like their flocks, were impoverished; few had access to schools for their children and many had the status of serfs; some of the feudal restrictions and obligations of serfdom were legally lifted from the Orthodox clergy in 1609.

[110]   The worship of Jesus began to replace the worship of Zalmoxis and Mithra among the Dacians as Christianity was introduced by soldiers and other Romans in the third century A.D., and it became widely adopted under the influence of Byzantium/Constantinople. Grumeza speculates that the worship of Zalmoxis, who may have been an only god and who gave promise of resurrection after death, may have led Dacians to be particularly open to Christianity (Grumeza 2009).

[111]   In Poland-Lithuania, the Orthodox Church was banned after the Union of Brest, although it regained partial legal status in 1607.

In Transylvania (including Maramureş at the time), after the Act of Union the Orthodox Church had a contradictory status. On the one hand, the Act of Union transferred all Orthodox rights and properties to the Uniat Church and declared all Orthodox to be Uniat; on the other hand, in 1699 Emperor Leopold I allowed Orthodoxy to exist, albeit only with its previous status as a "tolerated" religion with inferior status, and adding certain restrictions (such as not actively opposing Uniat doctrine, and continuing to tithe to the Uniat church of their communities) and without a return of its former properties. In practice, during the seventeenth century, Orthodox practitioners in Maramureş and Transylvania faced severe oppression from Uniat, Catholic, and civil authorities, including imprisonment and deportation. (Bonkalo, who was a Hungarian patriot, offers an alternate viewpoint, claiming that Orthodox priests "fiercely attacked the Roman and Greek Catholic clergy" (Bonkalo 1990, 87)). The Uniats in Transylvania, meanwhile, were not given full civil rights equal to those of Magyars, Szeklers, and Saxons until 1743.

[112]   Conflicts between Orthodox and Greek Catholic clerics and their followers became especially violent in eastern Poland-Lithuania regions (today's Ukraine) during the 1620s, when they were fighting over which Church would have which churches, monasteries, and associated lands. Hundreds of clerics on both sides were killed. Some Orthodox moved to or pleaded with Moscovy for support.

[113]   About two-thirds of the Orthodox in Poland-Lithuania converted to Uniat soon after the Union of Brest. Fewer converted in Transylvania

after the Act of Union, as Protestant Princes and elite strongly opposed the Union, actively worked against it (seeing it as a victory for Catholicism), and continued struggling against their Catholic Habsburg overlords, sometimes with the martial aid of Uniat and Orthodox Vlachs and Ruthenians.

[114] The "slow legal revival of Orthodoxy": As mentioned, one year after the Act of Union, Leopold I allowed Orthodoxy to exist. By the time of the reign of Maria Theresa in the Habsburg Monarchy (1740) there were some 124,000 Orthodox families in Transylvania and "... their constant petitions for proper spiritual oversight could no longer be safely disregarded" (Dampier 1905, 55). Thus in 1759 Maria Theresa forbid the persecution of Orthodox believers, and in 1761 she appointed a (non-Orthodox) bishop to "oversee" the Orthodox Romanians in Transylvania. In 1783, Emperor Joseph II appointed a Serbian Orthodox bishop for the "non-United Romanian Church," although it was still considered only a "tolerated" religion without full legal rights. In 1791, the Transylvania Diet granted a "legal position" to the Orthodox Church (Dampier 1905). In 1810, Emperor Francis I allowed the Orthodox Church in Romania to "elect" their own archbishop (i.e., nominate three candidates from which the Emperor would choose).

[115] The regimes of Hungary and Yugoslavia were the only Communist regimes in Europe that did not ban Greek Catholicism.

[116] In Slovakia, the Greek Catholic Church was legally restored before the fall of Communism, during the "Prague Spring" of 1968. After this happened, 205 out of 292 Orthodox parishes voted to return to Greek Catholicism; most Orthodox properties were not transferred to the Greek Catholic Church, however.

[117] In the Romanian census of 2002, about 61,000 people declared themselves of Ukrainian heritage, most living in Maramureş and Bukovina.

[118] Around 116,000 Jews perished in the Holocaust in northern Transylvania (151,000 lived there before the war); around 260,000 perished in Romania (about 600,000 lived there before the war) (Gido, in Zoltani 2013, 113).

The northern forty percent or so of Transylvania was then (again) a part of Hungary. It had been returned via the Second Vienna Award of 1940, arbitrated by Germany and Italy to keep the peace between two of their allies, Romania and Hungary—a development certainly consistent with Hitler's desire to smash the mold of Europe sculpted by the Allied victors of World War I. After the partition, more than 100,000 Hungarians and Saxons relocated from southern Transylvania to the north, more than 100,000 Romanians moved the other way, and there were two massacres of Romanian civilians by Hungarian troops during the re-occupation of the north.

[119] Our knowledge of Menumoret comes from the *Gesta Hungarorum* (The Deeds of the Hungarians), one of the earliest chronicles of Hungarian history written by an anonymous and not necessarily completely reliable self-described notary of King Bela, sometime in the twelfth century.

[120]   "Royal free" cities in the Kingdom of Hungary were cities in which the citizens were granted limited autonomy from the control of Hungarian nobles.

[121]   Satu Mare had a population of around 110,000 in 2005, but it is declining, dropping to around 95,000 by 2011.

UKRAINE

[122]   The forests of the northern plain of Ukraine—a region known as Polissia, which extends into Belarus and includes many lakes, low hills and a large wetland known as the Pripet Marshes—are comprised mostly of pine, oak and birch, while beech, fir and spruce dominate the Carpathian Mountains in the southwest; the forest-steppe zone in the country's center consists of rolling open grasslands and farmlands interspersed with stands of mixed, mostly deciduous trees, oak being most common.

[123]   (Subtelny 2000, 5).

[124]   Some contemporary Ukrainian historians maintain that the word "Ukraine" had the meaning "homeland" rather than "borderland" throughout most of the region's history—one of the many controversies regarding the history of the country.

[125]   In this book I will use the most common transliteration of the modern Ukrainian spelling of "Kyiv." The most common transliteration of the Russian spelling, and of the older Ukrainian spelling, is "Kiev." For the early medieval state, I will use the transliteration of the old Ukrainian spelling of "Kievan Rus'."

[126]   (Batt and Wolczuk 2002, 166).

[127]   Oblasts in Ukraine are administrative units, roughly equivalent to provinces (or states in the USA). There are twenty-four of them, plus an autonomous republic (Crimea—now claimed by Russia without international recognition) and two special status cities: Kyiv and Sevastopol (located in Crimea). Oblasts and the special cities are further divided into districts (*raions*). Each oblast has an administrative centre which is usually also its largest city. Districts are further divided into district-level cities, urban settlements, and villages.

[128]   (Batt and Wolczuk 2002, 168).

[129]   According to the most recent census of 2001, ethnic Russians make up about 17% of the population of Ukraine; they are a majority in Crimea, the two easternmost administrative districts of Luhansk Oblast, and several eastern cities; they make up a significant minority in roughly the eastern quarter of the country. 29.6% of Ukrainians speak Russian as their native language, and a majority do so in Crimea, parts of the Odessa Oblast, and far southeastern and northeastern regions. Most Ukrainians can speak Russian as a second language.

In 2012 the Ukrainian parliament passed a bill sponsored by the Party of

Regions allowing the use of "regional" languages in courts, schools, and other government institutions in administrative districts where at least ten percent of the population speaks the language. Given the demographics of Ukraine, the measure was primarily intended to apply to the Russian language in southern and eastern regions of the country, although three small communities subsequently invoked the rule for Romanian, Hungarian, and Moldovan (the first in a village near Rakhiv and the second in a town in the southwestern corner of Transcarpathia).

The bill had sparked intense passions, including protests in the street and fistfights in parliament. It was opposed by the Western-leaning political opposition and those afraid it would reopen a social and political division of the nation, discourage Russian-speaking people from learning Ukrainian, and even lead to the eventual extinction of Ukrainian. Fear was (and is) just as strong on the other side: It was fear of losing the right—provoked especially when the Ukrainian parliament passed a repeal of the bill shortly after Yanukovych fled the country during the upheaval in February 2014—that helped energize a separatist movement in the east and trigger direct Russian involvement, including the seizing of Crimea in March. The repeal of the minority language bill, however, was quickly vetoed by the acting president and condemned even by some western-leaning politicians, including Yulia Tymoshenko.

[130]   The economy of Ukraine is also somewhat dichotomous, primarily as a result of former central Soviet planning: The east is dominated more by industry and the center and west more by agriculture.

[131]   The Ukrainian journalist who was murdered—in September, 2000—was Georgiy Gongadze. He was co-founder of the online newspaper that later helped Yushchenko get the word out about the Orange Revolution protests, *Ukrainska Pravda* (Ukrainian Truth). His body was found decapitated and doused with dioxin. Kuchma was implicated when a politician (Oleksandr Moroz) produced excerpts from audio tapes made by Kuchma's bodyguard in which Kuchma seems to declare that Gongadze should be silenced; the authenticity of the recordings have been questioned and Kuchma has claimed the tapes are misleading due to selective editing. Three former government intelligence officials were later charged and convicted of the murder. An official investigation of Kuchma by the General Prosecutor of Ukraine's Office begun in 2011 has been tied up by a court ruling that the audio tapes are inadmissible as evidence since they were made illegally.

[132]   According to international and domestic NGO election observers, earlier in 2004 an Our Ukraine candidate for mayor of the west Ukrainian city of Mukacheve had lost an election as a result of voter intimidation, vote-buying, and fraudulent counting (Report by the Congress of Local and Regional Authorities of the Council of Europe. May 4, 2004: https://wcd.coe.int/ViewDoc.jsp?id=747961&Site=COE&BackColorInternet=C3C3C3&BackColor Intranet=CACC9A&BackColorLogged=EFEA9C]

[133]   The international community also expected problems in the Ukraine presidential election of 2004, as exemplified by a letter from President Bush

to President Kuchma delivered by Senator Richard Lugar earlier in the year that stated: "You play a central role in ensuring that Ukraine's election is democratic and free of fraud and manipulation. A tarnished election, however, will lead us to review our relations with Ukraine."

[134]   Foreign observers declaring the second round of the Ukrainian presidential election of 2004 to be fraudulent included the Organization for Security and Cooperation in Europe (OSCE) and the Council of Europe.

[135]   (Chivers 2005).

[136]   (Kristof 2004).

[137]   The first round of the election in October, 2004 had 2,455 international observers; the revote of the second round on December 26 had 13,644.

[138]   After these events, politics continued Ukrainian-style. In 2010, Yanukovych became president, and his most significant opponent, Tymoshenko, was imprisoned (accused of forcing the Ukrainian natural gas company to accept a deal too much in Russia's favor when she was Prime Minister in 2009), only to be released after Yanukovych fled as a result of the Maidan protests in 2014. The United States and several European countries considered her imprisonment an example of selective justice at best. In any case, the schizophrenic situation intensified with the separatist movement and the active involvement of Russia including the seizing of Crimea in 2014.

[139]   The Bush administration had to walk a fine line between its support for democracy and preference for the western-leaning faction in Ukraine, and its goal of improving relations with Putin-led Russia. It probably also did not want to create a potential backlash from appearing to be overly partisan. Thus it did not publically declare a preference for either candidate. Its preference was obvious, however, and one that Yanukovych supporters tried to expose and exploit.

[140]   Established in 1968, the Carpathian Biosphere Reserve is a collection of protected areas in the Transcarpathian region of Ukraine that totals 53,630 hectares; it is a member of UNESCO's World Network of Biosphere Reserves. The Reserve's territory —about 90% of which is covered by forests, most of it old growth—is divided into four functional zones: protected (core), buffer, regulated protected regime, and anthropogenic. The Reserve harbors 64 rare or endangered indigenous plant species and 72 rare or endangered animal species. See http://cbr.nature.org.ua/new_e.htm.

[141]   All these ranges are part of what is variously called the Eastern Beskids or Ukrainian Carpathians, which in turn are part of the Outer Eastern Carpathians.

[142]   The Bukovel Ski Resort, which is located about fifty kilometers across the Carpathian divide to the northwest is planned to become one of the largest ski resorts in the world, with 35 lifts and 100,000 beds of lodging. As of 2015 it had 15 lifts.

[143]   See the city of Rakhiv's website for two legends associated with the glacial lakes near Rakhiv: http://www.rakhiv.com/index_en.php?page=Lake&lang=en

144   During the early 2000s, some 270,000 Transcarpathians worked abroad on the black labor market in the EU (Batt and Wolczuk 2002, 183). Slovakia has given special status to foreigners "... recognized as Slovak," intended to allow people of Slovak heritage to more easily live and work in the country." This has led to a large increase in the number of Transcarpathian residents who claim Slovak heritage: from 7,000 in the census of 1991 to 70,000 in the census of 2001 (the last census in Ukraine), or about 5.6% of the population of Transcarpathia. (Batt and Wolczuk, 2002) and (*About number and composition population of UKRAINE*, the State Statistics Committee of Ukraine: http://2001.ukrcensus.gov.ua/eng/results/general/nationality/).

145   The population of Ukraine is declining due to a low birth rate and emigration. By 2014 it was down to 45 million.

146   *Trembitas* are made of pine or spruce that hopefully has been struck by lightning. They can be over four meters long and can be heard by humans for up to ten kilometers, and even further by most animals.

147   (Bonkalo 1990, 60-61).

148   In Ukraine, earlier versions of the *bartok* were called *tshakan* and *kelepa,* which were true battle axes used in large-scale combat such as revolts against foreign feudal lords and landowners between the sixteenth and mid-nineteenth centuries. According to Bonkalo, the Hutsul *bartok* was also called a *toporets'* (Bonkalo 1990).

149   Genetic evidence seems to suggest that Carpathian ridges have imposed a greater impediment to sexual liaisons than they have to the exchange of highland lingo, beliefs, and fashion, as Hutsuls, Boykos, and Lemkos have remained comparatively genetically distinct from each other relative to their proximity as the crow flies (Nikitin et al. 2009).

150   The White Croats were a tribe or collection of tribes with a murky history believed to have lived somewhere just north or northwest of the northern rim of the Carpathians by at least the sixth century A.D. Modern scholars propose homelands anywhere from Bohemia in the west to the headwaters of the Dniester in the east. There are references to White Croats in legends and early historical accounts of the northern Carpathians, who during the sixth century began settling the northern valleys of the Carpathians and then crossed the passes and settled the southern slopes within a hundred years. During the seventh century they perhaps spread as far eastward as Maramureş and began building strongholds throughout the region. It is generally assumed the White Croats while still north of the Carpathians were Slavic, but based on linguistic evidence some scholars suggest they may have had Sarmatian roots as well, perhaps forming from a Sarmatian elite that was overwhelmed by Slavic locals.

The White Croats are also the legendary ancestors of the Croats, who ended up in Dalmatia along the Adriatic coast in the western Balkans by the eight century. Byzantine writers of the tenth century (e.g., Byzantine Emperor

Constantine VII) offer differing versions about how the Croats got there that include mythological elements and the suggestion that they were invited by the Byzantine Emperor Heraclius (575-641) in order to buffer Avar power on the Empire's northern border (possibly an invention to justify Byzantine rule over the region). In any case, when they reached Dalmatia, they teamed up with any other Slavs who may have already been there and overthrew the Avar yoke, with or without prompting from Byzantium.

A remarkably similar story was told by Constantine VII for the origin of the Serbs: coming from "White Serbia," located next to "White Croatia" along the northern Carpathians (a place also "called by them 'Boiki'") they migrated to the land that would be called Serbia, just east of their former neighbors in Dalmatia (the other side of the Dinaric Alps).

[151]   The Tivercians (or *Tivertsi*) were an East Slavic tribe living along the Dniester and up into the northeast Carpathian foothills by at least the ninth century A.D.

[152]   The Ulichs (or *Ulichi*) were an East Slavic tribe living along the lower Dnieper and Bug Rivers by at least the eighth century A.D. who were pushed into the Carpathian Mountains by Magyars and Pechenegs during the tenth and eleventh centuries.

[153]   The genetic study of Nikitin et al. confirms an east-Slavic ancestry for the Hutsuls, also with Hungarian, Romanian, and Croatian descent; the latter seems to confirm White Croat roots (Nikitin et al. 2009).

[154]   (Bonkalo 1990, 18).

[155]   Ibid, p. 64.

[156]   "*Opryshky*" was the local Ukrainian Carpathian name for the mountain-based version of "outlaws" known as *hajduki* throughout Central and Eastern Europe. Coming in two essential forms, *hajduki* may have been either ruthless bandits terrorizing for selfish purposes, or small, independent bands of rebels (not rightly considered "brigands") fighting on behalf of peasants against the feudal oppression of Ottoman, Habsburg, Polish, or Romanian (or Transylvanian) nobility. Of course the reality may have been anything in between, but in folklore the *hajduki* and especially the *opryshky* are usually portrayed as being motivated by social justice rather than personal greed (the label "avengers" has been used).

[157]   (Heisler and Mellon 1946, 55).

[158]   During and just after World War II, the Ukrainian Insurgent Army fought against whichever forces it believed were the biggest obstacle to Ukrainian independence, which included at various times the German army, the Soviet Army, and both the Communist and Underground Polish armies; it also allied itself with the Polish anti-communist resistance after the war.

[159]   The joint hoisting of the 2012 UEFA European Soccer Championship by Ukraine and Poland was intended in part to symbolize the transcendence of past hostilities.

[160]   During the feudal era, many Carpathian villages were granted

autonomy provided they made periodic payments to their lords, usually in the form of sheep. In other words, they were not enserfed, but they were taxed.

[161]   (Sparks 2010, 194).

[162]   The embodiment of Kupala into a god or goddess may be a case of a festival leading to a deity rather than vice-versa, in a relatively recent interpretive leap by enthusiasts associated with a revival of interest in Slavic mythology. While there are plenty of references to Kupala as a deity in modern sources, as far as I know there are none in pre-modern historical or ethnographic sources.

[163]   According to one theory that attempts to reconstruct Slavic mythology by analyzing vestige folkloric elements scattered throughout Slavic literature and current folklore and integrating them unto the broader context of ancient Indo-European mythology, Ivan Kupala Day may have started as a wedding celebration for a (mostly west-Slavic) god of fertility, vegetation, and spring—Jarilo—and his sister, Morana, a goddess of winter, death, and nightmares.

[164]   (Barford 2001, 192).

[165]   Internet Encyclopedia of Ukraine. http://www.encyclopediaofukraine.com/display.asp?AddButton=pages\K\U\Kupalofestival.htm

[166]   In addition to bringing good luck, the fern flower was believed to provide its possessor with magical abilities, such as foretelling the future, reading minds, understanding the languages of animals and plants, becoming invisible, inspiring romantic love in the heart of another, and being able to find buried treasure (or it marked the site of buried treasure itself) (Yoffe and Krafczik 2003). But to seize the fern flower requires stalwart resolution, for you have to draw a magical circle around the plant and remain within until it blooms while demons try to entice you out with a terrible ruckus and clamor, and if you step outside without the flower you will be devoured.

While real ferns do not flower, the legend may have arisen from the attribute of one species, *Osmunda regalis,* that produces golden-red fertile fronds.

[167]   Non-medicinal herbal powers were also believed to be enhanced for herbs collected on Kupala Night, including the powers used by witches for black magic. Other examples of non-medicinal herbal powers, as reported in Transcarpathia during the early twentieth century, include: a plant known as *tancuvnyk,* which shakes and dances in the wind, could help young women dance; and *devjatosyl* (genus *Ononsis,* or restharrow), which is difficult to uproot, could make men strong (Bogatyrev 1998).

[168]   Speculation localizing the origin of the Proto-Indo-European language comes from a process of linguistic reconstruction (analyzing the current forms, content, and distribution of languages) along with archeological and genetic evidence used to establish prehistoric migration patterns. The conclusions are not without significant uncertainty.

[169]   Modifying the vowel in the middle of the stem (e.g., *ran* past tense of *run*) was probably the more typical way to indicate tense in proto-Indo-European (Anthony 2007, 4).

[170]   Dates in this section and its endnotes are estimates proposed by

Anthony (Anthony 2007), who gives a range of between 4,500 B.C. and 2,500 B.C. as the earliest and latest possible dates for when the Proto-Indo-European language was spoken in its original homeland. Other scholars propose dates ranging from as early as 7,500 B.C.

[171]   The Proto-Indo-European language is the common ancestor of several hundred languages and dialects today, including most of the current major languages spoken in Europe (excepting the Uralic languages, such as Hungarian and the Finnic languages), southwest Asia, and the Americas. PIE and proto-Uralic themselves may share a common ancestor language spoken by pre-agricultural foraging people living between the Carpathians and the Urals at the end of the last Ice Age.

[172]   The name for the chief sky god of the Proto-Indo-Europeans (more specifically, the daylight sky god) has been reconstructed to be *Dyēus* (or *dyew pəter* in Proto-Indo-European, literally "Sky Father"), who eventually became the Greek Zeus, the Latin Jupiter, and the Indian Dyauspitar (father of Indra).

[173]   We do not know where the wagon was invented, and it may have been invented at multiple places and times, but the earliest depiction of a wagon—an image engraved on a clay cup—was found near Krakow, Poland, in the northern foothills of the Carpathian Mountains.

[174]   In the nineteenth and early twentieth centuries, who the original Indo-European speakers were and who they became were matters of particular fascination. The Nazis called all of them Aryans—a term which the authors of the earliest religious writings of an Indo-Iranian branch, the *Rig Veda* and the *Avesta*, used to refer to themselves— and tried to use an alleged "pure" descent from them (without credible evidence) to justify horrific policies, consequently giving the term "Aryan" a bad name.

[175]   Anatolian languages may have evolved by about 4,200 B.C.

[176]   The Tocharian language may have evolved by about 3,700 B.C.

[177]   The Proto-Balto-Slavic language may have evolved by about 2,800 B.C. and diverged into the Slavic and Baltic languages by 2,500 B.C. (Anthony 2007). Other scholars propose later dates, although most are significantly earlier than the first millennium A.D., and the latest being around 500 A.D. Anthony proposes that Proto-Balto-Slavic may have begun from interactions between several forest, forest-steppe, and steppe peoples (possessors of Corded Ware, Globular Amphora, late Sredni Stog, and Yamna cultures) in the area of the middle Dnieper River beginning around 2,800 B.C.: the language of those who migrated north and east to the upper Dnieper and upper Volga basins evolving into Baltic, and the language of those who stayed in the middle Dnieper region evolving into Slavic (Anthony 2007, 377-380).

[178]   Germanic may have begun diverging from Proto-Indo-European by about 3,300 B.C. Anthony proposes that it began in the upper Dniester region along the northeastern foothills of the Carpathians, only about 500 kilometers to the west of the Proto-Balto-Slavic homeland, through interactions between

possessors of the PIE-speaking Usatovo culture and possessors of a series of local client cultures, including the late Trichterbecker culture (located between the Dniester and Vistula Rivers); these collected peoples may have then evolved or acquired a culture called Corded Ware (which also was influenced by the Yamna culture).

[179]   Proto-Italic-Celtic may have evolved by about 3,000 B.C. south and west of the Carpathians as carriers of the Yamna culture from the steppes east of the Carpathians immigrated up the Danube Valley and interacted with possessors of local cultures such as the Costofeni; it may have diverged into pre-Italic in southern regions and pre-Celtic in northern regions by around 2,500 B.C. The language may have gotten off on a mellow footing: not far from Bucharest near the Danube the earliest evidence of cannabis burning was found, dating to around this time.

[180]   The Balkan Indo-European languages may have diverged by around 2,500 B.C. Illyrian, Thracian and Phrygian are now extinct.

181 There is controversy regarding the relationship between the Dacian and Thracian languages, ranging from being separate languages to being closely related dialects of the same language. Conclusions about the Dacian language are speculative since it has survived only in the names of a few fauna and flora (maybe), toponyms, personal names, perhaps a few other words in Romanian and Albanian, and maybe one inscription.

[182]   The Armenian language may have evolved by about 2,800 B.C.

[183]   The Proto-Indo-Iranian language may have evolved by about 2,200 B.C.

[184]   (U.S. Department of State 2008).

[185]   (U.S. Department of State 2008).

[186]   (Shuster 2010).

[187]   (Stern 2009).

[188]   FEMEN is a feminist protest group founded in Ukraine in 2008, which has gained notoriety for flamboyant, often topless protests against the exploitation of women in many varied forms.

[189]   (Bogatyrev 1998).

[190]   (Eliade 1972).

[191]   (Wilson 2002).

[192]   The first archeological evidence of modern human presence in Ukraine consists of artifacts from the Gravettian culture found in the Crimean Mountains dated at about 32,000 years ago. This cultural tradition lasted for about 10,000 years. There may have been anatomically modern humans living in the area as early as 40,000 years ago, possessing a culture known as Aurignacian.

[193]   Recent genetic analysis suggests that modern humans and Neanderthals interbred to some extent. The newcomers were probably much more numerous than the indigenous Neanderthals, and their characteristics more adaptive, since

those with modern human characteristics or predominately modern human characteristics greatly out-propagated those with specifically Neanderthal features, which is why we, the surviving descendants, more closely resemble the early modern humans than the Neanderthals; in spite of early popular depictions, however, Neanderthals stood up straight and may have been fair-skinned and with no more body hair than modern humans. Analysis shows that between 1% and 4% of the non-African genetic code of modern humans comes from Neanderthals, including genes important for immune systems and for living in cold climates.

[194]   The large "super-towns" of the Cucuteni-Trypillian culture were not really cities. They had a central plaza but left no evidence of a palace, temple, or administrative center. They also did not have a surrounding defensive wall or moat, although at least one had an outer ring of houses that would have provided a two-story barrier cut by only a few defendable streets. Inside the towns, many houses were organized into groups of five to ten surrounding a larger central house, just as the smaller C-T settlements.

[195]   Archeology reveals a gender distinction between western and eastern Proto-Indo-European devotional practices from early on, the west being more female-centric and the east more male-centric—perhaps under the influence of neighboring cultures. In any case, Anthony speculates that this dichotomy may have led to the gender distinctions of PIE grammar (Anthony 2007).

[196]   The bridal payment theory is proposed by Anthony (Anthony 2007, 239).

[197]   There is evidence of trade between the C-T and Proto-Indo-Europeans, but beginning around 4,100 B.C., about ten percent of C-T villages became fortified with earthen banks and ditches, and some contain direct evidence of violence—especially litter of arrow and mace heads—but only for a period of a few hundred years. Additionally, a few late C-T sites in western Ukraine became heavily fortified with thick stone walls. A period of colder and drier climate has also been proposed as a factor that may have tipped the balance toward the herding economy and therefore the culture of the Proto-Indo-Europeans, but this occurred only during the earliest times of the transition.

[198]   The earliest use of copper, bronze, and iron spread through Europe generally in a westward direction, so the metallic ages occurred earlier in the Carpathian region than in western Europe. In fact, western Europe essentially skipped the age in which only unalloyed copper was used. A few small iron artifacts have been found in eastern Ukraine dated to as early as 2,500 B.C., earlier than what is considered the earliest Iron Age cultures of the Near East by around twelve hundred years.

[199]   The Cimmerians, Scythians, and Sarmatians were probably collections of related tribes rather than a single tribe. It is believed that they all spoke variants of Indo-European languages. As mentioned previously, "Scythian" became a generic term used by the ancient Greeks and Romans to refer to all the (nomadic) peoples living north and east of the Carpathians and

east of the Vistula River.

200   (Hippocrates, Part 17)

201   Celts arrived in the Carpathian region of southwestern Ukraine at the time of their maximum expansion eastward, around 275 B.C. Reversing the earlier metallurgic trend (which was east to west), the Celts brought advanced smelting technology into the Carpathians, including the manufacture of high-quality weapons, which they sold to customers such as the Dacians.

At least some of the Celtic cultural presence in the eastern reaches of its expansion was definitely the result of the migration of people and not just culture. The Romans describe a force of some 40,000 Celts from Gaul, about half of whom could be classified as fighting men (the other half being children, women, and elderly), raiding and fighting their way through Greece and Macedonia and then crossing into Asia Minor, where they settled (in Anatolia) and continued raiding and served as mercenaries and became known as Galatians.

202   It is unclear whether the Costoboci (as labeled by the Romans) had Dacian, Sarmatian, Scythian, Celtic, proto-Slavic, or Germanic origins; the material culture of the region at the time—labeled the Lipița culture by archeologists—provides evidence of Celtic and Roman influences among the upper class. In any case, Greek and Roman geographers place their homeland to the north or northeast of Dacia, between the Dacians and the Bastarnae further to the northeast, probably including the Dniester basin as well as the Carpathian uplands near the headwaters of the Tisza and Prut Rivers. The Costoboci took advantage of revolts in Slovakia (the Marcomannic Wars) to raid the Empire into the Balkans as far as Greece, until Vandals came to the rescue of Rome around 170 A.D. The Costoboci were driven back into the Carpathians, including into the lands of the Carpi along the eastern foothills, where they gradually disappeared as a distinct people.

203   Ethnic designations are never simple, and they may be used to designate a collective history (which may be in part mythical), territory, culture, ancestry (identifiable now through DNA analysis), physical phenotype, language, or any combination of these. In pre-modern times, ethnic identity may have often been limited only to the consciousness of the social, political, and economic elite inhabiting a given region. Given the size and diversity of the people to which it applies today (around 270 million Slavic language speakers and around 400 million people of Slavic descent), the term "Slav" may be most appropriate as a linguistic term. It first shows up in the historical record (in reference to a people) in writings of East Roman Empire and Ostrogoth chroniclers in the sixth century A.D.

204   See for example Polianskii in (Best, Decerbo, and Maksimovich 2012, 355). Polianskii was an intense Rusyn patriot.

205   Based on archeological evidence, most scholars now believe that the rapid migration of Slavic tribes most likely began in or near the northeastern fringes of the Carpathians; see for example (Heather 2009, 396). This is also

consistent with the first historical references to (most likely) Slavic people by East Roman historians writing in the mid-sixth century A.D., referring to raids south of this region, coming across the Danube from southern Moldavia and eastern Wallachia—that is, from along the eastern edge of the Carpathians— as well as somewhat later Frankish references to Slavs showing up on the western sides of the Carpathians by the seventh century (where they were called *Wends*)—see endnote 219 and Appendix F.

As with (and sometimes along with) Slavic ethnogenesis, however, there are alternative theories. Dismissing early historical accounts, Curta proposes that the Slavic identity didn't really coalesce until the assorted collection of peoples north of the lower Danube in the early sixth century had organized themselves enough to conduct their raids against the East Roman Empire. In other words, Curta suggests, the Slavic identity first arose just southeast of the Carpathians rather than northeast, and in the sixth century rather than the fourth, as a result of the organizing activities of a military elite and the labels given to them by the East Romans (i.e., *Sclaveni* and *Antes*), and that the subsequent rapid spread of the culture was more from the movement of a small political-military elite rather than the mass migration of people (including, importantly, the showering of emblematic adornments on their aristocratic female companions). Curta's proposal is controversial.

[206]   The early Slavs used iron-headed and wooden-handled axes to clear the land, wheeled plows with iron knives and ploughshares to plow the land, and iron-headed and wooden-handled sickles and scythes to harvest the crops.

[207]   How high in the mountains the early Slavic migrants ventured is unclear. Most maps of archeological sites and historical references and the consequent deduced areas of ancient cultural complexes leave the highest lands of the Carpathians blank: sort of a long, white comma surrounded by the dots, x's, o's and shaded areas that define speculative cultures that only cover the foothills and the long stretch of rolling land that slants up to the mountains from the Dniester. But surely there have always been lovers of heights and the peace and quiet they promote. More difficult to scrape a living from the slopes, perhaps, but land less in demand can be easier to hold onto when strange folk are about. As well, some of the archeological and historical gap may be due to lack of digging on the difficult slopes and lack of contemporary interviews with or reports by reticent highlanders.

[208]   Archeologists refer to the distinctive culture identified by artifacts from around the end of the fifth century A.D. prevalent along the northern and northeastern corner of the Carpathians, and almost surely left by Slavic inhabitants, as the *Korchak Culture*. Its primary characteristics are log huts sunk a few feet into the ground with stone ovens located in a corner opposite the door (often a north corner), rather simple pottery, and cemeteries of cremation urns (most flat, some covered with barrow mounds). It is the subsequent spread of Korchak relics, and those of several closely related and evolved variants, along with the scant historical references, that is used to

reconstruct the expansion of the Slavs.

209   Slavic immigrants into the North European Plain of Poland and Germany started perhaps as early as the late fifth century A.D. and continued into the seventh, filling a vacuum created by departing Goths, who left the material remains of what archeologists call the *Przeworsk Culture*. There is some evidence that a nearly simultaneous Slavic expansion occurred in an east-west direction through the northern forests of Poland from the area of Belarus, or even, as proposed by some Polish historians (particularly Kostrzewski), that an indigenous Slavic culture (a second Slavic homeland?) existed west of the Vistula prior to the sixth century, which would have existed underneath a Germanic elite during most of the first half of the first millennium (Barford 2001; Heather 2009, 412-414). In any case, the expansion of the Korchak culture into much of this area was initially scattered, indicating infiltration into an existing indigenous population.

210   Slavic culture in the middle Danube basin, which began perhaps as early as the early sixth century A.D. and continued until the end of the seventh, may have also been brought by Slavs migrating from the lower Danube, in company with Avar overlords. Both archeological and historical evidence suggests Slavic-Avar mixing along the middle Danube basin at this time.

211   Slavic culture west of the Moravian Gate, which arrived throughout the sixth century A.D. and was fairly saturated, may have come from the northern or southern slopes of the Western Carpathians, or from the middle Danube basin, or all three. The settlement northwards along the Elbe basin to the Baltic occurred by the late seventh century.

212   Slavs may have already been resident in the forests and forest steppe zone of western Ukraine, to the east and northeast of the Carpathians—perhaps their earliest homeland—but if so the newer Korchak culture spread among them from the west, beginning in the early sixth century and reaching the Pripet and Dnieper Rivers by mid-seventh century.

213   There is evidence of Slavic presence along the Mureş River by mid-seventh century A.D.

214   Archeological evidence suggests that the Slavs living on the Great Hungarian Plain by the seventh century were mixed with Avars.

215   It is unlikely that all or even most of the areas the Slavs expanded into were completely unoccupied, even given the earlier exodus of Germanic tribes from north-central and eastern Europe during the Great Migration. How many people actually left for Roman opportunities to the southwest is uncertain. Most of the political, military, and social elites probably did, but perhaps not most, and certainly not all, of the obscure folks living off the land—people more concerned with scraping a living than with politics, war, and social identification and therefore willing to adopt new cultural norms. They may have even been attracted to the relatively simple, materially modest, egalitarian, and land-based lifestyle of the new arrivals, to whom they were no longer forced by a militarized elite to give up their surplus.

As well, there is historical evidence that the early Slavs as they expanded were welcoming to outsiders, at least where they were not contending with major powers. For example, according to *Maurice's Strategikon*, after an initial period of enslavement, prisoners were given the choice to integrate as equal members of the tribe or to leave—with "a small recompense" no less! (Dennis 1984). (This magnanimity, rare for its time, would dissolve by the ninth century A.D. into the lucrative effluent of the slave trade.) Judging by the cases of Samo in Moravia (see the next volume, Slovakia chapter) and Rurik in Novgorod, the Slavs seem to have also been open to retaining non-Slavic leaders when deemed advantageous. Its attraction for indigenous peasants along with the Slav's welcoming attitude surely hastened the expansion of Slavic culture, the scope and pace of which is nearly impossible to explain by internal demographics alone.

[216]   (Procopius, 7.14.27).

[217]   The term "democratic" comes from Procopius (Procopius, 7.14.22). Barford believes that "democratic" may have had a somewhat different connotation for the East Roman writers than it does for us today, implying "disorder" typical of barbarians compared to the disciplined "civilized" world, and that given the size and scope of the later Slavic raids into Byzantine lands, some significant hierarchical military leadership must have developed at least in the south by the late sixth century (Barford, 2001). Curta also supports this view (Curta, 2001). Procopius's language about "democracy" seems clear, however, as he goes on to say: "...consequently, anything that involves their welfare, whether for good or for ill, is a matter of common concern" (or "referred to the people," according to another translation).

In any case, the only "king" mentioned during this period is a reference by Jordanes to an earlier king of the Antes named Boz, but there is doubt as to the veracity of this report; Jordanes may have been drawing from earlier sources who were trying to boost the reputation of a common enemy: the Goths) (Barford 2001). Other contemporary sources say that these early Slavs had only "petty chiefs." On the other hand, Curta posits a controversial theory that it was a political-military elite that was the key to forming a Slavic identity amongst an ethnically mixed crowd raiding in the lower Danube and Balkan provinces during the early sixth century A.D. (Curta 2001).

[218]   The term "sensitive" comes from *Maurice's Strategikon* as translated by Dennis (Dennis 1984, 120); another translation is "chaste" (Barford 2001, 68). Maurice adds that the suicidal wives "smothered" themselves.

[219]   The first extant descriptions of the Antes and Sclaveni come from the works of the Roman historians Jordanes and Procopius, writing around 550 A.D. about raids into East Roman territory. The quote "swamps and forests for their cities" comes from Jordanes (Jordanes, translated 1908, 5).

Jordanes states that Antes and Sclaveni are the names of the two largest subdivisions of a wide-ranging people known as *Venedi* (see Appendix F). Procopius states that the Antes and Scalveni have been alike in their "institutions and beliefs" since ancient times, and that they speak the same language; he also claims that they were both called "Sporoi" in ancient times (which he suggests came from the word "sporadic," referring to the nature of their habitation—in other words, "wanderers") (Procopius, 7.14.29).

There is evidence that the Antes may have been established east of the Carpathians as early as the second century A.D., possibly originally organized by a Sarmatian (possibly Alan) elite that became absorbed into a Slavic majority as they migrated northward into the forest-steppe zone northeast of the mountains (the term *Antes*, for example, does not seem to be Slavic). In any case, while the Antes and Sclaveni may have been sometime allies, they also sometimes were not. The Antes ended up allying with the Byzantine Empire and were essentially destroyed by the Avars in 602 A.D., at least as a tribal polity.

220   Procopius states that Slav warriors were especially adept at hiding behind rocks and bushes from where they ambushed their enemies and cites an incident wherein one such warrior, working for the Romans against Goths, was able to "[draw] his body into a small shape." (Procopius, 6.26.22). *Maurice's Strategikon* recommends attacking the Slavs only during winters "...when they cannot easily hide among bare trees, when the tracks of fugitives can be discerned in the snow, when their household is miserable from exposure, and when it is easy to cross over the rivers on the ice" (Dennis 1984, 122).

221   Procopius puts it this way: "...some of them do not even wear a shirt or a cloak, but hitch their trousers as far as their private parts and so enter battle with their opponents" (Procopius, 7.14.26).

222   The Slavs had a complex relationship with the Avars. Some Slavs, such as the Sclaveni, were part-time allies of the Avars and some, such as the Antes, were part-time enemies. For a time, the Romans contracted with Avars to keep Slavs at bay. Bulgars also got into the mix, employing Slavs along their northern borders to keep Avars away, and hiring them in the south to help in disputes with Romans. As the Avars took over the entire Pannonian basin and Transylvania during the latter sixth and seventh centuries, they took Slavs with them to do most of their fighting. Thus, Avars brought Slavs to the northwest, where the Danube meets the mountains at the western end of the Carpathians and where Slavic subjects were surely motivated to escape into Dalmatia, Carinthia, Moravia, Bohemia and through the Moravian Gate to points further north. Dalmatia became the center of resistance of the Croats, and Serbia of the Serbs, and Moravia and the southern slopes of the Carpathians of the Moravians (Slovaks). Meanwhile, so important and numerous were the Slavs to their Avar overlords, the Slavic language became the *lingua franca* of the Avar Khagnate.

223   This expansion of an originally obscure group of farmers, shepherds, and lumberjacks from some small patch of misty and hilly woodland on the northeast fringe of the Carpathians to cover much of Central and Eastern Europe in something under four hundred years is amazing—almost mysterious—and historians have been hard pressed to explain it. The picture I paint herein presents the highlights of the more or less most accepted view as extracted by

historians from scant written sources (none for events north of the Carpathians) and an archeological record consisting mostly of broken pottery, rotted hut foundations, crumbling stone ovens, and buried urns filled with the ashes of ancient cremated peasants. The lack of data leaves lots of room for alternate theories of what was surely a complex and varied process driven by multiple motivations. Debates have raged about whether the Slavic explosion was mostly an unorganized and relatively peaceful movement of human beings who absorbed indigenous populations as they went (seems to be the case in the Carpathians and the Sudetes), or was mostly an organized and violent displacement (seems to be the case in the Balkans, at least initially, and the northeastern forests, at least later), and whether it was mostly the movement of peasants, or of an evolving elite or warrior class, or was mostly the transmission of habits, technology, and language. There is evidence and argument for all at various times and places, but one thing seems clear: the Carpathian Mountains played a major role in shaping the distribution, lifestyle, and character of the Slavic people.

[224]   Church Slavonic is the later form of the original language (called Old Church Slavonic) used in the liturgy at the beginning of the Christian missionary in Slavic lands (specifically, Great Moravia) in the ninth century A.D. (more about this in the next volume: *The Western Mountains*). Old Church Slavonic is the first Slavic language put in writing. Church Slavonic is still used in the liturgy of some Orthodox churches.

[225]   The *Wielkopolska Chronicle*, written around 1400.

[226]   The original founding of Kyiv is shrouded in legend, but a settlement may have existed at the site as early as the fifth century A.D. The primary tribes in the area (between the Dnieper and Don Rivers) at that time were the Polianians and Derevlianians. Legend has it that the city was founded by a Polianian leader named Kyi and his three younger siblings: brothers Shchek and Khoryv, and sister Lybid.

[227]   The original founding of Novgorod is also shrouded in legend. Several medieval chronicles, including the Russian Primary Chronicle, refer to Novgorod as existing by the mid-ninth century A.D. and being the site to which the legendary Rurik moved the primary political and commercial roles of two earlier settlements (i.e., his "capital"): *Holmgard* and *Ladoga**. The chronicles were written a few centuries later, however, and dendrochronology (tree-ring dating) dates Novgorod's earliest buildings and wooden streets only to the late tenth century A.D.—over a hundred years later than the time of its legendary role. Thus the legendary details are suspect, but in any case, upon its building or soon after, Novgorod did indeed become the political center of the northern Rus' realm; and thus its name, which means "New City."

* Holmgard and Ladoga were among the first outposts taken over (or built) by the Vikings, who were expanding eastward from the Baltic, and used as trading centers, first to gather goods from the people of the local forests for customers in western Europe, and later for what would become a trading route "to the Greeks" (i.e., Byzantium and other southern empires).

Holmgard was located very close to Novgorod along the northern shores of Lake Ilmen at the egress of the Volkhov River. Archeology establishes that Holmgard was built by the mid-ninth century, making it a likely candidate for the later references to Novgorod, and legend makes Rurik its builder. The name *is* Scandinavian, it features prominently in certain Norse sagas, and it was built of stone rather than the more typical wood, with walls three meters high and three meters thick. Thus it was probably in fact founded by Varangians.

Ladoga was located along the Volkhov River a few miles upstream from where it flows into Lake Ladoga, about 200 kilometers north of Novgorod. Dendrochronology establishes that Ladoga was founded about 100 years earlier than Holmgard, its first houses built around 737.

[228] The term "Varangian" is imprecise and may have referred to most or all water-borne travelers, merchants, and pirates migrating across the Baltic from the Scandinavian Peninsula; it is derived from the Old Norse word for "faithful companion," but the label may have first been used in Byzantium in reference to the Scandinavian adventurers.

The etymology of the term "Rus'" is a matter of some controversy that has important connotations for those concerned with the historical roots of Russia. Evidence seems to establish that the term originally referred to a subset of Varangians probably from what is now Sweden, although perhaps only to those who first settled in the area of Lake Ladoga and whose political-economic center became Novgorod—maybe originally only to the princely family and retinue of Rurik. It may have ultimately derived from a Finnish label for Swedes ("*Ruotsi*"), or from the ancient Swedish (Old Norse) word for a crew of warrior-oarsmen.

[229] Trade along the Volga route had begun as early as the seventh century A.D. Trade along the Dnieper did not seriously get underway until the Rus' were established at Kyiv in the ninth century and the Khazars had been pushed back.

[230] By the Early Middle Ages the Slavic peoples were being held as slaves by people on all sides: north, east, south, and west:

North: Not all slaves were sold by the ninth and tenth century Rus' invaders; some were kept by them.

East: Slaves from Slavic territories had been sold to Arab and Khazar slave traders since at least the eighth century.

South: Slavic slaves were captured by or sold to the Byzantine Empire, and later, various Islamic polities.

West: German-based dominions captured and enslaved their eastern Slavic neighbors beginning at least by the tenth century (e.g., Otto the Great of the Holy Roman Empire).

[231] Examples of favorable trading terms forced from the Byzantine Empire: Rus' merchants would be fed and sheltered, be free from taxation, be supplied for their return journeys, and be given access to baths. In return they had to refrain from committing crimes.

²³² The report of ten percent of profit going to the Grand Prince of Kievan Rus' comes from Ahmad ibn Fadlan, an Arab chronicler writing in the tenth century.

²³³ The fact that the Scandinavians were always a small minority is clear from the fact that there are very few Scandinavian place names in the region and very little influence on East Slavic languages from Scandinavian languages.

²³⁴ The first Grand Prince to take a Slavic name was Sviatoslav, who reigned from 962 until 972.

²³⁵ Volodymyr had to claim the throne of Kievan Rus' by force from his brothers with the help of an army raised in Sweden.

²³⁶ The enumeration of Volodymyr's concubines comes from the Russian Primary Chronicle (Cross and Sherbowitz-Wetzor 2012, 94).

²³⁷ Volodymyr may have converted to satisfy political and romantic as well as spiritual needs: The Byzantine co-emperors at the time insisted upon it as a prerequisite for the Rus' prince's marriage to their sister. Volodymyr wanted close ties with Constantinople—in fact, he had just helped out the Byzantine emperors win a civil war—and since marriage at the dynastic level was often a vehicle for establishing or strengthening political ties in those days, both the marriage and the conversion would help achieve this goal. Unlike today, the personal motivations of leaders was not well reported in those days, so we cannot know the relative weight of politics, love, and faith involved in Volodymyr's conversion, although he did subsequently resist Byzantine control of the Russian church to the point of armed conflict.

The Russian Primary Chronicle offers a legendary account of Volodymyr's conversion in which he carefully considers the four major faiths surrounding his realm—Byzantine Christianity, Roman Catholic Christianity, Judaism, and Islam—before ruling the latter three out for some rather nonspiritual reasons, and then finally converting to Christianity when his wife-to-be declares that the only cure for his recently lost eyesight (due to an illness) is to be baptized—which promptly happens.

²³⁸ Volodymyr apparently always recognized the role that religion could play in promoting state governance and social unity. When he first came to power he consolidated various local pagan traditions into a more uniform cult to help unify the many tribes of the realm. He put the thunder-god firmly in the lead and publicly honored Perun and five other leading Slavic deities with large wooden statues erected on a hill near the palace in Kyiv.

²³⁹ Volodymyr's feats earned him a central position in *byliny*—epic folk poems sung at East Slavic festivals and family gatherings at least until the nineteenth century. In these stories the Prince is often portrayed as a venerable grandfatherly figure. Akin to King Arthur, he or his court spur fantastic, quirky quests by up-and-coming, younger heroes. Antagonists are stylized as "Tartars," dragons, vampires, werewolves, or other monsters over whom the sometimes overconfident heroes, known as *bogatyri*—

mighty knights on even mightier steeds (who morph into Cossacks in later Ukrainian tales called *dumy*)—often but not always triumph. Sometimes they are brought down by their own pride and boastfulness. The *bogatyri* often also get the girl, but sometimes it's the other way around: sometimes remarkable female warriors known as *polyanitzi* come to the rescue, exceeding their male counterparts in guile and strength.

240   The defense of Kyiv against the Mongol invasion of 1240 was led by Dmytro, whose leadership was so valiant that Batu uncharacteristically spared his life. Dmytro was sent by Danylo Halytskyi, the prince of the principality of Galicia-Volhynia, one of the centers to where power had spread with the dispersal of Rurik princes and the decline of Kievan Rus'. Danylo (or *Daniel*) had consolidated several principalities and acquired responsibility for Kyiv in 1239. After the fall of Kyiv, Daniel was forced to acknowledge the overlordship of Batu, but he continued to work to subvert the rule of the Mongols. He obtained Papal sanction for his resistance and thus became the first Rurik to transcend mere princedom, being crowned the first "King of the Rus' Kingdom" in 1253 (which at the time meant Galicia-Volhynia, including the Carpathians north of the divide). He never received the Papal troops he needed to completely shake off Mongol rule, however. He was the founder of the city of L'viv, which he named after his son, Lev, who took parts of Transcarpathia from Hungary and added them to the Rus' kingdom.

241   There is a mythology that delves even deeper into prehistory that claims that Ukrainians, and maybe all Slavs for that matter, ultimately descend from Magog, son of Japheth, son of Noah—a story especially popular during the seventeenth century. Many other European nationalities have proponents that similarly claim descent from Japheth, to whose lot, according to the Russian Primary Chronicle, "...fell the northern and western sectors." The first century A.D. Jewish historian Flavius Josephus specifies pretty much the entire region surrounding the Black Sea as the destination of the sons of Japheth.

242   The east Slavic tribes that comprised Kievan Rus' may have already been diverging before the formation of the state in a way that contributed to the later genesis of the three nationalities. Thus it may be that the Ukrainian national heritage is more derived from the earlier Slavic tribes of Polianians, Volhynians, Derevlianians, Severiane, Ulichs, White Croats, and Tivercians (the latter two in the Carpathian region); the Belarusian heritage more from the Krivichians and Dregovichians; and the Russian heritage more from the Viatichians and Slovienienes.

243   The traditional magical rites performed when the sheep and shepherds were first sent up the slopes each spring included practices such as circling the flock three times carrying axes and torches, putting nettles into the wooden casks that will carry milk, and measuring the milk produced on departure day to divine the season's production (Bogatyrev 1998, 73-74).

244   The institution of serfdom evolved gradually in Eastern Europe,

beginning in the fifteenth century, about when it was dying out in Western Europe. Starting with the right to judge them, nobles and landowners gained more and more control over the lives of the peasants, including the imposition of increasingly onerous labor obligations (known as *corvée*), until, with a decree in 1505 by the parliament of the Polish-Lithuanian Commonwealth (known as the *sejm*), which ruled most of the area of Ukraine at the time, peasants essentially became enserfed since they could no longer leave their village without their lord's permission. By the time of emancipation in the Russian Empire in 1861, about 42% of the people of Ukraine were privately owned serfs (about half the peasantry) and most of the rest (including about one million former Cossacks) were "state peasants"—a bit better off than privately owned serfs, but still bonded, albeit to the state instead of to individual lords. Serfdom was rare in the Carpathian highlands, however, where labor was scarce and so concessions required. The few serfs in Transcarpathia, which was ruled by Hungary rather than Russia, were emancipated in 1848.

[245]   By the nineteenth century, language, perhaps more than any other cultural attribute, ultimately defined what it meant to be Ukrainian. Russian imperial authorities knew this and attempted to extinguish the concept of Ukraine by extinguishing its language:

In 1863, the minister of internal affairs (Petr Valuev) banned the use of Ukrainian in all scholarly and religious publications.

In 1876, in a ruling known as the "Ems Ukaz," Tsar Alexander II closed Ukrainian newspapers and completely banned the publication and import of books written in Ukrainian, the use of Ukrainian on stage, and the teaching of Ukrainian in elementary schools.

[246]   The village teacher was the *precentor* of the village—a layperson in the Ukrainian Orthodox or Greek Catholic churches who assisted in church activities. He was also the person who taught Shevchenko to read.

[247]   Luckyj, cited in (Subtelny 2000, 233).

[248]   An earlier writer, Ivan Kotlyarevsky, is generally credited with being the first to publish a work in what is considered modern Ukrainian, in the late eighteenth century. Shevchenko's work is considered to represent a more mature and sophisticated linguistic progression. Shevchenko honored his literary predecessor with his poem, "To the Eternal Memory of Kotlyarevsky."

[249]   Romanticism is a categorization of artistic expression that began in Europe in the late eighteenth century and peaked in the early nineteenth century that emphasized emotion as a fundamental source of human experience and nature as a primary source of aesthetic inspiration. A reaction to industrialization and rationalization, Romanticism was a look back to what was perceived as a purer and nobler past, an attempt to restore the relevance of folk art and ancient customs and the importance of imagination and spontaneity in inspiring and guiding human thought and behavior.

[250]   (Yasinsky and Pashkova 1998).

[251]   Saints Cyril and Methodius were Byzantine Greek brothers and

Christian missionaries, first to Arabs and Khazars and then to Slavs during ninth century. They are credited with devising the Glagolithic alphabet, which used a Greek-like script along with symbols they created or derived from Hebrew to express Slavic phonetics so they could transcribe the Bible into the Slavic language (which was less divergent than it later became). The Cyrillic script and its variants that are used today for many of the Slavic national and regional languages of Eastern Europe and Central Asia are descended from the Glagolithic alphabet. More about Cyril and Methodius when we get to Slovakia.

There are some claims of a pre-Glagolithic script among the Slavs by some Ukrainian historians, of which there are supposed sample traces on display at the St. Sophia Museum in Kyiv, but more extensive examples have never been found (Wilson 2002, 32)—unless one accepts the authenticity of the Book of Veles (see endnote 300).

[252] The Shevchenko Literary Society later evolved into the Shevchenko Scientific Society. The organization had a turbulent legacy as it faced suppression. Many of its members were arrested and imprisoned or executed by the Soviet Red Army when they occupied L'viv in 1939 and forced it to disband. It was resurrected in 1989 and is the publisher of the online Encyclopedia of Ukraine: http://www.encyclopediaofukraine.com/

[253] (Dennis 1984, 121).

[254] The karst caves of Uholsko-Shyrokoluzhanskyi include the Druzhba ("Friendship") Cave, which has nearly a kilometer of corridors and one great hall of dripstones, and the Molochnyi ("Milk Stone") Cave, where Paleolithic humans once took shelter in the milky white rooms under reams of stalactite daggers. Paleolithic human occupants of the Milk Stone Cave left stone tools and fireplaces, and some researchers suggest they were hunters of the cave bears whose bones were associated with the artifacts; at least one researcher questions this conclusion, however (Ridush, B., 2012).

[255] Since such dogs have hung onto the outskirts of villages for millennia without much interference from humans in their breeding choices, they may have diverged less from wolves than those dogs that were selectively bred. See (Ratliff 2012).

[256] Elina Sawicki. "Wolves harm people." *Express*, 11-18 July 2013, p. 14 (the largest circulation newspaper in Ukraine).

[257] *Verkhovyna* may refer generically to the upper slopes just below the Carpathian crests in Subcarpathia, or more specifically to the extreme northcentral and northwestern region of Transcarpathia, the traditional homeland of the Boykos.

[258] The traditional Boyko homeland includes both the northern and southern slopes of the Ukrainian Carpathians, including areas in today's Zakarpattia, Ivano-Frankivs'k, and L'viv oblasts. It includes ridges north of the Carpathian divide that are also called the High Beskyds (or Skole Beskyds) and Middle Beskyds, as well as a southeast-northwest line of lower hills and valleys called the Mid-Carpathian Depression that separates the Beskyds from

the main Carpathian chain; south of the divide, it includes the Volovets' district and the northwestern Mizghiria and far northern Velykyi Bereznyi districts of the Zakarpattia Oblast; it extends to the west as far as the valleys of the Solinka and upper San River valleys in southeastern Poland (Magocsi 2006).

259   Genetic evidence suggests Boyko origins dating as far back as the Linear Pottery Culture, which existed in the region about 7,000 years ago (preceding the Cucuteni-Trypillian culture) (Nikitin, et al. 2009). The Boyko word of affirmation, "bo-ye," along with other unique aspects of their dialect is also taken by some scholars as evidence of an autochthonous heritage for the Boyko. An alternative but less accepted theory posits Boyko origins in the ancient Celtic Boii tribe: an obvious similarity of diction, but most scholars consider this only a coincidence.

260   (Nikitin, et al. 2009).

261   The Magyars displaced most of the Slavic presence from the Carpathian region south of the drainage of the Tisza (i.e., from Transylvania—essentially the southern half of the Carpathians) as far as the Danube, as well as from the Carpathian Basin (i.e., Wallachia and Pannonia). This created a gap between northern Slavs (who further split into East and West) and the southern Slavs living in the Balkans. The Slavs of Transylvania did however leave some of their vocabulary, place names, and perhaps other cultural influences such as embroidered clothing and egg painting.

262   See (Heisler and Mellon 1946) for example.

263   Multiple families living in Boyko huts were reportedly common in the nineteenth century. The families were typically those of the sons of the house. (Bonkalo 1990, 72).

264   (Bonkalo 1990, 75).

265   (Bonkalo 1990, 120).

266   That the Magyars came down the valley of the Latorysta is confirmed by Bonkalo (Bonkalo 1990, 12).

267   (*Gesta Hungarorum*, 18).

268   Laborets' as defender of the Castle of Ungvár is first mentioned in the *Gesta Hungarorum*—the earliest chronicle of Hungary written in the thirteenth century about the arrival of the Magyars—though not exactly as a stout defender. It just says that he fled and was captured and hung. The heroic legends seem to have come later, and Bonkalo claims they were created to establish a Rusyn cultural heritage and presence predating the arrival of the Magyars (Bonkalo 1990, 54). In any case, the *Gesta Hungarorum* makes it clear that the people living in the region when the Magyars arrived were Slavs, and so presumably was Laborets'. The nearby Laborec River in eastern Slovakia was named for him.

269   As part of the Arpad Line, the Veretsky Pass was also the scene of intense fighting during World War Two.

270   In some traditions, before becoming full-fledged *rusalki*, the unquiet

souls spend seven years in another purgatorial state called *navki*, manifesting as birds that cry out like babies and jealously harassing pregnant women as they search for someone to baptize them. Also in some traditions the *rusalki* could shape-shift into animals, like werewolves.

271   In some traditions the eyes of the *rusalki* were as black as the void, while in others they glowed greenish or red.

272   Some traditions have the *rusalki* beginning their nightly extra-aqueous adventures on Green (Maundy) Thursday (the Thursday before Easter) and lasting until the first thunderstorm of the season.

273   In some traditions, *rusalki* spirits could find peace: if they were a murder victim and their killer was apprehended.

274   An iconic monument to *Berehynia* towers over the Maidan (Independence Square) in Kiev, although for most Ukrainians it is a symbol of an abstract "national matriarch" (akin to "Lady Liberty") rather than a pagan goddess.

275   Food and Agriculture Organization of the United Nations Statistics Division http://faostat3.fao.org/browse/rankings/countries_by_commodity/E

276   Ukraine generally produced about 25% of the grain produced in the Soviet Union. During the Holodomor, it was officially required as a matter of law to produce one third.

277   The wide range in estimates of Holodomor deaths (which prior to recent research was even larger, between 1.8 and 12 million) is due to the lack of records. The higher end of the range includes deaths in southern Russia east of the current border of Ukraine, in a region called Kuban where many ethnic Ukrainians lived. Ukrainians were not the only victims: many thousands of Belarusians, Russians, Moldovans, and Kazakhstanis also suffered and died.

278   Peasants were identified (or misidentified for reasons of incompetence, envy, or grudge) as *kulaks* and "exploiters of the people" by a local *troika* consisting of the head of the village Soviet (council), the local Communist party secretary, and a secret police representative.

279   There were two kinds of Ukrainian minstrels, the *kobzari* and the *lirnyky*, depending on the instrument they played; the *kobzari* played a *bandura*—a kind of asymmetrical lute, and the *lirnyky* played a *lira*—a kind of hurdy-gurdy. The *kobzari* were pretty much limited to the region of Ukraine whereas the *lirnyky* ranged further. They probably started out less formally, at least in part as blind people trying to earn a living, but by the nineteenth century they had become organized into professional church-affiliated guilds, which provided training, apprenticeship, and enforced a requirement of blindness and competency. They specialized in long performances of epic folktales based on Ukrainian historic events. Most of the minstrels were executed during the 1930s under the order of Stalin. There is no official record, but the story is told that most were murdered when they came to attend a convention arranged by the authorities in 1932 or 1933 (some sources say 1939).

280   The Soviet collectivization of farms eliminated private ownership of

the land. Farms were worked collectively with the produce owned by the state. Food was rationed back to the farmers after quotas were met. Not completely ignoring the natural human motivation invoked by incentives, rations would be increased for meeting or exceeding quotas and reduced for not; the rewards were taken away during the Holodomor. Lenin-inspired economic theory believed that such a system would ensure optimum production and a more certain supply of food for urban workers, and Soviet propaganda encouraged the latter to believe it was so.

Ironically, in addition to poor productivity in the early days, the emphasis on trying to maximize short-term production along with the natural disinterest that results from non-ownership led to the abuse of landscapes—overuse of fields and overcutting of forests leading to soil erosion as well as the drainage of wetlands. Fortunately, collectivization was limited in the remote Carpathians.

An example of the disincentivizing effect of the Soviet collectivization of farms can be seen from statistics in 1970. At that time, in addition to the collectivized land, farmers were allowed to own private one-acre plots upon which they could do whatever they wanted—albeit on their own time. Although privately owned land was only 3% of the land under cultivation, it produced 33% of the USSR's meat, 40% of its dairy products, and 55% of its eggs and provided 36% of family income in Ukraine (Subtelny 2000, 528.

[281]   Approximately 2,500 people were convicted of cannibalism during the Holodomor.

[282]   The Joint Declaration at the United Nations on the 70th Anniversary of the Great Famine of 1932-1933 in Ukraine (Holodomor), November 10, 2003. The Declaration cites a figure of between 7 and 10 million for the number of people who died.

[283]   (Bonkalo 1990, 35).

[284]   Bonkalo, writing in the politically turbulent 1930s, claims that "The Czechs did not let in the grain and food collected in Hungary." Bonkalo's work is highly slanted, however, with an agenda of denying the Carpathian Rusyns any kind of national history, making them rather into Hungarians, and he takes all kinds of shots at non-Hungarian influences (e.g., Ukrainian, Russian, Czechoslovakian). So although his work is a valuable source of rare information about early twentieth century Carpathian Ruthenia, some of his conclusions and even "facts" have to be taken with a grain of salt. I have not found confirmation elsewhere that it was a policy of the Czechoslovakian government to starve the Rusyns living in their country.

[285]   The Chernobyl Exclusion Zone is a 2,600-square-kilometer (1,004-square-mile) area spanning Ukraine's northern border with Belarus, created in 1986 after the nuclear power plant explosion. Originally a circle with a radius of 30 kilometers (18.6 miles), it has since been adjusted to reflect measured radiation levels. The entire population—some 200,000 people—was eventually required to evacuate, and all but around 200 mostly

elderly residents remain excluded today. Nevertheless, although radiation can negatively affect individuals, and studies have found genetic abnormalities in field mice, insects and birds, as well as a reduction in the density and diversity of insects and birds in the most contaminated areas, what was a disaster for people has apparently been a boon for populations of many species of wildlife. Populations of wolves, wild boar (these first two especially), roe deer, red deer, foxes, badgers, raccoon dogs, ferrets, moose, beavers, lynx, and brown bears are all believed to have increased significantly (the latter four from almost none), and European bison (*Bison bonasus*) and Przewalski's horses (*Equus ferus przewalskii*) have been successfully reintroduced (Sparks 2013).

[286] Studies have shown a wide variation in the rate of mortality that can be sustained by wolf populations, depending on environmental and demographic factors and when during the year and which wolves are killed (breeding pair or not). The majority of studies, however, indicate sustainable harvest rates under 50% (Fuller at al., in Mech and Boitani 2003, 184-185).

[287] In 2012 the official rates of poverty and unemployment in Ukraine were 24 percent and 7.4 percent, respectively, but in reality each is much higher.

[288] Except for a few in the Chernobyl Exclusion Zone, the other two large predators of Ukraine, European brown bears and Eurasian lynx, are pretty much confined to the Carpathians. The official estimate of the number of brown bears in Ukraine is approximately 400, a number that is considered fairly accurate by independent wildlife experts. This implies a bear density about one third the overpopulated density of Romania. Bears can be legally hunted in Ukraine; few permits are issued, but poaching is significant. The overall trend for the bear population in Ukraine since 2000 is believed to be slightly decreasing, although increasing in certain areas.

The official estimate of the number of lynx in Ukraine is 350; independent experts believe the actual number is somewhat higher. Lynx is the most sensitive of the large carnivores and therefore is completely protected in Ukraine, although poaching is considered a threat. The population is believed to have been relatively stable since 2000. All official large carnivore population figures for Ukraine are from (Zibordi, et al. 2012) and reflect numbers provided in 2010.

[289] www.carpathianconvention.org

[290] (Zingstra H.L. 2009).

[291] (Batt and Wolczuk, 2002).

[292] One mythological motif portrays Perun (male sky) as impregnating the feminine earth (Mokosh) with his seed (rain).

[293] Mythology can manifest as a state-sanctioned or elite-sanctioned "official" religion, which has some chance of being written about, or as folklore, which is mostly oral (until recorded by folklorists or appearing in literature). Neither is static, and folkloric mythology in particular can vary almost by village. After all, if the religion of a people has not been cast in writing, or

is not enforced by a state or a rigorous and unified religious elite, then all it takes is the imagination of a single oral poet, storyteller, or minstrel to inject a mythological detail into the body of folklore.

In the case of pre-Christian Slavic mythology, the earliest written glimpse may be the werewolves of the Neuri, reported by Herodotus, although it is not certain that the Neuri were Slavic.

The earliest *certain* source is Procopius, the East Roman historian writing about the Slavs who were attacking the Empire in the sixth century A.D., who gives a brief description of a Slavic deity who sounds a lot like Perun. In 922 A.D., Ahmad ibn Fadlan describes Rus' praying to a "large post with a face like that of a man" who also sounds a lot like Perun (Barford 2001, 173).

The next sources are mostly Christian clerics and missionaries writing with agendas: For East Slavs, the author(s) of the *Russian Primary Chronicle* writing in the twelfth century about events as early as the ninth century; and for the West Slavs: Thietmar of Merseburg writing around 1012-1018 about events in 908-1018; Helmold of Bosau writing in the late twelfth century about events beginning around 800; Saxo Grammaticus writing in the late twelfth and early thirteenth centuries about the Slavic "Wends" who were attacking Denmark at that time; and Saint Otto of Bamberg, writing in the early twelfth century. Of these, only Saxo was not a cleric.

Thus, scholars of Slavic mythology have been forced into extracting inferences about Slavic gods and goddesses from very little written source material, all of which is secondhand and most of which was written by folks more interested in eradicating pagan beliefs than in accurately reporting them. Sometimes all we have about a particular deity is a single sentence in a single indirect source. In other cases, scholars infer from place names that a particular deity was probably at least known in the region.

The lack of written sources has resulted in a flexibility that has allowed for numerous interpretations, as well as inventions, of Slavic mythology, and there have been recent attempts to reconstruct Slavic mythology from an analysis of folkloric elements scattered throughout literature or recorded by folklorists, comparative Indo-European mythology, and folklore that is still told in the hinterlands.

[294]   Perun is not mentioned in any of the earliest chronicles about West Slavic paganism, although Helmold refers to a cult site for a deity called "Proven," which may be Perun. Also, the Polish word for lightning and thunderbolt is *piorun*. Thus Gasparini, for example, posits that Perun as thunder god was universal among the Slavs (Gasparini).

[295]   Procopius put it this way: "They believe that one god, the maker of lightning, is alone lord of all things" (Procopius, 7.14.23).

Helmold of Bosau in his *Chronicle of the Slavs* reports that the Slavic peoples living in the area of northwestern Poland during the twelfth century believed in a single heavenly deity who delegated the operation of the world to spirits "begotten" by him (Gasparini). Some scholars have thus argued that early Slavic worship consisted of "pantheism tending towards monotheism" and therefore its adherents were especially receptive to conversion to Christianity (Wilson 2002, 35).

[296]   Other derivative Indo-European thunder gods include the Norse god Thor (an instance of the wider Germanic deity Donar), the Baltic god Perkūnas, the Greek god Zeus, the Roman god Jupiter, the Celtic god Taranis, the Thracian god Zibelthiurdos, possibly the Dacian god Zalmoxis (and/or Gebeleizis, who may be the same), and the Hindu god Indra.

[297]   Envisioned by the newly converted as "... [riding] across the sky in a fiery chariot striking the earth with lightning bolts as he pursued the unclean force" (Ivanits 1989, 29), St. Elijah easily absorbed the characteristics of Perun. Like Perun, he brought water to the fields, spilt from his chariot as he carried it to the other saints, and if angry could flatten the crops with hail.

[298]   Details about Perun—his characteristics, feats, and role—are largely derived from folklore and were not universal, likely varying by both geography and time. The earliest written references to Perun, for example, say nothing about his axe/hammer. Was it a later absorption from Thor? The story of imprisonment by demons during winter (Yoffe and Krafczik 2003) may not have been universal. Folklore also gives Perun various wives: the Sun, (occasionally stolen by Veles, and completely contradicting the Sun as a male god such as Dazhbog); Mokosh; and Dodola (also called Perperuna), a goddess of rain.

[299]   Gasparini claims the Perun and Svarog may have been the only two deities common to all Slavs (Gasparini); Phillips and Kerrigan make the same claim for Svarog, Svarožič, and Dazhbog (Phillips and Kerrigan 1999).

[300]   There doesn't seem to be a natural connection between cattle, abundance, and death, and it may be that the name Volos (or Veles) or variants of it referred to different gods in different times and places; thus Volos of Cattle may not have been the same as Volos the Lord of the Underworld and enemy of Perun.

Volos's name was also invoked for the most famous forgery of Slavic history: *The Book of Veles*, although it does not focus on the underworld god. Claimed to be a translation of a text carved into wood planks in pre-Christian times (sometime prior to the tenth century A.D.) in an ancient and lost Slavic script, the book presents historical and religious tracts describing events and beliefs going back as early as the tenth century B.C., including the migration of the Slavs into the Carpathian Mountains. The original wood planks were allegedly found in Ukraine in 1919 by a Russian soldier (Fedor Izenbek) who handed them over to a Russian scholar (Yuriy Mirolyubov) who subsequently studied and translated them over a 15-year period. Such is the story first told either by the scholar, or the editor of a Russian émigré magazine in the United States where the translation was first published, or by the professor work who submitted it for publication, or all three. The original planks, if they ever existed, have been lost, and almost all modern scholars of Slavic mythology and linguistics who have analyzed it believe the work is a forgery. Nevertheless, *The Book of Veles* is assumed by some Neo-pagans today to be an authentic pagan Slavic religious text.

301   In Ukraine, *Koliada* originally referred to a series of winter rituals. Today, in many Slavic countries *Koliada* is associated with Christmas, and often refers specifically to the door-to-door caroling by young people on Christmas Eve. There are speculations that *Koliada* was also a Slavic sky goddess.

302   The philologists who reconstructed the tale of the battle between Perun and Veles are Vyacheslav Vsevolodovich Ivanov and Vladimir Toporov. There are secondary descriptions of this reconstructed myth all over the internet, but the only primary source I could find is an obscure reference to a 1973 article by Ivanov and Toporov entitled (translated) "The Problem of Authenticity of Late Secondary Sources in Relation to Mythological Studies (The Data on Veles in the Traditions of Northern Russia and Critique of Written Texts)." The natural cycles that supposedly get explained include the water cycles and the seasons.

303   The only pre-modern written reference to Svarog comes from a medieval Slavic translation of an Egyptian history written by a Greek historian, John Malalas, in the sixth century. The Slavic translator replaced the names of certain classical gods with names that are presumed to refer to existing Slavic deities that are equivalent (or roughly so), in this case *Svarog* for the Greek god *Hephaestus,* which thereby gave Svarog his more limited terrestrial roles. There is, however, additional indirect and etymological evidence for the existence of an independent Slavic sky-god called Svarog, to whom folklore and some modern scholars give the more celestial and primary roles described here; some give him the role of original Creator and some do not.

304   Some references also portray Dazhbog as a god of wealth and plenty, while others suggest a dark side, portraying him more as a demon than a god. Some southern references link Dazhbog with a Serbian god that was a "Shepherd of wolves," a god who ruled the underworld.

305   The name Svarožič is the diminutive of Svarog and as such can be interpreted as either "little Svarog" or "the son of Svarog" (or both). Original written mythologies not being available, it is uncertain whether Svarožič was considered a literal progeny of Svarog by all Slavic worshippers everywhere, or even whether Svarog, Dazhbog, and Svarožič were considered different gods or different aspects of one god. Or perhaps Svarog as the original sky god devolved over time into the two sons, gods of celestial and terrestrial fire. It may be that for some Slavic worshippers, Svarog represented the "old" dying sun prior to the winter solstice, Dazhbog the "new" rising sun after the solstice, and Svarožič the terrestrial fire. In any case, there are references to Svarožič in both the east and west; in the east he was definitively referred to as the god of fire; in the west among Elbe Slavs near the Baltic coast he had his own temple, which was destroyed probably sometime in the eleventh or twelfth centuries.

Hudec, whose work has a west-Slavic emphasis, takes a contrary tack for Svarožič and keeps him aloft as charioteer of the sun and supreme ruler of the other gods after being given the role by his father Svarog, who then curls up and sleeps inside the sun (Hudec, 2000).

306   In the tradition of Svarog as Creator, all the gods and goddesses have their genesis in Svarog, but Dazhbog and Svarožič are usually presented as the only *primary* progeny. Yoffe and Krafczik, however, also present Perun as a primary offspring of Svarog, essentially a specific manifestation of "Svarožič" (son of Svarog) (Yoffe and Krafczik, 2003).

307   In one tradition attributed to "Polish mythology," Simargl is the name of a "doomsday" hound bound to the northern star, who is guarded by two sister deities—the *Zorya*—one being the evening star and the other the morning star, and who also serve Dazhbog. If Simargl ever breaks loose, it will devour the constellation of Ursa Minor and the world will end.

(Hudec 2000) presents Simargl as a two-headed, female bird who was messenger of the gods and persecutor of poachers. As mentioned, Slavic mythology is rich with varied stories, some of which have been invented since pre-Christian times.

308   Moist Mother Earth may be the Slavic label for the eldest of Eurasian deities, the ubiquitous and vital fertility goddess, perhaps represented by the feminine figurines that are common in the archeological record before the coming of Proto-Indo-Europeans.

309   Several aspects of Ivan Kupala Day have been linked with Perun, and in one folkloric story, Perun is rescued by Zaria and nurtured with her tears of morning dew after falling from the sky on the shortest night of the year; some versions have Perun being thrown down by a demon of drought.

310   Some scholars identify Rod instead of Perun as the original supreme Slavic god, the creator of all existence, and it may be that Perun replaced the more indigenous Rod as a result of Scandinavian influence. In fact Rod has been adopted as the top Slavic god by some modern Slavic-Neopagans, who call themselves Rodnovers.

311   The temple of Svetovid was located on Rügen Island, just off the Baltic coast. It was supposedly well-defended and housed the tribe's treasury. Although historical references link Svetovid only to this island, a 2.5-meter tall limestone statue of the god was found in western Ukraine, and his name made it into most Slavic languages.

312   According to one reconstruction, Jarilo was a son of Perun. He was celebrated in springtime festivals and eventually evolved into Saint George.

313   Radegast was mentioned by a few German chroniclers in the eleventh and twelfth centuries as being worshiped by the Luticians, a west Slavic tribal confederation living in what is now northeastern Germany. Details are lacking, but perhaps due only to the meaning of his name (something like "valued guest"), modern Slavic mythological reconstruction has cast Radegast as a god of hospitality. Hospitality being a very important attribute of traditional Slavic folk custom, Radegast has made enough of an impression in the modern Czech Republic that he has a beer named after him and a rather impressive statue carved of him

Although there is no evidence, and although they share no attributes in common that I can discern, the name "Radegast" is very close to J. R. R. Tolkien's wizard Radegast the Brown, and it seems unlikely that the English scholar of Northern European languages had never heard of Radegast.

314   There are very few stone statues and very little evidence of temples in the Slavic pagan archeological record. The few that have been found were probably relatively late innovations, made around the time of contact with Christian societies. Many of the stone statues are polycephalic: multi-headed representations of multi-gods. Could these be expressions of at least an intuitive belief in the unity underlying the multiplicity in the divine (if not also the profane) world?

315   According to written reports, offerings to Perun (or in the case of Procopius's report, to "...the one god, the maker of lightning") included cattle, beer, and wine (Procopius, 7.14.23). Folklore also includes goats and suggests that red roosters were symbolic of Perunian fire and lightning and were sacrificed into the fires. Two incidents of human sacrifices to "the gods"—Perun and/or Volos are implied—are mentioned in the Russian Primary Chronicle, although they may be inventions by writers who were writing with an agenda to discredit paganism. Helmold's *Chronica Slavorum* also mentions the sacrifice of Christian captives to the Slavic pagan gods, although he was writing about the (necessary) conversion of Polabian Slavs (Yoffe and Krafczik 2003). ibn Fadlan mentions the sacrifice of bread, meat, onions, and milk to a large wooden post with a face, accompanied by prayers beseeching a good price for trade goods (Barford 2001, 173).

316   It seems likely that Slavic mythology included the World Tree metaphor, since most early Indo-European religions did, and there are secondary sources that claim such, but I have not found any primary sources or references to primary sources. The cosmology of the nearby Norse certainly did, although the roots of their tree, Yggdrasil, did not extend to the underworld.

317   Reverence of river spirits, nymphs, and other nature spirits (in addition to the one god of lightning) was reported by Procopius as already being of ancient tradition among the Slavs in the sixth century A.D. (Procopius, 7.14.22-24).

318   Purification by the smoke from "living fire" and special amulets could also defend against unclean forces.

319   The souls of the recently deceased were believed to lurk around the homestead for some days (some traditions specify forty) before departing on their epic journeys to the otherworld, for which purpose coins and the deceased's most familiar and practical items used in life, such as a hat, might be placed with the body.

320   Witches and sorcerers were believed to continue operating as sort of vampires after their time in living form had passed, continuing their mischief during the dark hours as reanimated bodies, but not necessarily feeding on flowing human blood.

321   *Domovyky* were often mischievous and capricious and required placating to remain benevolent; otherwise they could play various tricks on the household, although usually not seriously damaging ones: banging pots, closing doors, tangling needlework, or upsetting farm equipment and such. If they were pleased, they would protect livestock and crops and warn of impending dangers (Malko). They could also shape-shift into animals, and in some places in Poland they commonly took the form of snakes (Phillips and Kerrigan 1999). They may have evolved from strictly ancestor spirits after ancestor worship became discouraged by Christianity, and in some areas a new house could not be considered safe until after the ghost of its first master could take on *domovoy* duties. Some traditions, on the other hand, had them originating from the spirits of the trees used in the construction of the house. Other household vegetal spirits found shelter and honor in sheaves of grain or sprigs of birch or thistle kept under the Christian icons (Gasparini).

322   *Kikimory* might be spirits of girls who died unbaptized, who instead of going out to the stream like the *rusalki* stayed around the household. They lived in the cellar or behind the stove and came out at night to spin, or tangle spinning, depending on her judgment, and help keep well-kept houses or further disrupted unkempt ones, and maybe sit on a sleeping person to cause breathing problems or nightmares. These seem obviously related to the more generic *mora* of European folklore.

323   For example, feasts called *dziady* were held on several specific days throughout the year (from three to five depending on location) to commemorate the dead.

324   Belief in witches, etc. (wizards, magicians, fortune-tellers, seers, spiritual healers, and sorcerers are often included under the term) was widespread throughout Europe during the early modern era (fifteenth to eighteenth centuries); fortune-telling (considered a sin after the arrival of Christianity) and the work of magicians in calling up demons were reported in the Russian Primary Chronicle as occurring as early as the eleventh century. It was believed that some witches were born into the craft; having no choice in the matter of their supernatural powers, these witches were prone to help. Other witches chose the profession, obtaining their powers through pacts with the "unclean force" (or devil); these witches usually had malicious or at least selfish intent. In either case, it was believed that witches could remain active after death.

The benign work of witches included: healing both humans and livestock, especially by warding off the spells of other witches or evil spirits; enhancing the fertility of the fields; warding off crop failures and bad weather (e.g., hailstorms); attracting good weather (i.e., good for crops: rain when needed); enhancing the production of milk; finding lost objects, animals, treasure, and money; fortune-telling; exposing thieves and other witches; and communicating with the dead. The fertility and weather functions were especially important in the highland landscapes of the Alps, the Carpathians, and the Balkans (Pocs 1999, 8). See endnote 77 for examples involving the

"werewolf warriors," which in the east may have evolved from a Slavic Perun/
Veles shamanism rather than, or alongside, or after, a Norse Odin shamanism
(Pocs 1999, 131).

The malicious work of witches included causing illness; stealing crops and
milk; and reducing the fertility of the fields via insects, disease, bad weather,
or stealing "the dew" (rain).

Witches' tools included potions, incantations, spells, ritual purification
with fire and water, the "evil eye" (a malicious glance), and appeals to Christian
saints.

In addition to hiring other witches, defenses the non-magician could use
against witches included onions, garlic, amber, incense, keeping windowsills
decorated and clean, appeasing with gifts, and in the most extreme cases, aspen
stakes. It was believed that witches would often take, or make others take,
the forms of animals—magpies and wolves being favorites—and thus many
innocent animals were killed as witches.

[325]   Early on (seventh to twelfth centuries), Christianity was adopted by
the rulers and urban elite but didn't make it much into the rural countryside.
As Christianity began extending its reach into the countryside beginning in
the thirteenth century, the churches, both the Western (Catholic and later
also Protestant) and Eastern (Orthodox) did their best to stamp out paganism,
persecuting *volkhvy* (pagan priests) and extolling their flocks against belief in
pagan gods and goddesses, nature spirits, and magical practices. Meanwhile,
although the rulers and urban elite officially denied the reality of pagan beliefs
such as witchcraft, many of them took precautions, especially as some *volkhvy*
sowed discontent and threatened retaliation. Some Orthodox clerics in fact
"did not doubt the existence of demons [as opposed to gods] but tried to forbid
their cults" (Barford 2001), and some in the remote rural villages even hired
magical healers themselves.

The Western churches' efforts were ultimately more dogmatic, brutal,
and successful, culminating in the witch trials that began in the fifteenth
century (which also made it east). In remote rural areas of Eastern Europe,
however, pagan beliefs and rituals hung on well into the twentieth century, at
least. Legal proceedings against those accused of causing deleterious effects
through spells persisted as late as the nineteenth century.

[326]   Many pagan festivals became linked to Christian celebrations, and
many pagan deities morphed into Christian saints: Perun became St. Elijah;
Mokosh /Moist Mother Earth gave her attributes to St. Paraskevi and the
Virgin Mary; Jarilo transformed into St. George. Volos's benevolent aspect
merged into the Byzantine St. Blasius, while his malevolent aspect was given to
the devil. Some Biblical accounts were also subtly influenced by a pre-Christian
heritage in legends and stories told by the peasants, if not by the clergy. For
example: God having to battle powers of darkness in order to create the world;
and the many spirits that influence the world (*domovoi, leshy, rusalki*, etc.)
being minions of Satan that descended with him when he was banished from
heaven).

327 For example, Christian saints, whose power might be concentrated in sacred icons and images, were appealed to for relief from dark forces, even by sorcerers; St. Nicholas—the precursor of Santa Claus—was especially helpful to peasants. Since the Western churches were more successful at suppressing paganism than the Orthodox Church, *dvoeverie* was more common in Orthodox countries. It was also especially favored by women, perhaps reflecting their natural desire to preserve the more matriarchal aspects of the pagan beliefs.

APPENDIX A

328 There can be ambiguity in defining the breadth of a complexly shaped mountain range, depending on how one defines the axes of the chain (perpendicular to which is its breadth). In the case of the Carpathians, for example, if one considers the Western Romanian Carpathians to be a northerly broadening of the Southern Carpathians, rather than a branch off of the main chain with its own longitudinal axis, then one would take a southeasterly-northwesterly measurement of breadth and get a measurement of about 400 km (250 mi).

329 If you take a much wider view, the Carpathian Mountains appear as one of several southeast-to-northwest aligned collections of mountains lying along the northeastern periphery of the "Alpide belt" (or Alps-Himalaya System), a huge system of mountains that stretch along the southern edge of the Eurasian tectonic plate, from Java in the southeast to the coast of Spain in the northwest. Another is the Caucasus chain, on the other side of the Black Sea.

330 For a concise yet thorough summary of the geologic aspects of the Carpathians, including nomenclature, I refer the reader to http://www.carpathians.pl/carpathians01.html

APPENDIX C

331 The Carpathian Sich had only a few thousand members (with even fewer actually bearing arms), many of whom were Ukrainian nationalists who came from Galicia on the other side of the Carpathians (then a part of Poland). They performed policing duties and even ran a theater company during the short existence of Carpatho-Ukraine. Under sway of ultra-nationalists they began to defy their own government, and some 600 Carpathian Sich fighters, in hope of achieving Ukrainian independence, went on to assist the Nazis in the invasion of Poland.

APPENDIX E

332 Rusyn International Media Center. Accessed May 21, 2015: http://web.archive.org/web/20080729193053/http://www.rusynmedia.org/News/2007/rimc310507.html

333 (Kristoff, 2014).

APPENDIX G

[334] There is debate about whether Rurik may have originally been a Danish Viking by the name of Rorik who ruled a region known as Friesland along the North Sea coast (now northeastern Netherlands and northwestern Germany) between 841 and 873. The name and the time seem about right.

[335] A written Byzantine source (the *Chronicle of George the Monk*) confirms a Viking raid on Constantinople around 860, although the origin and leaders of the attackers are not specified. A Rus' raid on Byzantine outposts that may have occurred even earlier in the ninth century, known as the Paphlagonian expedition of the Rus', is described in the *Life of St. George of Amastris*.

[336] The Russian Primary Chronicle says that in taking Kyiv, Oleg had the aid, voluntary or otherwise, from several Finnic tribes—Chuds, Meria, and Vesh—in addition to his own Varangian warriors and northern Slavic allies (the Sloviene and Krivicy).

[337] The *Russian Primary Chronicle*, which original title is translated literally as the "Chronicle of Bygone Years," was traditionally (since the thirteenth century) believed to have been written by a monk named Nestor, the sure author of several other works. The original manuscript is lost, and subsequent analysis has cast doubt on this theory, painting a less certain and more complex picture of the original authorship. It was probably compiled over a period of a few decades, beginning perhaps as early as the late eleventh century, with the author (or authors) relying on oral history and perhaps some short chronicles kept in the Crypt Monastery of Kyiv from as early as the late tenth century. With an agenda to present the foundations of the state in impressive, unified, and divine terms in order to legitimize the current ruling dynasty and also promote the unity of princely descendants during a time of disintegration, its reports have a slant and some of its earliest stories are certainly semi-mythological. On the other hand, most if not all the major events have their basis in fact (as proven by ultimate results, archeology, and sometimes by neighboring written histories), the stories becoming more reliable the closer they are to the time of writing.

[338] Legends invented by later dynastic cheerleaders added a descent from Augustus Caesar to Rurik's credentials.

[339] Including, for example, restrictions against theft, nonpayment, and murder by citizens of one polity on the other, provisions for mutual defense (against nomads), extradition agreements, mutual return of escaped slaves, mutual assistance of citizens in trouble, inheritance of property owned by ex-pats who die, allowance of mercenary services, and punishments for violations (for example, theft compensation equal to three times the value of stolen property).

[340] Reports of human sacrifices by pagan Slavs tend to be dismissed by historians, who suspect religious agendas by chroniclers, especially since no supporting archeological evidence has been found.

³⁴¹ The Rurik princes could, however, seize the land of peasants who died without male heirs.

³⁴² The lack of a strong centralized power and system of vassalage is blamed for the relative inability of medieval Central and Eastern European states to resist foreign domination: Generally, a single prince could not gain enough power to coalesce all the resources of the state in order to thwart invaders. Later, well after Kievan Rus' fell to the Mongols, true feudal systems did develop in Central and Eastern Europe, and then the situation reversed as far as the lower classes—the peasants and serfs—were concerned: conditions for them became more rigid and harsh than for the corresponding classes in the West.

³⁴³ The pride of many Ukrainians, the Holy Sophia Cathedral of Kyiv is a UNESCO World Heritage site.

³⁴⁴ The body of written law first established by Iaroslav the Wise is known as the *Rus'ka Pravda* ("Rus' Justice"). It evolved over time, and among its rather liberal and humane features (for the time): fines were a more common form of punishment than bodily injury, imprisonment, or execution; women were given some inheritance rights and could own land; some reasonable methods were specified for gaining evidence (as were some unreasonable ones, such as trial by hot iron for the crime of murder if no witnesses were available). As was common for the period, however, justice was discriminatory by social class (for example, the fines for injury or death to the lower classes were much less than those applicable to the higher classes).

³⁴⁵ Succession of the title of Grand Prince of Kyiv officially went to the oldest surviving male member of the dynasty (such as a brother) rather than to the eldest son of the current prince, although this was a rule that was sometimes overridden by martial might. In any case, it was a strategy that probably exacerbated dynastic conflict.

³⁴⁶ According to the *Russian Primary Chronicle*, Vseslav was born with a caul, and he was presented as a werewolf in the epic poem *The Tale of Igor's Campaign* (originally composed perhaps during the twelfth century and recorded anonymously during the thirteenth) and other *byliny* (East Slavic folkloric poems). He had a reputation for magical powers and sorcery as he fought against his uncles, sons of Iaroslav, for control of Kyiv.

BIBLIOGRAPHY

Anonymous. *Gesta Hungarorum*. Translated by Martyn Rady. University College London. Accessed May 9, 2015. http://eprints.ucl.ac.uk/18975/

Anthony, David W. 2007. *The Horse, the Wheel, and Language: How Bronze-Age Riders from the Eurasian Steppes Shaped the Modern World*. Princeton: Princeton University Press.

Aslund, Anders and McFaul, Michael. 2006. *Revolution in Orange*. Washington, D. C.: Carnegie Endowment for International Peace.

Barford, Paul M. 2001. *The Early Slavs*. Ithaca, New York: Cornell University Press.

Baring-Gould, Sabine. 2008 (first published 1865). *The Book of Were-Wolves*. Forgotten Books.

Batt, Judy and Wolczuk, Kataryna. 2002. *Region, State and Identity in Central and Eastern Europe*. New York: Frank Cass Publishers.

Best, Paul; Decerbo, Michael; and Maksimovich, Walter; translators. 2012. *A History of the Lemko Region of the Carpathian Mountains in Central Europe, by Fr. Ioann Polianskii (writing as I. F. Lemkyn)*. Higganum, CT: Carpathian Institute.

Bogatyrev, Petr. 1998. *Vampires in the Carpathians: Magical Acts, Rites, and Beliefs in Subcarpathian Rus'*. Translated by Stephen Reynolds and Patricia A. Krafcik. New York: Columbia University Press.

Boia, Lucian. 2001. *Romania: Borderland of Europe*. Translated by James Christian Brown. London: Reakton Books.

Bonkalo, Alexander. 1990 (reprint). *The Rusyns*. Translated by Ervin Bonkalo. Fairview, NJ: Carpatho-Rusyn Research Center. Distributed by Columbia University Press, New York. Originally published in 1940 by Franklin-Tarsulat, Budapest.

Carpathian Large Carnivore Project. Annual Report 1999.
———. Annual Report 2000.
———. Annual Report 2001.
———. Annual Report 2002.

Carpatho-Rusyn Society. 2014. *Letter of Appeal*. http://carpatho-rusynacademy.org/pdf/World%20Academy%20ZakOblRada%20endorsement%20May%202014.pdf

Chivers, C. J. "How Top Spies in Ukraine Changed the Nation's Path." *New York Times*, January 17, 2005.

Cross, Samuel H. and Sherbowitz-Wetzor, Olgerd P, translators and editors. 2012 (original 1953). *The Russian Primary Chronicle (Laurentian Text)*. Cambridge, Massachusetts: The Medieval Academy of America.

Curta, Florin. 2001. *The Making of the Slavs: History and Archeology of the Lower Danube Region c. 500-700*. New York: Cambridge University Press.

Dampier, Margaret G. 1905. *History of the Orthodox Church in Austria-Hungary*. London: Rivingtons.

Dennis, George T., translator. 1984. *Maurice's Strategikon: Handbook of Byzantine Military Strategy*. Philadelphia: University of Pennsylvania Press.

Douglas, Adams. 1992. *Beast Within: A History of the Werewolf*. New York: Avon Books.

Dvornik, Francis. 1962. *The Slavs in European History and Civilization*. New Brunswick, NJ: Rutgers University Press.

Eliade, Mircea. 1978. A *History of Religious Ideas: From the Stone Age to the Eleusinian Mysteries*. Chicago: The University of Chicago Press.

Eliade, Mircea. 1972. *Zalmoxis The Vanishing God: Comparative Studies in the Religions and Folklore of Dacia and Eastern Europe*. Chicago: The University of Chicago Press.

Fermor, Patrick Leigh. 1986. *Between the Woods and the Water*. New York: New York Review Books.

Gasparini, Evel. *Slavic Religion*. Encyclopedia Britannica, Accessed August 25, 2013. http://www.britannica.com/EBchecked/topic/548484/Slavic-religion

Gheorhgiu, Olimpiu. "Thousands of ethnic Hungarians call for autonomy." *Associated Press*, October 27, 2013.

Gerard, Emily. 1888. *The Land Beyond the Forest: Facts, Figures, and Fancies from Transylvania*. New York: Harper & Brothers. Reprint by Forgotten Books (2012).

Grumeza, Ion. 2009. *Dacia: Land of Transylvania, Cornerstone of Ancient Eastern Europe*. New York: Hamilton Books.

Heather, Peter. 2009. *Empires and Barbarians: The Fall of Rome and the Birth of Europe*. New York: Oxford University Press.

Heisler, J. B., and Mellon, J. E. 1946. *Under the Carpathians: Home of a Forgotten People*. London: The Travel Book Club.

Hippocrates. *Hippocrates Collected Works I: Air, Water, and Places*. Edited by W. H. S. Jones. Perseus Digital Library, Tufts University. Accessed February 24, 2015. http://www.perseus.tufts.edu/hopper/text?doc=urn: cts:greekLit:tlg0627.tlg002.perseus-eng2:17

Hudec, Ivan. 2000. *Tales from Slavic Myths*. Wauconda, Illinois: Bolchazy-Carducci Publishers, Inc.

Internet Encyclopedia of Ukraine. http://www.encyclopediaofukraine.com/default.asp

Ivanits, Linda J. 1989. *Russian Folk Belief*. New York: M. E. Sharpe, Inc.

Jenkins, Simon. 2009. "The forgotten Saxon world that is part of Europe's modern heritage." *The Guardian*, October 1, 2009. Accessed May 21, 2015. http://www.theguardian.com/commentisfree/2009/oct/01/romania-saxon-conservation-village

Johnson, Lonnie R. 2002. *Central Europe: Enemies, Neighbors, Friends*. New York: Oxford University Press.

Jordanes. 1908. *The Origins and Deeds of the Goths*. Translated by Charles C. Mierow. Hard Press, 2006. Kindle Edition. (Originally published by Princeton University Press, 1908.)

Kononenko, Natalie. 2007. *Slavic Folklore: A Handbook*. Westport, Connecticut: Greenwood Press.

Kozloff, Nikolas. 2014. "Ukraine Crisis: Hands Off Transcarpathia!" *The World Post*, May 20, 2014. http://www.huffingtonpost.com/nikolas-kozloff/ukraine-crisis-hands-off_b_5358893.html

Kristof, Nicholas D. "Let My People Go." *New York Times*, December 4, 2004.

Kutal, Miroslav and Rigg, Robin, editors. 2008. *Perspectives of wolves in Central Europe, Proceedings from the conference held on 9th April 2008*. Olomouc, Czech Republic: Hnutí DUHA Olomouc.

Machal, Jan. 1916. *Slavic Mythology*. A Chapter in: Gray, Louis Herbert, Ed., *The Mythology of All Races. Vol. 3 of 13*. Boston: Marshall Jones Company. Forgotten Books reprint (2013).

Maenchen-Heflen, Otto J. 1973. *The World of the Huns: Studies in Their History and Culture*. University of California Press.

Malko, Roman. "Fabulous creatures of Ukrainian folklore—is there more to them than just superstition and old beliefs?" *Welcome to Ukraine* website accessed May 19, 2015. http://www.wumag.kiev.ua/index2.php?param=pgs20043/70

Magocsi, Paul R. 2006. *The People from Nowhere: an illustrated history of Carpatho-Rusyns*. Uzhgorod, Ukraine: V. Padiak Publishers.

Magocsi, Paul R. and Krafcik, Patricia A., editors. 1993. *The Persistence of Regional Cultures: Rusyns and Ukrainians in Their Carpathian Homeland and Abroad*. Fairview, NJ: Carpatho-Rusyn Research Center. Distributed by Columbia University Press, New York.

McCallum, M. L. 2007. "Amphibian Decline or Extinction? Current Declines Dwarf Background Extinction Rate." *Journal of Herpetology*. 41(3):483–491.

Nikitin AG, Kochkin IT, June CM, Willis CM, McBain I, Videiko MY. 2009. "Mitochondrial DNA sequence variation in the Boyko, Hutsul, and Lemko populations of the Carpathian highlands." *Human Biology*. 81(1):43-58.

Plato, *"Charmides."* The Internet Classics Archive: http://classics.mit.edu/Plato/charmides.html

Phillips, Charles and Kerrigan, Michael. 1999. *Forests of the Vampire: Slavic Myth*. Amsterdam: Time-Life Books.

Pilkington, Ace and Olga. 2010. *Fairy Tales of the Russians and Other Slavs*. Forest Tsar Press.

Pocs, Eva. 1999. *Between the Living and the Dead: A Perspective on Witches and Seers in the Early Modern Age*. Budapest: Central Europena University Press.

Procopius. 2014. "History of the Wars of Justinian," in *Prokopios: The Wars of Justinian (Hackett Classics)*, translated by H. B. Dewing, revised by Anthony Kaldellis. Indianapolis/Cambridge: Hackett Publishing Company, Inc. Kindle Edition.

Ptolemy, Claudius. 1932. *Geography of Claudius Ptolemy*, translated by Edward Luther Stevenson. New York: Cosimo, Inc.

Quinn-Judge, Paul and Zarakhovich, Yuri. "The Orange Revolution." *Time Magazine*, November 28, 2004.

Ratliff, Evan. 2012. "The Forever Dog." *National Geographic Magazine*, February 2012.

Reznikova, Zhanna. 2007. *Animal Intelligence: From Individual to Social Cognition*. Cambridge University Press.

Ridush, Bogdan. 2012. "Palaeogeographic records in sediments of karst caves in Ukrainian Carpathians." *GEOREVIEW* Vol. 21 (2012).

Rigg, R. and S. Findo. 2000. Wolves in the Western Carpathians: past, present and future. *Presentation at Beyond 2000: Realities of global wolf restoration symposium*. Duluth, Minnesota, 23–26 February.

Shuster, Simon. 2010. "Prostitution: Ukraine's Unstoppable Export." *Time Magazine*, October, 2010.

Sparks, Alan E. 2010. *Dreaming of Wolves: Adventures in the Carpathian Mountains of Transylvania*. Blaine, Washington: Hancock House Publishers.

Sparks, Alan E. 2011. "The Wolves of Transylvania." *International Wolf Magazine*. Spring 2011 (Vol. 21. No. 1).

Sparks, Alan E. 2013. "The Wolves of Ukraine." *International Wolf Magazine*. Winter 2013 (Vol. 23. No. 4).

Stern, David. 2009. "'Sex pats' discover Ukraine's alluring women." *GlobalPost*, June 9, 2009. http://www.globalpost.com/dispatch/russia-and-its-neighbors/090608/sex-tourism

Stoker, Bram. 1897. *Dracula*. Great Britain: Archibald Constable and Company.

Strabo. *Geographica, Book 7*. Perseus Digital Library, http://www.perseus.tufts.edu/hopper/

Subtelny, Orest. 2000. *Ukraine: A History (Third Edition)*. Toronto: University of Toronto Press.

Summers, Montague. 2003 (first published 1933). *The Werewolf in Lore and Legend*. Mineola, NY: Dover Publications, Inc.

U.S. Department of State. 2008. *Trafficking in Persons Report, 2008*. http://www.state.gov/j/tip/rls/tiprpt/2008/105389.htm

Weatherford, Jack. 2004. *Genghis Khan and the Making of the Modern World*. New York: Three Rivers Press.

Webster, Robin; Holt, Suzie; Avis, Charlie. 2001. *The Status of the Carpathians: A report developed as part of The Carpathian Ecoregion Initiative*. World Wildlife Fund.

Wilson, Andrew. 2002. *The Ukrainians: Unexpected Nation (Second Edition)*. New Haven, CT: Yale University Press.

Vincenz, Stanislaw. 1955. *On the High Uplands: Sagas, Songs, Tales, and Legends of the Carpathians*. New York: Roy Publishers.

Yasinsky, Bohdan and Pashkova, Valentyna. 1998. *Taras Shevchenko in the Library of Congress: A Bibliography*. The Library of Congress. http://www.loc.gov/rr/european/shevchenko.html#Intro

Yoffe, Mark and Krafczik, Joseph. 2003. *Perun: The God of Thunder. [Studies in the Humanities Vol. 43]* New York, NY: Peter Lang Publishing.

Zibordi, Filippo; Mustoni, Andrea; Ionescu, Ovidiu. 2012. *Large Carnivore Conservation.* Task Force Protected Areas—Permanent Secretariat of the Alpine Convention. ALPARC.

Zingstra H.L.; J. Seffer, R. Lasak, A. Guttova, M. Baltzer, I. Bouwma, L. J. Walters, B. Smith, K. Kitnaes, G. E. Predoiu, B. Prots, G. Sekulic. 2009. *Towards and Ecological Network for the Carpathians.* Wageningen International, PO Box 88, 6700 AN Wageningen, Netherlands.

Zoltani, Csaba K., editor. 2013. *Transylvania Today: Diversity at Risk.* Budapest: Osiris Publishing

INDEX

CPSIA information can be obtained
at www.ICGtesting.com
Printed in the USA
LVHW01s1355160917
548574LV00001B/16/P